W9-BZX-518

look up Giuseppe

Xindian

Youth Park

Botanical Garden

Zhongzheng Bridge

Huazhong Main Bridge

Huanhe East Road

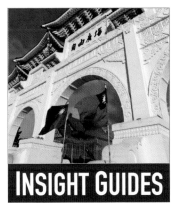

INSIGHT GUIDES

TAIPEI

HOW TO USE THIS BOOK

This book is carefully structured both to convey an understanding of the city and its culture and to guide readers through its attractions and activities:

◆ The Best Of section at the front of the book helps you to prioritize. The first spread contains all the Top Sights, while the Editor's Choice details unique experiences, the best buys or other recommendations.

◆ To understand Taipei, you need to know something of

its past. The city's history and culture are described in authoritative essays written by specialists in their fields who have lived in and documented the city for many years.

◆ The Places section details all the attractions worth seeing. The main places of interest are coordinated by number with the maps.

◆ Each chapter includes lists of recommended shops and restaurants, bars and cafes.

◆ Photographs throughout the book are chosen not only

to illustrate geography and buildings, but also to convey the moods of the city and the life of its people.

◆ The Travel Tips section includes all the practical information you will need on your trip, divided into four key sections: transportation, activites (including nightlife, tours and sports), an A–Z of practical tips, and language.

◆ A detailed street atlas is included at the back of the book.

PLACES AND SIGHTS

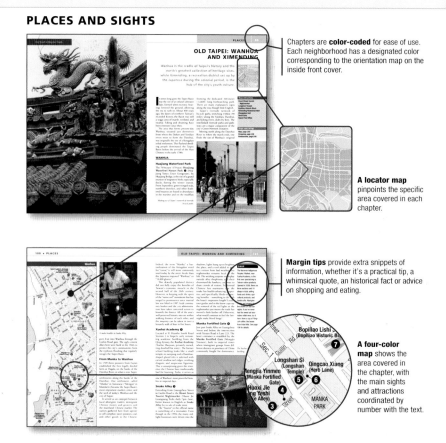

Chapters are **color-coded** for ease of use. Each neighborhood has a designated color corresponding to the orientation map on the inside front cover.

A locator map pinpoints the specific area covered in each chapter.

Margin tips provide extra snippets of information, whether it's a practical tip, a whimsical quote, an historical fact or advice on shopping and eating.

A four-color map shows the area covered in the chapter, with the main sights and attractions coordinated by number with the text.

PHOTO FEATURES

Photo features offer visual coverage of major sights or unusual attractions. Where relevant, there is a map showing the location and essential information on opening times, entrance charges, transport and contact details.

SHOPPING AND RESTAURANT LISTINGS

Taiwanese

Hai Feng Can Ting (Sea Breeze Restaurant)
17 Zhongzheng St. Tel: 02-2621 2365.
Open: daily 11am–11.30pm. $$$
This famous Taiwanese eatery is a legend in Danshui. There is no menu; guests select their freshly caught seafood from among the ice-covered offerings in the front. This is classic Taiwanese seafood, with flash-fried oysters, grilled snapper,

Shopping listings provide details of the best shops in each area. **Restaurant listings** give the establishment's contact details, opening times and price category, followed by a useful review. Bars and cafés are also covered here. The grid reference refers to the atlas section at the back of the book.

TRAVEL TIPS

By bus/coach

Long-distance bus travel is popular with locals because of the low cost – a bus ticket from Taichung, in central Taiwan, to Taipei is only about NT$300. In addition, since most bus terminals are right around Taipei Railway Station, connection to the MRT and...

Travel Tips provide all the practical knowledge you'll need before and during your trip: how to get there, getting around, and what to do. The A–Z section is a handy summary of practical information, arranged alphabetically.

THE BEST OF TAIPEI: TOP ATTRACTIONS

At a glance, the Taipei attractions you won't want to miss, from sky-scraping architecture and colorful temples to hot springs and buzzing nightmarkets.

◁ **Taipei 101.** Until recently the world's tallest building, standing at 508 meters (1,667ft), this iconic tower is a wonder of design and engineering. Be sure to inspect the massive Tuned Mass Damper. See page 152.

▽ **Longshan Temple.** In the heart of the old Wanhua District and filled day and night by those seeking divine aid. Check out the icon of the main goddess Guanyin, which miraculously survived direct bombing hits in World War II. See page 102.

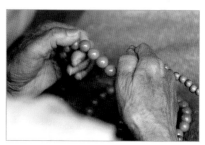

▽ **Beitou Hot-Springs area.** A lovely valley carved by a bubbling hot-springs stream dotted with new and old resorts, public baths, and large sulfur pits and pools. See page 179.

▽ **Shilin Nightmarket.** Taiwan's biggest and best nightmarket, with pretty much every type of traditional snack food eaten in Taiwan and China since, it seems, the beginning of time. A tremendous feast for the senses. See page 174.

▷ **National Palace Museum.** With well over half a million rare documents and artifacts, this museum is home to the world's greatest treasure vault of Chinese artifacts. See page 190.

△ **Maokong Gondola.** For a breathtaking sensation of gliding through the sky over Taipei take a ride in a Crystal Cabin. See page 169.

▷ **Puppetry Art Center of Taipei.** Discover a remarkable collection of Taiwanese string puppets, shadow puppets, and glove puppets. See page 154.

◁ **Muzha Tea Plantations.** In a steep hill valley in Taipei's southeast corner, scores of plantations with highly personalized teahouses dot the slopes, serving up "tea cuisine," and faraway views. See page 166.

▷ **Chiang Kai-shek Memorial.** This complex was built on an imperial scale and rivals Beijing's Forbidden City for awe-inspiring grandeur. The roof of the National Theater was modeled after Beijing's Hall of Supreme Harmony. See page 124.

▽ **Yangmingshan National Park.** The world's largest national park within a city's limits is perched on a mountain and offers hiking, hot-springs soaking, picnicking, flower gardens, giant fumaroles, historic sites, and much more. See page 194.

THE BEST OF TAIPEI: EDITOR'S CHOICE

Setting priorities, saving money, unique attractions... here, at a glance, are our recommendations, plus some tips and tricks even locals don't always know.

BEST WALKS

Butterfly Corridor. The most popular trail on Yangmingshan, a beautiful mountain park filled with trails and hot springs, plus hundreds of butterfly and bird species.See page 197.

Qingtiangang. Also found high on Yangmingshan, this plateau with ocean views features fumaroles and idyllic pastures of water buffalo. See page 199.

Tianmu Steps. An easy pathway up the

Taipei life on Ximending's pedestrian streets.

side of Yangmingshan from the Tianmu expat enclave. Popular with families. See page 178.

Taipei Botanical Garden. Take a leisurely stroll past exotic flora and linger by a huge lotus pond. See page 130.

Guandu Nature Park. This boardwalked marsh brings one close to birds and other species seen nowhere else. See page 184.

Dadaocheng and Wanhua. Let an historical walk through two of Taipei's oldest districts – lined with old shophouses and heritage sites – transport you back in time to the heyday of immigrant settlements and river trade. See pages 99 and 113.

Ximending. A walk down pedestrianized Wuchang and Emei streets provides some retail therapy, and insight into the latest youth crazes and fashions. See page 105.

Taipei offers good family activities.

BEST FOR FAMILIES

Taipei Water Park. A perfect place for kids to frolic in water-based amusements. See page 165.

Science Education Center. Here, science is taught through interactive displays and 3D movies. Next door, the Astronomical Museum has iWERKS and IMAX theaters. See page 175.

Taipei Zoo. Has a Children's Zoo, an ever-popular koala sanctuary, live-in pandas, and a butterfly conservation area. See page 170.

Miramar Entertainment Park. The giant

rooftop Ferris wheel here is Asia's second largest. See page 185.

Children's Art Museum in Taipei. Where all the masters are young and the paintings interactive. See page 141.

Su Ho Paper Memorial Museum. Papermaking workshops make this fun for young ones. See page 141.

Riverside Bike Paths. The city is encircled by easy-grade bike paths meandering through parks, with cheap bike-rental kiosks. See page 252.

PLACES OF WORSHIP

Taipei Confucius Temple. One of Taipei's grandest, the temple comes alive on Teachers' Day, when age-old rites are performed at dawn. See page 120.

Ciyou Temple. The annual birthday celebrations for Mazu, patron saint of seafarers, are most elaborate here. See page 155.

Taipei Grand Mosque. The country's main mosque, built with Saudi Arabian funding, is open to guided public visits for Muslims and non-Muslims alike. See page 163.

Xiahai City God Temple. This becomes a sea of raucous activity during the City God's birthday procession. See page 115.

Xingtian Temple. Dedicated to Guan Gong, patron saint of businessmen, this is one of Taiwan's richest temples, famous for the efficacy of its *shoujing*. See page 139.

Zhinan Temple. In the hills of Muzha, always thronging with devotees of Lü Dongbin, one of the Eight Immortals. See page 170.

Tianbula.

Baosheng Festival warrior.

FAMOUS FOOD

Tianbula. A Taiwanese version of tempura, this snack features fried tubes of fish paste, dried beancurd, and pig's blood cakes, dunked in a sweet and spicy sauce.

Stinky tofu. You either love or you hate this fermented beancurd snack, often called "Chinese cheese." Found at nightmarkets.

Soy braised foods. Called *luwei*, from tofu to tongue, all manner of foods are stewed for long hours in sauce and spices for a deep, rich, salty flavor.

Pearl milk tea. This cold beverage comes in myriad flavors with a dollop of chewy "pearls" made from tapioca flour.

Pineapple cakes. Cube pastries with pineapple paste filling, invented in central Taiwan. A delicious gift. See page 68.

Aiyu. Chilled *aiyu* is a "cooling," jelly-like dessert made from the eponymous fruit. Exclusive to Taiwan. See page 176.

Shaved ice. A generous heaping of crushed or shaved ice, topped with red beans, yam, or fresh fruits, then drizzled with condensed milk.

Three Cup Chicken. Perhaps Taiwan's most representative dish, meats and other tasties slowly pot-simmered in a cup of soy sauce, rice wine, and sesame oil. See page 64.

At the Shung Ye Museum of Formosan Aborigines.

ONLY IN TAIPEI

Shung Ye Museum of Formosan Aborigines. One of the best places in the world to learn about the aboriginal tribes of Taiwan. See page 177.

Taipei Robot Pavilion. Located at the Taipei Expo Park, the pavilion hosts a collection of androids who can dance, play music and wrestle. See page 138.

Nightmarkets. These are the places to get your nightly grease fix, cheap clothing, and an authentic taste of local street life. See page 86.

Temple festivals. Birthday celebrations for deities such as Mazu are conducted in the streets of Taipei, with processions, firecrackers, and huge effigies. See page 52.

Bihu Weaving House. Intricate bamboo architecture of exquisite beauty, and a piece of contemporary landscape art. For the best experience visit the place at sunset or after dark. See page 186.

Betel nut stands. Glass kiosks with scantily-attired girls selling betel nuts, which are mildly intoxicating "Chinese chewing gum," pepper the outskirts of the city. See page 234.

BEST BARS AND PUBS

Blue Note. Taipei's homey home for jazz-lovers. Brings in talent, has a house band, and features regular jam sessions. See page 249.
Carnegie's. A big venue open to the street, one of the city's only nightlife spots with alfresco seating. Wide bartops, made for dancing, are well used. See page 161.
EZ5. Taipei's best-known dinner club, renowned for hosting the top homegrown club singers from Taiwan and around, who like to sing their favourite English tunes here. See page 249.
The Pig & Whistle. This venerable neighborhood British pub in the heart of the Tianmu expat enclave offers all the beloved UK foods and sports. See page 189.

Carnegie's is a hugely popular bar, known for its lively atmosphere and wide selection of shooters.

BEST VIEWS

Four Beasts Mountain. From the westernmost peak of this mountain on Taipei's east side, the whole city sits before you like a giant scale model. See page 153.
Muzha Tourist Tea Plantations. The city sparkles at night from the teahouses on the highest slopes here. See page 166.
Mt Qixing. From here, Yangmingshan's tallest peak, the ocean and Taipei Basin is laid out before you. See page 198.
Taipei 101 Observation Decks. Catch stunning views from the main 89th-floor Observatory and 91st-floor outdoor deck. See page 152.
Jiufen. This small town, on the slopes of Mt Jilong, provides panoramic views of the mountains and sea from teahouse decks. See page 221.
Wulai Cable Car. Soars high over a hot-springs valley, brushing past a waterfall that bursts from the bluff-top you fly to. See page 233.

A detail at the Baoan Temple.

BEST ARCHITECTURE

Longshan Temple Dragons. In the graceful, ornate southern Chinese style, the temple is famed for its dragon carvings, notably the writhing pillars. See page 102.
Baoan Temple. It's not easy to beat Longshan Temple for color and decorative intricacy, but this Unesco-recognized temple does; the *koji*-pottery roof work is magical. See page 120.
Presidential Office Building. A red-brick neo-Renaissance edifice built by the Japanese on a scale worthy of any head of state. Its tower was the tallest structure during the colonial era. See page 126.
Shihsanhang Museum of Archaeology. Located outside of the city, in the town of Bali, is this distinctively angular building that garnered the Far East Architecture Award in 2003. See page 207.
Taipei 101 Fengshui. A wonderful example of traditional *fengshui* symbolism in action, the bamboo stalk shape symbolizing people's fortitude, ancient coin symbols inviting wealth. See page 152.

An amazing view of the Taipei 101 tower and city skyline from Four Beasts Mountain.

TOP SHOPPING

Eslite Bookstore, Dunhua Branch. Open 24 hours daily, this is a nice alternative nightlife option, with thousands of English-language titles and superb people-watching. See page 148.

Guang Hua Digital Plaza. One of the best places in the city to buy or just window-shop for state-of-the art electronic goods. In mid-2015 another electronics shopping mall, the Taipei Information Park, will open next door. See page 141.

Holiday Jade Market. This jade-lovers' mecca is one of the Asia's largest markets to buy this green shiny stone. See page 143.

Nanmen Market. Taipei's renowned and biggest day market. The city's number one spot to shop for traditional sausages, snacks and cookies. See page 130.

MONEY-SAVING TIPS

Cheap food and drink. Though the food at Taipei's nightmarkets may be slightly too greasy for sensitive stomachs, it is clean, tasty, and dirt cheap. Visitors can feast on all sorts of traditional Taiwanese snack foods and drinks and still come away with change from an NT$500 bill.

Biandang are Taiwan's answer to the lunchbox. During lunch hour, locals move out in droves to the ubiquitous *biandang* outlets, where for merely NT$50–80 you're given a bed of rice in a disposable, sealable box, and allowed a choice of three or four toppings from a buffet selection of 15–20 dishes. Cheap and tasty.

Almost all bars and clubs in the city have a daily happy hour that lasts at least a couple of hours. Some will water the drinks to preserve profit margins, but the majority play a fair game. The most popular happy hour with the old-time expatriate crowd is at the Front Page bar in the Imperial Hotel on Linsen North Road. A free snack buffet is provided, consisting mainly of traditional fried Taiwanese bite-sized morsels. Get there early, for the regulars are very much intent on getting their evening fill.

Many bars and clubs also have a weekly Ladies' night, generally on Wednesdays. The usual deal is one free drink and a waiver of the cover charge at venues where there is canned or live music.

Free views. Rather than pay for entry into the observatories at the city's two tallest man-made structures, head for one of two hillside stairways that lead to views just as uplifting. Both start from easily accessible trailheads, and are calm and pleasant 20-minute hikes. The first is up Elephant Mountain, just south of the Taipei 101 skyscraper and 15–20 minutes on foot from Taipei City Hall MRT station. The other is up Yuanshan behind the Grand Hotel, just 5 minutes from Jiantan MRT station.

Refunds. Foreign travelers who make purchases of at least NT$3,000 on the same day, and from the same Tax Refund Shopping (TRS)-posted store, are eligible for a refund of the 5 percent VAT paid (see page 70).

Magazines. Pick up free copies of the tourist-oriented *Travel in Taiwan* from all Tourism Bureau service centers, *Discover Taipei* at City Hall and mrt stations, and *This Month in Taiwan* from hotels and other public places.

Museums and attractions. Many museums and attractions in Taipei do not charge admission, including the Discovery Center of Taipei, Beitou Hot Springs Museum, and the Ketagalan Culture Center, the Chiang Kai-shek Memorial Hall, Lin An Tai Historical House and Museum, Sun Yat-sen Historic Events Memorial Hall, and the National Revolutionary Martyrs' Shrine.

Parks and Gardens. The city's many public parks, such as Daan Forest Park, 228 Memorial Peace Park, Sishoushan Community Forest, Dajia Riverside Park, Yangmingshan National Park's hiking trails, and the Botanical Garden, do not charge admission fees.

Temples. Three is an open invitation to the city's scores of Taoist, Buddhist, and Confucian places of worship, large and small.

Festivals. Plangent pageants of color and ceremony, all of Taipei's temple festivals are free, as is the Taipei Lantern Festival and other secular celebrations throughout the year.

Concerts. Check the local newspapers for free concerts at Daan Forest Park's amphitheater, or Taiwanese celebrity appearances in *Ximending*.

View from above of Zhongxiao West Road.

Trendy Ximending couple.

NEW TAIPEI

In many ways, Taipei is a tale of two cities. The old city was crowded, polluted, and chaotic. But the modern city is very different. It has evolved over the years, and is now staking a claim as one of the best in Asia. Call it the New Taipei.

When Chiang Kai-shek's government set up camp on the island in the late 1940s, the idea was that it was temporary and its members would go back to mother China shortly. Little thought was put into beautifying their capital, defined by row after row of unsightly cement-block residential buildings hastily put up to accommodate the new arrivals.

Since the lifting of martial law in the late 1980s, and the burgeoning of disposable incomes as a result of the economic miracle of the 1960s and 1970s, the improvement of the city has been a key goal. Taiwan is now the fourth-richest country in East Asia in terms of per capita income and enhancing quality of life has become the primary pursuit. Indeed, the pace of change has been startling. Metro lines have opened, and new

Taipeiers are keen on the latest technology.

freeways move traffic briskly, while tough pollution laws have throttled the two-stroke scooters that once belched the city's signature pollution. Two large squatter villages were razed, and are now leafy parks filled with in-line skaters and tai chi practitioners.

The Taiwanese love sophisticated IT gadgetry, and the new Taipei is a hyper-modern city, thanks to the billions of dollars the government has poured in. Almost the entire city is WiFi accessible, and the city government aims to bring fiber-optic internet to most households, with targets of 80 percent coverage in 2015.

The city's important heritage sites are no longer being torn down in the headlong pursuit of maximum lucre; many are being restored and given a second lease of life. A key government program is to create a "necklace of cultural pearls" through the city – a long line of irreplaceable historical sites.

The new Taipei is big (it rivals any capital city), but not too big (you can cross town in 20 minutes by Metro). It's exotic, but not too exotic. It's crowded enough to be *renao* (literally "hot and noisy"), buzzing with restaurants, nightclubs, and boutiques, but not chronically gridlocked like, say, Bangkok.

But best of all are the friendly residents who cheerfully direct visitors to the Metro station and write down Chinese characters for the taxi driver. They are the *Xin Taiwanren*, or New Taiwanese, and the heart and soul of the city.

Girls hit the town in trendy Ximending.

PEOPLE

The educated and well-traveled residents of Taipei have higher incomes and greater fashion consciousness than their countryside kin, but at heart they still embody the Taiwanese spirit of *renqingwei*, or "human feeling."

Since late imperial times, Taipei has been the center of political and economic power on the island. It has long been the norm for people of ambition and talent to move here from their hometowns in the central, southern, and eastern regions. On top of this demographic imbalance, a common complaint is that for too long the Kuomintang (KMT) government poured an unfair share of financial resources into the capital city's development, leaving the other regions to fend for themselves.

There is some truth to these accusations. When Chiang Kai-shek's Nationalists landed on the island in the late 1940s, most of the 2 million or more mainlanders who came settled in and around Taipei. Though it was still somewhat backward by international standards then, it was Taiwan's leading city. The Kuomintang government saw Taipei as its base, and other areas as populated by outsiders and Japanese sympathizers. It hoarded resources for itself and the city.

Since the end of martial law in 1987, things have been changing. Political leadership is moving towards greater ethnic and geographical representation, and resources are in turn being spread out more evenly.

It is also recognized that given its limited land area, Taipei is far too heavily populated; since 1968 and the era of Taiwan's "economic miracle," the population has increased 63.5 percent and the number of households 1.73 times. Recent initiatives such as the creation of satellite cities and what are called "new towns" have aimed to encourage Taipei residents to move to

Crowds of scooter-riders stuck in traffic hint at the city's population density.

outlying areas – or at least to deflect the influx of citizens from other areas.

Population size and density

In 2013 Taiwan's overall population was 23.3 million. In 2014, the greater Taipei area housed 6.95 million people, and the city alone was home to 2.69 million (over a million households). With about two-thirds of the island mountainous, Taiwan trails only Bangladesh in population density among states with a population over 10 million, and it's the 16th most densely populated country in the world. The problem is exacerbated in Taipei, ringed as it is by mountains and plunked down in the small Taipei Basin. With approximately 9,900 people per square kilometer, this is one of the world's most crowded cities. Heavily residential Daan District is the most crowded, with 27,600 people per square kilometer.

In the 1980s, almost all of the city's green areas had been built over. Since then the city administration has been working hard to increase public green spaces, and the city has been growing upward instead of outward. Stand-alone single homes are almost non-existent except on Yangmingshan, where the richest live. Most citizens live in residential high-rises, packed side by side in solid rows, in units akin to what Westerners would call a condominium. Whereas in the 1980s most such high-rises were only 3–5 stories tall, today they are 8–10 stories, and even higher downtown. Elevators are common only in the newer residential buildings.

The tradition of the extended family, with parents living in the house of the eldest male offspring (or vice versa), is breaking down in

A trendy Taipeier.

2014 interview poll run by the National Chengchi University revealed that over 60 percent of country's inhabitants identified themselves as Taiwanese, up from merely 13.6 percent in 1991, while 32.6 percent

Taipei. A major reason is that sons and daughters have left their parents behind in central and southern Taiwan in order to take advantage of Taipei's better work prospects, especially for those with tertiary qualifications.

Stereotypes

Taipeiers tend to see themselves as more sophisticated than the residents of the island's other areas. The schools tend to be better, and the salaries and disposable incomes are higher. The monthly household income in 2013 was about NT$128,700 (up from just NT$6,159 in 1971), with an average consumption expenditure of NT$84,500. Taipei citizens also travel overseas more, and doggedly pursue international trends in fashion, with a noted preference for

Longshan Temple, one of Taipei's most important.

Enjoying quality time in the Dajia Riverside Park.

conspicuously displayed brand names. There is also greater sophistication with regards to animal welfare, eco-friendly living, and other issues.

The Taiwanese in general tend to see the people from the erstwhile motherland of China as backward and dishonest, and those with enough disposable income to travel to Taiwan as somewhat loud and gauche. The Taiwanese will also mention racism seen in the West, and maintain that Taiwan suffers no such discrimination, offering as proof the very open-minded religious tolerance found here. However, what is not recognized is that the Han Chinese homogeneity of local society is extant in large part because of a lack of acceptance of outsiders other than those of white skin from rich Western nations. Overseas guest workers from Southeast Asia, in particular, are often looked down on, and accounts of exploitation are regularly reported in the papers. The same is true of the increasing number of foreign spouses, mostly women from China and Vietnam, who only in recent years have been granted the right to work and are now slowly organizing and fighting for their rights.

Population breakdown

Taiwan's population profile is approximately 97.71 percent ethnic Han Chinese and 2.29 percent aborigine; according to statistics, aboriginal population has increased by over 30 percent since 2001. Among the Han Chinese, about 70 percent are Fujianese, 14 percent are Hakka, and 14 percent mainlander. In local parlance, a "mainlander" is someone who came to Taiwan from China with the KMT in the late 1940s and early 1950s, or a descendant of such an individual. A member of the Hakka community is one whose ancestors came to Taiwan during imperial times from the mountainous areas of Guangdong Province in China. The ancestors of the Fujianese came almost exclusively from the southern part of Fujian Province, or "south of the Min River," and their language is still referred to as *Minnanyu* (Southern Min) today, though some variation now differentiates the mainland China and Taiwanese dialects.

Taipei's demographics do not match the island's overall ethnic breakdown. Though there has been much intermarrying between mainlanders and Taiwanese – comparatively few women came over in the great exodus of the 1940s – identity remains strong through patrilineal descent, and today about half the city's population identify themselves as mainlanders. As a result, the two main parties that seek eventual reunification with China, the Kuomintang and the People First Party, have unusually strong political bases here.

The Hakka population in Taipei is close to 8 percent. They are a tightly knit community that has traditionally frowned on

POPULATION MOVEMENTS

The imbalance in Taiwan's population is most evident in the run-up to the Chinese New Year holidays each year. Normally bustling Taipei becomes eerily quiet as people vacate en masse for parents' hometowns in the island's center and south. A drive south to Kaohsiung that might normally take 5 hours may take as long as 15; buses, trains, and planes are booked months ahead.

This phenomenon is now evolving, as the elderly parents of Taipei residents are now passing away, and the Taipeiers who moved to the city in the 1960s and 1970s have become parents and grandparents, shifting the center of familial gravity to the city.

Commuters line up at an MRT station.

intermarriage. Even during the "economic miracle," comparatively few moved from traditional farming villages in the foothills to the cities. This isolation is now breaking down in the information age, and the growth of the middle class among the Hakka is growing.

IDENTITY

Ask four citizens of Taipei who they are and you'll likely get four different answers. Much of the population now sees China as politically distinct, so do not like the term *Zhongguoren*, literally "people of China." Many of those whose ancestors arrived during imperial times now simply refer to themselves as *Taiwanren*, "Taiwanese." Some mainlanders who arrived after World War II, however, do not use this term. Many Taiwanese themselves wish to identify with the shared Chinese cultural legacy, so *Huaren* is often used, a term derived from the more literary designation for China. The term *Hanren* is used to emphasize Chinese ethnicity, meaning "Han people," referring to China's Han Dynasty.

The city's aborigine community is small, with just 15,391 individuals in mid-2014, 0.57 percent of the total population. There is no concentration in any district. The Ketagalans of the Taipei Basin have long been absorbed into the Chinese community, or have moved into the hills to the south and been absorbed by the native peoples there. Like other native populations around the globe, the aborigine community is in crisis. Its members are failing in the school system, and the school system is failing them. They remain uncompetitive in the job market because of lack of necessary skills, limited ability in the major languages, alcoholism, and discrimination.

The majority of aborigine residents are blue-collar laborers who work on large-scale construction projects, moving back and forth between Taipei and their home villages, especially when the projects end and work temporarily dries up. Members of the island's tribes constitute Taipei's poorest communities, subsisting at or below the poverty line, and living in close proximity to each other. The majority of Taipei families own their own homes, but few aborigine families do.

Shopping in Ximending.

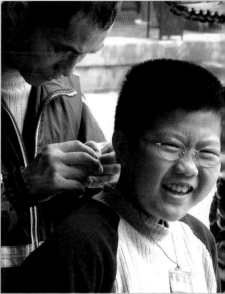

Traditions at temples are kept alive among both young and old.

National psyche

The Taiwanese people are well known for being hardworking. Among the Chinese, a long history of economic instability has given rise to a belief in hard work and saving up to weather the inevitable hard times. Traditionally, trust was only placed in family and a small circle of friends.

This is now changing, with the younger generation not having known poverty and, in the eyes of more senior generations, assuming that money grows on trees. Young workers are often called "strawberries," meaning they go all squishy when given even the slightest pressure. The "strawberries" are considered too demanding, wanting extra pay first before they are willing to take on job pressures, rather than proving themselves first in order to receive the award of a higher salary.

A national identity is also slowly emerging. In imperial times, the Chinese moved to Taiwan to escape oppressive Chinese officialdom. Here they developed an independent streak, akin to that of the American pioneer. In fact Taiwan was once something of a "Wild, Wild East." During the Japanese colonial era,

> The Taipeier understands the concept of going Dutch, but here someone will always *qingke* or play host. Counting one's individual due, down to the penny, is seen as demeaning.

the rulers tried to "Japanize" the population. Later, during the martial-law period, the KMT tried to remake the population as citizens of China – no local languages in schools, no TV, radio, or movies in Taiwanese. In spite of this, a "Taiwan first" attitude is now shared by many locals, whether they support unification with China, formal independence, or the status quo.

Social etiquette and behavior

The norm of the family unit is shifting, with the extended family being replaced by the nuclear family, and younger people becoming increasingly individualistic. But traditional values still predominate in social life. Where this is most obvious to the overseas traveler is in the spirit of *renqingwei*, which loosely translates as "human feeling." The city's people, as do all Taiwanese, see themselves as *reqing*, which roughly means "warmhearted."

Once a personal connection is made with a local, the importance of being *haoke*, or a

> You won't see much touching between the sexes here, save for some youths. Follow the local lead, avoiding even innocent, friendly contact. Many a Western male has been secretly labeled a selang, or "color wolf."

"good host," comes to the fore. The visitor will be taken out and any small favor asked will be quickly handled. Be wary of idly commenting how much you like a person's jewelry, clothing, painting, and so on, because they may well turn around and give it to you. If you are taken out, be sure to invite the person out yourself before leaving the island. Not to do so may be seen as being manipulative, or at the least ill-mannered. If unsure of where to host a gathering, simply explain the situation to your guest, who will be glad to help. The Taiwanese embrace with open arms the foreigner who tries to understand the local culture, and will forgive almost any faux pas.

Locals are aware that the tradition of being *haoke* goes all the way back to the time of Confucius, who taught "Do not do unto others what you would not have them do unto you." Ergo, you should be a good host at all times, for would you not want to be treated the same way if you yourself were traveling?

But though denizens of Taipei are known for their inviting warmth and friendliness, travelers may be disconcerted by the inconsiderate behavior they witness in public. Many a visitor goes away with an image of even well-dressed and obviously educated people jostling others without apologizing, refusing to allow other drivers to merge, or illegally edging vehicles through crowds of pedestrians as they try to cross the street.

Taipei's working professionals.

Young Taipeiers making the most of a day out in Danshui.

An aboriginal artisan at work.

There is a healthy political participation by Taiwan's citizens, seen here at the 2004 elections.

The root, say anthropologists, is the woefully turbulent history of the Chinese people. The constant social instability and little or no legal protection for the individual may well have bred a somewhat overzealous sense of self-interest.

Thankfully things are changing quickly in light of Taiwan's high level of education, increasingly trusted official enforcement of the individual's legal rights, and government campaigns, especially prior to international events for which the city is serving as host. In 2004 then-mayor of Taipei Ma Ying-jeou (Taiwan's President since 2008) bemoaned the unacceptable level of dirt seen in public areas, even as Taipei strives to become a city of international caliber. He expressed hope that the city's sparkling MRT system could serve as a model to encourage greater public cleanliness, and this hope has slowly become reality. The newer areas of the city, such as Xinyi District with its gleaming office towers, were a glimpse of things to come. The introduction of a rigorous mandatory recycling system with the pay-as-you-throw scheme has created an infinitely cleaner and tidier city. As of 2014, Taipei seems to be a capital highly committed to green living and ecology, and despite the city's rapid economic growth, the waste production is falling.

As prosperity has increased, the Taiwanese have embraced their leisure time.

DECISIVE DATES

From prehistory to the Qing dynasty

5000 BC to 2000 BC
Neolithic Tapenkeng people inhabit the Taipei area.

4000 BC
The island is settled by peoples of Austronesian ethno-linguistic stock, the ancestors of today's aborigines.

AD 200–1500
The Taipei area is inhabited by the Shihsanhang people, a non-Chinese race possibly related to the Austronesians.

1544
Portuguese sailors passing Taiwan call it Ilha Formosa, "Beautiful Island."

1622
Dutch traders establish a base on Penghu in the Taiwan Strait.

1628
Spanish troops build Fort San Domingo in Danshui, with the intention of further territorial expansion.

1642
The Spanish are driven from Taiwan and the Dutch take over.

1662
Koxinga, or Zheng Chenggong, a Ming dynasty loyalist, drives the Dutch from Taiwan, and Taipei falls under Chinese control.

1737
Immigrants, mostly from China's southern Fujian Province, continue to settle in the Taipei area, which soon hosts a number of prosperous trading centers.

A woodblock print depicting the Japanese takeover in 1895.

Leaders including Chiang Kai-shek, Franklin Delano Roosevelt and Winston Churchill at the Cairo Conference in 1943, which addressed the Allied position toward Japan during World War II.

1858
The Treaty of Tianjin, resulting from the Second Opium War, opens several ports, including Danshui, to foreign trade. Taipei prospers.

1885
Liu Mingchuan becomes the first Qing dynasty governor of Taiwan. He moves the capital from Tainan to Taipei, and launches a series of modernizing reforms.

Japanese presence
1895
China loses the First Sino-Japanese War, and cedes Taiwan to Japan under the Treaty of Shimonoseki.

1930
The Wushe Uprising, the last major aboriginal rebellion against the Japanese, is forcibly suppressed.

1935
An Exposition to commemorate Japan's administration of the island is held, showcasing the great improvements made to the colony's infrastructure and economy.

1937
The Second Sino-Japanese War begins.

1943
Franklin Roosevelt, Winston Churchill, and Nationalist leader Chiang Kai-shek meet in Cairo, and declare that when World War II ends, Taiwan will be returned to China.

1945
World War II ends. The Japanese surrender. Taipei returns to Chinese control.

The Republic of China
1947
The 2-28 Incident sparks off protests in Taipei and across the island. Nationalist troops kill up to 28,000 civilians in response. The event launches the White Terror, an era of harsh political repression.

1949
The communist People's Republic of China (PRC) is proclaimed under Mao Zedong. Chiang Kai-shek and the defeated Kuomintang (KMT) flee to Taiwan, where the Republic of China (ROC) is established, with Taipei named as its temporary capital.

1950s
The US Seventh Fleet deters an all-out war across the Taiwan Strait, despite the ferocious 1954–55 and 1958 bombardments of Quemoy (Kinmen Island).

1960s
Taiwan starts to become an exporting powerhouse, launching four decades of spectacular economic growth.

1965
The National Palace Museum opens on the outskirts of Taipei.

1971
The UN admits the PRC as the legitimate representative of China, and expels the ROC.

1975
Chiang Kai-shek passes away, paving the way for political reform.

1978
Chiang Kai-shek's son Chiang Ching-kuo becomes president of Taiwan.

A Taipei pro-independence rally.

1988
Lee Teng-hui becomes the first Taiwan-born president of Taiwan. Opposition parties are legalized.

1992
Taiwan and China loosely agree that there is "One China," but disagree on what that means, exactly.

1995–96
China launches missile tests near the coast of Taiwan, and some of the missiles land in the ocean near Taipei. US warships move closer to Taiwan.

1979
The US switches recognition to the PRC, and ends formal diplomatic relations with Taiwan. The US Congress then passes the Taiwan Relations Act, which implies that the US will defend Taiwan in the event of an attack by mainland China. The Kaohsiung Incident galvanizes opposition to martial law.

1980
The Hsinchu Science Park is established near Taipei, and becomes a driving force in Taiwan's high-tech economy.

1986
The opposition Democratic Progressive Party (DPP) is founded.

1987
Martial law is lifted. The Taiwanese are allowed to travel to China.

1996
Lee Teng-hui wins a landslide victory in Taiwan's first presidential elections. The first Taipei Metro line opens. Police shut down 188 sex parlors in a week, and pledge to close the rest.

1997
The opposition DPP wins 12 out of 23 mayoral and county seats, and for the first time receives more votes than the KMT.

1999
President Lee Teng-hui abandons the fuzzy "One China" principle, and declares "special state-to-state" relations. China again threatens to retake Taiwan by force. A devastating earthquake, measuring 7.6 on the Richter scale, kills over 2,300 people, injures over 8,000.

Taipei continues to have a thriving technological industry, exhibited here at Hsinchu Science Park.

Modern politics

2000
Chen Shui-bian is elected president, temporarily ending 50 years of KMT rule. Taiwan becomes a member of the WTO.

2001
The Dalai Lama arrives for a spiritual visit. Tropical storm Nari causes widespread flooding and kills at least 66 people.

2002
Authorities impose water rationing in Taipei for the first time in 22 years as drought reduces reservoirs to historically low levels. President Chen Shui-bian declares that Taiwan is "not someone else's province." This sparks an uproar in China and at home, prompting him to back away from his rhetoric. China surpasses the US as Taiwan's top trading partner.

2003
Taipei is gripped by the SARS epidemic, and the economy suffers. After three months of drama, the WHO declares the infection contained.

2004
The Taipei 101 tower, then the world's tallest building, is completed, a status maintained until late 2009, when it is surpassed by Dubai's Burj Khalifa. Chen Shui-bian and Annette Lu are shot and wounded in a bizarre assassination attempt a day before the presidential election. Chen narrowly wins re-election, but the

The Taipei 101 tower, which held the record for being the world's tallest building for five years.

results are disputed, and half a million people swarm into Taipei to protest. Chen is eventually affirmed as the winner.

2005
KMT politician Lien Chan pays a landmark visit to China, and is received by president Hu Jintao.

2008
The DPP loses national elections after many supporters lose faith in the party because of spreading

scandals. The KMT's Ma Ying-jeou is elected president, and immediately moves to bring Taiwan closer to China.

2009
Typhoon Morakot lashes Taiwan, bringing a deluge of rain and causing over 600 deaths, largely in the south. Former President Chen Shui-bian is given life in prison after a corruption trial.

2010
Taiwan and China sign a free trade pact, regarded as the most important bilateral agreement in 60 years of separation.

2012
Ma Ying-jeou of KMT is re-elected President of Taiwan.

2014
A new services-trade pact with China raises concerns that it will hurt Taiwan's industry, and provokes opposition protests.

President Ma Ying-jeou.

A 1930s poster advertising the Taiwan Expo.

A MODERN MIRACLE

With its turbulent past and location at the crossroads of East Asia, Taipei has, at one time or another, been seized and shaken by history's major forces and trends. Today it is experiencing a period of political ambiguity but great prosperity.

The Taipei area has undergone successive cycles of colonization – by the Spanish, Dutch, Chinese, and Japanese – and has suffered the virtual extinction of its native peoples. It has gone through lawless periods, when warlords, pirates, and clan families fought over the area's spoils.

Natural disasters have been frequent, such as the devastating quake of September 21, 1999 and the 2009 typhoon-induced deluge that killed 600 people. Nor has Taipei been spared the ravages of war. During World War II, Allied bombs pounded the city before the Japanese surrendered the island. This was followed by a period of bitter oppression under the tyrannical rule of Generalissimo Chiang Kai-shek.

But the city has enjoyed good times as well, and in the past few decades, riding the crest of Taiwan's transition from rural backwater to economic powerhouse, Taipei has blossomed. It now boasts a fully democratic government and an excellent infrastructure. It nurtures a rich flowering of culture, and its educated populace enjoys a higher quality of life than at any other time in history.

Aboriginal inhabitants

The history of human inhabitation in what is present-day Taipei began perhaps 7,000 years ago, when it was settled by the Tapenkeng people. These Neolithic aborigines, like later settlers, were attracted to the lush Taipei Basin, a fertile land that enjoyed steady and predictable rainfall, was good for growing crops, and was rich in clams, fish, deer, and other food sources. But the Tapenkeng were succeeded by the Ketagalan aborigines.

Detail from a 15th-century Chinese map depicting Taiwanese aborigines hunting deer.

When ethnic Chinese immigrants first arrived four to five centuries ago, they encountered these and other Austronesian ancestors of today's aboriginal groups. The 19 tribes on the island lived in large communities and practiced agriculture, but those in and around Taipei were eventually almost entirely assimilated or extinguished by successive waves of newcomers.

Western traders

In 1544, Portuguese sailors passing the island dubbed it *Ilha Formosa*, meaning "beautiful island," a name that belied the terrifying

Busy Dadaocheng port in the 19th century.

The battle between Koxinga and the Dutch.

reputation the island soon acquired. Sailors shipwrecked on its coasts were seized and robbed of everything, lucky to escape with their lives. More often than not, they were speedily killed by head-hunting aborigines.

In the early 1600s, the Dutch East India Company arrived in the Taiwan Strait. They were followed soon after by the Spanish, whose troops built Fort San Domingo in Danshui in 1628. Over the following decades, the Dutch and Spanish vied for control of the Taipei area. Under Dutch rule, rebellious aboriginal groups were forcibly suppressed, converted to Christianity, and schools were set up. It was also this period that saw the overhunting and extinction of Taiwan's indigenous species of deer to fuel Dutch trade. Eventually, in 1662, the Dutch were driven from Danshui by the Ming dynasty loyalist Koxinga, or Zheng Chenggong. Zheng had hoped to retake China from its new Qing dynasty rulers using Taiwan as his base, but that did not happen.

Danshui River communities

After Taiwan came under Chinese control, settlers poured into Taipei, most of them from Fujian Province, just across the strait from Taiwan.

In those days, the Danshui River was still deep enough for river transport, and settlements sprang up along its banks. Wanhua, in the southwest corner of today's Taipei, prospered as a trading center, as did adjoining areas. Expansion was steady, and by the mid-1700s, Taipei had become a collection of prosperous farming and trading neighborhoods. The fertile basin produced staples like rice and vegetables, while the rich seas off Danshui provided abundant fish. Business was brisk, with tea and camphor from the hills above Taipei creating a lively market for overseas trade after the 1858 Treaty of Tianjin.

A tough environment

Like the rest of Taiwan then, Taipei was only loosely governed by the Qing administration. During the 1700s and 1800s, it was not a city as such, but a series of small fiefdoms carved out by local warlords, trading companies, and large clan families. Forced to contend with invasions from rival gangs of immigrants and

A Taipei street scene during Japanese rule.

from aborigine attacks in outlying areas, each neighborhood in Taipei built narrow stone gates to seal itself off, a hallmark of those lawless times.

But Taipei was also a city of great opportunity. Far from the regulations of imperial China, Taiwan was a sort of untamed frontier, where immigrants who had vision and energy could prosper. Farmers with landholdings amassed fortunes, as did moneylenders and traders in tea, camphor, and opium. In their wake came craftsmen, laborers, and fortune-seekers from China.

Chinese control

Life took a turn for the better in the late 1800s. In 1875, Taipei was named a prefectural city, and in 1885 Taiwan became an official province of China. A city wall was built from 1882 to 1884. In 1885, an ambitious governor named Liu Mingchuan moved the provincial capital from Tainan to Taipei, and launched reforms. He brought electricity to the city – the first in China to have it – and laid a railway from Taipei to the port of Keelung, about 30km (20 miles) away.

Alas, the period of reform was short-lived. In 1894–5, far to the north, the Japanese pounded the ill-equipped Chinese troops in the First Sino-Japanese War. One of the spoils of Japan's easy victory over the crumbling Qing dynasty was Taiwan, ceded under the 1895 Treaty of Shimonoseki.

> Owen Rutter writes of mid-1800s Taiwan in Through Formosa: An Account of Japan's Island Colony: "The government was corrupt…the country was ravaged by bands of brigands…sanitary conditions were filthy…"

Qing supporters among Taiwan's ruling class tried to prevent Japanese occupation of the island by declaring a Republic of Formosa, but the plan fell through when troops from China began rampaging. Japanese soldiers soon restored order, and sporadic native resistance over the years was eventually quelled.

Propaganda during the Chinese Civil War.

Japanese rule

The Japanese were harsh rulers, forcing the Taiwanese to learn Japanese, and strip-mining the island's resources for imperial Japan. Still, some historians argue that the Japanese occupation was the dawn of modern Taiwan, and that stern discipline was necessary to bring the fractured Chinese together under one

---

COLONIAL TAIPEI

Eager to make a success of their first colony, the Japanese built majestic theaters, lively restaurants and bathhouses, and tree-lined boulevards. They carved out a prime piece of riverfront property – today's Ximending – and declared it a pleasure zone. Many of the classic buildings in Taipei date from this era, including the Presidential Office Building, the Red Theater, and others. Owen Rutter, who visited in 1923, describes the city as such: "Taihoku [Taipei] is undoubtedly laid out on a finer scale than any other city in the Japanese empire, with wide streets, spacious parks, and public buildings that would not disgrace any capital in the world."

---

government. The Japanese rigorously enforced their laws – then a new concept to the people of Taipei – and ended the ceaseless plundering, gang violence, and bandit/aborigine raids that had plagued the city.

The Japanese tore down the old city walls, a traffic-stopping anachronism, and also built roads, harbors, railroads, and crucially, power plants, giving birth to the city's first light industry. They also established banks and standardized the monetary system. They built schools islandwide, and many Taiwanese received a formal education for the first time. The unpleasant open sewers and outhouses that typified Taipei life were replaced by modern underground pipes.

Civil war in China

But the era of Japanese rule did not last. When World War II ended in 1945, Taiwan was formally returned to Chinese rule under terms previously agreed upon in Cairo between Allied leaders Winston Churchill, Franklin Roosevelt, and Chiang Kai-shek, who was then nominal leader of China's government. Events on the mainland would once again determine the island's fate.

In the years leading up to World War II, even as Taiwan enjoyed peace and stability, China had entered a period of chaos. The Qing dynasty collapsed in 1911, and the Republic of China was established the following year, under the leadership of revered revolutionary Sun Yat-sen. However, Sun was unable to maintain his hold on power, and for the next three decades, various warlords and factions fought for control of China.

> *The arriving Nationalists treated Taipei citizens with contempt, seeing them as Japanese sympathizers and citizens of a defeated nation. Indeed, many men had fought China beside the Japanese.*

Eventually, the struggle was dominated by two groups: the Nationalists, or Kuomintang (KMT), under Chiang Kai-shek, and the Chinese Communist Party, under Mao Zedong. The two sides briefly ceased open hostilities under an uneasy truce during World War II, but in 1946, as the world watched, China was once again plunged into a civil war between the American-backed Nationalists and the Russian-backed Communists.

The February 28 Incident

On October 21, 1946, Chiang Kai-shek visited Taiwan on a groundswell of goodwill and hope. The crowds were happy to welcome Chinese rulers after 50 years of Japanese occupation. However, their smiles turned to shock and dismay when they saw the ragged soldiers who accompanied Chiang, many of whom were rude, dirty, uneducated, and penniless. The Taipei people, accustomed to rule by the clean and orderly Japanese, were aghast.

Preoccupied by the ongoing civil war with the Communists, Chiang returned to China and appointed the corrupt Chen Yi to govern Taiwan. Trouble was not long in coming.

On February 27, 1947, officers from the Monopoly Bureau in Taipei tried to stop an elderly widow from selling black-market cigarettes, and she was wounded. A crowd gathered, a scuffle broke out, and the officers opened fire, killing a man. The next day, on February 28 (which later became known as the 2-28 -Incident), crowds gathered to protest, and were met with resistance. This ignited a violent uprising that spread throughout the island. Governor Chen Yi sent for reinforcements, and a massacre began. Thousands of unarmed Taiwanese were shot and killed, and thousands more were dragged from their homes and later disappeared. The brutal suppression took between 18,000 and 28,000 lives, according to a government report released in 1992.

Nationalist exodus

Meanwhile, after a protracted struggle on the mainland, the Communists seized control of China, establishing the People's Republic of China (PRC) in 1949 under Mao Zedong. Chiang Kai-shek fled to Taiwan in the same year with the defeated Nationalists – more

Chinese Nationalist soldiers head for Taiwan, bearing the Republic of China's flag.

than 2 million ragged immigrants from mainland China. Most of them settled in Taipei – which became the base for Chiang Kai-shek's Republic of China (ROC) – filling the spacious Japanese parks with squalid shanty towns.

> The immigrants from China in 1949 were mostly male, giving Taipei a high ratio of men to women. The city's sex gap widened further after abortion became legal in 1985.

Since taking over the island the KMT had treated the city as its own, illegally annexing property owned by the Taiwanese. Because officers and other well-connected immigrants had no land and no jobs, they were given all the top government positions; the regular troops were largely left to fend for themselves, especially after demobilization was commenced. The people of Taipei had no role in government and no voice in political affairs, though many were educated and

Woodcut depicting events of the 2-28 Incident.

wealthy. Resentment grew over the nepotism of the new government. Given Chiang's propensity for ruthless and autocratic rule, well established in mainland China, it soon became clear that he would continue the period of oppression known as the White Terror, not end it.

The White Terror

The 2-28 Incident set the tone for the White Terror that followed, a frightening era that was typified by executions without trial, midnight knocks on the door, long prison terms for political dissidents, and strict suppression of everything Taiwanese, including the native languages. Chiang Kai-shek's secret police were unpredictable and arbitrary, and his victims had no legal recourse. Chiang himself is said to have signed at least one execution order every day, and sometimes up to 10, for almost a decade. In this way, many of Taipei's best and brightest – students down to high-school level, professors, doctors, and scholars – were imprisoned or killed.

The White Terror repression was sweeping. A few of the victims were avowed communists, seduced by the same spell that had captivated mainland China. More were critics who spoke out against the inefficiency and corruption of the Chiang dictatorship. Others were innocent students who shared the same campuses with the communists and critics.

Chiang and his Nationalist government were, during the first 15 years of their rule, obsessed with retaking mainland China. They saw Taipei as merely a temporary capital and a launchpad. Thus, they paid little attention to the utilities, transportation, housing, parks, and other amenities that make life easier and more pleasant. As it grew, the city became crowded and dirty, snarled in traffic, and hamstrung by civic mismanagement. This gave Taipei a lingering, bad reputation, a sorry situation that did not change until the 1990s, when the elected government finally turned its attention to the capital city's infrastructure and made much-needed improvements.

Eventually, it became clear that the Nationalists had no chance of retaking mainland China, and Taiwan turned its full attention to the economy, where it had great success.

Building a road in the early days of Chiang Kai-shek's Republic of China.

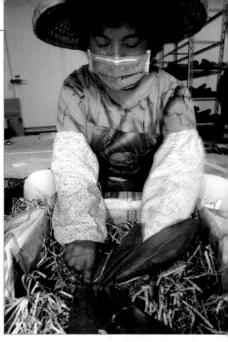

A worker at a flower farm; Taiwan is one of the leading exporters of orchids.

Building a model economy

In the 1950s, the government promoted agriculture through land reforms. Because Chiang had no power base in Taiwan, he had no entanglements to overcome or special interests to protect, and was able to introduce sweeping changes. Sharecroppers were given sharp rent reductions, public lands were sold to tenant farmers at 2.5 times the value of one year's main crop, and a land-to-tiller program forced landlords to sell land they did not farm themselves. By leveling the playing field and sowing the seeds of equal economic opportunity, the land reform launched Taiwan on the road to prosperity.

In the 1960s, using its prosperous agriculture as an export base – especially of sugar and pineapples – Taiwan shifted to light industry, the government emphasizing the manufacture of labor-intensive exports such as textiles, paper, and electrical goods. With its low labor costs and hardworking people, Taiwan soon became a successful exporting country.

In the 1970s, to fuel the transition to more advanced industry, the focus was on infrastructure, and several projects were initiated, including the North-South Freeway and the Chiang Kai-shek (now Taiwan Taoyuan) International Airport, plus railways, roads, harbors, and a nuclear power plant. Then, as land and labor costs rose, Taiwan moved into high-tech manufacturing and shifted labor offshore, much of it to China.

In 1980, in a stroke of far-sighted genius, and long before other countries in Asia caught on, Taiwan realized the importance of electronics, and government planners launched the Hsinchu Science-based Industrial Park (today the Hsinchu Science Park), which would become the epicenter of Taiwan's electronics industry and a global leader in semiconductor manufacturing. As the capital of a rising economic power, and home to many corporate head offices and regional headquarters, Taipei found its niche as a services center and became the administrative hub of the country.

Taiwan's smooth transition from rural backwater to powerhouse high-tech exporter makes it, in many ways, a model economy.

Chiang Ching-kuo (left) and Lee Teng-hui (right).

Today, Taipei is a high-tech, modern city.

Losing political clout

Politically, however, things were not going as well. In the 1970s, several critical changes altered Taiwan's relationship with the world. The government-in-exile had long been considered the legitimate administration of China, and was supported by the world's anti-communist powers. Taipei hosted a succession of world leaders, and considered itself a capital city of global stature.

SPARKLING MRT

Used by over two million passengers every day, the Taipei MRT, or metro, is the epitome of the country's modern miracle. Opened only in 1996 with the 10.5km-long (6.5 mile) Muzha line and just 12 stations, it has experienced rapid development. Every few years a service on a new line begins operations, and as of 2014, the network is 134.6km-long (83.6 mile), has eight lines (Xinyi and Songshan are the newest), and 113 stations. Several new routes are under construction and the long-term vision is that the MRT system will be extended to more than 270 kilometers (167.7 miles).

All that changed in 1971, when the UN admitted China and expelled Taiwan. A year later, President Richard Nixon made his landmark visit to China, paving the way for formal US recognition of the People's Republic. Following this watershed 1979 announcement, Taipei was gripped for days by anti-American riots that engulfed the US embassy. Uneasily, Taiwan was forced into playing second fiddle to China, a huge and unpredictable country of growing political and military influence.

Long road to democracy

At the time of Chiang Kai-shek's death in 1975, the country was prospering, but the Taiwanese, whose ancestors arrived more than three centuries ago, still considered the China-born Nationalists as outsiders. Despite the persecutions of martial law, dissent percolated throughout the island, finally boiling over with the Kaohsiung Incident, a landmark event in the development of Taiwan's democracy.

It occurred in December 1979, when a pro-democracy journal called *Meilidao*, "Formosa Magazine," organized a rally in Kaohsiung. The

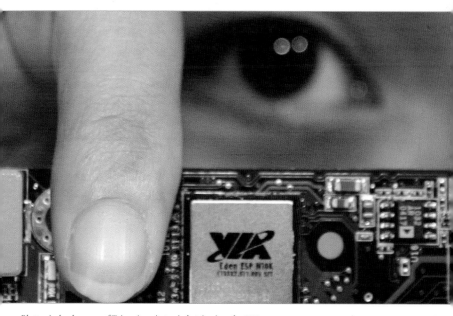

Electronics has been one of Taiwan's mainstay industries since the 1980s.

rally was repeatedly interrupted by riot police and tear gas, and it soon became a violent confrontation. The rally organizers, including famous dissident Shih Ming-teh and Annette Lu, who later became vice-president, were charged with sedition. They were defended by a team of lawyers that included Chen Shui-bian, who later became president, and Frank Hsieh, who later became premier. The riots and subsequent trial galvanized the people of Taiwan against martial law. It was the crucible in which the opposition Democratic Progressive Party (DPP) was forged, and a turning point in modern Taiwan's history.

After the Kaohsiung Incident, the situation had to change. Chiang Kai-shek's son, Chiang

ELEGY OF SWEET POTATOES

In Taipei, as elsewhere, political repression spawned a generation of heroes. Among them were well-known dissidents like Peng Ming-min and Bo Yang, men who were imprisoned for their beliefs and later became outspoken advocates of freedom. But the tyranny also created quieter heroes, including the remarkable Tsai Tehpen, author of an extraordinary work of prison literature called *Elegy of Sweet Potatoes: Stories of Taiwan's White Terror*.

Tsai spent 13 months in the Nationalist gulag, beginning in October 1954, and he recounts his nightmare in a straightforward style that is as much of a pleasure to read as possible. Accused of owning a book about Mao Zedong, Tsai's ordeal began with five days of fatigue investigation, without sleep or water, and ended in a re-education camp, where he was forced to recite propaganda about the greatness of Chiang Kai-shek. In the end he was acquitted, but not before spending many terrifying months in prison.

The book is filled with gripping and tragic stories from fellow inmates, combined with acute observations about prison conditions, guards, and lifestyles. The horror of the White Terror was carefully chronicled by Tsai, for which students of Taiwanese history have a profound gratitude. The Chinese edition of the book has garnered three major literature awards.

Ching-kuo, had become president in 1978. Unlike his father, the younger Chiang was friendly and personable. He also clearly saw the need for reform. Across Asia, the tide was turning in favor of democracy; martial law under autocrat Ferdinand Marcos was lifted in the Philippines, and pro-democracy protests were under way in Korea and China. International pressure to end martial law in Taiwan was increasing, particularly from the US. In 1987, Chiang announced the lifting of martial law, and the people were allowed to travel to China for the first time since 1949. Chiang died in 1988, and the ban on political parties was formally ended the following year.

Lee Teng-hui became the island's first Taiwan-born president in 1988, and, in 1996, its first president ever elected by popular vote. His triumphant march through the streets of Taipei, to a rising chorus of heartfelt cheers, was a momentous event for the people.

Coming of age

Taiwan's 2000 presidential election was a contest between Nationalist candidate Lien Chan,

The city's iconic Taipei 101 tower.

Taiwan remains a major goods exporter with busy ports.

independent James Soong and DPP candidate Chen Shui-bian. Chen eventually won, ending 55 years of Nationalist rule on the island. This was a milestone in Taiwan's long journey from dictatorship to democracy. Chen served two terms, but an ever-widening whirlpool of scandals brought the DPP low in the 2008 elections, with middle-of-the-road voters turning to the KMT en masse and bringing Ma Ying-jeou to power. Despite growing concerns that Taiwan's sovereignty was eroding under Ying-jeou's rule, he was re-elected president in 2012.

Taipei itself has entered something of a golden age. The city's infrastructure has been greatly improved: a series of road and rail projects has alleviated the city's once-notorious traffic problems. In the Xinyi District, now the most glamorous neighborhood in town, the Taipei 101 tower soars at record-breaking height. Modern Taipei, at long last, has turned into one of the most agreeable cities in Asia. It may bear the indelible marks of its turbulent history, and manifest the spirited frisson of its diverse throngs, but the city of Taipei today is assuredly blazing a path into a new age.

Cross-strait tensions

The ongoing tension between Taiwan and China is one of the world's biggest headaches – a hotspot that could potentially ignite a global conflict.

The two countries have an emotive relationship: mainland China has a deep desire to retake Taiwan, which it considers a breakaway province, and has repeatedly threatened to take it by force. But polls show that the majority of people in Taiwan prefer the status quo – that is, de facto independence from China. That stance has toughened since the 1990s, as China-born "mainlander" immigrants have lost influence, and a Taiwanese identity has emerged. Many Taiwanese see no compelling reason to join China, which they view as a poorly governed country where laws and courts are suspect, personal freedom is limited, and quality of life is not as good.

The two states are far apart politically, but economically they are comfortable bedfellows. Taiwanese investments in China have surged since 1990, with current estimates reaching US$14 billion. Two-way trade has grown from just US$5 billion in 1990 to over US$165 billion in 2013. Over 750,000 Taiwanese, businesspeople and dependants, now live in China at least 180 days a year. Importantly, China is Taiwan's largest trading partner.

With the Kuomintang's return to national power in 2008, the economic doors to China have been thrown open, and the two sides are moving closer politically. The business sector is pleased with events, but pro-independence advocates are aghast, seeing all efforts at rapprochement as appeasement and setting the stage for an eventual attempt at reunification. Nevertheless, there are now direct flights between the two countries, and Chinese tourists are allowed to enter Taiwan territory.

Throughout the 1990s, the Taiwan-China dialogue was shaped by politician Lee Teng-hui, who did a lot to further pro-independ-ence sentiments; China had little success with him. In 1996, as Taiwan prepared to hold its first popular presidential election, China tried to derail Lee's campaign by launching missiles near the island, but the move backfired, and Lee won the majority.

The third major player in the conflict, the US, does not support Taiwan's independence. But the Taiwan Relations Act, an agreement signed between the US and Taiwan in 1979, implies that America will defend Taiwan against attack. As the stalemate drags on, Taiwan continues to act like an independent country, electing its own leaders and pursuing its own foreign policy, though the current administra-

Taiwanese military maneuvers in 1996.

tion does nothing to displease Beijing. It maintains a strong military and service is mandatory for males (however, conscription is to be ceased by 2017); approximately 215,000 soldiers currently serve full time in the armed forces.

Meanwhile, on the streets of Taipei, the existence of a distant threat does not dampen the spirit of overall prosperity.

In Dalongdong Baoan Temple.

The intricate interior at the Zhuchi Temple in downtown Sanxia.

RELIGION

Taipei is one of the most religiously tolerant cities on Earth; every god is welcome and represented here. Buddhism, Taoism, and Confucianism are the main formal religions, but the old folk customs, beliefs, and superstitions guide daily life and permeate all levels of society.

Religious freedom in Taipei has lent the city a colorful atmosphere that can be found nowhere else, and certainly not in China, where many temples were destroyed and religions almost hounded out of existence during the Cultural Revolution. Many ancient Chinese rituals and ceremonies are still practiced with great pomp and pageantry in Taiwan, though they have all but disappeared in China and been reduced in scale elsewhere. The city is filled with an astonishing variety of temples and monasteries that welcome visitors and provide vivid local color. Exuberant festivals, such as a deity's birthday celebrations, take place year round.

> *In the hills around Taipei, Buddhist groups build huge monasteries, which on weekends are filled with city dwellers seeking peace through meditation.*

Paper money to be burnt for the gods.

Buddhism and Taoism are Taipei's main religions, while Confucianism provides a daily code of ethics for many of its citizens. At the same time, Christian missionaries walk the streets, and churches and mosques dot the neighborhoods.

According to Ministry of the Interior statistics, in 2011 there were over 15,300 places of worship in the country, including nearly 12,000 temples and over 3,300 churches. A total of 27 different religions are recognized by the government, no mean feat considering that religious groups must meet certain requirements – such as having a minimum number of local believers and sufficient funds – to achieve official recognition.

Traditional customs, beliefs, icons, and old superstitions permeate all levels of society in Taipei. Most adults – even those who may not profess a particular religion – routinely worship at a church or temple, and engage in spiritual activity. It is common to see homes and shops with an illuminated shrine, or people burning incense to honor a deity, hero, or ancestor. Most families perform ancestor worship, and at important times – such as when a son or daughter takes a university entrance exam – parents will visit a temple to burn incense, light candles, and solicit divine help. Many drivers in Taiwan adorn their cars with charms, statuettes, and religious invocations for protection against accidents.

The role of folk religion

In his book *Private Prayers and Public Parades: Exploring the Religious Life of Taipei*, Mark Caltonhill observes: The "Han-Chinese, who form the vast majority of Taipei's population, tend to say they are people of 'Three Religions' *(San Jiao)*… Confucianism *(Ru Jiao)*, Daoism *(Dao Jiao)*, and Buddhism *(Fo Jiao)*… [It is not] that these religions are not important in the lives of many Taipei citizens, but rather, that the day-to-day religious practices seen around the city really belong to a 'folk' or 'popular' tradition that runs alongside, beneath, or above these Three Religions."

Most people in Taipei subscribe to a kind of folk religion that has its roots in Buddhism, Confucianism, and Taoism, but also includes a broad mixture of other mystical and superstitious beliefs, and a vast pantheon of deities, beings, and spirits, both fearsome and benevolent. An important component is ancestor worship. Many Taiwanese believe that upon death,

Preparing offerings for the Baosheng Festival.

A supplicant at Longshan Temple.

a person becomes a spirit, and that the spirit has the same needs as a person on Earth: food, shelter, money, and a place to live. So when a loved one passes away, members of his or her family will burn "hell money" and miniature paper houses, and offer food and other items of use in the afterlife.

> Taiwan folk traditions are opportunistic. Whereas faiths like Christianity require believers to adhere exclusively to their doctrines, most Taiwanese embrace a deity or practice that brings them succor.

A pragmatic approach to prayer

The approach to prayer in Taipei is essentially pragmatic: What has this god done for me lately? If a god fails to deliver – usually money, marriage, or a promotion – the petitioner may turn to another deity. But it works both ways. Worshippers can ask gods for divine assistance, but they usually must express gratitude by burning paper money, lighting incense and candles, offering fruit or drinks or food, or even

A worshipper lights incense.

Buddhist, Taoist, and folk icons reside together. The key gods will always be located in the main hall, which will be fronted by a courtyard, and most lesser folk gods, who have origins in Chinese antiquity, are located in the rear of the temple complex.

Buddhist temples are quieter than their Taoist counterparts, and are geared more toward reflection than worship. Many are located in hillside monasteries, and these have a more hushed and reverent tone. Visit Shandao Temple for an example within the city. By Western standards, they may not be that quiet, yet they are not the hives of activity that Taoist temples are. Guanyin, the Goddess of Mercy, is featured in many Buddhist temples.

Buddhism is expanding rapidly overseas, and the epicenter of this global Buddhist renaissance is Taiwan. The island may seem like an unlikely place for a religious revival, but it makes sense: Taiwan is rich, and it has religious freedom. As elsewhere, many people in Taiwan are finding that material wealth does not satisfy their spiritual needs and are going in search of enlightenment.

performing penitential rites during a festival. If a petitioner fails to return a favor, bad fortune may follow.

To witness the role of religion in the daily life of the city, a visitor should head straight for one of the temples. These intoxicating places are filled with atmosphere – and thick incense smoke – and are the focal point of the city's religious life. Most temples in Taipei are mixtures of different deities, practices, and rituals.

FAMILY ALTARS

A family altar sits in the main room of most Taiwanese homes. This is where household gods and ancestors are worshipped in an ancient tradition that has changed little over the centuries. On the altar are small statues of the household god(s), and to the left are the ancestral tablets that contain family records, including the names of ancestors dating back many generations. Incense is offered daily, and on special days, offerings of food are placed on the altar. The set-ups take many forms: in some homes a simple shelf hangs on the wall, while others boast large, intricately carved shrines that take up a great deal of space.

The icon of Mazu at Baoan Temple.

The Guandu Temple's ornate roof.

Catholic worshippers at St Christopher's Church.

A new brand of Buddhism

Taiwan's Buddhism is not the gentle philosophy of self-denial and meditation that Westerners may associate with Buddhism; its powerful groups have come down from the mountains and into the world, so to speak, with the mission of practicing a compassionate religion suited for modernity. Powered by Taiwan's economic prosperity, they have extended their vision of "Buddhism in the human realm" far beyond the island's shores.

They are rebranding this ancient religion, and transforming it into a dynamic force that can compete with other faiths for the hearts and minds of the world's religious believers.

There are five main Buddhist organizations in Taiwan, each led by a charismatic nun or monk. All five groups are wealthy and have built extravagant temples, but also founded schools, hospitals, and charities. They are Fo Guang Shan, Chung Tai Chan, Tzu Chi, Ling Jiou Mountain

MAZU, PATRON OF SEAFARERS

Mazu, the patron saint of seafarers, is perhaps the most popular folk deity in Taiwan. According to legend, Mazu was born in the Song dynasty (960–1279) as Lin Mo, the daughter of a fisherman, on an island off the coast of China's Fujian Province. One day, her father and brothers were caught in a typhoon while at sea, and their ship sank. The young Lin Mo saw them in a dream, and tried to save them using mystical powers. Upon waking, she learned that her brothers, but not her father, had been miraculously saved. She died at 28, but continued to save other seafarers, often through miraculous means, and she soon became known as Mazu, or "maternal ancestor."

Because the Taiwan Strait is a treacherous body of water, early immigrants from the mainland carried with them statues of Mazu, or incense ash from one of her temples. Upon arrival in Taipei, or elsewhere, they erected temples in her honor. The icon of Mazu is usually immediately recognizable by her dark blue visage. She is flanked by a pair of dramatic statues with huge, exaggerated eyes and ears, called Eyes that See a Thousand Miles, and Ears that Hear upon the Wind, who help the goddess locate sailors in distress. Her birthday celebration, observed on the 23rd day of the 3rd lunar month, is one of Taiwan's most important religious festivals.

Buddhist Society, and Dharma Drum Mountain. Fo Guang Shan is the biggest, with over 200 branches in 30 countries. Chung Tai Chan (*chan* is Mandarin for Zen) is maybe the most esoteric, with its unusual young monastery in central Taiwan, complete with giant TV screens to greet visitors, to bolster its mission to tend to the spiritually and physically needy. It has over 90 meditation centers all over the world, including eight in the United States.

The third is Hualien-based Tzu Chi Foundation, mostly a charity organization that runs one of the world's largest registries of bone-marrow donors, plus a string of hospitals and an international relief organization that has rendered aid everywhere from Afghanistan to tsunami-struck Indonesia. Ling Jiou Mountain, the fourth, opened the Museum of World Religions in 2001 in suburban Taipei, while its large and still expanding "sacred mountain" complex is on the northeast coast. The fifth is Dharma Drum Mountain, which opened the massive Dharma Drum Mountain Nung Chan Monastery complex just north of Taipei in 2005, and in 2012, added the Water-Moon Dharma Center. The focal feature of the center's scenery

is a mirror-like pool in front of the main hall. The mission of Dharma Drum Mountain – embodied by its ecological seminars, social welfare programs, and meditation retreats – remains to "build a pure land on Earth."

The growth of Christianity

Aside from these essentially Asian beliefs, a large number of people in Taipei are practicing Protestants (as was Chiang Kai-shek himself) and Catholics. Christianity was first brought to Taiwan by the Dutch and Spanish, who occupied the island in the 1600s. With the traders came the missionaries, who learned the native languages and converted the aborigines. Mark Caltonhill writes: "Missionaries were particularly successful among the indigenous population, perhaps because of the egalitarian nature of their approach compared with the discriminatory policies of the Japanese administration and the entrenched prejudices of the Han-Chinese majority." Even today, many Christians are descended from the native peoples of Taiwan. Today, more than 95 percent of Taiwan's 537,000 aborigines belong to a Christian denomination.

A newly married couple pose at the Museum of Drinking Water.

Buddhist nuns in Jinguashi.

FESTIVALS AND CELEBRATIONS

The capital hosts a calendar of celebrations that shed light on Chinese culture and provide a dramatic spectacle for visitors.

Most religious festivals adhere to the Chinese lunar calendar, so dates vary from the Gregorian calendar (see page 261). The first annual event – and most important – is the Chinese Lunar New Year, greeted with firecracker blasts to scare away ghosts. The traditional 15 days of feasting, reunion, and visiting are largely conducted among family and friends, and the city becomes quiet during the holiday from work, which may last the entire first week. But the festival run-up, when shops sell traditional *nianhuo* (New Year goods), is interesting for tourists. In summer, the Dragon Boat Festival is celebrated (see pages 78 and 244). Equally interesting is the Mid-Autumn Festival, dedicated to the harvest moon. Among the grand celebrations are more solemn observances. During Ghost Month, after Hell's Gates open on the 1st day of the 7th lunar month, the city is filled with incense smoke from offerings and the superstitious tread lightly. Throughout the year, the various gods' birthday festivals are significant for religious Taipeiers.

The birthday of Confucius is observed on Teacher's Day at Taipei's Confucius Temple. During this highly ritualized event, the main celebrants of the ceremony – often high-ranking government officials – welcome the spirit of the great sage with rites, incense, and offerings.

Giant puppets (shenou) such as this, representing various supernatural beings, are often seen at religious processions. Another eerie practice sometimes seen is the self-flagellation of temple mediums who enter a trance.

During the ritual fire-walking, those fulfilling penitential vows race across burning coals carrying a deity's palanquin.

Performers wear papier maché masks at Baosheng Festival.

Intricate and precisely choreographed mass displays are a highlight of the National Day celebrations, which take place in front of the Presidential Office Building in westside Taipei.

NON-RELIGIOUS AND THEMED FESTIVALS

Experience Chinese culture at a local event.

Taipei plays host to many secular festivals. The best known is National Day, or Double Tenth Day, a countrywide event on October 10 that honors the founding of the Republic of China in 1912 by Dr Sun Yat-sen. The event starts with a public parade through Taipei, the president of Taiwan gives a policy speech, and firework displays light up the city.

One of the most anticipated annual events is the Taiwan Culinary Exhibition, held at the Taipei World Trade Center every August. With dramatic chef contests, food for sale, cooking classes, and pavilions featuring Taiwanese and regional Chinese cuisines, this fair is one of the island's exhibition highlights. Another key annual event is the Taipei Film Festival, launched in 1999 and held every summer. It showcases work by Taiwan's talented movie-makers and also screens dozens of overseas movies. Taipei also boasts smaller festivals, such as the Yangmingshan Flower Festival in spring and the Yingge Ceramics Festival in summer. At the ceramics festival, visitors can tour working kilns and watch artisans at work.

The Lantern Festival is the cheeriest annual celebration in the city, as downtown Taipei turns into a swirling sea of colorful lanterns. It marks the final night (Yuan Xiao) of the Chinese New Year celebrations, and is traditionally a night for singles looking for love.

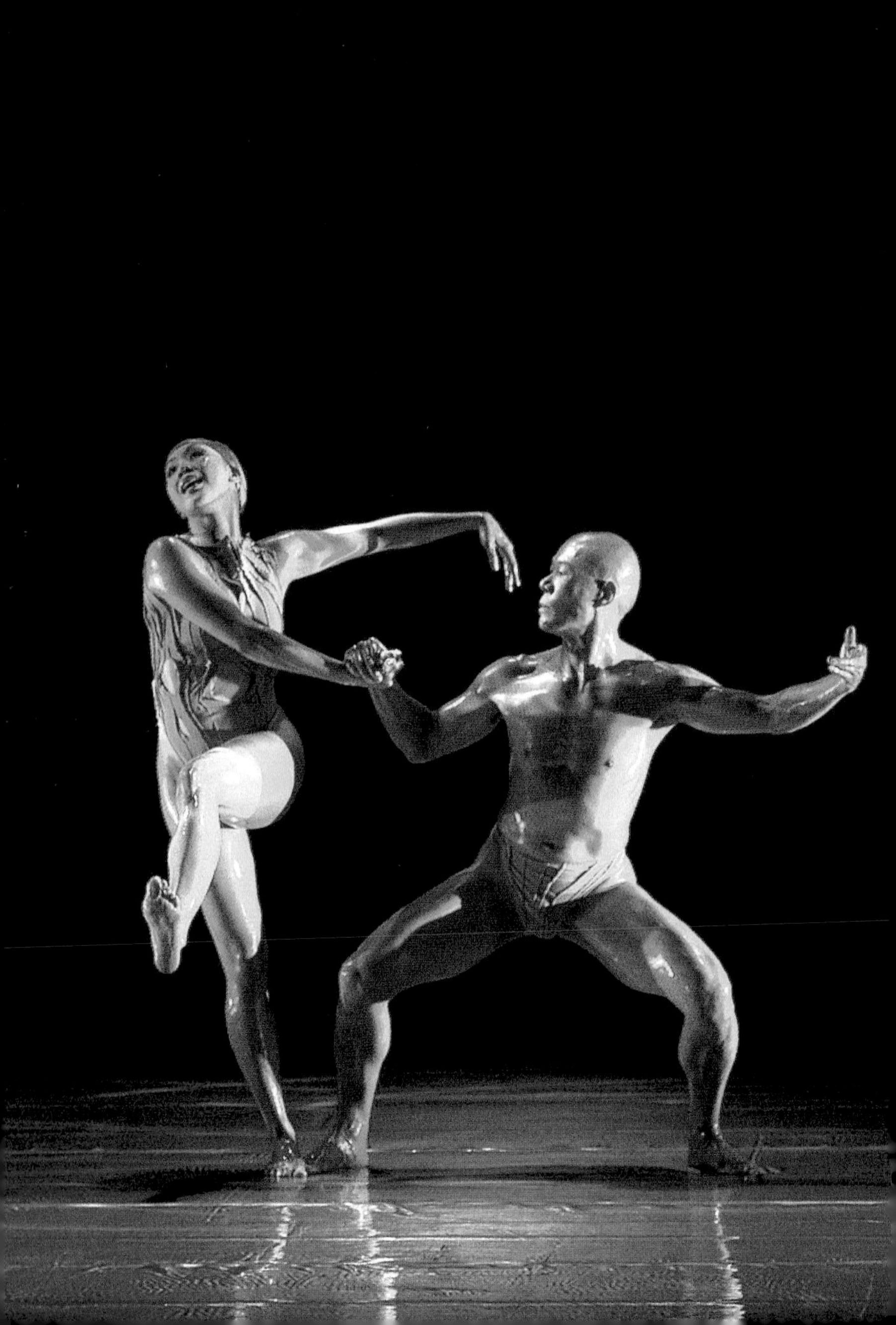

A performance of the Taipei Dance Circle.

THE ARTS

Taipei's lively arts scene, while respecting the antiquity of Chinese tradition, is distinguished by its New Wave cinema and modern dance, and enlivened by its minority-language literature, experimental theater, and a vibrant gallery scene.

When most people think of the arts in Taiwan, they call to mind the National Palace Museum, the world's premier collection of imperial Chinese art and antiquities. Indeed, the museum remains a must-see for visitors to the country, but bear in mind that the treasure trove of artifacts on display there forms just the tip of Taipei's artistic iceberg.

Today, the arts have become a medium for the Taiwanese to explore the issues of identity so often fought over in Taipei's rambunctious legislature. Many of the arts that speak of the greatness and antiquity of Chinese heritage are nowadays joined by arts that revel in the emergence of a local Taiwanese culture, adding dynamism to the city's cultural mix.

> According to the International Publishers Association, Taiwan ranks second in the world in terms of new book titles published in 2013 per citizen, second only to the United Kingdom.

Preserving traditions

For much of the second half of the 20th century, the Chinese Communist Party on mainland China directed waves of social movements aimed at obliterating tradition and modernizing the country, dealing crippling blows to the arts there. As such, Taiwan became something of a custodian of traditional Chinese culture, and its capital is in some ways a better place to get a glimpse of traditional Chinese art and performances.

Traditional hand-puppet show at the Lin Liu-hsin Puppet Theatre Museum.

Beijing opera in its original form lives on, with almost nightly performances alternating among Taiwan's pre-eminent troupes, of which the leading one is the Fu Hsing Academy. Taipei's National Theater and National Concert Hall, as well as the Novel Hall for Performing Arts, regularly schedule full-length operas and dance performances. The Taipei Chinese Orchestra, which performs Chinese instrumental music, plays regularly at Zhongshan Hall. There are new, state-of-the-art performing venues in the works too, with Taipei Performing Arts Center housing

TaipeiEYE performance of Chinese opera.

three theaters from 2015 and Taipei Pop Music Center opening in 2016.

Traditional Taiwanese puppet theater, a delightful folk art performed in the Taiwanese dialect, also survives. Performances can be caught at the Lin Liu-hsin Puppet Theatre Museum, where the curator and director of

TAIWANESE LITERATURE

Taiwan has produced no Mishimas or Murakamis – that is, no writers well known internationally. One reason, of course, is that very little Taiwanese literature has been translated into English. Another reason, however, is that for most of the 20th century the island's literature was circumscribed first by the Japanese administration and then by the KMT government, which encouraged writers to work around themes of nostalgia for mainland China and other politically safe issues. One of the few Taiwanese classics available in English, and a chilling indictment of traditional chauvinism and sexual violence, is Li Ang's *The Butcher's Wife*.

the resident Taiyuan Theatre Puppet Company is Dutchman Robin Ruizendaal, and at the Puppetry Art Center of Taipei.

For a tourist-friendly sampler of these performing arts, the TaipeiEYE holds weekly revues showcasing a bit of everything – Beijing opera, puppetry, Chinese acrobatics, musical ensembles, and even some indigenous Taiwanese dance pieces – with English subtitles where required. This condensed art is well suited to travelers on short visits.

Transitional forms

Taipei is very much a city in transition and is home to a lot of bold experimentation with traditional forms. Prominent examples of the more experimental theater groups that incorporate modern approaches into **traditional Chinese** opera and drama – usually featuring the inclusion of contemporary issues and settings – are Ping Fong Acting Troupe and the Green Ray Theater, among a host of others. Ya Yin Ensemble's style is usually labeled "avant-garde" Beijing opera, and while following the

Yang San-lang's oil painting "Sound of Waves."

performances can be a strain, they are a fascinating example of the ways in which Taiwan is redefining itself culturally.

Contemporary movements

When martial law was lifted in 1987, Taiwan began to look simultaneously inwards and outwards. Waves of young Taiwanese went abroad to study and work, bringing new ideas back with them when they returned to Taiwan.

Meanwhile, the increasingly pluralistic political environment that eventually led to the defeat of the Nationalists by the pro-independence Democratic Progressive Party in the 2000 presidential elections has also given rise to a more lively arts scene. Cinema and dance have reached new heights, and minority-language literature, experimental theater, and the gallery scene have been enlivened.

By all means take in the traditional arts when in Taipei, but don't miss out on the experience of a modern dance performance, a local film screening, or a tour of some excellent modern Taiwanese art.

Visual arts

Take a stroll along Anhe Road in Taipei's dynamic eastern district, and the many hole-in-the-wall galleries scattered here will attest to the city's thriving contemporary art scene. But for a comprehensive overview of the directions Taiwanese artists have been taking in the visual arts over the past century, there is just one destination: the Taipei Fine Arts Museum. The temporary exhibits here are varied – as likely to feature French Impressionists as the Taiwanese oils of the Japanese colonial era – but the permanent exhibition represents a unique opportunity to see Taiwan's emergence from both colonialism and one-party rule through the eyes of its painters.

For a comprehensive view of what Taiwanese artists have been doing in the contemporary arts over the past few months, past few weeks, or even the past few days, head to the Museum of Contemporary Art Taipei. Few museums in the world are as contemporary (or, for that matter, temporary) as this one. MOCA Taipei presents no permanent exhibitions, only special exhibitions, nor does it purchase works by the artists it exhibits. Going even further, most displayed works are created specially for the exhibitions in which they appear, and many cease to exist except as photographs in the MOCA catalogues when the exhibitions end, which can never capture the experience that the artworks produced in life. The only solution is to make frequent visits whenever the museum changes its galleries.

The Meiji-era Japanese artist Ishikawa Kinichiro (1871–10) is generally credited with being the "father of modern Taiwanese art." His influence gave rise to a first generation of so-called Western–influenced artists, who paid tribute in watercolors to the natural beauty of Taiwan and its then still rustic environment. Chief among these artists are Yang San-lang (1907–95) and Liao Chi-chun (1902–76); the latter's landscape work *Uluanpi Lighthouse* has become emblematic of the era's art.

By the 1920s and 1930s, Japanese experimentation with Expressionism started to take

Taiwanese director Ang Lee clutches his Academy Award for "Brokeback Mountain".

A still from Tsai Ming-liang's 2009 movie "Face."

hold in Taiwan, and Taiwanese artists began to apply bold oil colors to their celebrations of the Taiwanese countryside and rural life. The movement was put on hold by the turbulence of World War II, the eventual surrender of Japan and its withdrawal from Taiwan, and the arrival of the Chinese Nationalists. Taiwan's new government put the island under martial law and embarked on a program of fostering only traditional art forms. The inevitable backlash came in 1957, when two art societies were formed with the self-appointed task of modernizing Taiwanese art. The result was avant-garde approaches to traditional forms, such as pen-and-ink landscapes, the most famous exponent of which was Lin Kuo-song (b. 1932).

The 1970s saw yet another backlash, with artists of the "native soil" movement returning to the themes – and to a certain extent even the techniques – of the Japanese era. It is a style that has retained a certain popularity to this day, particularly among the so-called "unschooled" rustic artists, who are best and most famously typified by artist Hung Tung

Director Tsai Ming-Liang collects an award at an event in his honour during the Deauville Asian Film Festival, 2014.

(1920–87), who in his day drew enormous critical acclaim. But it is also a style that has been forced to find its niche in a bustling marketplace of artistic ideas that today draws on influences both local and international. Many contemporary Taiwanese artists are more likely to be experimenting with installation art and multimedia than extolling the pastoral splendor of rural Taiwan in oils and canvas.

Work by Taiwanese photographers has also received attention lately, as evidenced by the Taipei Fine Arts Museum's recent spending spree over the past decade to amass a collection of such work.

> Taipei has been appointed the World Design Capital 2016. The city has a bustling culture scene, is driven by design, yet it wants to find a balance between cutting-edge innovation and respect for nature.

Cinema

In the 1980s, a new generation of directors, notably Hou Hsiao-hsien and Edward Yang, aided by the Central Motion Picture Corporation, began making movies that collectively came to be known as the Taiwanese New Wave. Hou, in particular, between 1985 and 1989, was behind a series of internationally acclaimed and award-winning films, such as *Dust in the Wind, A Time to Live and a Time to Die*, and *City of Sadness*, whose evocative neo-realistic depictions of Taiwanese rural life won more fans in overseas art-house cinemas, unfortunately, than at home. Yang's 1985 effort, *Taipei Story*, on the other hand, was a bleak representation of dislocation and urban ennui among young Taiwanese adults.

With the 1990s came Taiwan's so-called Second New Wave of directors. The most internationally well known of these is the multiple award-winning Tsai Ming-liang. His early trilogy of movies about urban decay filmed between 1992 and 1997 – *Rebels of the Neon God, Vive L'Amour* (winner of the Golden Lion at the 1994 Venice Film Festival), and *The River* – are formally beautiful and very sparing with dialogue.

Hou Hsiao-hsien continued to be a major force in the 1990s, with *Puppet Master*, which won the Jury Prize at Cannes in 1993, and *Flowers of Shanghai* (1998), cumulatively garnering him the accolade of "Director of the Decade" in a 1999 poll of movie critics by the New York weekly *The Village Voice*.

Meanwhile, the Second New Wave saw the emergence of a young director who was to take his work decidedly into the mainstream. Ang Lee launched his career with *Pushing Hands* (1991), *The Wedding Banquet* (1993), and *Eat Drink Man Woman* (1994). *The Wedding Banquet* raised eyebrows in conservative Taiwan with its depiction of a gay couple, one of whom is forced into a heterosexual marriage of convenience. But then the movie was a hit overseas, winning the Golden Bear at the 1993 Berlin Film Festival. Lee has gone on to further international success, directing *Crouching Tiger, Hidden Dragon, Brokeback Mountain*, and *Life of Pi*, as well as the Chinese-language *Lust, Caution*. In contrast to Ang Lee's mainstream successes, both Hou and Tsai have continued to make movies

Yun-Fat Chow in the box-office smash, "Crouching Tiger, Hidden Dragon."

in the styles that have made them darlings of the art-house circuit. Tsai's *Wayward Cloud* (2005), a movie that combines the musical, dance, and pornographic genres, created a sensation at the Berlin Film Awards, where it premiered. It raised so many questions that it earned itself the distinction of having the

BOX-OFFICE TIGER

Ang Lee's 2000 film *Crouching Tiger, Hidden Dragon,* which was produced with about US$15 million, was the first non-English movie to make more than US$100 million in the US, and the first ever A-list kung fu movie, starring Michelle Yeoh and Yun-Fat Chow. Lee has continued to break down boundaries in his work, following *Crouching Tiger* up with *Brokeback Mountain* in 2005, which won the Golden Lion at Venice, four Golden Globes, and three Oscars, including for Best Director. Lee garnered the Academy Award for Best Director the second time for the 2012 film, *Life of Pi,* which received 11 nominations in total and collected four Oscars.

longest press conference in the awards' 55-year history. It went away with the FIPRESCI Prize and the Silver Bear.

Hou's *Café Lumière* (2003) was nominated for a Golden Lion at the 2004 Venice Film Festival, while his ode to love, *Three Times* (2005), was nominated for the Palme d'Or at the 2005 Cannes Film Festival.

In 2008 and 2009, Wei Te-Sheng's music-drama *Cape No. 7* was an unprecedented box office success in Taiwan, surpassing such Hollywood blockbusters as *Jurassic Park* and *The Lord of the Rings*. It won 15 awards in total and led to the revival of Taiwanese cinema. Subsequent huge hits with the Taiwanese audience have included Giddens Ko's romance *You are the Apple of My* Eye and Fung Kai's *Din Tao: Leader of the Parade* (both 2012).

However, it's Tsai Ming-liang that continues to be one of the most acclaimed Taiwanese film-makers in the world. His 2013 drama *Stray Dogs*, shot in Taipei, was another success, winning a Grand Jury Prize at the Venice Film Festival. In recent years, the capital of Taiwan also served as a backdrop for the Hollywood science-fiction movie *Lucy* (2014), directed by Luc Besson and starring Scarlett Johansson.

Dance

The "matriarch of Taiwanese dance" is perhaps the legendary Tsai Jui-yueh, who learned modern dance in Japan and brought it back to Taiwan, founding the China Dance Arts Institute in 1953. Her talents were neglected in the early days of Nationalist rule, when traditional Chinese dance was promoted over all other forms. But as the island inched towards liberalization in the 1960s and artists began to look to foreign influences again, Tsai began to train a new generation of Taiwanese dancers in a modern idiom. She retired to Australia in the early 1980s. Tsai passed away in 2006. Her lovely Japanese courtyard-style former Taipei studio complex, which was gutted by fire in 1999, has been refurbished and renamed the Tsai Jui-yueh Dance Studio – Rose Historic Site and declared a national heritage spot.

Tsai's influence is rivaled by Liu Feng-hsueh, who established a studio in 1967 and then went on to set up the Neo-Classic Dance Company in 1976, which continues to perform today. Meanwhile, as Liu was emerging as a major influence on modern dance in Taiwan, Lin Hwai-min was in the US, studying under Martha Graham – a woman whose influence on dance has been compared to Picasso's on painting and Stravinsky's on music. The result was the Cloud Gate Dance Theatre (www.cloudgate.org.tw), which Lin formed after he returned to Taiwan in 1973. His early themes were taken from Chinese legend, but he was quick to turn to the subject that has concerned so many other Taiwanese artists – the question of identity. His first major work on this subject was the 1978 production Legacy, an epic which told the story of Taiwan's early pioneers.

Lin's work, while continuing to evolve, has dodged back and forth between intimate local subjects – such as his 1997 show *Portrait of Families*, a sweeping story of life in Taiwan under Japanese rule – and themes that draw on a diverse range of sources in India, Southeast Asia and China, such as the eclectic *Songs of the Wanderers* (1997), which has

Dance is one area of the arts in which Taiwan has drawn international acclaim. The island's most famous troupe is Cloud Gate Dance Theatre, directed by Lin Hwai-min, considered one of the world's top choreographers.

been performed to great acclaim in Europe. These remain key works in the Cloud Gate repertoire.

Lin has been a formidable influence in Taiwan, and many former members of his troupe have broken away to form schools of their own. Notable among these are Lin Hsiu-wei, whose Taigu Tales Dance Theatre (www.taigu-tales.com) performs stark meditative acts that are redolent of Japan's *butoh* tradition. Another Cloud Gate breakaway was Liou Shaw-lu, who formed the Taipei Dance Circle in the 1980s. Following his death in 2014, the troupe was taken over by his wife, Yang Wan-rung.

A performance at the annual Tsai Jui-yueh Dance Festival.

Steamers of dumplings and buns at the famous restaurant Din Tai Fung.

CUISINE

Like much else in Taipei, dining has undergone a renaissance since the 1990s. The old-school restaurants serving authentic regional specialties are increasingly joined by a new wave of stylish outlets that excel in pan-Chinese fusion. Meanwhile, the humble street snack still satisfies late-night cravings.

Not so long ago, a dinner in the capital meant a visit to a Chinese restaurant with red and gold decor, spartan tables and chairs, but wonderful food and friendly old waiters. These are the old favorites that secured Taipei's culinary reputation as one of the best in Asia. Word of mouth is the best way to find one of these small and nondescript places tucked in the neighborhoods. People in Taipei are not fixated on the "great restaurant" concept, and they do not give out stars and awards. The food at these traditional establishments is regionally "pure": East never meets West, and fusion cuisine is not an option. Shanghainese is heavy and stewed, Sichuanese is hot and spicy, Cantonese is fast-cooked and fresh, and Taiwanese is mild and tends toward seafood – exactly the way they were meant to be.

But eventually, visitors may want to forgo the Formica tables and fading decor, and head uptown for the next generation of restaurants, whose excellent fare and elegant interiors have raised the bar for the city's eateries.

Fine dining at the Grand Hotel.

> What's that smell? It must be stinky tofu: every nightmarket is suffused with its pungent odor. But those who love this unusual food swear that getting past the odor rewards one with a great flavor.

The new wave of dining

The 20- and 30-somethings who have led the latest dining trends may have abandoned their parents' restaurants, but they have not abandoned their parents' food. Why would they? Chinese food is still king, but the new restaurants have lost the strict ethnic divisions, and serve a pan-Chinese fusion cuisine that is heavy on flavor but light on oil. Waitstaff are uniformly young and the ambience sophisticated. The newest trend is for Western-style service, with one dish served at a time rather than the all-at-once approach of the typical Chinese culinary experience (literally 20 minutes of flying chopsticks and it's all over).

By 2005, the nouveau restaurant trickle had become a flood, and today Taipei is awash with new and buzzing venues, filled with eye-catching designs and clientele. The food is typified by

Tucking into dumplings, a feature of Shanghainese cuisine.

superb, judiciously used ingredients. The menus are often small, featuring expertly cooked dishes. But don't be fooled by the upscale settings: even at the most chic places diners can let the chopsticks fly and drip sauce on the tablecloths. These restaurants may pour highballs and serve vodka shots, but this is still Taipei – they will put ice cubes in your beer unless you tell them not to.

If that is one too many bowls of *bai fan* (white rice) for you, Taipei also offers an array of non-Chinese cuisines. Trendy but simple Italian food has replaced the richer and more complex cuisine of France in some Asian cities, but not in Taipei. The city boasts numerous excellent French restaurants, all serving the fattest goose liver this side of the Seine, and most with wine lists as thick as a phone book.

Taipei also has simple, alfresco Italian bistros, Western sandwich shops, burger joints, excellent Indian restaurants, and all the other culinary virtues that accompany wealth and a cosmopolitan populace. Visitors are spoiled for choice.

THREE CUP CHICKEN

San bei ji or "Three Cup Chicken," an island specialty most often experienced by foreigners in local beerhouses, is perhaps Taiwan's most representative dish. It was perfect for farming folk in pioneer days because it allowed them to be away in the field.

The ingredients are simmered in an earthenware pot for hours, meaning no need for constant attention to a hot fire, in a "three cup" sauce, one of soy sauce, one of rice wine, one of sesame oil. Simple. Some substitute cane sugar for the sesame oil. The traditional recipe also calls for ginger and basil leaves, perhaps a more surprising ingredient. The dish is served in the pot when the sauce is almost fully absorbed into the meat, the chicken sizzling – almost popping with the heat – just the right side of burning. This original slow-cook dish is then eaten with rice or congee.

Locals say that a place that can't prepare *san bei ji* properly is not a true Taiwanese eatery. They also like to try such variations on the chicken as pork and dried beancurd, as well as more exotic options, such as frog, squid, and so on. Local males – each a self-confident Chinese-food expert – will also tell you that eating their favorite *san bei ji* without cold Taiwan beer is not a true three-cup experience.

Stinky tofu is a classic nightmarket dish.

Cooking sizzling eggs in bulk.

Taiwanese cooking

Among the various Chinese regional cuisines, Taiwanese cuisine, or *Taicai*, is less well known and more difficult to find beyond the island's shores, so visitors may not even know it exists. This may be due to Taiwan's long political isolation, or perhaps to the simpler, more rustic character of this style of cooking.

Descended from the culinary traditions of southern Fujian Province, Taiwanese cooking evolved in response to the geographical, economic, and agricultural conditions the island's early immigrants faced. Abundant seas and mountainous terrain gave rise to a reliance on fish and seafoods. Squid is routinely grilled or stir-fried, oysters added to vermicelli soup or omelets, clams are eaten raw, and dried anchovies are fried with peanuts. Hardship and scarcity in the early days gave rise to humble fare. Watery rice congee was filled out with sweet potatoes and accompanied by salted radish omelets and braised pig's trotters. An interesting local innovation is the use of basil to flavor dishes, as exemplified by the famous *san bei ji*, or "Three Cup Chicken".

Street snacks

Some of the best known and most loved local foods, however, are the *xiaochi*, or "small eats." Throughout town, many of the city's devoted foodies will be found in neighborhood nightmarkets, perched on plastic stools and eating hot snacks from temporary tables. Unlike in Singapore and Hong Kong, these street stalls have not been herded indoors into sterile malls and oil-stained parking lots. Save for Shilin Nightmarket, vendors ply their trades outdoors, under strings of bright lights, with flames a-leaping and wafts of smoke ascending skyward.

The food is invariably freshly cooked because the turnover is high. Many stands concentrate on a single dish, and the variety is remarkable. A

Tianbula is a local nightmarket standard, a unique Taiwan version of Japanese tempura. The art of batter-frying meats was taught to the Japanese by early Spanish and Portuguese missionaries.

The fast and flaming wok of Cantonese cooking.

Taipei nightmarket is a movable feast of congee, oyster omelets, stinky tofu, scallion pancakes, soup noodles, pork buns, roasted corn, dumplings, and piles of soy-braised tongues, innards, and other more exotic offerings. The grilled squid, brushed in sesame oil, hoisin and chili sauce, and dusted in cayenne pepper, is especially delicious.

But the real street classic of Taipei, sold from mobile carts all over town, and the local equivalent of the New York hot dog, is the humble barbecued sausage. Many a late-night drinker has emerged from a pub and walked straight to one of the town's ubiquitous sausage vendors. The sausages are cooked over the hot coals until the fat sputters and smokes; the smell of these salty-sweet sausages is as much a feature of Taipei as the motor-scooter exhaust smoke.

Regional cuisines of China

Just about every regional cuisine of China is available in Taipei, including steamed Shanghai dumplings, Northern Chinese wheat-based staples, Mongolian barbecue, Sichuan hot pot, Cantonese dim sum, dried Hunan ham – the list is virtually endless.

Taiwan's turbulent history is largely responsible for this happy culinary miracle. When soldiers and other immigrants poured into Taipei after the civil war in China in the late 1940s, they brought with them their favorite foods from all over the mainland. Many of the best restaurants in Taipei were first opened by newly arrived expert chefs who had previously worked in private households.

TIME TO EAT

Restaurants that serve breakfast will do so from about 7.30am to 9.30am. Kitchens will be open for lunch from noon until 2pm, and most people will eat dinner between 5pm and 7pm, though restaurant kitchens will be open from about 5pm to 9–9.30pm. The Taiwanese do not have a brunch tradition, and most eateries following a Western-style schedule, closing in between the main mealtimes, will not be open at this time. Several restaurants, especially those in international hotels, now offer afternoon tea. Note that many restaurants will remain open all day once their kitchen is open; in such cases detailed hours are given in the Restaurant listings.

Sichuan cuisine

The star of this popular cuisine is undoubtedly the Sichuan pepper, or *hua jiao*, a spice infamous for imparting a "numbing" sensation to the tongue. Together with black pepper and chili pepper, it has given Sichuan cooking its reputation for spiciness. But the chili oils and hot sauces used by Sichuan cooks to season their foods are not always strong, and the dishes usually have a sweet or sour flavor as well to provide balance. *Gongbao jiding*, known in the West as "Kung Pao Chicken," is a classic dish of chicken cubes stir-fried with chili and peanuts. Also famous is *mapo* tofu (spicy bean curd with minced pork), and *yin si juan*, a fried bread roll that sometimes serves as a substitute for rice.

Shanghainese cuisine

Taipei's version of this cuisine is lighter, less oily, and not nearly as sugary sweet. A perennial favorite is Beggar's Chicken. A tender spring chicken is stuffed full of ham, dried shrimp, mushrooms, scallions, soy sauce, Shaoxing rice wine, and a hint of black pepper; the juice from these fillings marinates the bird. Another favorite is sautéed beef with ginkgo nuts; the chunks of beef are marinated, then stir-fried with ginger and black pepper.

Don't miss the *dong po rou*, that famous marbled pork that warms body and soul on a winter day. The artery-clogging layers of meat and fat are salty, sweet, and tender, and literally melt in the mouth. It's not health food for sure, but it does taste good.

Deservedly or not, Shanghai also gets credit for one of the most delicious of Chinese foods, the *xiao long bao*. The slightly chewy skins of these mouth-watering "little dragon" dumplings contain a juicy filling of succulent minced pork and a delightfully warm and fragrant burst of gingery soup.

Related to Shanghainese cuisine is the fine, light food of Hangzhou, considered the most refined regional food in China. Hangzhou cookery stresses fresh ingredients and mild spices, plus the hallmark flavors of red vinegar and rice wine. A beautiful introduction to this delicate cuisine is freshwater shrimp with Longjing tea. The shrimps have a tight, crisp texture and a mild sweet flavor, while the tea leaves add a slightly bitter note.

Fragrant soup.

A vendor grills corn at a street stall.

Northern cuisine

The salty, mild, and lightly seasoned Northern Chinese stews and braised foods use vinegar and garlic as key flavorings. In Northern cooking, wheat flour largely replaces rice, and many of the dishes are served with pancakes or sesame seed-coated buns.

The signature dish is, of course, Peking duck. Slices of crispy roasted duck skin, light and crunchy as wafers, are served with mild spring onion and sweet sauce on a pancake. Another good choice is stewed preserved cabbage with sliced pork, made in a rich soup stock with tender streaky pork, aged chicken, and sour preserved cabbage.

Jiang rou, a stewed meat served cold with a *wasabi*-like mustard, and *la pi*, a cold noodle dish, are worth trying, as are the chicken strips dipped in egg white and cooked with sweet peas – mild but full of subtle flavor.

Cantonese cuisine

Because so many immigrants from Guangdong Province in Southern China settled in the West and opened restaurants, Cantonese food is

> *The pineapple cake is a central Taiwan concoction that is today a top local courtesy gift choice. Available at traditional-style bakeries, it is a bite-sized pastry with a chewy filling of fragrant pineapple paste.*

the one most often associated with China. In Cantonese cooking, the freshness of the ingredients is of paramount importance. Fish, for instance, should ideally still be swimming just before it is cooked. Seasoning tends to be light, and preparation quick. A classic dish is steamed fish with a mild garnish of cilantro, ginger, pepper, sesame oil, and soy sauce. For stir-fried dishes, the "breath of the wok" is all-important, and the mark of a master chef.

For some reason, Cantonese food is not as popular in Taipei, although all of the classic dishes can be found here. These include beef and broccoli with oyster sauce, diced chicken with cashew nuts, barbecued pork, steamed lobster, shark's fin soup, abalone and bok choy, and the numerous kinds of dim sum.

Delectable fresh fruits for sale.

Delicate dim sum.

Taiwan is home to some of the best teas in the world.

Tea

With its sun-drenched mountain slopes – the island has dozens of peaks over 3,000 metres (10,000ft) high – Taiwan is perfect for tea growing, and it produces some of the world's finest teas. Taipei itself is filled with teahouses and tea drinkers.

Taiwan's most famous tea is Dongding Oolong, which comes from the rolling foothills of Taiwan's Central Mountain Range. These humid peaks are often covered in cloud and mist. Tea needs this cool climate; if the weather is hot, the tea leaves grow too fast, and become tough and bitter. Mountain teas are famous for their mildness, and Dongding Oolong is no exception. It is gentle and refreshing, with a hint of springtime.

A more unique variety of tea is Baihao Oolong, also known as "Oriental Beauty" (*Dongfang Meiren*). This tea has a robust, perfumed flavor, like an Earl Grey but earthier and more natural.

Also notable are the lightly fermented Baozhong, and the more heavily fermented Tie Guanyin (Iron Goddess), which has a caramel color, a full, mature flavor, and a sweet aftertaste. These are just a few of the varieties available in the capital, and the tea one drinks can depend upon the time of day, the time of year, and which part of Taiwan one is currently visiting.

Sipping tea at a Chinese teahouse involves more than just a beverage. The methodical brewing of a pot of tea is a soothing practice and a cultural experience in its own right.

As Taipei prospers, the locals continue to refine their palates and sharpen their desire for fine food. As a result, modern Taipei boasts the sort of uniform dining excellence found only in the world's great culinary cities, and you will find that eating out is indeed the city's top form of recreation.

KAOLIANG WINE

Visitors to Taipei may encounter a wickedly strong drink called Kaoliang wine. This fiery distillate is a banquet favorite. Many Taiwanese men have a soft spot for it, which they associate with their youthful days of military service on Kinmen Island, where the most famous brand is brewed.

Kaoliang wine is made from sorghum steamed in vats for 2 hours, then fermented in bins for 10 days. The sour mash is then squeezed, and the resulting liquid distilled into raw liquor. Like olive oil, the first press is the best. Kaoliang-drinking etiquette forbids sipping – the entire shot glass must be tossed back in one big gulp. *Gan bei!* – literally, "dry glass"!

SHOPPING

As in many other Asian cities, similar businesses tended to cluster together in the Taipei of old. While specialist shopping areas still exist, modern Taipei offers consumers an alluring array of destinations at which to spend their cash.

Upmarket designers can be found in the Xinyi shopping district.

Shopping in Taipei used to be a simple affair. If you wanted the best selection of shoes, you went to the shoe street, which was literally lined with shoe shops and nothing else. Another area might specialize in furniture, say, or cameras.

The air-conditioned shopping mall was a foreign concept that took a while to catch on, but malls are now found everywhere (although in some malls, you will find very similar businesses side by side – recalling the old days of Taipei shopping).

In fact, the free-spending Taiwanese have come to love shopping malls and department stores so much that Japanese company Mitsukoshi has built four of them in eastern Taipei's modern Xinyi District, a short walk south of the Taipei City Hall MRT station, forming the popular Xinyi New Life Square complex. Overkill, perhaps, but heaven for mall fans. There are two more malls within walking distance, including one at the base of the Taipei 101 tower.

The Xinyi malls are not all identical though; each is aimed at a different clientele. An upmarket outlet operated by Mitsukoshi is packed with luxury chains like Chanel and Louis Vuitton, while the New York New York mall offers lower prices, and is popular with 20-somethings and hip teens. Even though clothing – particularly women's fashion – dominates sales floors in the area, you will find a wide range of other goods, including books, consumer electronics, audiovisual equipment, and appliances, courtesy of

---

VAT REFUND

Foreign travelers who make purchases of NT$3,000 or more on the same day from the same Tax Refund Shopping (TRS) store are eligible for a refund of the 5 percent VAT paid.

To claim the refund, an application must be made – within 30 days of the date of purchase – at the port of departure. The goods must be shown to be taken out of the country. Visit the "Foreign Passenger VAT Refund Service Counter" at the airport or seaport.

For more details and information, including a useful list of TRS retail outlets, visit the Tourism Bureau website at www.taiwan.net.tw.

Dedicated followers of fashion shopping on into the evening.

The best clothing bargains are found at markets rather than malls.

chains like FNAC. Most of the malls have a wide selection of eateries in their basements.

Couture connection

The Xinyi malls are ideal if you are in a hurry and want to shop in air-conditioned comfort, but much of what you see will be the same familiar brands you might find in New York, Singapore, or London – and the prices will seem familiar too. For more variety and better bargains, you will have to venture further.

Clothes are sold all over Taipei – from night-markets, where you can outfit yourself in polyester brand-name knockoffs for little more than spare change, to Asian chain stores like Giordano and Hang Ten, which are full of reasonably priced apparel. But the more statuesque foreign visitor might have trouble finding sizes that fit. A Taiwanese "L" is more like a US or European "M."

Expatriate residents head for the export shops in the Tianmu area in north Taipei. On Zhongshan North Road Section 7, just north of Tianmu East Road, are a number of shops selling clothing originally manufactured for export to the US and Europe.

Not only will you find larger sizes, but some real bargains too. Many of these shops sell factory seconds and out-of-season items at tremendous discounts. You may even see noted brands like Calvin Klein and Donna Karan – usually with the labels partly snipped out to indicate they are not for export. While most are indistinguishable from garments selling for 10 times more overseas, you should check these carefully, because you will occasionally spot flaws like missing buttons, torn seams, or minor variations in the cloth color.

Those with a penchant for the pop star-inspired, youth-oriented street fashions of the moment will be amply rewarded in the side streets of Ximending (see page 104) or the wholesale haven of Wufenpu (see page 155).

High-tech haul

Taiwan is one of the world's largest manufacturers of high-tech electronics, so many visitors to the island expect to find personal computers and other gadgets cheaper than they are at home. Whether or not you go home with a bargain, however, depends very much on what you are looking for. Generally, products that are cheap in other developed nations will be even cheaper in Taiwan, but high-end items are actually more expensive in Taiwan. This is

> *Small stores are the best places to buy cutting-edge electronics. Department stores and a few specialist chains offer them, but prices are higher, selection is limited, and staff not as well informed.*

because there is not much demand locally for top-of-the-line products (due to slightly lower average incomes than in the West), so they retail in smaller quantities and at higher prices.

At the corner of Xinsheng North Road and Civil Boulevard is the Guang Hua Digital Plaza (see page 141), a six-story building packed with literally hundreds of shops selling computers, computer parts, digital cameras, music players, and other electronic gadgets. The vendors from the famous old Guanghua Market, a labyrinth under a nearby expressway flyover that has been demolished because of safety concerns after a major earthquake, are located on the second and third levels. The fourth and fifth floors house vendors from another now defunct electronics market, and the sixth floor is home to a number of specialist repair shops.

Another electronics mall, the Taipei Information Park, opened in mid-2015 right next to the Guang Hua Digital Plaza. The city government's intent is to make the district the world's number one location to shop for cutting-edge electronics, greater than the famous Japan's Akihabara Electric Town.

Thriving markets

Oddly juxtaposed with the modern offerings of Guang Hua Digital Plaza are smaller markets selling jade and antiques. Most can be found on the east side of Xinsheng South Road. The casual antiques buyer might prefer the antiques shops on Yongkang Street (close to the corner of Jinhua Street), which is also a delightfully bustling neighborhood area. Antiques buyers should keep a sharp eye out for the high-quality fakes and over-restored items that abound.

The area around Yongkang Street is also home to a few stores selling local and foreign handicrafts. Unlike, say, Thailand, Taiwan does not produce large amounts of attractive, low-cost handicrafts aimed at foreign tourists. But recently there has been a surge of interest in traditional arts and crafts combined with more

The section of Boai Road where there is a high concentration of camera shops.

Treasures at Bai Win Antiques.

A piece of liuli glass art.

contemporary styles. The large government-sponsored Chinese Handicraft Mart is very useful for travelers, although it has prices higher than private shops, because it houses the many types of representative Taiwan handicrafts under one roof, has English-speaking personnel, and ships overseas (see page 129).

Glass and porcelain art

Opinion is divided as to whether it is true art or expensive kitsch, but the often colorful glass art known as *liuli* certainly has a distinctive esthetic, and remains a unique product of Taiwan that has come to international attention in recent times.

Artist Loretta Yang, owner of Newworkshop (Liuli Gongfang), is a former actress of great regional fame who stunned fans in 1987 by turning to an art form where, as she has explained, aging brings respect rather than rejection. Her works are true to Chinese classical and Buddhist themes, with functionality of minor importance.

Artist Heinrich Wang, of Tittot, is a former movie director and actor who dropped celluloid for glass in 1987, and more recently, dropped glass for porcelain. His works, which are attractive while being functional around the home and office, have won prizes and acclaim around the world.

Exotic teas

Plenty of high mountain slopes and a local market where almost everyone is a -connoisseur have combined to make Taiwan home to some of the finest-quality Chinese teas in the world. In fact, certain prized Oolong varieties are only produced and sold in Taiwan, such as Baozhong, Dongding, and Baihao (Oriental Beauty). The best way to shop for tea is to visit one of the many teahouses, such as Wang De Chuan Fine Chinese Tea (95 Zhongshan N. Rd, Sec. 1; daily 10am–9pm; tel: 02-2561 8738, www.dechuantea.

RECEIPTS AND WARRANTIES

Many small stores will not give you an official receipt as they operate under small business laws that allow them to avoid paying sales tax. This even applies to big-ticket items like personal computers. On request, they will usually write out a bill of goods, listing the items you have bought and the purchase date.

Products are rarely sold with an international guarantee. Local guarantee terms are usually as follows: free replacement with an identical item if you encounter problems within the first week, and full parts and service guarantee for the first year – but check the details if possible, as terms can vary considerably.

A selection of Taiwanese teas for sale, presented in elegant tins.

com), cha FOR TEA (152 Fuxing N. Rd; daily 7.30am–10.30pm; tel: 02-2719 9900, www.cha fortea.com.tw), or one of the establishments on Hengyang Road off Chongqing South Road Section 1. Here you can sample different varieties before deciding which to buy, and owners are steeped in tea expertise.

The best tea is sold loose, not pre-packaged. Any local expert will recommend the spring crop, which is handpicked from the finest young tea leaves grown at elevations above 1,500 meters (5,000ft). Most of this tea is organically grown. Spring tea is always in short supply and can easily cost NT$3,350 for a *catty* (about 600g or 21oz). The famous and costly Oriental Beauty will set you back no less than NT$3,000 for a *catty*. Tea of "ordinary" quality generally costs around NT$1,350 for the same amount, good enough for the tea neophyte and still far better than the tea dust that finds its way into Western tea bags. Most teahouses also sell the full set of equipage for brewing, but the town of Yingge (see page 236) is renowned for its ceramic tea sets.

PAY THE NAMED PRICE

A word of advice about bargaining in Taipei: Don't. This is not China or India, and inflated "tourist prices" are almost unheard of. There are very few exceptions to this rule, and haggling is often only necessary for unique items like antiques. Sellers may be offended by hard bargaining, especially over small sums of money, since this implies they are being both inhospitable to a guest (you), and impecunious enough to be concerned about a dollar or two. Where prices are not marked, a polite request for a discount is acceptable. Shopkeepers will occasionally even reduce the price for you if you forget to ask.

Nightmarkets

If you find the glass and marble malls too sterile for your tastes, then Taipei's bustling and sweaty nightmarkets (see page 86) offer a dizzying variety of products, as well as bizarre – but useful – local inventions like electrified fly swatters (they look like tennis rackets). However, the quality of nightmarket products tends to be as low as the prices. Visitors will enjoy the nightmarkets more if they go to look and savor the atmosphere rather than buy.

See also the Shopping boxes in Places chapters for more information on where to shop.

Jade Market

Jade has traditionally been valued in Chinese societies as highly as gold has been in the West. This gemstone offers a combination of toughness and physical beauty.

What's more, jade is believed by the Chinese to protect against evil spirits and misfortune, which is why you will often see a jade pendant dangling from the rearview mirror of one of Taipei's speeding taxis (as it races through a red light).

Whether you get there by taxi, or at the more sedate pace of the MRT (the market is a 10-minute walk from Zhongxiao Xinsheng station), you will find a whole world of jade (see page 143) at Taipei's Jianguo Holiday Jade Market, in the cool shade of the Jianguo Expressway flyover.

Gnarled stallholders squint at veined stones of lustrous green, pearly white, and blood red. Rickety tables hold an assortment of bracelets, earrings, pendants, figurines, and just about anything else imaginable – even delicate carved jade flowers and oddities like popular cartoon characters.

Contrary to popular belief, jade occurs in a wide variety of colors, and not just green. Its coloring also tends to become more vivid with age, particularly when warmed and polished by wearing close to the skin. Traditionally this phenomenon is explained as the jade absorbing the bad luck that would otherwise have afflicted the bearer.

Good-natured arguments break out over an item's value. It is generally seen as accept-able to improve the color of cheaper jade pieces by bleaching, and to firm up the structure by impregnating it with wax or resin, but these techniques considerably reduce the value; it is tricky for the inexperienced shopper to spot the difference.

Jade shopping for beginners

The pace of business is relaxed and stallholders offer cups of tea to customers. With the most prized jade pieces fetching tens of thousands of US dollars, they can afford to bide their time. But do not be discouraged; there is something for everyone here. You can easily pick up a simple but attractive jade necklace or bracelet for between NT$500 and NT$650.

Bargaining is advisable for the most expensive items, but less effective with the cheapest pieces. The Jianguo Holiday Jade Market Council have a desk at one end of the market, and it is worth consulting them if you are considering an expensive item. They speak little English, but will try to help.

Some of the Jade Market's wares.

The weekend market is the most fun for the visitor, but is not the only place to buy jade in Taipei. Another much smaller market is open every day a short walk north, at the corner of Xinsheng South Road and Bade Road. Jewelry shops also offer a selection, generally of higher quality and price than found in the markets; many will provide certificates of authenticity on request.

Baseball practice at Taipei's Tianmu stadium, the epicenter of the nationally beloved sport.

SPORTS, FITNESS AND PASTIMES

Taipei may not be the biggest sporting town, but it does have one very popular spectator sport – baseball – and a number of interesting participant sports, ranging from solemn early-morning tai chi gatherings to quirky late-night ballroom dancing.

Of Taipei's spectator sports, baseball is the most popular. The Chinese Professional Baseball League (CPBL, www.cpbl.com.tw) games are loud, energetic contests, played with enthusiasm and gusto.

The city also has an on-again, off-again professional basketball league. Basketball games were popular in the mid-1990s, but attendance declined, and the league folded in 1997. However, in 2004, the league was revived as the Super Basketball League (SBL), and is today thriving.

Taipei also has its favorite participant sports. Among these, nothing can touch the martial arts for popularity.

> Taoism, with its philosophy of non-aggression, is a key element of the martial arts. "The best soldier is not soldierly," wrote Taoist philosopher Lao Tzu. "The best fighter is not ferocious; the best conqueror does not take part in war."

Basketball remains popular with locals.

Baseball

Visitors seeking an enjoyable Taipei cultural experience, but with a touch of the familiar, should attend a professional baseball game. The rules are the same as elsewhere – nine-inning games, four bases, three strikes and you're out – but the spectacle is quite different.

There are no true "home" teams in the CPBL. The four teams have a regional base, but wander the island playing many "home" games in many different stadiums. This curious set-up guarantees that fans of both teams show up at every game. They carry whistles, trumpets, and drums, and greet every play with a crescendo of raucous noise. The cheering is organized and synchronized, and is led by hyperactive, self-appointed cheerleaders.

The food is different as well: replacing the famous hot dog is the local lunch box, with meat, rice, and cold vegetables. Another choice is grilled sausage, which comes not in a bun, but with a clove of raw garlic. The beer and soft drinks are the same, though, and so is the relaxed and happy atmosphere.

Dragon boat teams race for the finish.

A venerable history

More than 100 years ago, the Japanese taught the Taiwanese to play baseball, and the locals later beat their colonial masters in a landmark game in 1930. The sport surged in popularity in the 1960s and 1970s, when Taiwan's little league team began to dominate the world, eventually winning 17 world titles.

In the 1990s, baseball really took off. The CPBL played its first season in 1990, and then, in 1992, Taiwan's national team won a silver medal in the Summer Olympics in Barcelona. The CPBL quickly grew in popularity, and in 2001, Taiwan hosted the World Cup of Baseball. The home team took third place, beating Japan in the bronze medal game. That victory ignited a joyful celebration, as thousands of fans took to the streets and staged a spontaneous parade.

That dramatic moment was followed by another key national victory, this time against

DRAGON BOATING

For one day each May/June, Taipei's Jilong River becomes a hive of activity, filled with brightly colored boats, pounding drums, and splashing paddles. This is the Dragon Boat Festival. The festival has its origins in Chinese antiquity, but today's races are ultra-modern, and attract teams of local and international competitors. Many of the boats are paddled by highly fit racers who train for months prior to the event. Most boats have 18 paddlers, plus a drummer – the heartbeat of the dragon – and a helmsman. In Taiwan, a 21st person rides on the prow to snatch the victory flag at the end of the course. The distance of a standard dragon boat race is 500 meters (1,640ft).

The Dragon Boat Festival is traditionally held on the 5th day of the 5th lunar month, on or near the summer solstice. It was originally believed that this season of oppressive heat was prone to pestilence and drought. Water-borne festivities thus evolved to counteract this.

With time, the festival has become more associated with the tragic story of Warring States patriot Qu Yuan, who drowned himself in a river in despair over being discredited by rivals for the emperor's favor. It is said that concerned citizens threw zongzi, rice dumplings, into the river to prevent the fish from eating Qu Yuan's body. The festival is thus also celebrated with the eating of zongzi.

In November 2017, Taipei will host the XXIX Summer Universiade, or the World Student Games, an international sports event for university athletes from more than 160 countries.

arch-rival Korea in 2003, which catapulted Taiwan's baseball team – playing under the moniker of Chinese Taipei – into the 2004 Summer Olympics. During the fraught game against Korea, groups of people huddled around their radios throughout Taipei, and erupted into loud cheers when the 5-4 victory was finally secure.

In recent years the league has been reduced to just four teams and around 2009 regular-season attendance dropped to about 3,000 per game as a result of two games-fixing scandals. In 2013, however, the average attendance had increased to 6,000 per game. During playoff games noise regulations are still sometimes broken in Tianmu Stadium, forcing a decision to play only on weekends. The many fans who cannot watch from within the modern 10,000-seat venue catch broadcasts outside the ballpark, on a giant screen set up by the city government.

Martial arts

Percolating through Taipei life, everybody seems to have some connection to the martial arts – a mother-in-law who is a devotee of tai chi, perhaps, or a colleague who competes in wushu. In fact, many of China's most accomplished martial artists sought refuge here following persecution on the mainland.

Martial arts is a broad term that includes many disciplines. In the "hard arts" like Long Fist and Wing Chun, force is opposed by force, concentrating on points of attack, and focusing energy into punches and kicks. In tai chi, Xingyiquan, and other "soft arts," force is turned against the attacker. These focus on movement principles, relaxing one's body, and circulation of *qi*, or vital energy.

Each one has various schools, with its stylized rituals and fighting applications. And all have health benefits. According to a study

Martial arts retain many devotees here.

A morning tai chi session in the park.

Enjoying some alfresco ballroom dancing, a popular pursuit in Taipei.

done in Taipei, seniors who perform tai chi regularly have less than half the decrease in oxygen uptake, compared to a control group. In other words, tai chi practitioners tend to be more limber and fit. Tai chi also performs a social function, as the practitioners often go to the same places every morning to practice, where they talk and socialize. Early-rising visitors to Taipei will see evidence of this in many local parks.

The steady popularity of martial arts in Taiwan is partly explained by its spiritual dimension; more than a sport, these self-defense disciplines are both a lifestyle and a philosophy. Western forms of unarmed combat, such as boxing and wrestling, are effective as fighting techniques, but lack the philosophical core.

Ballroom dancing

Curiously enough, another popular sport in Taipei, albeit among middle-aged and older folk, is ballroom dancing. Dance sessions take place not in dancehalls or ballrooms, but in outdoor parks, on summer evenings. At about 9pm, the dancing lessons begin, a night-time version

of the morning tai chi classes. Instructors turn on their tape players and set up shop, as couples whirl and waltz in the semi-darkness, under the trees and into the night, making for an unusual and memorable sight.

Climbing and hiking

Rock climbing is another sport that has surged in popularity in the last few years. Unlike some other sports, climbing does not require a large body size. The Chinese physique, often small and strong, is well suited to it. On weekends, many climbers head for Longdong, on the Northeast Coast about 90 minutes from Taipei, to climb the sheer rock walls that soar above the ocean.

Hiking is also popular, and on weekends, people head to Yangmingshan National Park (see page 194). It is not as wild or spectacular as other mountain getaways, but Yangmingshan has one great advantage: it is right on Taipei's door-step. That means a day hike in Yangmingshan can end with a hot dinner in the leafy suburb of Tianmu, rather than in a windswept tent at 3,000 meters (10,000ft).

Traditional remedies

In Taipei, a city that celebrates its heritage, traditional Chinese medicine is alive and well, and highly regarded by the people, who use it to enhance their well-being.

The city's many strange-smelling apothecaries are filled with row after row of drawers containing exotic animal, mineral, or plant extracts. Among the ingredients are cinnabar and amber to calm the nerves, antelope horn to relieve pain, peach pits and safflower to promote circulation, and ginseng to fortify the lungs.

Indeed, the use of herbal mixtures is one of the key treatment strategies of Chinese medicine. The prescriptions often feature four or more ingredients – some are agents, others help counteract side effects, and others promote general good health – that a patient takes home and boils for hours to get a potent and usually bitter brew. The herbal remedies are extensive, with more than 2,000 in the literature, and about 150 commonly used.

Concepts

Chinese medicine is rooted, like the martial arts, in the theory of yin and yang, the concept of qi, or vital energy, and the Five Elements, said to classify the properties of all things. Traditional Chinese doctors aim to maintain the smooth passage of qi, and the proper equilibrium of yin and yang and the Five Elements, by using acupuncture, herbs, massage, and other methods. Unlike Western medicine, which concentrates on alleviating symptoms, Chinese medicine aims to keep a patient in good health by targeting any underlying imbalances. The physician performs an external diagnosis by observing a patient's complexion, taking the pulse, and peering at his or her tongue. This stems from a belief that one's internal systems can be observed from the exterior.

Besides herbal therapy, another popular treatment is massage, or tuina, which unclogs meridians of qi, relieving problems like joint injuries and muscle sprains. More dramatic is baguan, or the technique of using suction cups to stimulate circulation. The cups are heated inside with a wad of flaming cotton to create a vacuum, then placed upon a few vital points of the body. The flesh swells into the cup, causing superficial bruising. This treatment is said to be effective for respiratory problems.

Chinese medicine is gaining acceptance worldwide, and it has shown promise in treating chronic conditions like diabetes and heart disease. Acupuncture is becoming more common in the West, and

Preparing a Chinese herbal prescription.

its use as an anesthetic is no longer news. Chinese phy-sicians also do not dispute the superiority of Western medicine in the treatment of acute pathology such as traumatic injuries. Like the many Taiwanese who visit both Chinese and Western-trained doctors, they see traditional remedies as a complement to Western medicine, not a substitute.

NIGHTLIFE

With none of Bangkok's restrictive closing hours or the expatriate exclusiveness often seen in Hong Kong, Taiwan's capital has developed a winning diversity of evening entertainment in recent years.

Happy punters.

Old-timers complain Taipei's nightlife heyday is but a memory. Certainly the city has matured and lost edginess, but to say it is past its prime is to fail to be attuned to all that Taipei has going for it after dark.

Nightmarkets

When Taiwanese abroad get nostalgic for home, they miss the *renao* – heat and noise – of the nightmarket. After all, before there were bars, pubs, and hip-hop clubs – dancing was outlawed under martial law nearly 30 years ago – there was the local nightmarket

(see page 86). But if you're hankering for more raucous late-night action, read on.

Beerhouses

For many foreigners beerhouses, or *pijiuwu*, are Taipei's after-hours highlight. Rowdy and come-as-you-are, the quintessential Taiwan beerhouse has cavernous halls, big picnic tables, greasy nightmarket foods, watery draft beer in kegs of many sizes, and low, low prices.

Let's go singing

When the Taiwanese want to loosen up with colleagues or friends, they're more likely to say "let's go singing" than "let's have a drink" – though the singing is usually accompanied by lots of rapid-fire toasting and quaffing of alcohol. Karaoke is a Japanese import, of course, but the Taiwanese have taken to it as if it were their own, and Taipei is studded with palatial karaoke chains that do booming business. One of the most popular, Cash Box, has outlets with lobbies so opulent that some newcomers mistake them for five-star hotels. Even if nervous singing in public, when you get an invitation from Taiwanese friends to go out singing, accept – all the big KTVs have a selection of English-language hits.

Bars and clubs

In times past, the "Combat Zone," centered on Shuangcheng Street behind the Imperial Hotel, was Taipei's prime cluster of expatriate watering holes. Sometimes called "Sugar Daddy Row," this stretch had its heyday before 1979, when the US military had a base nearby.

Partying at loud and lively Carnegies, which is renowned for its lengthy shooter menu.

Beerhouses are a quirky Taiwan feature.

The formula was Western pub food, imported beer, canned retro-rock, and friendly female bar staff. Today, the area looks more than a little tired, and much of the action has moved to alternative locations.

That said, the Combat Zone is far from deserted, particularly on Fridays and Saturdays, and is a relatively welcoming place for out-of-towners unfamiliar with Taipei. It is convenient, too, insofar as most watering holes are clustered on Shuangcheng Street itself and a small alley running off it.

A long-standing alternative to the Combat Zone has been the Shida university district. Popular with foreigners studying Chinese or teaching English in Taipei, this area has enjoyed a minor renaissance in recent years, after a period of decline. On weekend nights you'll see crowds of foreigners gathering in the Shida Nightmarket area for a quick bite before heading off to their chosen music venues.

The main players are the Blue Note, a cozy jazz-venue icon at the corner of Shida and Roosevelt roads, 45 Pub on Heping East Road, and the sprawling Roxy 99, a basement nightclub on Jinshan South Road (see page 249).

The long section of Anhe Road that runs between Heping East Road and Xinyi Road, along with the alleys running off it, is the area that is upstaging Taipei's traditional nightlife districts. In the early 2000s, in what seemed the blink of an eye, it became home to countless

BARBERSHOPS

Taipei once had a certain reputation for its seedy nightlife, and in particular its notorious "barbershops." Only a complete Taiwan newbie would wander into one of these establishments for a haircut – they were well known to be fronts for prostitution. But times have changed. Very few of these "barbershops" have survived the major clean-up operations that two of Taiwan's most recognizable politicians imposed on Taipei during their terms as mayor of the city: Chen Shui-bian, who was elected mayor in 1994, and Ma Ying-jeou, elected in 1998. A sprinkling of such places still exist on Yanping Road near Ximending.

There is no shortage of drinks on offer at this trendy Taipei lounge bar.

Girls on the town.

drinking venues, ranging from the big and brash Carnegies – renowned for its bar-top grooving patrons – to hole-in-the-wall lounges featuring ambient beats and some impressive selections of wine and spirits. Some of the choicest lounge-bars are down the alleys, so be a little adventurous. Note that they tend to be better for couples than for single drinkers looking to strike up conversation with like-minded people.

The shift to Anhe Road in recent years has been accompanied by increasing sophistication. Lounges and fashionable DJ clubs are more and more the kind of places that Taipei's fashionistas like to flaunt their iPhones. Cool hideaways like Room 18 and Organo are occasionally graced by celebrities and are the kind of places considered hip spots to relax before heading on to a club.

As for the club scene, it has evolved from one of marginal interest, having gone through a phase of frequent police crack-downs, to finally becoming mainstream with the seemingly permanent presence of Luxy

(see page 248), which frequently has big-name guest DJs from Europe and the US on its schedule, and Myst (see page 248), a chic nightclub with a waterfall and pond inside, usually fully packed out.

Pop and rock

Taiwan is arguably the pop music capital of the Mandarin-speaking world, churning out a steady stream of hits that are warbled by fans in KTV parlors throughout the Chinese diaspora. Such is the music's popularity, it is often necessary to hold concerts in stadium venues to accommodate the crowds. Check the local newspapers for information.

The more recent development has been the explosion of Taiwan's band culture. The independent music scene was kick-started by the Spring Scream music festival in 1995 in Kending, in southern Taiwan. Today this ongoing festival is complemented by the Ho-Hai-Yan Music Festival, three to five days of live music, which is held over annually in July at Fulong Beach on Taiwan's northeast coast.

Taiwan's pop culture

To many ordinary Chinese, Taiwan is a breeding ground for new talents waiting to be discovered and a place to fulfill superstar aspirations.

The territory has produced numerous pop icons in the Chinese entertainment industry, from evergreen singer Teresa Teng to screen goddess Brigitte Lin Ching-hsia and Taiwanese tourism ambassador, singer Zhang Huimei (affectionately known as "a MEI").

Of course, this inevitably makes for a love-hate relationship between the stars and entertainment journalists. Taiwan has become a hunting ground for the juiciest gossip and fodder for hundreds of Asian tabloids. As in Hong Kong, Taiwanese paparazzi spare no effort to get the best headline for the front page. Celebrities know the rules of the game and craft the symbiotic relationship skillfully. Those not in the know have disparaged these reporters as "vile pigs." Robbie Williams unwittingly pushed up the tabloid circulation numbers when he pointed at journalists at Chiang Kai-shek (now Taiwan Taoyuan) Airport and said, "I didn't insult your country, I will insult you."

An all-important element of Chinese television has always been the drama serial. In recent years, however, it has undergone a transformation. Insipid melodramas are no longer the norm; instead, youth-obsessed "idol dramas" have become de rigueur on channels. Only the good-looking need apply. JVKV (formerly F4), Taiwan's answer to boyband One Direction, has driven thousands of pre- and post-pubescent teens to high-octave screaming in airports and hotel lobbies, and elevated "groupism" into an art form. This group of four attractive men with their long hair and fairy-tale princely personas has created a multimillion-dollar industry, spawning a wave of copy-cat boy (and girl) bands, with groups like 5566, Fahrenheit, Ice Man, JPM, Lollipop F, and S.H.E. competing for a slice of the burgeoning teen market. When it comes to solo acts, Jay Chou and Jolin Tsai have long occupied the thrones of pop royalty.

Teen culture

Taiwan teens have never embraced Japanese pop culture in a bigger way than now. In the ultra-funky district of Ximending, "coolness" and "in-your-face" attitudes are defined with bold use of colors in hair, tattoos, and exaggerated accessories. American musical genres like R&B and hip hop have been eagerly accepted as well: youngsters decked out in baseball caps and oversized jeans are a common sight.

While the Taiwanese are still traditional in other aspects of life, Western pop influences have created a more liberal attitude in the local media. Steamy bedroom talk, poking fun at politicians, and humiliating celebrities are almost obligatory in the highly popular variety and talk shows televised by satellite across Asia.

A Mei at a press conference in Taipei, 2014.

NAVIGATING THE NIGHTMARKETS

These nightly bazaars – unique, unplanned, and colorful – offer traditional snack foods, shopping, and an authentic taste of crowded local street life.

According to a survey by the Tourism Bureau, nightmarkets are one of the most popular attractions on the island, rivaling even the National Palace Museum. And it seems like every neighborhood in Taipei has one. Admittedly, one has to put up with a lot of jostling, clamor, and grease. But with an irresistible combination of bright lights, big crowds, fresh food, carnival games, and hawker stalls, the city's nightmarkets never fail to entertain.

The top attraction is, of course, the local snack foods – often unhealthy, but usually very tasty. Browsing the merchandise on sale is another highlight. But don't overlook the other options – from fortune-tellers to seal-carvers, acupuncturists to blind masseurs.

For overseas visitors, the most famous of Taipei's nightmarkets has always been the so-called "Snake Alley" in Wanhua (see page 101). Snake Alley, however, has seen better days and is now something of a tourist trap. For a more authentic experience, head over to one of the other nightmarkets around town, mentioned individually in the Places chapters.

A mannequin at a nightmarket stall advertising mole removal services. The Chinese believe that moles on one's face and body may augur well or ill for the person, depending on their position on the body. Moles that attract bad fortune are removed to avert this.

A colorful and brightly lit Chinese gate serves as the main entrance to Raohe Street Nightmarket, lending a festive ambience. Nightmarkets catering to tourists, both local and foreign, often feature these gates, and have a large number of permanent stalls. Other nightmarkets without permanent outlets only spring up at night.

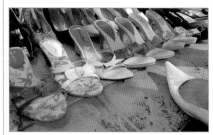

Shoes on sale at Shilin Nightmarket. Shoppers are often spoiled for choice. Though fashion accessories, clothing, lingerie, and shoes dominate the selection, one can also find watches, tin toys, stuffed animals, carvings, and all manner of trinkets. Prices are low, and bargaining is possible, but all purchases are strictly caveat emptor, for the quality of the products may be low too.

A young couple consulting a traditional Chinese fortune-teller at Raohe Street Nightmarket. With the aid of the Chinese almanac and a person's date and time of birth, the fortune-teller is able to provide astrological forecasts of one's career, romance, health, and other aspects of life. They are also frequently consulted to determine if the astrological signs of two persons planning to marry "clash," or will result in a happy union.

A stall at Miaokou Nightmarket in Keelung selling freshly made runbing, another traditional Taiwanese snack food. Five or six ingredients, mostly vegetables, are rolled in a soft flour skin. Unlike chunjuan or spring rolls, which they resemble, they are not fried.

A stall at Shilin Nightmarket selling piping hot shengjian bao. Filled with minced pork or a peppery vegetable filling, these buns are first steamed, then pan-fried to create a crispy bottom crust. Besides this, some of the most popular street foods include yan su ji ("salt crispy chicken"), nuggets of chicken deep-fried and seasoned with spices; hujiao bing, a bun filled with minced meat and pepper then baked; herbal pork rib soup; o-a-mi-sua, a congee of vermicelli and oysters; herbal jelly (xiancao) with tapioca pearls; and much more.

An alternative to shopping for food or clothes is to pick up a cheerful jade souvenir.

Taipei traffic.

The Taipei skyline at sunset the day before a typhoon arrives.

INTRODUCTION

A detailed guide to Taipei and its surroundings, with principal sites numbered and clearly cross-referenced to maps.

Recognizing that most travelers to Taipei come on business, the travel authorities are encouraging longer stays to take in the sights. The city is also improving communications in English; today there is a wealth of information available to those interested in seeing more of the city.

The key to exploring the metropolis is understanding the personalities of its various districts. In the west, by the Danshui River, the old hubs of Wanhua and Dadaocheng are where it all began. Filled with the city's oldest cultural, historical, and religious sites, the cores of these neighborhoods remain much as they were a century ago. In the central districts, the old walls built by the Qing dynasty imperial government may no longer stand, but the area is graced by

Leisure time in Danshui.

architectural monuments in Western styles built by Taiwan's erstwhile colonial rulers, the Japanese.

In the east, the Xinyi District is Taipei's bright new shining star and the center of economic activity. The most sophisticated department stores, theater complexes, and nightlife venues, all built on the grandest of scales, collectively swirl around Taipei 101, the city's defining visual icon.

North of the Jilong River are some of Taipei's most popular tourist attractions, including the priceless artifacts at the National Palace Museum, the best traditional Taiwanese snack foods at Shilin Nightmarket, and the cosmopolitan flavor of Tianmu, a suburban expatriate enclave.

Yangmingshan, just 30 minutes from downtown, is a true rarity – a national park within city limits, with a network of mountain trails and hot springs. South and east of the city, in Muzha and Nangang, tea plantations perfume the hills.

Being surrounded by mountains and hills means that the physical expansion of the vibrant metropolis has been upwards rather than outwards. Today the visitor sees a forest of futuristic structures reaching for the sky, standing side by side with heritage architectural works such as Wanhua's renowned Longshan Temple. Perhaps this best defines the personality of the city – living with the comforts of the old and familiar while enthusiastically embracing the new.

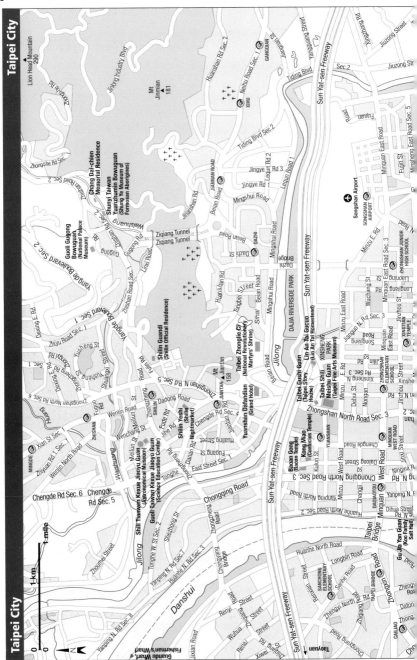

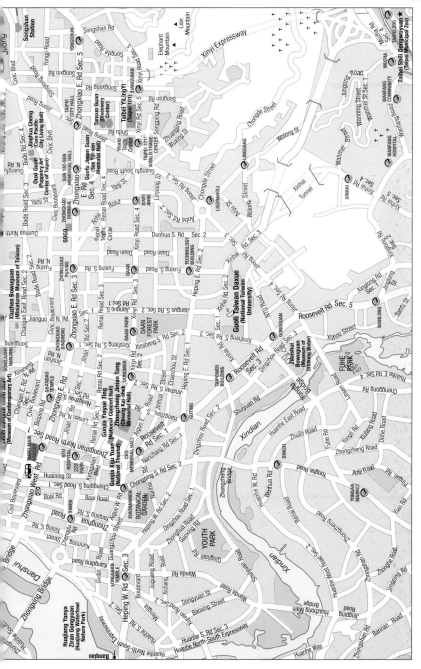

OLD TAIPEI: WANHUA AND XIMENDING

Wanhua is the cradle of Taipei's history and the north's greatest collection of heritage sites, while Ximending, a recreation district set up by the Japanese during the colonial period, is the hub of the city's youth culture.

In times long gone the Taipei Basin was the site of an inland saltwater lake, formed when tectonic heavings lowered the ground, allowing the sea to rush in. About 400 years ago, the dawn of northern Taiwan's recorded history, the Basin was still a soggy area of marsh, wetland, and swamp. Silting and draining have been extensive since then.

The area that forms present-day Wanhua, situated just downriver from where the Dahan and Xindian rivers meet to form the Danshui, was originally the site of a Ketagalan tribal settlement. This flatland-dwelling people dominated the Taipei Basin before the arrival of the Han Chinese in the early 1700s.

WANHUA

Huajiang Waterfowl Park

The 70-hectare (170-acre) **Huajiang Waterfowl Nature Park** ❶ (Huajiang Yanya Ziran Gongyuan), by Huajiang Bridge, is the site of a grand reunion of migratory birds, especially ducks, during the winter season. From September, green-winged teals, northern shovelers, and other feathered beauties are found in abundance in the marshes and on the mudflats

Making use of Taipei's network of riverside bicycle paths.

fronting the dedicated 500-meter (1,640ft) long birdwatching path. There are many explanatory signs along the way, though little English.

Taipei's riverside network of bicycle paths, stretching 150km (90 miles) along the Xindian, Danshui, and Jilong rivers, slides by here. The interlinked riverside parks and pathways are a major component of the city's Green Network initiative.

Moving north along the Danshui River to where the marsh ends, one finds the site of Wanhua's original

Main Attractions
Huaxi Street Tourist
  Nightmarket
Longshan Temple
Bopiliao Historic Block
Ximending Pedestrian Mall
Zhongshan Hall
North Gate
Taipei Post Office

Maps and Listings
Map, page 100
Shopping, page 106
Restaurants, page 109

Wanhua

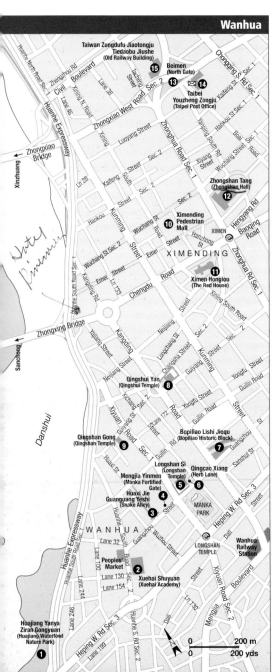

A snake handler in Snake Alley.

port. Exit into Wanhua through the Guilin Road gate. The ugly cement dikes here were built in the 1960s to protect the city's communities from the typhoon flooding that regularly ravages the Taipei Basin.

From Manka to Wanhua

In 1709 three pioneers from Fujian established the first legally deeded farm at Dagala, on the banks of the Danshui River, in what is now Taipei. More followed, concentrating their settlements along the banks of the Danshui. One settlement, called "Manka" in Taiwanese ("Mengjia" in Mandarin), became the Taipei Basin's most important market center, and the seed of today's Wanhua and the city of Taipei.

It served as an entrepôt between local aborigine traders, immigrant Chinese miners and growers, and the mainland Chinese market. The natives gathered here from upriver to sell camphor, sweet potatoes, coal, and other goods to the Chinese.

Indeed, the term "Manka," a bastardization of the Ketagalan word for "canoe," is still more commonly used today by the area's locals than the Japanese-imposed "Wanhua," or "10,000 glories."

This densely populated district did not fully enjoy the benefits of Taiwan's economic miracle in the second half of the 20th century. However, in keeping with the spirit of the "native soil" movement that has surged to prominence since martial law was lifted in 1987, local community leaders and the city administration have taken concerted action to beautify the district. All of the area's well-preserved historic sites are within walking distance of each other, and the majority can be taken in over a leisurely walk of four to five hours.

Xuehai Academy ❷

Located at 93 Huanhe South Road Section 2 is Taipei's only remaining academic building from the Qing dynasty, the **Xuehai Academy** (Xuehai Shuyuan; privately owned, ring doorbell for entry). The former school building looks like a small temple; its sweeping roof of bamboo-shaped glazed tiles is adorned with carved swallow-tail ridges, writhing dragons, and auspicious figurines. This is unsurprising given the reverence the Chinese have traditionally had for learning. Today it serves as the ancestral shrine for the Gao clan, one of Wanhua's most powerful families in imperial days.

Snake Alley ❸

Extending from Guangzhou Street to Guilin Road is the **Huaxi Street Tourist Nightmarket** (Huaxi Jie Guanguang Yeshi; daily 7pm–2am), better known in English as **Snake Alley** for its sale of snake meat.

The "Tourist" in the official name is something of a misnomer. Even though in the 1990s the many red-light businesses were driven into the shadows, lights hung up to brighten the place, and a roof added to protect visitors from bad weather, this nightmarket remains local to the hilt. The writhing serpents on display outside alley shopfronts, and their showman-like hawkers, continue to draw crowds of visitors. Traditional Chinese lore maintains that the snake has health-enhancing properties, and specifically, libido-enhancing benefits – something to do with the beast's impressive length! Locals, tour guides, and in-the-know cops say the removal of the red lights at the nightmarket just means the trade has moved a little further off. Otherwise, what would continue to fuel the late-night snake blood binge?

Manka Fortified Gate ❹

Just past Snake Alley on Guangzhou Street and before the intersection with Xiyuan Road is Lane 223. The lane's entrance is straddled by the **Manka Fortified Gate** (Mengjia Yinmen), built in imperial times when immigrant groups from different districts or provinces of China commonly fought for dominance.

SHOP

The Naruwan Indigenous Peoples' Market, near Xuehai Academy, is the first ever specializing in Taiwan-native products. Opened in 2008, there are three sections and 10 shops in total, selling foods and drinks, agricultural products, and handicrafts. Aborigine artists and singers stage live shows on Sat/Sun nights. If you've never had the sweet yet sour native millet wine, try it here. Have a cup of *Pangcah* coffee, the beans from tribal hills. See page 106 for details.

The Xuehai Academy building.

Divining or oracle blocks are pairs of kidney-shaped red blocks, each with one convex side and one flat side. The rattle of these wooden blocks hitting the floor is a characteristic sound heard in many a Chinese temple.

DIVINING BLOCKS

A Longshan Temple and other Chinese temples around Taipei, you'll see people throwing down divining blocks to seek advice from the gods. First they stand before the icon and burn three incense sticks. Then while holding the divining blocks, they silently state their name, birthdate, and address, and present their petition in the form of a question. The blocks are then dropped. If one convex side and one flat side show, the answer is positive. Two convex sides are "angry blocks" – the answer is negative. If two flat sides show, no answer has been given, and the supplicant must try again, with the question framed a different way.

Longshan Temple packed with worshippers.

This bloody intercommunal conflict did not subside until the latter half of the 1800s, when most of the land was already settled and titled, and there was general prosperity. Every night, and in times of emergency, such fortified gates would be closed and guarded. As was often the case in towns, there were no community walls, but houses were clustered tightly, facing inward, to create effective wall-like perimeters.

Longshan Temple ❺

Address: 211 Guangzhou Street, www.lungshan.org.tw
Opening Hrs: daily 6am–10.20pm
Entrance Fee: free
Transportation: Longshan Temple

Just west of Xiyuan Road is **Longshan Temple** (Longshan Si), one of Taiwan's most important places of worship and of priceless historical importance. The temple was first built on a much smaller scale in 1738. The much expanded incarnation seen today is renowned for its exquisite woodcarvings, as well as for its stone sculptures, a noteworthy example of which are the 12 major support columns in the main hall, twined by auspicious dragons hewn from solid stone.

Long ago, a merchant from Quanzhou in Fujian Province stopped here to relieve himself, then forgot his sacred protective incense pouch. Later, locals saw a bright light emanating from the pouch, and found an inscription inside that claimed it came from the renowned Longshan Temple in Quanzhou. This was a clear sign to build a replica, and Taipei's version soon came into being.

Early on, the temples in Wanhua were commonly used as military bases by the market town's rival immigrant groups. Soon, Longshan Temple became the seat of the area's religious, judicial, social, and commercial affairs. In 1885, as French marines stood ready to attack Taipei during the Sino-French War, the local militia rushed to the city's defense. Their banners carried an image of Longshan Temple, their military headquarters.

The temple's main deity, Guanyin, the Goddess of Mercy, has over the years proven to be powerful and protective. The area was devastated by an earthquake in 1815, but it is said that the icon of Guanyin sat through it serene and safe. During World War II, Allied planes hit the temple (Japanese troops were often billeted in places of worship). The bombs and ensuing fire razed the main hall but somehow missed the goddess. Even though the iron railings around Guanyin had melted, nothing more than her toes were singed. This really got the people's attention, and today devotees come to her from morning to night with requests for clarity and assistance.

Herb Lane ❻

Along the eastern wall of the temple is **Herb Lane** (Qingcao Xiang), a short, covered alley lined with retail and wholesale outlets (daily 8am–10pm). Piled high in canvas sacks, display boxes, or loosely in heaps, are countless fresh or dried herbs, roots, and medicinal plants. Some are leafy, others knobby or spiny, in shades of green or brown. The aroma of the place is bracing.

The market sprang up beside Longshan Temple in 1738. Food, textiles, and embroidery were originally sold, and later, baked goods and candles for worship. The herbs on sale today are used in traditional food recipes, tonics, and medicines.

Bopiliao Historic Block ❼

Located just to the east, **Bopiliao Historic Block** (Bopiliao Lishi Jiequ) is the block running both sides of Lane 173 off Kangding Road, just north of its intersection with Guangzhou St (Sun–Thu 10am–5pm, Fri–Sat 10am–7pm). This is one of Taipei's oldest sections, and with Dihua Street in Dadaocheng, among its most intact, stretching back 200 years. The entire block of

Huaxi Street Tourist Nightmarket is a world of traditional eateries, antique and curio shops, foot-massage parlors, and the infamous snake flesh, blood, and bile soup vendors.

WHERE

If you seek advice more specific than the divining blocks can reveal, another type of divination available at Longshan Temple is *qiuqian*, or "drawing lots." After addressing the query to the deity, one draws a bamboo sliver at random from a container. This is exchanged at a counter for a corresponding slip of paper with the oracular advice written on it.

One of the stalls on Herb Lane.

Zhongshan Hall was something of an experiment for its Japanese architect; some of its decorative features were influenced by elements of Hispano-Moorish architecture.

Icons at Qingshui Temple.

old buildings, done in the imperial Chinese style and featuring arcades to protect customers from the elements, has been spruced up in recent years to serve as a time portal; it looks like Taipei of half a century ago and more. Some of the shopfronts have been done up to look exactly as they did in the 1980s, for use as backdrops in the local movie *Monga*, released in early 2010, which tells the story of 1980s Manka and Wanhua and of the city in general. The name "Bopiliao" literally means "peeling off bark," referring to the main business here in the 1800s when timber would be unloaded at the nearby port and brought here for processing. The block is now being developed as an arts and culture zone.

Qingshui Temple ❽

Address: 81 Kangding Road
Opening Hrs: daily 6am–9.30pm
Entrance Fee: free
Transportation: Longshan Temple

Further east, Guangzhou Street intersects with Kangding Road. Turn north, and a short distance away is ornate **Qingshui Temple** (Qingshui

Yan), erected in honor of Song dynasty Taoist monk Chen Zhaoying. Chen is revered for selflessly providing medical care to the poor and for successfully praying for rain when drought threatened. The temple has seven iconic images of Chen, who is also known as the "Divine Progenitor" (Zushi). The most famous statue has its nose in the process of dropping off – a sign of impending disaster. Another shows the nose jumping back on when the crisis has passed. These in no way indicate anything untoward will happen when the visitor is in the building; they are merely didactic devices, believers say, to show what has happened here in the past. Skillfully wrought and extremely detailed depictions of scenes from famous mythological tales concerned with moral guidance enrich the exterior and interior walls and support beams of the temple.

Qingshan Temple ❾

Address: 218 Guiyang Street Sec. 2
Tel: 02-2382 2296
Opening Hrs: daily 5.30am–9.30pm
Entrance Fee: free
Transportation: Longshan Temple

Just west of Xiyuan Road Section 1 is **Qingshan Temple** (Qingshan Gong). It is known especially for its magnificently carved beams and murals. The small hall at the rear of the temple's courtyard has a shrine to the King of Qingshan. Besides dispelling pestilence, he is believed to dispense justice in the underworld, thus having a direct role in deciding the fate of newly deceased mortals. The temple erupts in plangent birthday celebrations for the King of Qingshan on the 22nd day of the 10th lunar month.

XIMENDING

Ximending is the compact area of narrow streets just north of Wanhua, west of Zhonghua Road, and south of Zhongxiao West Road. *Ximen* means "west gate," and *ding* is the

Mandarin pronunciation of the Japanese character for "district." The west wall of the old walled city was where Zhonghua now runs, and the West Gate stood precisely above where Ximen MRT station is today.

The old city walls were torn down by the Japanese, and the area over which Ximending is now spread, once marshy and malarial, was cleared. A well-planned shopping and recreation hub in a precise grid of streets was established. Today the Japanese influence is still evident in several important heritage buildings and, strangely enough, in the fact that the district concentrates on Japanese-inspired youth fashion. The city has accentuated the flavor by adding street decor that evokes Tokyo's Shibuya district.

The core of Ximending is the intersection outside Ximen MRT station, from which the major streets run at angles outwards, like the rays of the sun on the Japanese naval flag. On weeknights and weekends, Wuchang and Emei streets are closed to vehicles, becoming the **Ximending Pedestrian Mall ❿**.

A leisurely stroll through the streams of happy, young, and thrill-seeking shoppers brings you past countless downmarket boutiques, shops selling Hello Kitty dolls, and the panoply of pop star-inspired youth fashion musts of the moment. You will also see teens intently devouring

WHERE

Ximending Pedestrian Mall is frequently the venue for celebrity appearances or free outdoor concerts by Taiwanese pop stars such as Jay Chou. To experience the screaming fandom, check local press listings for information.

Crowds shopping in bustling Ximending (below and left).

SHOPPING

The contrast in the Ximending and Wanhua shopping experiences is like going on visits to two different worlds. Wanhua has a heritage feel, and is Taiwan's best place to see the old Chinese preference for clustering scores of shops selling the same thing in one compact area. Ximending decidedly exists in the here and now, chock-a-block with sellers of anything and everything fashionably new and trendy, providing all the eclectic and kitschy paraphernalia that the local youth require in the quest to express their individuality.

Arts and crafts

Small Garden
70 Emei St., www.taipei-shoes.com
Tel: 02-2311 0045. p268, A2
This shop has sold beautiful hand-crafted, embroidered shoes for more than six decades. The designs are delicate and colorful.
The Red House
10 Chengdu Rd.
Tel: 02-2311 9380. p268, A2
Houses artist boutiques in the main building, and has an artist and designer bazaar each weekend. Concentrates on trendy youth-oriented items.
Tuo Yi Hang
311 Heping W. Rd., Sec. 3
Tel: 02-2304 0359. p268, A3
Carries local-style handicrafts of all kinds for household use, plus some for religious worship.

Cell-phone accessories

ESGM
4F-22, 70 Xining S. Rd., www.esgm.tw
Tel: 02-2375 5432. p268, A2
Taiwan folk are crazy about the latest electronic gadgets, and youth often turn over their cellphones every few months. This is Ximending's first outlet providing cellphone skin services. The style range seems infinite.

Jewelry

Chyh Jiun
2F-6, 70 Xining S. Rd.
Tel: 0966 135 925. p268, A2
Specializes in trendy, sleek-design silver jewelry, and has its own design workshop on-site. Several items are low-cost, with prices starting at just a few hundred NT dollars, moving up into the thousands.

Magazines

Mag Freak
1-2F, 7 Wuchang St., Sec. 2
Tel: 02-2389 6728. p268, A2
A true paradise for magazine lovers, or those who just want to see what the local kids are reading. This spot has thousands of local and imported titles, the latter mostly from Japan, but many from the West. There is a heavy emphasis on popular culture. Taiwan stores don't mind customers standing and reading for hours.

Models

Model King
4F-1B32, 70 Xining S. Rd.
Tel: 02-2312 2355. p268, A2
Stuffed to the rafters with toy models, with 30,000-plus model selections, mostly what young folk would like, such as comic-book and cartoon figures, action heroes, and fighter planes.

Markets

Huaxi Street Tourist Nightmarket
Huaxi St.
All the downmarket standards, including clothing and curios, plus antiques shops that will handle shipping.
Naruwan Indigenous Peoples' Market
102 Huanhe S. Rd., Sec. 2
Tel: 02-2720 8889, ext. 2013.

Ten shops sell a variety of arts and handicrafts, and produce from all around Taiwan's tribal areas. Buy traditional millet wine, native coffees, mountain teas, fresh organic fruits and vegetables, jewelry, and more. There are also authentic hot foods.

Photography

Flower Waves
70-8 Xining S. Rd.
Tel: 02-2370 5852, 0966-321-250. p268, A2
Uses advanced photography in wedding, individual, and pet portraiture, plus much more. Customers from overseas can have all photography done in the styles of their homelands. Price range is around NT$4,000 for a suite of 20 custom-tailored photos.

Themed areas

Lane 159, Dali St.
p268, A3
You'll find around 36 stores here specializing in clocks, watches, and accessories such as straps. Prices are in the mid-to-low range. Many of the timepieces you see in the night-markets have been sourced here; it is also a wholesale market.
Xiyuan Road Sec. 1
p268, A2
Sometimes referred to as "Buddhist Street" by locals, this area near Longshan Temple has about 20 stores selling religious crafts, all of which are for sale. Expert craft-workers sometimes do the intricate embroidery on the spot.
Ximending
p268, B2
Virtually this entire section of the city, shooting off from Ximen MRT Station, is dedicated to youth wares. Mid- and low-priced clothing and jewelry stores, music outlets, movie theaters, and tiny retail outlets peddling MP3 players, digi-cams, and cell phones.

comic books in the many small shops that specialize in Japanese-style *manga* (*manhua* in Mandarin).

The Red House ⓫

Address: 10 Chengdu Road, www.redhouse.org.tw
Tel: 02-2311 9380
Opening Hrs: Sun–Thu 11am–9.30pm, Fri–Sat 11am–10pm, closed Mon
Entrance Fee: free
Transportation: Ximen

The Red House (Ximen Honglou) is a two-story octagonal building with walls of bright red brick built by the Japanese in 1908. It sits directly outside the southwest exit of Ximen MRT station. It was originally constructed to house Taiwan's first modern market, specializing in the Japanese foods and goods that the island's colonial masters missed so much. This became the core of the district, attracting other retailers and recreational outlets – including droves of red-light businesses. In its various guises since the Japanese left in 1945, it has served as a movie theater and a venue for traditional folk performances.

Today the main floor houses the classy **Cho West** café (see page 109), a display area on the site's history, and a clutch of cozy shops given over to independent artists to sell their creations. The second level is an attractive 200-seat venue devoted to traditional folk performances, in particular puppetry and children's theatre (admission charge). The impressive recessed ceiling is held up by hefty timber support beams original to the building. In 2007, the Cruciform Building attached to the main octagonal building was also developed, housing numerous artist workshops and with a market for artists and designers. In the cobblestoned squares on either side of the complex you will find the **Moonlight Movie Theater**, for flick-watching under the stars on weekends, and the **Outdoor Café**.

The complex in its entirety is also referred to simply as The Red House.

Zhongshan Hall ⓬

Address: 98 Yanping Road, www.csh.taipei.gov.tw
Tel: 02-2381 3137
Opening Hrs: Mon–Fri 9am–5pm, Sat–Sun 2pm and 4pm
Entrance Fee: charge, free audio guides
Transportation: Ximen

North of Ximen MRT station stands the visually imposing **Zhongshan Hall** (Zhongshan Tang), with its back facing Zhonghua Road and its front on Yanping South Road. The grandiose edifice, built by the Japanese to serve as Taipei City Hall, was started in 1932 and completed in 1936. This was where the Japanese military governor signed the articles of surrender in 1945, turning the island over to the Allies.

There are two large performance halls within and productions are also staged in the large plaza in

The fashion trends embraced by Ximending's peddlers and shoppers may not appeal to the non-teenaged crowd, but the area is still great for people-watching.

The rather incongruously placed North Gate.

Red Theater.

Inside Zhongshan Hall.

North Gate ⑬

Five minutes on foot north of Zhong-shan Hall, the **North Gate** (Beimen) sits forlornly in the traffic circle where Zhong-hua, Yanping, and other roads meet; the Zhongxiao flyover comes incongruously within inches of its upper level. This important heritage site is one of the four surviving city gates, and is the only one with its original appearance faithfully maintained. It was built in 1884 in the Northern Chinese style, highly unusual in a land where almost all structures from the imperial era had Southern Chinese designs.

The gate faces the area's highest point, the peak of Mount Qixing on Yangmingshan. By conventional Chinese geomantic principles, the main city gate was supposed to face south. But because Dadaocheng was in its prime in the 1880s and most of the commercial traffic came from the north, the city's blueprints were flipped. In order to balance the *feng-shui* and block baleful energy from flowing in from the north, the main gate was therefore oriented north-east instead.

front of the building, notably during the Taipei Traditional Arts Festival in spring, for which the hall is the main venue. The facility is home to the much-lauded Taipei Chinese Orchestra, Taiwan's first fully professional orchestra dedicated to Chinese music. There is also a spacious coffee shop within, laden with historical accoutrements and serving high-quality imported brews.

Taipei Post Office ⑭

Directly across the street from the North Gate is the old **Taipei Post Office** (Taibei Youzheng Zongju; Mon–Fri 7.30am–9pm, Sat 8.30am–4.30pm, Sun 8.30am–noon). Built in 1929, this old darling is no faded star but a proud and functioning facility.

This edifice manifests the transitional style the Japanese architects experimented with in the 1930s (they "practiced" in their colony before utilising novel concepts in the motherland). Its neoclassical design harmonized with the streamlined simplicity found in the modern buildings of the time. The original structure had three stories. Its front entrance was bracketed by four pairs of symmetrical columns whose Corinthian capitals showed an elegant Egyptian palm

design. After Retrocession in 1945, an extra floor was added to accommodate demands for space, and the magnificent first-story terrace was replaced with today's black marble entrance, giving the facade its remarkably unusual two-tone character.

Old Railway Building ⑮

Standing on the northwest corner of Zhong-xiao and Yanping roads is the huge, stately **Old Taiwan Railway** **Administration Building** (Taiwan Zongdufu Jiaotongju Tiedaobu Jiushe; no entry). It was built by the Japanese in 1919 to serve as the nerve center of a rapidly expanding railway network. Stylistically, it incorporates elements of Tudor and 19th-century Victorian architecture. The first story is covered in the bright red brick that was so popular at the time of construction, while the second story is constructed of white limestone.

The Old Taiwan Railway Administration Building.

RESTAURANTS, BARS, AND CAFÉS

PRICE CATEGORIES

Prices for an average meal for two persons, including drinks.
$$$$ = above NT$2,000
$$$ = NT$1,000–2,000
$$ = NT$500–1,000
$ = under NT$500

Restaurants

Taiwanese

Ah Chung Noodle Shop
8-1 Emei St. Tel: 02-2388 8808. Open: daily 10am–11pm. **$** p268, B2
A simple, cheap, yet tasty bowl of noodles will surely satisfy your hunger. The place is immensely popular, so be prepared to line up.

Emei Iced Fruit House
4 Emei St. Tel: 02-2388 0588. Open: daily 11am–10pm. **$** p268, B2
The owners here have created the house sauces, all made fresh on-site. Over 100 shaved-ice selections.

Tainan Tan Tsu Mian
31 Huaxi St. Tel: 02-2308 1123. Open: daily L & D. **$$$** p268, A3
The most pricey version of noodle dish *danzai mian*, served here on Wedgwood china and silverware.

Bars and cafés

Cho West
10 Chengdu Rd. Tel: 02-2311 9380. Open: Sun–Thu 11am–9.30pm, Fri–Sat until 10pm, closed Mon. **$$** p268, A2
A chic and eclectic place, with leather chairs, wood tables, traditional cups and pots, and old Taiwanese music playing. A good range of coffees, teas, and spirits, including non-Western choices like sake and plum wine. Serves light meals and Western desserts.

Fortress Café
2F, 98 Yanping S. Rd. Tel: 02-2381-9551. Open: Daily 11am–11pm, closed first Mon each month. **$$$** p268, B2
Located in the Zhongshan Hall historic site, this is an expansive, cultured spot, yet with reasonable prices. The menu is wide-ranging, including tapas, seafood, and tasty desserts.

CHINESE TEMPLE ARCHITECTURE

Beneath its brilliant colors and intricate craftsmanship, the Chinese temple is built in a formalized layout, without any nails or adhesives.

Look beyond the thick incense smoke and mystic apparatus of a traditional Chinese temple, and you will discern an architectural ethos that has been preserved for over 2,000 years.

Chinese temples were traditionally constructed of wood, and, like other important buildings, were raised on platforms. Stylistically, its most noticeable feature is its magnificent roof, and indeed, during imperial times, the different roof forms were codified and their uses regulated.

The spatial planning of a classical Chinese building complex revolves around the principles of insularity (the courtyard concept), axiality, symmetry, and geomancy (fengshui). The halls of a temple or dwelling face inward onto one or more open courtyards, and the halls and courtyards are arranged along a central longitudinal axis. The left and right sides of the complex are symmetrical along this axis. By conventional geomantic principles, a building faces south (a practice that arose in North China to take advantage of the warmer southeasterly winds and avoid the colder, sand-laden northerly winds), but subtle reorientations in response to the local topography are sanctioned to maximize the unobstructed flow of good qi (vital energy).

An example of a main hall dedicated to Mazu. The icon itself is on an altar in a recessed area. In front of it is a table for ritual offerings, and before that an incense urn. Beside the incense urn are divination implements. A plaque above expresses a benediction for calm seas.

Most temples have a large urn facing the main hall for worshippers to place incense sticks in for the main deity. Another urn, facing the entrance instead, is for the Jade Emperor, who is not represented by any icon. Don't be surprised to see worshippers praying in this direction!

Temple doors are usually painted (sometimes carved) with the images of door gods (men shen), who prevent baleful spirits from entering the temple. Additionally, the doors have raised thresholds as it is believed that ghosts cannot step over them. The central doors of many temples remain shut except during important festivals, as it is believed that these portals are only for the deities' use. Mere mortals enter by the side gates.

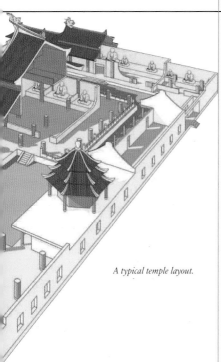

A typical temple layout.

ALTARS AND THE HEAVENLY HIERARCHY

Chinese temples almost always play host to more than one deity, and just as the social hierarchy governed the layout of a classical Chinese dwelling, the divine hierarchy determines how a temple's various deities are enshrined within. The temple's main deity is invariably given pride of place on the central altar of the main hall. The deity's attendants or guardian spirits flank him/her on the altar. Altars to the left and right of the main deity hold secondary (but important) deities. Lower ranking deities are enshrined in the rear hall, with the most important one(s) in the center and the less so on the left and right. The side halls house the lowest ranking deities or spirits, if any. Often, they are used to enshrine ancestral tablets, or are used as monks' quarters or administrative offices. The roof forms of a temple reflect this hierarchy, with the highest roof reserved for the main hall and the lowest roofs for the side halls. Pay attention to the "circuit" that a devotee makes through a temple, and you will see that the gods are worshipped in order of rank. A point of etiquette to note when visiting a temple: Avoid pointing at the icons. It is generally considered impolite and believed to draw the ire of the deity.

Undoubtedly one of the most impressive features of a classical Chinese building is its raised-beam construction technique, whereby the roof is supported by successive tiers of transverse beams resting on columns. An intricate system of canti-levered brackets and trusses (dougong), fitted together precisely using mortise and tenon joints rather than nails or adhesives, supports the generous overhang of the roof eaves. These wooden members not only provide structural support for the massive roofs, but also afford an avenue for some of the most intricate carvings, intensely colored lacquer, and lustrous gold inlay.

In contrast to the more rigid Northern style of such structures as the National Theater (see page 125), Taiwan's oldest temples are built in the floridly decorated Southern Chinese style, the most distinctive feature of which is the gracefully upturned roof ridge ending in "swallow tail" finials. The roof ridges – and indeed most available surfaces – are vehicles for spiritually symbolic ornamentation. The dragon, a symbol of power and bringer of rain, was revered in the traditionally agrarian Chinese society. Also often seen on temple roofs are phoenixes, pagodas, and the gods of Prosperity, Happiness, and Longevity.

OLD TAIPEI: DATONG

Like many aging communities in other modern cities, Datong District's neighborhoods were left behind during Taiwan's modern economic progress. Redolent of the past, these areas are now attracting notice for their living heritage.

At the core of Datong District are two of Taipei's oldest communities, Dadaocheng and Dalongtong, both long ago absorbed into the expanding city. In many ways, life goes on here as it did 100 years ago. Everywhere one looks, one is staring at history, and the legacies of the hardworking people that brought life to the place.

Dadaocheng

Dadaocheng can be literally translated as "large open space for drying rice in the sun." In the 1850s, the lower sections of the Taipei Basin had been taken over by Han Chinese farming folk. Along the stretch of the Danshui River occupied today by the Taipei metropolis sat two thriving Chinese market settlements, each with over 10,000 inhabitants: Mengjia, today called Wanhua (see page 99), and Dalongtong (see page 120). Dadaocheng, the large undeveloped area between these towns, was where farmers brought their rice to spread out for drying.

In 1853, old tensions between Chinese immigrant groups erupted in Wanhua, this time with more blood spilled than ever before. The losers – their homes, ancestral halls and places of worship in ruins – straggled to Dadaocheng to begin life anew.

Dihua Street

The settlers' leaders were members of the merchant guilds, the de facto source of leadership among the Chinese communities in Taiwan at the time, as imperial officials were not present or not trusted. Each guild was made up of immigrants from the same part of China. These men set up the standard commercial establishments of those times in shophouses, on what

Main Attractions
Dihua Street
Xiahai City God Temple
Lin Liu-Hsin Puppet Theatre Museum
Chen Tian-lai Residence
Dadaocheng Wharf
Taipei Circle
Museum of Contemporary Art Taipei
Baoan Temple
Taipei Confucius Temple

Shopping at dried-food stores along Dihua Street.

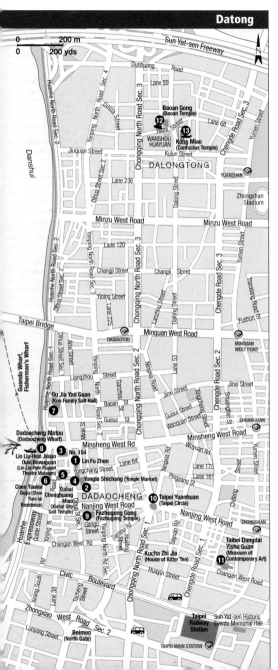

Datong

has become today's dynamic **Dihua Street**, the spiritual and commercial center of Dadao-cheng. Exodus leader Lin You-zao's shophouse remains today, at No. 105, on the corner of Minsheng West Road, where the Lin family still lives and runs the shop. Evidence of the bitter 1853 exodus is reflected in its name, **Lin Fu Zhen** ❶ ("Lins Restore Order").

The sections of Dihua Street just north and south of Minsheng are among Taipei's best-preserved streets. This was the core of the original settlement area, and has been the island's most important distribution center for traditional dried foods, herbs, medicines, and other goods since before the turn of the 20th century. Wholesalers still hawk many of the same goods that people have flocked here to buy for over 100 years. Chinese medicine shops cluster around the Xiahai City God Temple (see page 115) and stretch north to Minsheng, while dried-food suppliers predominate north of Minsheng, a one-stop-shopping area for dried mushrooms, tree fungus, dried fish, and shredded squid.

Both in and around the multistory **Yongle Market** ❷ (Yongle Shi-chang), near the temple, are numerous fabric stores, tailors, curtain makers, and upholsterers (Tue–Sat 10am–6pm).The prices here are not as low as can be found in the side streets of Hong Kong but are reasonable, and old-style textile patterns are available in abundance. The Chinese New Year season is the best time to visit and jostle with the crowds.

Dihua's shophouse facades

Among the historic architectural specimens along Dihua Street are many shophouses with neo-Baroque facades. These were added to extant structures in the 1880s and 1890s as part of the reforms encouraged by governor Liu Ming-chuan, whose goal was to learn from the West and modernize. The buildings serve as a wonderful metaphor for the reality that such emulation went only skin-deep; beyond the Western facades, the cramped interiors of the buildings are very much that of the traditional shophouse, with a family's multiple generations living in the back and working in the front.

Of particular interest is the single-story shophouse at **No. 154** ❸, built in the open fields in 1851 by Lin Lantian, an entrepreneur. The decrepit structure has had many make-overs through the years, and deserves another, but Lin's descendants still live in the back and rent out the shopfront.

Xiahai City God Temple ❹

Address: 61 Dihua Street Sec. 1
Opening Hrs: daily 6am–7.30pm
Entrance Fee: free
Transportation: Shuanglian

In 1859 things were going well, and Lin You-zao built the **Xiahai City God Temple** (Xiahai Chenghuang Miao). The refugees had brought their resident City God, or Chenghuangye, out of Mengjia. Each urban agglomeration in China had its own City God, who watched over the citizens in the district and decided a person's fate after death.

Today this temple remains the area's religious and social center, and one of Taipei's most important places of worship. It retains much of the same look and trappings as it did in the latter 1800s, for the resident priests believe any change will alter the *fengshui* that has brought so much prosperity to the community. One of its many notable features is the **Martyrs' Memorial Hall** set up in memory of the 38 young men slain protecting the sacred image during the 1853 clash.

The celebration of the City God's birthday, on the 13th day of the 5th lunar month (usually in June or July), has been called "North Taiwan's No. 1 Festival." The parade of the god's effigy through the streets is, in particular, a boisterous and exuberant pageant of bone-shaking loudness attended by thousands.

Lin Liu-Hsin Puppet Theatre Museum ❺

Address: 79 Xining N. Road,
www.taipeipuppet.com
Tel: 02-2556 8909
Opening Hrs: Tue–Sun 10am–5pm
Entrance Fee: charge
Transportation: Shuanglian

WHERE

Goods spill out of the shops along Dihua Street, lining the arcades, and hawkers freely distribute samples, so you can try anything that is unfamiliar. Note that goods are generally sold by the *jin*, not the pound or kilogram, equal to about half a kg. The street assumes a carnival-like atmosphere as Chinese New Year approaches, festooned with bright lights and decorations, displays taking up the street and vehicles banned, shops staying open till midnight, and people thronging in.

The City God's icon at Xiahai Temple.

The Lin Liu-Hsin Puppet Theatre Museum (Lin Liu-Hsin Jinian Ouxi Bowuguan), which serves as workshop, playhouse, and museum, is run by a Dutchman, Robin Ruizendaal, whose doctorate is in Chinese marionette theater. This delightful facility is filled with folk art masterpieces – over 6,000 creations from around the globe – and is his contribution to the revival of traditional arts. Lin Liu-Hsin was one of Taiwan's great puppet masters, and the two historical buildings in which the museum and its Nadou Theatre are located were donated by his widow, along with many Taiwan-puppetry treasures. Guided tours in English with special performances are available for groups, with advance notice required. There are also regular scheduled shows. All performances have English and Chinese text projection, with interactive encounters afterward.

Guide Street

Short **Guide Street** (pronounced "gway-duh") runs south from Minsheng and parallel to Dihua Street. This lane once fronted the river, and was called "Western Houses

The Chen Tian-lai Residence on Guide Street.

At Lin Liu-Hsin Puppet Theatre Museum you can try out the traditional hand puppets.

Street" because it was lined with the factories of rich local and foreign merchants. Generally, warehouses were on the first level, offices and other rooms on the second, and the factor's or owner's residence on the third. Liu Ming-chuan, Taiwan's first governor, convinced rich local families to invest in raising many of the buildings along this street to attract international trading firms, part of his efforts at modernization.

A prime example of the results is the **Chen Tian-lai Residence ❻** (Chen Tianlai Guju), at No. 73 (private property; no entry). Chen, a tea merchant, was fabulously rich for his time, his wealth deliberately reflected in the architectural motifs and appointments of this edifice. During Japanese rule, visiting members of the imperial family were brought to this "model Taiwanese residence" for a none-too-accurate glimpse of residential life in Taiwan.

Sprouting on the old neo-Baroque buildings are subtle architectural surprises such as elegant water pipes molded in the shape of bamboo. Almost all structures on Guide Street were raised on stone foundations to keep precious goods high and dry when the temperamental Danshui River flooded, common in the typhoon season. Xining North Road, between Guide and Dihua, was in fact a stream along which small boats plied in days of old. The stream helped with floodwater containment.

Koo Family Salt Hall ❼

One block north of Minsheng is Guisui Street. Down Lane 303 at No. 9 is the **Koo Family Salt Hall** (Gu Jia Yan Guan), an important heritage site both in terms of its architecture and its place in Taiwan's history (private property; no entry). Koo Xian-rong is renowned as the local merchant who met the Japanese forces on their march to Taipei in 1895. Alone, he asked them to hurry, as the leaderless, unpaid, and abandoned mainland Chinese forces had run amok. He almost lost his life, but thereafter he became a local the

Japanese trusted, and his fortune was made. He was granted a coveted salt-monopoly license, the guaranteed road to great riches, and for a time this was both the headquarters for the family salt business and the Koo home, and thus a center for power on the island. The Koo family remains one of Taiwan's most powerful today in business and in politics. The Baroque-style residence, restored to its original grandeur at significant family expense with some city help, now houses a kindergarten.

Dadaocheng Wharf ❽

Minsheng West Road ends at an ugly dike built in the 1950s, fronting the Danshui River. On the other side is **Dadao-cheng Wharf** (Dadaocheng Matou). In the days of shipping, dry goods such as tea and rice were trans-shipped from here to ocean-going craft downriver at the port of Danshui. Dadao-cheng's commerce exploded in the 1860s as a result of three factors. First, rival Wanhua's harbor became drowned in silt, a fate Dadaocheng would only suffer in the 1890s. Second, the river was opened to Western firms by the 1858 Treaty

A child plays on the anchors at the wharf.

Bitter tea served with sweet haw pellets.

BITTER TEA

Kucha, or bitter tea, is a "cooling" drink, meaning it has a *yin*, or cool, rather than *yang*, or hot, essence – even when served warm or hot. Locals do not drink *kucha* during cold weather. A single bowl of *kucha* is especially popular in summer, and is said to rid the body of many mild afflictions such as toothache, sore throat, and high blood pressure, all traditionally believed to stem directly from having too much heat in the body. Perhaps Taipei's favorite source is **Kucha Zhi Jia** (House of Bitter Tea), at Changan West Road and Chong-qing North Road. Thirty-six herbs are used in its *kucha*, which is boiled for six hours for maximum flavor and effectiveness.

A reproduction of a Qing dynasty ship is displayed at the Dadaocheng Wharf.

of Tianjin after the Second Opium War. Third, British trader John Dodd saw the potential of the nearby hills for growing Oolong tea for export, initiating the growing and processing that soon made tea the Taipei Basin's major export, followed by camphor.

Blue Highway (Lansi Gonglu) river cruises launch from Dadaocheng Wharf and head north for Guandu Wharf or Danshui's Fisherman's Wharf. The cruises offer a good way to get a clear sense of the mass and beauty of the mountains that surround the Taipei Basin. A bicycle path passes by the wharf, part of the city's larger network of bike paths that runs almost right around the city and on to the north coast at Danshui, along the Jingmei, Xindian, Danshui, and Jilong rivers.

Fazhugong Temple ❾

East of Dihua Street, down Lane 344 on Nanjing West Road, stands the unusual, multistory **Fazhugong Temple** (Fazhugong Gong; daily 8am–10pm), whose main altar is on the second story. The powerful icon housed within, Fazhu – a slayer of snakes and demons not widely worshipped in Taiwan – was brought from Fujian Province in imperial times by a tea merchant. With time, the god's ability to help devotees prosper in business and recover from illness became apparent, leading to the temple's role as a center of worship for Dadao-cheng's tea merchants.

On the 22nd day of the 9th lunar month (October or November), the raucous "Big Turtles Festival" is held to celebrate the deity's birthday. Suppliants ask Fazhu for red "turtle" cakes – made of glutinous rice or flour – representing a godly favor. If their request is granted, they are expected to "pay interest" by bestowing the temple with two such turtles at the next festival.

Taipei Circle ❿

Located in the traffic circle where Nanjing West and other roads meet,

Taipei Circle (**Taipei Yuanhuan;** www.taipeicircle.com; daily 10.30am–11pm) is the most recent incarnation of the old and beloved Jiancheng Circle Food Court, which was set up around 1910 as a community meeting area by the Japanese. It had, right into the 1970s, long been north Taiwan's most popular nightmarket, specializing in traditional snacks such as glutinous rice dumplings, oyster omelets, fishball noodles, and un-fried spring rolls. After a major overhaul completed in 2003, a failure, and a grand reopening in 2009 as the Taipei Circle, the market is now decidedly kids-oriented. It is housed in a circular two-story glass and steel structure, home to a traditional-style food court, arts and performance facilities, and a rooftop garden. During the reconstruction, a forgotten reservoir dating from World War II was unearthed, built by Japanese soldiers seeking to ensure water supply in the face of Allied bombing. History displays focus on the role of traditional snack foods in the culture of the city. One block south of the circle you will find the **House of Bitter Tea** (www.coteahouse. com.tw; see page 117).

Museum of Contemporary Art Taipei ⓫

Address: 39 Changan Road, www.mocataipei.org.tw
Tel: 02-2552 3720
Opening Hrs: Tue–Sun 10am–6pm
Entrance Fee: charge
Transportation: Zhongshan

On the eastern end of Changan West Road is the **Museum of Contemporary Art Taipei** (Taibei Dangdai Yishu Guan), which once served as the city hall. This heritage site was built in 1919 by the Japanese in a red-brick hybrid of Victorian and Edwardian styles. With 11 galleries spread over two floors and no permanent exhibits, MOCA Taipei regularly juxtaposes works by foreign and local artists, concentrating on the themes of art, design, and architecture.

SHOPPING

The Datong district is a heritage area, so it is no surprise that most shops specialize in goods that have been standards for a century and more — though a few places bring a new twist to old themes.

Arts and crafts

Lam Sam Yick Co.
58 Chongqing N. Rd. Sec 2. http://lamsam yick.mysinablog.com. Tel: 02-2556 6433. p272, A4
This family-run enterprise has been in place since 1912. Long famed for calligraphy sets and other traditional writing supplies of the highest quality.

Embroidery

Yuan Sheng Embroidery
21 Dihua St Sec. 1. Tel: 02-2558 1019.
p272, A4
Silk cloth embroidered in classical style is sold here. Many types are used for religious worship.

Fabrics

Yongle Textile Market
21 Dihua St Sec. 1. p272, A4
100-plus outlets for fabric on the second and third levels at Taipei's greatest galleria for textiles. Tailoring services also available.

Food

Lin Fu Zhen
105 Dihua St. www.linfuzhen.com.
Tel: 02-2557 6409. p272, A4
A heritage building run by descendants of Dadaocheng's founder. It specializes in traditional Chinese "north-south" goods, such as dried seafoods.
Vigor Kobo
76 Jiuquan St. www.taiwan-vigor.com.tw.
Tel: 02-2291 9122. p272, A1
Famed for its traditional bite-sized pineapple cakes, once named Taipei's best in a public contest, which come in delicate gift-boxes. Or try the inkstick-style cakes.

Tea

Wang's Tea
26, Lane 64, Chongqing N. Rd Sec. 2.
www.wangtea.com.tw. Tel: 02-2555 9164.
p272, A4
One of Taiwan's most respected tea purveyors, trading since 1890. Roasting is done on-site. Sells all of Taiwan's best teas, including Oolongs, and offers extensive tastings.

Dalongtong

The community of Dalongtong, at Datong District's north end, once rivaled Wanhua as a river port. The Danshui River used to flow closer by (where Yanping North Road Section 4 now runs), but silting in the late 1800s caused by rapid opening up of land upstream changed its course and cut off the community's economic lifeline. Save for visits to two magnificent cultural sites, this area is relatively quiet, largely bypassed by locals and visitors alike on their way to other districts.

Baoan Temple ⑫

Address: 61 Hami Street,
www.baoan.org.tw
Opening Hrs: daily 7am–11pm
Entrance Fee: free
Transportation: Yuanshan

Baoan Temple (Baoan Gong) formed and still forms the core of the old settlement; in early days the Danshui and Jilong rivers met immediately northwest of here. Begun in 1805, it took 25 years to complete. All the materials were brought over from mainland China, along with the artisans to work them. This architectural masterpiece

Tablets rather than icons represent the Great Teacher at the Confucius Temple.

A deity icon at the Baoan Temple.

is recognized as among Taiwan's most elaborate, and an overhaul brought an honorable mention in the 2003 Unesco Asia-Pacific Heritage Awards.

The temple's main deity is Baosheng Dadi, the God of Medicine, a real-life figure and legendary physician from the Song dynasty, born in Fujian Province's Tongan County, where the settlers in Dalongtong came from. Other important deities are Shennong, the God of Agriculture, and Mazu, Goddess of the Sea. It is believed that in the late 19th century, prayers to Shennong brought heavy rains, ending a drought lasting months. Grateful believers thereafter en-shrined the icon now in the hindmost court, honoring their otherworldly rescuer.

The temple's birthday celebrations for Baosheng Dadi and Mazu are among the island's most colorful festivals.

Taipei Confucius Temple ⑬

Address: 275 Dalong Street,
www.ct.taipei.gov.tw
Tel: 02-2592 3934
Opening Hrs: Tue–Sun and national

holidays 8.30am–9pm
Entrance Fee: free
Transportation: Yuanshan

Across from Baoan Temple is the **Taipei Confucius Temple** (Taibei Shi Kong Miao), set amid sculpted gardens in an expansive walled compound. Confucius was a man of simple living, it is said, so temples to the sage are places of dignity and simplicity: no icons, and little of the elaborate carvings and statuary seen on Taoist temples. However, the water dragons on the roof, said to protect the compound from fire, are characteristic of South China and Taiwan. Some believe there are no philosophical inscriptions because none dare compete with one of time's greatest literary masters.

Note the owl images on the main hall's roof. Owls are said to have been unfilial and vicious until educated by the Great Teacher. The grounds are usually quiet, but come to life each Teacher's Day, when solemn, time-honored ceremonies take place. Guided English tours are available.

The newest attraction is a 4D Theater screening two films that help understand both the Confucian system of belief and the Chinese culture (English subtitles, free). The full show takes 35 minutes during which viewers experience a full range of physical special effects, such as snow and wind. It's a fun way to grasp Confucian thinking.

TIP

A limited number of "first come first served" seats are available for Teacher's Day celebrations at the Taipei Confucius Temple, but you'll have to line up in the wee hours to have a chance. You'll have a much better shot at the full practice run the day before, also first come first served, held in the afternoon from 4–5pm.

RESTAURANTS, BARS, AND CAFÉS

PRICE CATEGORIES

Prices for an average meal for two persons, including drinks.
$$$$ = above NT$2,000
$$$ = NT$1,000–2,000
$$ = NT$500–1,000
$ = under NT$500

Restaurants

Chinese
Zui Hong Lou
9 Tianshui St. Tel: 02-2559 7089. Open: daily L & D. $$$ p272, A4
Near Dihua Street, here you'll find regional specialties such as Chaozhou-style lobster and shark's fin soup. English menu.

Indian
Himalaya
97 Yanping N. Rd Sec. 2. Tel: 02-2555 5552. Open: daily L & D. $ (daily specials) $$$ p272, A4
A "home cooking" restaurant with a wide range of vegetarian curries. The samosas and green chutney made in-house are spot-on. Daily specials are inexpensive for the amount served. Reservations necessary.

Japanese
Xiao Dong Ting
8, Lane 250, Nanjing W. Rd. Tel: 02-2555 2386. Open: daily 11.30am–9.30pm. $$ p272 A4
On an alley known colloquially among expats as "Alimentary Alley," this is in fact a collection of small eateries serving high-quality, unusually inexpensive sushi and sashimi, best enjoyed while sitting at an outdoor table nursing a cold beer.

Taiwanese
Kucha Zhi Jia
244 Changan W. Rd. Tel: 02-2558 0019. www.coteahouse.com.tw Open: daily 10am–6pm. $ p272, A4
Besides its bitter tea, the shop serves other "cooling" liquids such as jasmine tea, chrysanthemum tea, lotus seed soup, and taro soup.
Li Ting Xiang (Lee's Cake Headquarter)
309 Dihua St Sec. 1. Tel: 02-2557 8716. http://lee-cake.com Open: Mon–Sat 9am–8pm, Sun 9am–7pm. $ p272, A3
Traditional family-run bakery. House specialties include an shi bing, a cake eaten 1,000 years ago by soldiers.

Taipei Circle
Roundabout by Nanjing/Chongqing Rds. www.taipeicircle.com p272, A4
New incarnation of an old nightmarket, now a food court with classic snacks.

Bars and cafés

Bolero
308 Minsheng W. Rd. Tel: 02-2556 0710. www.bolero.com.tw Open: daily 10am–10pm. $$$ p272, A4
A café-cum-restaurant, this is a Taipei icon. During and long after the Japanese era this was a haunt for politicos, artists, and the literati, an introductory portal to Western culture for countless locals. A living time capsule, it serves fine Western meals interpreted the Taiwan way.
Kanpai
2-1, Lane 25, Nanjing W. Rd. Tel: 02-2555 6110. www.kanpai.com.tw Open: Sat–Sun 11.30am–3pm, daily 5–11pm. $$ p272, B4
A beerhouse with the trappings of a restaurant and – something different – Japanese nightmarket-style foods. There are nightly beer-quaffing contests and a Happy Hour on cocktails pre-7.30pm.

OLD WALLED CITY AND ZHONGZHENG

Formerly the seat of authority for the Qing and Japanese administrations in Taiwan, this area retains its grandeur through its majestic old buildings, dignified monuments, and wide boulevards.

The core of Zhongzheng District is the Old Walled City (Gucheng). Built in the early 1880s during the Qing dynasty, the east wall stretched along today's Zhongshan South Road, the south wall along Aiguo West Road, the west wall along Zhonghua Road, and the north wall along Zhongxiao West Road. In preparation for the naming of Taipei as capital of the newly created province of Taiwan in 1885, the walls were erected to house and protect the administrative seat of power.

The walls are long gone – torn down by the Japanese to facilitate troop movement and improve public sanitation after they took over in 1895 – but the sense of history lives on, as do four of the five original gates. The area is characterized by grand and imposing architectural edifices erected by the Japanese to engender awe and respect – or at least subservience – in their new subjects, and to showcase the model colony, Japan's first, for the Western colonial powers watching.

Today these buildings, all built in Western architectural styles, continue to fulfill practical civic functions, and impart an atmosphere of historical gravitas to the area.

To the south of the Old Walled City is a primarily residential area,

with communities centered around parks and gardens, most initiated by the Japanese on a grandiose scale. There is little commercial activity in Zhongzheng, and nights bring a blanket of quiet calm. Residents in need of raucous fun head west to Ximending (see page 104), or east to the malls and department stores of Xinyi District.

The area directly north of the Old Walled City used to be mostly scrubland or farm. The Japanese later decided to build a boulevard from where the east wall stood, straight

Main Attractions
Chiang Kai-shek Memorial
National Chiang Kai-shek
   Cultural Center
East Gate
Presidential Office Building
Taipei 228 Memorial
   Museum
National Taiwan Museum
Nanmen Market

Maps and Listings
Map, page 124
Shopping, page 128
Restaurants, page 131

The grand Presidential Office Building.

to the high perch where the Grand Hotel (see page 173) stands today, the location of the great Shinto shrine to which all royal visitors and appointed governors-general from the imperial homeland proceeded in grand procession upon arrival. The concourse – today's Zhongshan Road – was aptly called the Imperial Way.

Chiang Kai-shek Memorial Hall and Cultural Center ❶

Address: 21 Zhongshan S. Road Sec. 1, www.cksmh.gov.tw
Tel: 02-2343 1100
Opening Hrs: daily 9am–6pm

Entrance Fee: free
Transportation: Chiang Kai-shek Memorial Hall

The best place to begin a tour of Zhongzheng is at its most famous landmark, the **Chiang Kai-shek Memorial Hall** (Zhongzheng Jinian Tang), which has its own eponymous MRT station at the southernmost point of Zhongshan Road where it intersects with Aiguo Road. The hall was built in the late 1970s to memorialize the longtime leader of the Republic of China, Chiang Kai-shek. Its immaculate grounds feature lovely sculpted gardens and serene ponds.

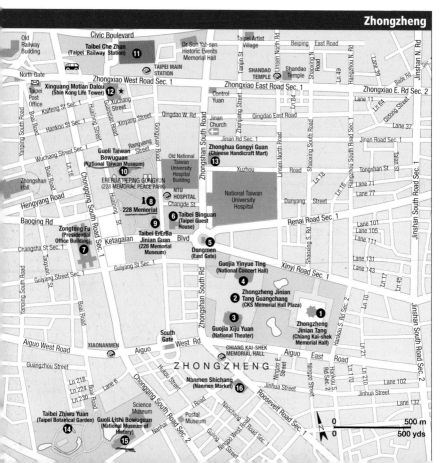

The magnificent structure, with a marble facade and a twin-eave roof of brilliant blue tiles crowned by a golden spur, is 76 meters (250ft) high. Inside, steps lead up to a dais three stories high, on which sits a massive statue of the Generalissimo. On the ground level are exhibits related to the former President's life, including personal effects, a mock-up of one of his offices, and a bulletproof Cadillac. English tours of the hall and grounds are available with advance application.

National Chiang Kai-shek Cultural Center

Address: 21 Zhongshan S. Rd Sec. 1, http://npac-ntch.org
Tel: 02-3393 9888
Opening Hrs: open for public performances only
Entrance Fee: charge varies per public performance
Transportation: Chiang Kai-shek Memorial Hall

The below performance halls are collectively called the **National Chiang Kai-shek Cultural Center** (Guoli Zhongzheng Wenhua Zhong-xin); both traditional and modern productions are regularly staged here.

The expansive **Chiang Kai-shek Memorial Hall Plaza** ❷ (Zhongzheng Jinian Tang Guangchang) – think of Forbidden City scenes from the movie *The Last Emperor* – is always busy with visitors looking for grand vistas and lots of space to breathe. It is flanked by the massive and ornate **National Theater** ❸ (Guojia Xiju Yuan) on the south and **National Concert Hall** ❹ (Guojia Yinyue Ting) on the north, built and painted in brilliant Ming dynasty style. In fact, they are modeled after the Halls of Supreme Harmony and Preserving Harmony in the Forbidden City. The plaza's tremendous arched entrance, 30 meters (100ft) high and 80 meters (266ft) wide, faces China, the homesick Chiang's beloved birthplace.

East Gate ❺

The impressive **East Gate** (Dongmen) stands in the center of the traffic circle off the northwest corner of the memorial hall grounds. Especially pretty when lit at night,

One of Taipei's many wedding salons. If you're planning to tie the knot in Taipei, be aware that auspicious dates on the Chinese calendar often result in "peak" periods for nuptials.

The Chiang Kai-shek Memorial Hall Plaza gate.

Zhongzheng, which roughly means "central uprightness," is the courtesy name of Chiang Kai-shek, memorialised here; it is also the official name by which he is known in Taiwan.

The East Gate stands in front of the KMT Headquarters.

this was the largest of the five original gates. Today's ornate embellishments are not true to the original, however; renovation work was carried out in 1966 on what was originally a simple structure in Southern Chinese style.

An interesting fact about the East Gate is that this was where the Japanese military first entered the walled city in 1895 on their approach from nearby Keelung port to take possession of Taipei. History books show old photographs of Japanese officers on horseback marching proudly through the North Gate, but in fact, an advance party had slipped in through the East Gate the night before, led by local citizens who were concerned that the city was collapsing under the rampage of the mainland Chinese soldiers whose leaders had already run for home.

Taipei Guest House ❻

West on Ketagalan Boulevard, at the northeast corner of Gongyuan Road, is the exquisite **Taipei Guest House** (Taibei Binguan; www.mofa.gov.tw/tgh), considered the most elegant example of Baroque architecture in Taiwan, augmented with a roof in Mansard style and high Roman pillars. It was

built on between 1897 and 1901 to serve as the Japanese Governor-General's residence. Today the site is used by the President's Office for important functions, and is very irregularly open to public visits (public holidays 8am–4pm, no advance booking is required), announced beforehand on the website.

Presidential Office Building ❼

Address: 122 Chongqing S. Rd Sec. 2, www.president.gov.tw
Tel: 02-2311 3731
Opening Hrs: Mon–Fri 9am–noon
Entrance Fee: free; advance booking required
Transportation: NTU Hospital

Built by Taiwan's Japanese colonial masters in neo-Renaissance style, the **Presidential Office Building** (Zongtong Fu) was completed in 1919 and known as the Governor-General's Office. The heavy cost brought intense criticism from the Japanese parliament, but the elaborate red-brick edifice served its purpose, clearly demonstrating Japan's might. The central tower, 66 meters (215ft) high, served as a watchtower against attack. It was long and, by law,

National Taiwan Museum

Taipei's tallest structure. The building was bombed by the Allies in World War II. Today's huge entrance portico was added during post-war renovations. The building is partially opened and tours given on weekdays, and fully opened for the full day on a series of weekend dates throughout each year, listed on the official website. There is also an art gallery within the complex, featuring new exhibits every few months highlighting Taiwan's fine arts and crafts.

228 Memorial Peace Park

On the north side of Ketagalan Boulevard is the shady and forested **228 Memorial Peace Park** (ErErBa Heping Gongyuan). It was created by the Japanese in 1907 and was originally called Taipei New Park. In 1996 the present name was given in honor of those killed in the turmoil surrounding the infamous 2-28 Incident (see page 37) of February 28, 1947.

The park is busiest in the early morning, when it is filled with solemn practitioners of tai chi and other ancient martial arts, and senior citizens sitting under shady trees playing Chinese chess or engaged in songbird competitions. In the park's center, just inside the east entrance, is the towering **228 Memorial** ❽ (ErErBa Jinian Bei), a postmodernist steel spire held up by a base of three gigantic cubes standing on their vertices. The cubes are considered an "unnatural" shape, as opposed to the Chinese concept of the sphere as representing harmony and perfection, and symbolize the disturbance to nature represented by the 2-28 Incident. Remembrance ceremonies are held annually on February 28.

Taipei 228 Memorial Museum ❾

Address: 3 Ketagalan Boulevard, http://228.taipei.gov.tw
Tel: 02-2389 7228
Opening Hrs: Tue–Sun 10am–5pm, closed days after national holiday
Entrance Fee: charge; free Feb 28 & Dec 10, the latter Human Rights Day
Transportation: NTU Hospital

Near the sculpture is the **Taipei 228 Memorial Museum** (Taibei ErErBa Jinian Guan), in another heritage building built by the Japanese. It housed a radio station that was taken over by protesters in the 2-28 Incident, who broadcast demands for government reform from here. The museum has a number of poignant video presentations, with some English. Among the riveting displays on individual victims of the Incident and later White Terror, visitors can ponder the blood-stained shirt saved by a wife after her husband's execution and writings by survivors detailing the days their family members were either shot or forcibly taken from homes, never to return. There is no English translation in the displays, but the museum provides a good recorded English-language audio tour. Note that there is a simple,

cozy café and restaurant on-site looking inward into the park, with a quiet, friendly tree-shaded patio.

National Taiwan Museum ⑩

Address: 2 Xiangyang Road, www.ntm.gov.tw
Tel: 02-2382 2566
Opening Hrs: Tue–Sun 9.30am–5pm
Entrance Fee: charge
Transportation: NTU Hospital

Just inside the park's north entrance

SHOPPING

This area, primarily one of residential high-rises and public buildings, is relatively quiet. Its two retail hubs are along and just south of Zhongxiao East Road from Shin Kong Life Tower to near the Taipei Post Office, and along the Roosevelt Road, shooting off from the Chiang Kai-shek Memorial grounds.

Arts and antiques

Kander's Arts and Antiquities Gallery
25-27 Zhongxiao W. Rd Sec. 1. Tel: 02-2389 1212. p268, C1
Sells high- and medium-quality antique items and art. Seal engraving is also done on-site, starting at NT$1,000. Call ahead for English service.

Arts and crafts

Chinese Handicraft Mart
1 Xuzhou Rd. Tel: 02-2393 3655. www.handicraft.org.tw p268, C2
Specializes in high-quality works crafted in Taiwan, along with selected items from China. Has a very good selection of two iconic types of Taiwanese art, the colorful koji pottery and exquisitely hand-painted oil umbrellas from Meinong town. Overseas shipment can be arranged.
Taiwan Crafts Center
9/10F, 20 Nanhai Rd. Tel: 02-2356 3880. www.ntcri.gov.tw p268, B4

Stocks Taipei's best selection of traditional-style works by the island's best-known craftsmen. A good display of koji pottery, attractive woodcarvings, and art from Sanyi, Taiwan's woodcarving center. Limited English spoken.

Department stores

Shin Kong Mitsukoshi
66 Zhongxiao W. Rd Sec. 1. Tel: 02-2388 5552. www.skm.com.tw p268, B1
This Shin Kong Life Tower outlet has 14 levels of shopping and dining, targeting families and middle-income shoppers. There are other outlets in Xinyi and Tianmu and on Nanjing E. Rd. Each has an information counter where tourists can get English assistance with foreign exchange and the Taiwan Tax Refund system for shopping.
Taipei City Mall
Tel: 02-2559 4566. www.taipeimall.com.tw p268, C1
Runs under Civic Boulevard just north of Taipei Railway Station, then north to Zhongshan MRT station. A city under the city, with hundreds of retail outlets. Many close shortly after the evening rush hour.

Electronics

Camera Street
Boai Rd Sec. 1 near intersection with

Hankou St. p268, B1
Find a cluster of around 40 photographic equipment specialists here, officially designated Camera Street by the city. The shops seem small but are well stocked; not as cheap as Hong Kong stores, but competitive.
Nova
2 Guanqian Rd. Tel: 02-2381 4833. www.nova.com.tw p268, B2
The 130-plus shops here have very similar stock, allowing for comparison and bargaining. A local mecca for the latest gadgetry. Free Internet on the third floor. Known for great prices, usually lower by 10 percent or more than elsewhere; the best deals are generally cash only.
T-Zone Computer
54 Zhongxiao E. Rd Sec. 1. Tel: 02-2392 4442. http://tzonecomputer.en.ecplaza.net p268, C2
Big outlet selling computer equipment, cell phones, and all the usual gadgets. Original units are provided with international warranty.

Foods

Nanmen Market
8 Roosevelt Rd Sec. 1. Tel: 02-2321 8069. www.nanmenmarket.org.tw p268, C3
Taipei's largest traditional day market, a bazaar for such favorite traditional Taiwanese preserved foods as sausages, seafoods, pastries, and more.

is the imposing **National Taiwan Museum** (Guoli Taiwan Bowu-guan), built by the Japanese in 1915 in Greek Revival style. It was created to house the results of Japanese researchers' work on the natural history of their colony. Inside are well over 40,000 items collected over the past 100 years, with unmatched material on the lives of the island's original inhabitants; the indigenous peoples' trove contains over 7,000 pieces. Among the museum's most prized possessions is the original "Yellow Tiger Flag" created when local notables declared the short-lived Republic of Taiwan in 1895. Just outside the museum entrance is a pair of old steam engines that were two of the first to ply the island's railway network in colonial days, both shipped in from the West.

Shin Kong Life Tower

Just beyond 228 Memorial Peace Park's north entrance, and across from the mammoth **Taipei Railway Station** ⑪ (Taibei Che Zhan), which resembles the architectural giants the Soviets and Communist China once loved, stands the **Shin Kong Life Tower** ⑫ (Xinguang Motian Dalou; 66 Zhongxiao W. Rd Sec. 1). For several years, the 800ft (245-meter) structure with 51 stories was Taipei's tallest. It was only dwarfed by the Taipei 101 tower (see page 152) in late 2004.

At the base of the tower is a very posh and large (14 levels, two underground) **Shin Kong Mitsukoshi Department Store** (Xinguang Sanyue). At weekends, live outdoor concerts are regularly staged on the plaza fronting the tower, or on the grounds of the train station right across the street. Directly behind the tower are the cramped streets of the city's famous 'cram school' area, stuffed with specialist private schools helping students on weeknights and weekends to cram information into their heads in preparation for regular-school and TOEFL exams.

The main station district has been chosen as a construction site for one of the major Taipei projects. By 2018, it will be home to the **Taipei Twin Towers,** multifunctional space hosting offices, shops, and tourist hotels. The taller tower will measure 320.7 meters in height (1,052ft), while the smaller will be 241.5 meters (792ft) tall. Underneath, there will be a terminal station of the Taoyuan International Airport MRT. The development, which is one of the most expensive in the city, is expected to completely overhaul Taipei's old center as the surrounding area is fully revitalized.

A vase for sale at the Chinese Handicraft Mart.

Chinese Handicraft Mart ⑬

The **Chinese Handicraft Mart** (Zhonghua Gongyi Guan) has long been the city's most popular one-stop shop for foreign visitors looking to purchase traditional arts and crafts to take home (1 Xuzhou Rd; daily 9am–6pm; www.handicraft.org.tw; tel: 02-2393 3655). It is located just off Zhongshan South Road, almost equidistant from the NTU Hospital, Taipei Main Station, and Shandao Temple MRT stations. The large

Taipei Railway Station

A display at the National Museum of History (see page 130). English signage is sporadic; invaluable English-language tours are given at 10.30am and 3pm daily

In the Taipei Botanical Garden.

multistory facility stocks over 40,000 items, everything from porcelain, cloisonné, and oil-paper umbrellas to painted fans, woodcarvings, and crystal. Prices are reasonable as the government-run facility is seen as a public relations vehicle as much as a profit-making one. Overseas shipping services are offered. You will find English-speaking staff are on hand to assist you. The mart now has an online store offering special discounts.

Taipei Botanical Garden

Address: 53 Nanhai Road, http://tpbg.tfri.gov.tw
Tel: 02-2303 9978 ext. 1420
Opening Hrs: daily 5.30am–10pm
Entrance Fee: free
Transportation: Chiang Kai-shek Memorial Hall

South of the Old Walled City are two locations especially worth visiting. From the Presidential Office Building, walk south on Chongqing South Road for about 45 minutes.

Established by the Japanese in 1921, **Taipei Botanical Garden** (Taibei Zhiwu Yuan) is an oasis within the city where all sounds of

traffic are shut out. It is filled with plants and immense trees that were mere saplings when the Japanese started this experimental station and the city's airport still stood right by here, beside the Xindian River. Wide pathways meander through 17 sections of exotic plant life totaling 1,500 species. Most famous are the lotus varieties, which bloom in summer. Oddities include giant Amazonian water lilies big enough to support a man's weight, square bamboo, and two Bo trees (*Ficus religiosa*, or Sacred Fig), the type under which the Buddha achieved enlightenment.

Also found here is the Qing dynasty provincial governor's *yamen*, or headquarters, which was transported here from where Zhongshan Hall now stands.

National Museum of History

Address: 49 Nanhai Road, www.nmh.gov.tw
Tel: 02-2361 0270
Opening Hrs: Tue–Sun 10am–6pm, open Mon if a national holiday
Entrance Fee: charge
Transportation: Chiang Kai-shek Memorial Hall

Beside the Botanical Garden, and thus making for a fine afternoon outing together, is the **National Museum of History** (Guoli Lishi Bowuguan), which is less crowded than the National Palace Museum (see page 190) but has a collection that in many ways rivals it. It is home to about 10,000 one-of-a-kind Chinese artifacts dating from as far back as 2,000 BC. These works, unlike those in the National Palace Museum, were never in the imperial collection. The permanent exhibits on Tang dynasty tri-color pottery and Shang bronzes are especially noteworthy.

Nanmen Market

Just south of the CKS Memorial, **Nanmen Market** (Nanmen Shichang) is

長葉腎蕨
【Gleandraceae 腎蕨科】

Taipei's biggest and best-known day market, held on this spot for over a century (8 Roosevelt Rd Sec. 1; www. nanmenmarket.org.tw; daily 7am–8pm; tel: 02-2321 8069). "Nanmen" means "south gate," a reference to the nearby old walled city gate. It opened in the Japanese colonial era as a vegetable distribution center, called Qiansui (Thousand Year) Market. Originally a single-story structure, it was completely overhauled in 1983 and emerged multi-storied. In 2012, it was thoroughly refurbished yet again, and now it is bright, stylish, and air-conditioned in all areas.

Goods are brought in from all around Taiwan, and for many years the market has been a key Taipei source for Jiangzhe (China's Jiangsu and Zhejiang provinces) produce. Before Chinese New Year, the place is really hopping, for here you'll find some of the most popular holiday foods, such as sausages, traditional preserved hams, cooked foods, snacks, cookies, steamed mincemeat-stuffed buns, and steamed breads. If any one booth can be recommended it should be Yi-chang Yufang (Yi-chang's Imperial Workshop), which has won the Top Cooked-Food Vendor award during the Taipei Traditional Market Festival four times. It specializes in Jiangzhe cuisine and has over 100 cold and hot-prepared-food choices.

TIP

Google Street View now covers Taipei, allowing convenient 3D virtual travel through the city's lanes and alleys before you tackle them "live." Especially in the old sections of town, the cramped, narrow-artery neighborhoods can strike the newcomer as labyrinthine.

RESTAURANTS, BARS, AND CAFÉS

PRICE CATEGORIES

Prices for an average meal for two persons, including drinks.
$$$$ = above NT$2,000
$$$ = NT$1,000–2,000
$$ = NT$500–1,000
$ = under NT$500

Restaurants

Cantonese

The Dragon
B1, Sheraton Taipei, 12 Zhongxiao E. Rd Sec. 1. Tel: 02-2321 1818. www.sheraton grandetaipei.com.tw Open: daily L & D. $$$ p268, C2
Amid a modern Chinese setting, enjoy Cantonese fare with a special focus on classic dishes such as shark's fin and abalone. The dim sum selection is also very good. A treat is the special Palace Dinner, with dishes resembling those savored by emperors in the past.

Halal

Shao Shao Ke
15, Lane 41, Renai Rd Sec. 2. Tel: 02-2351 7148. www.shaoshaoke.com Open: Tue–Sun L & D. $$$ p268, D3
Contemporary and traditional Islamic dishes from China's

Shaanxi Province, with unleavened bread, lamb, and fragrant spices at its core. Excellent, inexpensive set meals for two. No English spoken.

International

Kitchen 12
1F, Sheraton Taipei, 12 Zhongxiao E. Rd Sec. 1. Tel: 02-2321 1818. www.sheratongrande taipei.com.tw Open: daily B, L & D, plus afternoon tea. $$ p268, C2
This airy buffet restaurant has an open kitchen and bakery, and 12 themed-cuisine areas. In a space with a 17-floor-high atrium, enjoy delicious Indonesian *nasi goreng*, Malaysian curry, Vietnamese spring rolls, or an American tuna melt.

Jiangzhe

Yi-chang Yufang
8 Roosevelt Rd Sec. 1. Tel: 02-2393 0383. Open: daily 10am–8pm. $$ p268, C4
In the Nanmen Market, this place specializes in foods from China's Jiangsu and Zhejiang provinces. Popular dishes include Dongpo pork, Shaoxing chicken, and lotus seeds in syrup.

Taiwanese

Lao Zhang Beef Noodle Shop
50-2 Nanchang Rd Sec. 1. Tel: 02-2396

8865. www.lao-zhang.com.tw $ p268, C4
"Old Zhang" is perhaps Taipei's most famous beef-noodle eatery, comfy and breezy. The shop won at the prestigious Taipei Beef Noodle Festival in 2006.

Bars and cafés

Café Astoria
2F, 7 Wuchang St Sec. 1. Tel: 02-2381 5589. www.astoria.com.tw Open: daily 10am–10pm. p268, B2
A famous heritage business opened post-World War II by a Russian émigré. Has a restored 1940s-salon ambience, quality international coffees, and Russian meal and sweet-treat classics.

The Lounge
1F, Sheraton Taipei, 12 Zhongxiao E. Rd Sec. 1. Tel: 02-2321 1818. www.sheraton grandetaipei.com.tw Open: daily 10am–1am. p268, C2
Equal parts bar and café, this has long been a popular rendezvous spot for the moneyed class. Two sides of walled glass look outside, while the inside looks into the lobby. Has quality coffee and alcohol lists, and a reputation for cocktails.

CENTRAL TAIPEI

Much of this area, while in a central part of the city, is not exactly "downtown." In fact, visitors looking to experience a sampling of heritage, culture, or just some green open spaces, will be amply rewarded.

Taipei residents tend to think of the Zhongshan District as the primarily open, green area of parkland on the southern bank of the Jilong River. In fact, this central district, bounded in the south by Civil Boulevard, covers a larger area.

From the 1950s until the late 1980s, tree-lined Zhongshan North Road was the epicenter of Taiwan's fashion scene, where the big clothing brands set up shop. The city's international hotels were also located here. But the temples of fashion have since migrated to the boutique areas east, and the newest big-brand hotels are also being built in the eastern business district. A stroll along Zhongshan Road from south to north reveals an area with a slightly more genteel flair – perhaps giving a better feel of the city's pulse than its more frantic environs.

Shandao Temple ❶

Address: 23 Zhongxiao E. Road Sec. 1, www.shandaotemple.org.tw
Tel: 02-2341 5758
Opening Hrs: Tue–Sun 9am–5pm
Entrance Fee: free
Transportation: Shandao Temple
Shandao Temple (Shandao Si) was opened in 1935; one of seven major temple sites constructed by Japanese

Buddhists during the colonial period. Today it is the largest of the city's seven most important Buddhist temples. The nine-story structure is architecturally quite unlike other Taiwan temples, faintly resembling a giant funerary tower in its stark austerity. Inside, it also lacks much of the clamor and jostle typical of other temples. There is a museum housing a first-rate vault of Buddhist artifacts, ranging from the Northern Wei (386–534) to the present. The pièce de résistance is undoubtedly a priceless

The meditative Shandao Temple hall.

Central Taipei

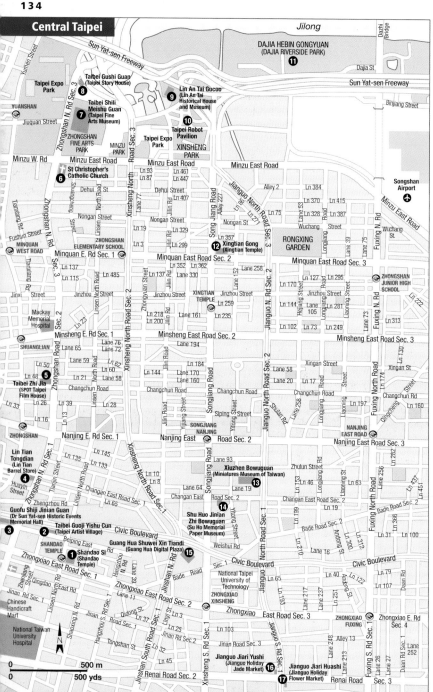

Jilong

Dazhi Bridge

Sun Yat-sen Freeway

DAJIA HEBIN GONGYUAN
(DAJIA RIVERSIDE PARK) 11

Dajia St

Sun Yat-sen Freeway

Binjiang Street

Yumei Street

Taipei Expo Park

Taibei Gushi Guan 8
(Taipei Story House)

Lin An Tai Gucuo 9
(Lin An Tai
Historical House
and Museum)

Zhongshan N. Rd Sec. 3

Taibei Shili Meishu Guan 7
(Taipei Fine Arts Museum)

YUANSHAN

Jiuquan Street

ZHONGSHAN FINE ARTS PARK

MINZU PARK

Road Sec. 3

Taipei Robot Pavilion 10

Songshan Airport

Taipei Expo Park

XINSHENG PARK

Minzu W. Rd

Minzu East Road

Minzu East Road

Minzu East Road

Minzu East Road

Fuxing N. Rd

Wuchang St.

St Christopher's Catholic Church 6

Ln 93
Ln 87

Ln 461
Ln 447

Jianguo North Road Sec. 3

Alley 2

Ln 384

Xinsheng North Road Sec. 2

Shuangcheng Street

Dehui St

Dehui Street

Alley 227

Ln 75

Lane 53

Ln 370
Ln 328
Ln 357

Ln 415
Ln 387

Fuxing N. Rd

Nongan Street

Nongan Street

Jilin Rd

Ln 407

Wuchang Street

Road

Fushun Street

Ln 19

Ln 329

Nongan St

Longjiang

Ln 75

MINQUAN WEST ROAD

ZHONGSHAN ELEMENTARY SCHOOL

Ln 3

Ln 299

Ln 357

Xingtian Gong 12 (Xingtian Temple)

RONGXING GARDEN

Tiantong Street

Zhongshan N. Rd Sec. 3

Minquan E. Rd Sec. 1

Minquan East Road Sec. 2

Minquan East Road Sec. 3

Jinxi Street

Ln 137
Ln 115

Ln 485

Linsen North Road Sec. 2

Zhongyilan Street

Ln 352 Ln 362
Lane 330

Ln 137 Rd

Jinzhou Street

Ln 258

Ln 132

Ln 170
Ln 144

Ln 127
Lane 105

Ln 295

Liaoning Street

Jinzhou Street

ZHONGSHAN JUNIOR HIGH SCHOOL

Ln 222

Jinzhou

Ln 23

Jinzhou Street

XINGTIAN TEMPLE

Ln 259

Hejiang Street

Longjiang

Ln 281

Liaoning St

Ln 73

Fuxing N. Rd

Ln 313

Mackay Memorial Hospital

Ln 218
Ln 200

Jilin Rd

Lane 161

Ln 235

Ln 102

Ln 73

Ln 249

SHUANGLIAN

Minsheng E. Rd Sec. 1

Minsheng East Road Sec. 2

Minsheng East Road Sec. 3

Lane 65

Lane 76
Lane 72

Lane 194

Taibei Zhi Jia 5 (SPOT Taipei Film House)

Ln 50
Ln 48

Lane 59

Ln 60

Ln 21

Lane 58

Ln 144

Ln 184
Lane 170
Lane 160

Jilin Road

Xingan Street

Xingan St

Ln 58

Ln 130

Ln 26

Changchun Road

Changchun Road

Lane 20

Ln 17

Ln 197

Changchun Rd

Ln 33

Ln 39

Ln 28

Lane 258

Ln 160

Ln 16

Ln 13

Sipling Street

Jilin Road

Yiting Street

Songjiang Road

Shulan Rd

Liaoning

Qingcheng Street

ZHONGSHAN

Nanjing E. Rd Sec. 1

SONGJIANG NANJING

Nanjing East Road Sec. 2

NANJING EAST ROAD

Nanjing East Road Sec. 3

Lin Tian Tongdian 4 (Lin Tian Barrel Store)

Ln 135
Ln 133

Ln 145

Xinsheng North Road Sec. 2

Ln 10
Ln 8

Lane 93

Zhulun Street

Ln 256

Ln 282

Huayin Street

Zhengzhou Rd

Changan East Road Sec. 2

Ln 62

Ln 65

Lane 64

Changan East Road Sec. 2

Xiuzhen Bowuguan 13 (Miniatures Museum of Taiwan)

Ln 46

Lane 19

Longjiang

Ln 63

Changan East Road Sec. 3

Ln 19

Bade Road Sec. 2

Ln 437
Ln 451

Guofu Shiji Jinian Guan 3 (Dr Sun Yat-sen Historic Events Memorial Hall)

Shu Huo Jinian Zhi Bowuguan 14 (Su Ho Memorial Paper Museum)

Ln 31

Ln 100

Taibei Guoji Yishu Cun 2 (Taipei Artist Village)

SHANDAO TEMPLE

Beiping East Rd

Hangzhou N. Rd Sec. 1

Jinshan N. Rd Sec. 1

Guang Hua Shuwei Xin Tiandi 15 (Guang Hua Digital Plaza)

Bade Road

Weishui Rd

Ln 210

Lane 16

Bade Road Sec. 3

Antong St

Ln 40

Ln 312

Ln 300

Ln 366

Ln 122

Ln 79

Shandao Si 1 (Shandao Temple)

Zhongxiao East Road Sec. 1

Zhongxiao East Road Sec. 2

Civic Boulevard

National Taipei University of Technology

Ln 65

Civic Boulevard

Ln 217
Ln 227

Ln 251

Ln 107

Zhengzhou Street

Qingdao St

Zhenjiang Street

Qingdao East Rd

Civic Boulevard

ZHONGXIAO XINSHENG

Zhongxiao

East Road Sec. 3

ZHONGXIAO FUXING

Zhongxiao E. Rd Sec. 4

Lane 252

Chinese Handicraft Mart

Jinan Rd Sec. 1

Jinan S. Road Sec. 1

Hangzhou S. Rd Sec. 1

Qidong St

Jinshan S. Rd Sec. 1

Ln 3

Ln 103

Jinan Road Sec. 3

Ln 248

Alley 13

Ln 213

Bade Rd

National Taiwan University Hospital

Shaoxing S. Rd

Ln 37

Ln 25

Ln 12

Ln 45

Renai Road Sec. 2

Jianguo Jiari Yushi 16 (Jianguo Holiday Jade Market)

Jianguo Jiari Huashi 17 (Jianguo Holiday Flower Market)

Xinsheng S. Rd Sec. 1

Songjiang Rd

Renai Road Sec. 3

Fuxing S. Rd Sec. 1

Ln 26
Lane 27
Daan Rd

N

0 — 500 m
0 — 500 yds

Song dynasty (960–1279) wooden icon of the Bodhisattva Guanyin that is exceedingly delicate in line and texture (it is occasionally on loan to the National Palace Museum).

Taipei Artist Village ❷

Address: 7 Beiping E. Road, www.artistvillage.org
Tel: 02-3393 7377
Opening Hrs: Tue–Sun 11am–9pm
Entrance Fee: free
Transportation: Shandao Temple

Located just 5–10 minutes on foot west of Shandao Temple is the **Taipei Artist Village** (Taibei Guoji Yishu Cun). It is housed in a heritage building that was constructed by the city's Public Works Bureau in 1953 and rescued and restored in 2001. At the Taipei Artist Village the focus is on experimental cross-cultural creation; local artists and overseas talents are brought together in an artist-in-residence program to stimulate and share their creative juices. These artistic practitioners are drawn from all disciplines: visual, literary, musical, moving image, photographic, performance. The facility has 10 live-in studios serving as artists' accommodations and work spaces. There are also two exhibition-cum-performance spaces, two gardens, and a courtyard where hands-on activities are held. Shows are frequently staged, and there is a mixed art and dining space where artists interact with visitors and works are for sale. In 2010, a twin artist village in the Treasure Hill was opened (see page 167).

Dr Sun Yat-sen Historic Events Memorial Hall ❸

Address: 46 Zhongshan N. Road Sec. 1
Tel: 02-2381 3359
Opening Hrs: Tue–Sun 9am–11.30am, 2–4.30pm
Entrance Fee: free
Transportation: Taipei Main Station

West of the Taipei Artist Village is **Dr Sun Yat-sen Historic Events Memorial Hall** (Guofu Shiji Jinian

Guan), a little oasis transplanted from old Japan into the middle of the modern metropolis whizzing by on all sides. Sun Yat-sen stayed here in 1913 when in Taiwan to drum up support to retake power in China from the usurping warlord Yuan Shikai. This was then the Umeyashiki Inn, one of Taiwan's few high-class accommodations. The walled compound features a small sculpted park in Japanese style, lined with footpaths, gurgling pools, and miniature bridges. Inside the wood-frame inn, paraphernalia on Sun's life and times are displayed. Incidentally, the inn was once about 50 meters (165ft) northeast, where Civil Boulevard now runs; it was shifted here decades ago when the railway line was moved underground.

The proprietor of Lin Tian Barrel Store still makes the wooden barrels with his own hands.

Lin Tian Barrel Store ❹

On the corner of Zhongshan Road and Changan West Road stands the **Lin Tian Barrel Store** (Lin Tian Tongdian), a renowned shop of important folk history pedigree (108 Zhongshan N. Rd Sec. 1; Mon–Sat 10am–8pm, Sun 11am–5pm; tel: 02-2541 1354). The Lin family has

Dr Sun Yat-sen Historic Events Memorial Hall.

TIP

Check out the bookstore at SPOT Taipei Film House for a fine collection of Asian films on DVD. Many of the arthouse choices are hard to find anywhere else.

been making traditional wooden barrels and other vessels since 1928. Most are made of high-quality red cypress. Though the shop is stuffed to the rafters with food steamers, tubs, flower stands, and even toilet seats – each painstakingly made by hand with traditional tools over two to three days – most larger items need to be ordered a month in advance. But you're sure to find some invaluable little item on any spur-of-the-moment visit.

SPOT Taipei Film House ❺

Address: 18 Zhongshan N. Road Sec. 2, www.spot.org.tw
Tel: 02-2551 7786
Opening Hrs: daily from 11am; bookstore closes at 11pm, café and SPOT Cinema at midnight, bar at 2am
Entrance Fee: charge (SPOT Cinema)
Transportation: Zhongshan

About 15 minutes north is the white stucco **SPOT Taipei Film House** (Taibei Zhi Jia). This heritage building was constructed around 1925 in a loose American-antebellum style. It was first used as the US consulate, then served as the

ambassador's residence for the US when Taiwan and the US still maintained formal diplomatic relations. Today the facility is dedicated to non-mainstream film, notably independent and arthouse works. The former garage has been converted into the cozy 98-seat SPOT Cinema, which has six screenings daily from noon to midnight.

In the main structure is a small Eslite bookstore with books and products related to film. Sixth Avenue, a wine lounge, is on the airy second level, and a café, SPOT Café Lumière, on the ground level and courtyard, is a wonderful spot for leisurely reading and people-watching.

Little Manila

Most days of the week, the area around Zhongshan Road and Dehui Street, about 15 minutes north of SPOT Taipei Film House, is quiet. But on Sunday, the weekly day off for the many Filipino workers, the area is transformed into their social turf, colloquially known as **Little Manila** (Xiao Manila) and centered on **St Christopher's Catholic Church ❻**

Taipei SPOT Film House.

(51 Zhongshan N. Rd Sec. 3; Sun 8am–dusk; tel: 02-2594 7914). The church offers services in English and is packed from mid-morning into the early afternoon with Filipino worshippers. Outside, temporary stalls are set up selling snacks and treats from the Philippines, English books and gossip rags from back home, bric-a-brac, and even cheap haircuts. There are also a number of permanent Filipino-owned grocery stores and eateries in the area. English and Tagalog fill the air for the day, as does music from the home islands, often accompanied by impromptu dancing. Best of all, however, is the sheer sense of joyful revelry that prevails. Little Manila is just a 10-minute walk east of Minquan West Road MRT station.

Taipei Expo Park

Created as the site for the Taipei International Flora Exposition in 2010, the Taipei Expo Park is a multifunctional performance and exhibition venue (www.taipei-expopark. tw; Tue–Sun 9am–5pm, Sat–Sun until 8pm; tel: 02-2596 1546). Apart from hosting the Taipei Fine Arts Museum, the Story House and Lin An Tai Historical House and Museum, it's also home to a number of sights, including the Expo Dome (whose architecture resembles a bamboo basket); the Expo Hall; the Pavilion of Aroma and Flowers, where you can shop for aboriginal items; the Pavilion of Dreams, whose galleries host various noteworthy exhibitions; the Pavilion of Angel Life, featuring a remarkable art gallery (www.angellifepavilion.com.tw); the Taipei Children's Recreation Center; and a 3D IMAX cinema. 2013 saw the opening of the Taipei Robot Pavilion, which houses a cutting-edge robotics-themed collection. By 2016 the Taipei Green Pavilion will also be constructed, offering office and retail facilities.

Taipei Fine Arts Museum ❼

Address: 181 Zhongshan N. Road Sec. 3, www.tfam.museum
Tel: 02-2595 7696
Opening Hrs: Tue–Sun 9.30am–5.30pm, Sat until 8.30pm
Entrance Fee: charge, free on Fri and Sat after 5pm
Transportation: Yuanshan

Situated directly across Zhongshan North Road from the Children's Recreation Center is the **Taipei Fine Arts Museum** (Taibei Shili Meishu Guan). The entry fee of just NT$30 is one of the city's best deals. It has over 4,500 pieces in its permanent collection of works by local and overseas artists. Most of the works are contemporary and are paintings. The second-level galleries reflect Taiwan's history through contemporary art – primarily oil paintings – in exhibits rotated every six months. Guided tours in foreign languages can be provided with advance notice, and there are also audio tours.

Taipei Story House ❽

Address: 181-1 Zhongshan N. Road

One of the Filipino grocery stores in Little Manila. Workers from the Philippines account for the second-largest group of foreign laborers in Taiwan.

A popular ride at the Children's Recreation Center.

FACT

In the 1980s, the Lin An Tai Homestead was moved to its Binjiang Street location piece by piece – all 20,982 planks, 38,096 bricks, 24,050 tiles, 95 windows, and 32 large carvings – from its original location on Siwei Street in east Taipei in order to make way for the widening of Dunhua South Road.

The fairytale facade of the Taipei Story House.

Sec. 3, www.storyhouse.com.tw
Tel: 02-2587 5565
Opening Hrs: Tue–Sun 10am–5.30pm
Entrance Fee: charge
Transportation: Yuanshan

Right beside the museum is the charming **Taipei Story House** (Taibei Gushi Guan), colloquially known as Yuanshan Villa after the hill just north of the river, on which today's Grand Hotel is perched. A mock Tudor mansion built in 1914 by a Dadaocheng tea merchant, it was used during the colonial period by the Japanese police to incarcerate and interrogate political activists. Today the building houses an art showroom and exhibits on the history of Taipei, focusing on the importance of the common working folk and the tea industry. Note that to ensure preservation of the heritage site the number of visitors is limited to 30 at any one time. Be sure to visit the superb Story Tea House for some refreshment, a teahouse/restaurant open to a courtyard featuring a sophisticated wood theme (see page 144).

Lin An Tai Historical House and Museum ❾

Address: 5 Binjiang Street, www.lin-an-tai.net
Tel: 02-2598 1572
Opening Hrs: Tue–Sun 9am–5pm
Entrance Fee: charge
Transportation: Yuanshan

About 15 minutes on foot east of the Fine Arts Museum is the **Lin An Tai Historical House and Museum** (Lin An Tai Gucuo). This is one of the few traditional courtyard complexes still extant in north Taiwan, and the best-preserved in Taipei. The Lins were a powerful merchant family from Fujian Province and their wealth is evident. They flouted imperial rules when they used swallow-tail roofs, then the exclusive privilege of high-level mandarins. In fact, many merchant families in north Taiwan scorned these rules and the representatives of the Qing court sent to keep an eye on things. Such families had private militias for protection since the officials were inadequate at keeping law and order. Building of the complex started in 1820, and the stone used was brought by ship from Fujian, as were the artworks and craftsmen. The flagstones of the wide forecourt before the main entrance were ballast from the Lin ships.

The large pool before the forecourt is a *fengshui* device; its shining surface deflects negative *qi* from sweeping in through the main portal. It also had practical functions, such as to raise fish, a water source for fires, to cool incoming breezes, and as a defense line if under attack. Be sure to pick up the brochure at the ticket office, the only information in English at the complex.

Taipei Robot Pavilion ❿

A very recent pavilion at the Taipei Expo Park features a remarkable collection of high-tech robots (Tue–Sun 9am–5pm, Sat–Sun until 8pm;

admission every 15 minutes, max 34 people per session; charge). The android machines will impress you with their dancing and wrestling skills, while they have also mastered playing the violin – as well as basketball. There are some hands-on-exhibits to get stuck into, too.

Opened in 2013 in the Xinsheng Park, the exhibition is a joint venture created by high-tech industries, research institutes, academic institutions, and the government.

Dajia Riverside Park ⑪

Dajia Riverside Park (Dajia Hebin Gongyuan) is a 12km-long (7-mile) green belt on the south bank of the Jilong River, starting from just east of the Taipei Fine Arts Museum and running all the way to Nangang Software Park. The section of the river nearest the museum was "straightened" in the mid-1990s to ease water flow and alleviate constant flooding. It is the venue for the city's annual Taipei International Dragon Boat Race Championships, which attracts teams from around the globe.

The city's bicycle-path network runs along both sides of the river, and bike rentals are available. Bikes can be dropped off at other kiosks along the network. The dike walls that shut off the park from the city proper are lined with attractive city-sanctioned graffiti art; the authorities paint over the walls every four months and the artists start again. There is food and drink available, from licensed vendors who drive in little catering-type trucks and set up temporary open-air eateries and cafés.

Xingtian Temple ⑫

Address: 109 Minquan E. Road Sec. 2, www.ht.org.tw
Tel: 02-2502 7924
Opening Hrs: daily 7am–9pm
Entrance Fee: free
Transportation: Zhongshan Junior High School

At the corner of Songjiang Road and Minquan East Road is the thriving **Xingtian Temple** (Xingtian Gong), a large complex built in the 1960s dedicated to Guan Gong, the God of War. Guan Gong was originally a mortal, a renowned general during the Three Kingdoms Period (184–280). His gift for strategy and tactics has also made him the patron deity of businessmen – hence the sleek cars often found parked in front of the temple. Black-bearded Guan Gong is easy to identify from among the Chinese pantheon of deities because of his red face, said to have been given to him in his youth by an immortal as a disguise after he killed a local bully. Known from folktales as a defender of the weak, and revered for his righteousness and loyalty, he is a key figure in the Chinese classic *Romance of the Three Kingdoms*.

In addition to the statue of Guan Gong, the temple compound is filled with other accoutrements of worship. In the front courtyard is an incense urn with two golden-winged dragons clinging to each side, acting as the handles, and a horde of dragons'

Bicycles can be rented for rides in Dajia Riverside Park.

The view from the riverside is even better at night.

A park food vendor.

Incense is required for the shoujing rites at Xingtian Temple.

heads stretching skyward from the two-tiered metal canopy. In the inner courtyard are three long tables sagging under the weight of offerings from the faithful. Among the offerings are fresh fruit such as pineapples and bananas, and traditional confections such as *migao*, a sticky, slightly sweet rice cake; meat is forbidden. The offerings are eventually given to the needy after the gods have partaken of their essence.

In the evenings the temple transforms into an ethereal world, as delicate small lanterns are lit and believers walk about with candles.

Just outside the temple, the underground pedestrian passages under the Songjiang-Minquan intersection are filled with fortune-tellers, who do a brisk trade. Within each stall, the faithful sit wide-eyed, intently listening to the prognostications of the oracles on matters such as the right time to open a business or sign contracts, when to hold a wedding or whether to hold one at all, how a child will do in an exam, and other pivotal moments in life.

Miniatures Museum ⑬

Address: B1, 96 Jianguo N. Road Sec. 1, www.mmot.com.tw
Tel: 02-2515 0583
Opening Hrs: Tue–Sun 10am–6pm
Entrance Fee: charge
Transportation: Nanjing E. Rd.

The **Miniatures Museum of Taiwan** (Xiuzhen Bowuguan) houses a superb collection of miniatures from around the world, brought together by the husband-and-wife owners. Instantly bringing out the inner child in adult visitors are the many wonderful works such as the tiny Roman ruins, a Lilliputian world, the inside of Buckingham Palace, and Thunder River, an old Colorado pioneer town regularly and convincingly hit by a particularly violent thunderstorm. But the museum's signature piece is perhaps the mini Rose Mansion by renowned miniatures artist Reginald Twigg, which took him four years and has been judged one of the most important miniature artworks in the US in modern times. The original mansion, now demolished, was for a long time a Los Angeles landmark.

Su Ho Paper Museum ⑭

Address: 68 Changan E. Road Sec. 2, www.suhopaper.org.tw
Tel: 02-2507 5535
Opening Hrs: Mon–Sat 9.30am–4.30pm
Entrance Fee: charge
Transportation: Zhongxiao Xinsheng

The Chinese have a love affair with the written word and the paper it is written on. Indeed, paper was considered one of the "Four Treasures of the Study" (*Wenfang Si Bao*) by classical Chinese scholars.

The **Su Ho Memorial Paper Museum** (Shu Huo Jinian Zhi Bowuguan) was founded by the Chen family in loving memory of Chen Shu-huo, one of Taiwan's last few masters of papermaking, who was killed in 1990 in a plane crash. There are exhibits here on the materials and processes of papermaking, its history in Taiwan, and the handmade papers of different periods and cultures. There is a fine mockup of a traditional handmade paper workshop, and guests can even try their hand at making their own paper mementos, as well as making the paper itself, and engage in science games to understand paper better. Reservations are required, which simply means a wait after you show up, as visitors are led in groups through the museum on a guided tour.

Guang Hua Digital Plaza ⑮

Housed in an attractive six-level building featuring state-of-the-art amenities, **Guang Hua Digital Plaza** (Guanghua Shuwei Xin Tiandi) is located on Civil Boulevard between Jinshan and Xinsheng roads (www. gh3c.com.tw; daily 10am–9pm; closed on the second and fourth Tue each

Making paper at the Su Ho Paper Museum.

SHOPPING

This upmarket district's shops tend to dress themselves up with elegant trappings, even those selling traditional-type goods, in emulation of the string of boutiques and high-end stores that have long lined Zhongshan North Road, which from the 1950s to the 1980s was the center of fashion for all of Taiwan.

Antiques

Cherry Hill Antiques
6, Lane 77, Zhongshan N. Rd Sec. 2. Tel: 02-2541 7575. http://cherryhill.antiques.com.tw p272, B3
Specializes in woodcarvings from China, wood furniture, ceramics, mirrors, and embroidery; also carries Taiwan antiques and rare Vietnamese embroidery. Range from inexpensive to very expensive. Masterly reproductions also available.

Baked goods

Taipei Leechi Cake Shop
73 Changan E. Rd Sec. 2. Tel: 02-2506 2255. www.taipeileechi.com.tw p268, E1

Guang Hua Digital Plaza.

This well-known shop sells a variety of Taiwanese traditional baked treats, many in attractive gift-box packaging. Signature creations are green-bean cakes, mushroom vegetable cakes, sun cakes, and pineapple cakes.

Books

Caves Books
103 Zhongshan N. Rd Sec. 2. Tel: 02-8792 5024. www.cavesbooks.com.tw p272, B3
The main branch of a small chain known for language-teaching books and English literature titles. Modest collection of English books on Taiwan.

Clothes

Grand Tailor
81-4 Zhongshan N. Rd Sec. 2. Tel: 02-2571 7431. www.grand-tailor.com.tw p272, B3
In business for over three decades, using infrared technology to complement traditional fitting. Comfortable with Western styles, specializes in suits, NT$10,000–20,000. Turnaround is about a week.
Hanching Cheongsams
53-6 Zhongshan N. Rd Sec. 3. Tel: 02-2586-6781. www.hanching.com.tw p272, B2
Specializes in *cheongsams* and *qipaos*, both traditional and personalized fashion-statement versions. Three to five working days are needed, with standard prices of NT$7,000–9,000. International mailings handled and they are used to foreign customers.

Electronics

Guang Hua Digital Plaza
8 Civic Boulevard Sec. 3. Tel: 02-2391 7105. www.gh3c.com.tw p268, E2
Laptops, notebooks, desktops, cell phones, PDSs, CD players, digital cameras, and more. Staff in the six-floor facility thrive on techno-speak.

Flowers and plants

Jianguo Holiday Flower Market
South side of Jianguo Rd & Renai Rd Sec. 3. www.fafa.org.tw p268, E3
Flowers of myriad variety; the local subtropical and tropical breeds are the main draws. Bonsai and other plants also sold, plus gardening paraphernalia of far-ranging choice. Open weekends only.

Jade

Jianguo Holiday Jade Market
North side of Jianguo Rd & Renai Rd Sec. 3. p268 E3
Good-quality jade jewelry and craftwork at reasonable prices. Other items sold here include Chinese macramé and Buddhist prayer beads and bracelets. Open weekends only.

Tea

Geow Yong Tea Hong
14 Changchun Rd. Tel: 02- 2502 0506. www.geowyongtea.com.tw p272, B4
With a pedigree going back to 1842, this specializes in Taiwan teas, believing local climatic and soil conditions to be the world's best.
Kung Fung Yung Tea Merchants
7, Lane 72, Sec. 2, Zhongshan N. Rd. Tel: 02-2563 2851. www.kfytea.com p272, B4
Stocks teas from China and Taiwan, offers own-recipe health teas, and carries an array of teapots and specially designed ceramic, porcelain, and bamboo tea utensils of sterling quality.
Wang De Chuan Fine Chinese Tea
95, Sec. 1, Zhongshan N. Rd. Tel: 02-2561 8738. www.dechuantea.com p272, B4
Displays of both Taiwan and China teas are on the first floor, with a tea salon upstairs. Famed for its teas in red canisters.

month; tel: 02-2391 7105). Most of the vendors from the old nearby Guanghua Market have moved in, plus vendors from another consumer-electronics market, and this new incarnation continues the tradition of being the city's best place to scout for computers and related gadgets and peripherals, pulsing with a steady stream of IT gadget-lovers fervently shopping for the latest electronics. There are hundreds of outlets, all stuffed to the rafters, and both buyers and sellers know their stuff. Many of the goods are Taiwan-made, and while prices don't match, say, Hong Kong, they are certainly lower than in Western countries. Many vendors can speak a little English – or rather, techno-speak. Another electronics shopping mall was, at time of writing, due to be opening in mid-2015 – the **Taipei Information Park**, located right next to the Digital Plaza. The intent is to make the district one of the world's most important sites for shopping for the newest high-tech electronic goods, superior to Tokio's Akihabara Electric Town.

Holiday Jade Market ⑯

Further south, on the north side of Renai Road under the Jianguo flyover, is the **Jianguo Holiday Jade Market** (Jianguo Jiari Yushi), which springs to life on weekends (Sat 9am–8pm, Sun 9am–6pm; see page 75). It is north Taiwan's mecca for lovers of this shiny stone, and with about 850 vendors, it is one of Asia's largest jade markets. On sale are crafted pieces both antique and contemporary, plus cut stones au naturel.

The myriad small pieces make good gifts. Prices are quite reasonable, and haggling is accepted for anything about NT$1000 or higher. The gift-buying possibilities are augmented by such handicrafts as woodcarvings, bambooware, and ceramic tea sets. Be prepared to brave

Bangles at the Jianguo Holiday Jade Market.

the crowds, as some 20,000 to 30,000 throng the jade and flower markets each weekend.

Holiday Flower Market ⑰

On the south side of Renai Road, also under the Jianguo flyover, is the **Jianguo Holiday Flower Market** (Jianguo Jiari Huashi; www.fafa.org.tw; Sat–Sun 9am–6pm), to which growers come from Neihu, Yangmingshan, or as far away as central Taiwan to sell their blooms. The scores of small stalls sell both common and exotic flowers and much more, such as pot-holders, vases, seeds, seedlings, garden tools, and many types of plants, including bonsai *(penzai)*. Prices are far lower here than at local florists. Some stalls have prices posted, but many don't to allow sellers to gauge buyer interest. Haggling is possible, and experienced buyers often wait until shortly before closing time to make a purchase, knowing sellers will be eager.

RESTAURANTS, BARS, AND CAFÉS

Restaurants

American

Robin's Grill
2F, Regent Taipei, No. 3, Lane 39, Zhongshan N. Rd Sec. 2. Tel: 02-2523 1321. www.regenttaipei.com Open: daily L & D. **$$$$** p272, A4
Prime location and a simple menu concentrates on the grill – prime cuts of Black Angus, succulent lamb, and tender breast of chicken. Large salad bar and dessert menu.

Chinese

Peng Yuan
2F, 380 Linsen N. Rd. Tel: 02-2551 9157. www.pengyuan.com.tw Open: daily L & D.

Many Chinese restaurants serve excellent seafood.

$$$ p272, C2
The original outlet in the "Peng's Garden" chain, this large, busy, and noisy place (private rooms available) concentrates on its good Hunan cuisine. The best dish is the rich and smoky *mizhi huotui* (Hunan ham with honey).

Szechuan Court
No. 63 Chung Shan North Rd Sec. 2. Tel: 02-2100 2100 ext. 2383. www.ambh.com. tw Open: daily L & D. **$$$** p272, C3
China-born chefs create noteworthy dishes including the *gongbao jiding* (stir-fried diced chicken with dried chili peppers) and *guaiwei ji* ("strange-tasting" chicken). The high prices are due to the food quality, the bigwig-clientele, and the service fit for emperors. Younger chefs are now slowly bringing in variations to old classics.

Tien Hsiang Lo
B1, Landis Taipei, 41 Minquan E. Rd Sec. 2. Tel: 02-2597 1234. http://taipei.landishotels resorts.com Open: daily L & D. **$$$** p272, C3
Authentic Hangzhou cuisine ("Southern ingredients, Northern style"), which specializes in fish and crustaceans, served in sumptuous surroundings, with seamless service. A signature dish is shrimp sautéed in *Longjing* ("dragon well") tea leaves.

Continental

Taipei Story Tea House
181-1 Zhongshan N. Rd Sec. 3. Tel: 02-2586 8628. www.storyhouse.com.tw Open: Tue–Sun 11am–7pm, Sat–Sun until 9pm. **$$** p272, C1
This comfy place has a wraparound, covered patio with lovely mountain views, perfect for rendezvous. Emphasized are rural European dishes such as Alsatian *sauerkraut*, pig's trotters, truffles, and spring chicken.

French

Le Bouquet
1F, Ambassador Hotel, 63 Zhonghan N. Rd Sec. 2. Tel: 02-2100 2100 ext. 2856.

www.ambh.com.tw Open: daily 10am–9pm. **$$** p272, B4
This small but popular café-boulangerie gets crowded when the breads and pastries come out from the ovens at 11am and 4pm daily. The ambience, aromas, and ingredients are all deliciously French. Favorites include the Ambassador Classic Pineapple Cakes.

Paris 1930
2F, Landis Taipei, 41 Minquan E. Rd Sec. 2. Tel: 02-2597 1234. http://taipei.landishotels resorts.com Open: Mon–Sat D, brunch Sat–Sun. **$$$$** p272, C3
Declared by some to be Taiwan's best French restaurant, with classic decor and sophisticated service. Try the foie gras on parma ham risotto. The award-winning wine cellar is the island's most extensive.

Hakka

Tung Hakka Cuisine
7 Minsheng E. Rd Sec. 3. Tel: 02-2518 2766. www.tung-hakka.com Open: daily L & D. **$$** p272, D3
With its clean and contemporary interior, this is the original location of a small Hakka chain. The menu includes such delicacies as pig intestines with ginger and vinegar. The quality of the preparation is dependable. Note that Hakka dishes tend toward saltiness, though you can ask for less to be used.

International

Azie
1F, Regent Taipei, No. 3, Lane 39, Zhongshan N. Rd Sec. 2. Tel: 02-7701 7722. www.regenttaipei.com Open: Mon–Thu noon–10.30pm, Fri noon–11.30pm, Sat 11am–11.30pm, Sun 11am–10.30pm. **$$** p272, C4
Its location in a large, sundrenched atrium makes Azie a favorite casual meeting place. The culinary offerings are a fusion of Asian and Western; the dim sum and Western desserts are recommended. Live music in evening.

Pouring a cold one at Malibu West.

Brasserie

1F, Regent Taipei, No. 3, Lane 39, Zhongshan N. Rd Sec. 2. Tel: 02-2523 8000 ext. 3870. www.regenttaipei.com Open: B, L, afternoon tea & D. **$$$** p272, C4

The marketplace-buffet here, with open kitchen, is themed "Festival Buffet." Get Chinese hot pot at one booth, or the city's best roast beef at another. Another is a veritable fishmarket of crab, eel, and tuna. Over 100 selections.

Lily Café

1F, Cosmos Hotel, 43 Zhongxiao W. Rd Sec. 1. Tel: 02-2311 8905. www.cosmos-hotel.com. tw Open: daily 9am–11pm. **$$** p268, C1

Open all day, with an after-10pm snack menu available. Decent sandwiches and traditional Taiwanese foods. Western cuisine combined with exotic flavors. Semi buffet.

SPOT Café Lumière

18 Zhongshan N. Rd Sec. 2. Tel: 02-2562 5612. www.spot.org.tw Open: daily 10am–midnight, Fri–Sat until 2am. **$$$** p272, B4

Located in the heritage SPOT Taipei Film House, this place serves light snacks, gourmet coffees, and fresh melt-in-your-mouth pud-dings. There is an outdoor patio with shady trees.

Japanese

Mihan

B3, Grand Formosa Regent, 41 Zhongshan N. Rd Sec. 2. Tel: 02-2523 1305. www.regenttaipei.com Open: daily L & D. **$$$–$$$$** p272, C4

Offering *shabu shabu* (hot pot), *robatayaki* (seafood and vegetables cooked on a charcoal grill), and *yakiniku* (grilled meat), Mihan is billed as Taipei's only three-in-one Japanese chargrill restaurant. A wide variety of seafood and US beef (three grades) is available, as is a cellar full of interesting sakes.

Robin's Teppanyaki

2F, Regent Taipei, No. 3, Lane 39, Zhongshan N. Rd Sec. 2. Tel: 02-2523 8000 ext. 3930. www.regenttaipei.com Open: daily L & D. **$$$$** p272, C4

Everything you expect from Japanese *teppanyaki* (grilled dishes), but with a decidedly Western twist. For instance, dishes include beef burger steaks, lobster, prawns and scallops in mustard sauce, or fresh-fruit crêpes.

Taiwanese

Ching Yeh Restaurant

1, Lane 105, Zhongshan N. Rd Sec. 1. Tel: 02-2551 7957. www.aoba.com.tw Open: daily 11.30am–2.30pm, 5–10.30pm. **$$–$$$** p268, C1

This perennially popular place is one of Taipei's best Taiwanese restaurants. It has been in business for over 40 years, and is best known for its traditional dishes. Specialties include stewed abalones, stir-fried shark's fin, grilled pork, and braised seafood noodle soup.. For dessert, try the deep fried taro balls with dry radish.

Bars and cafés

Malibu West

23-4 Shuangcheng St. Tel: 02-2592 8228 www.malibuwest.url.tw p272, C2

Another iconic bar in the Combat Zone. Good Western-style pub food: steaks, burgers, pizza, and pasta. There is a tropical theme to the decor while sports are shown on the TV, and pool and darts are available.

The Taipei 101 tower, the city's principal icon and formerly the tallest building in the world.

TAIPEI EAST

The city's east end is about money; this white-collar world pulses with the exuberance of those who know how to make it and those who have the insatiable desire to spend it. Further east, the skyscrapers give way to hillside tea plantations.

U p to the early 1970s, Taipei's eastern district was largely an area of sugar-cane fields and rice paddies. Then there was an upsurge of new construction on the east side of Fuxing Road. Residents from the west flocked to the new facilities in search of fun. Pacific SOGO Department Store went up in the early 1980s, attracting myriad other entertainment and retail enterprises and establishing the area as the city's financial, commercial, shopping, and entertainment core. In the mid-1990s, the remaining open area between Keelung Road and the mountains was developed, and it is this, the Xinyi District, that is the city's new heart and the island's definer of chic upscale fashion.

DINGHAO

The **Dinghao** shopping and entertainment area is concentrated along the main thoroughfares and back-alley mazes spreading out from the Dunhua North Road and Zhongxiao East Road intersection. *Dinghao* translates as "top best." The area grew eastward from SOGO, and that department store remains its fulcrum. Accessed via key bus routes and two MRT lines, this is the city's prime area for people to link up after

Staff of the Pacific SOGO Department Store.

work and on weekends. Here the visitor finds fashion boutiques serving upscale customers, more youth-oriented outlets, quality restaurants and inexpensive eateries, cinemas showing Western films, jewelry shops, art galleries, and more.

SOGO Department Store ❶

The original **Pacific SOGO Department Store** (Taipingyang SOGO Baihuo Gongsi) is located just outside the Zhongxiao Fuxing MRT station

The light-filled and airy central atrium of the Breeze Center, with its modern glass interpretation of the classical dome, imparts a touch of class intended to appeal to the mall's well-heeled clientele.

at 45 Zhongxiao E. Road Sec. 4 (www. sogo.com.tw; Sun–Thu 11am–9.30pm, Fri–Sat and the day before holiday 11am–10pm; tel: 02-2776 5555). The station is fed by two major lines and sees a tremendous flow of commuter traffic. SOGO launched the department store craze in the 1980s, leading to the super-mall craze that has gripped the nation since the late 1990s. Through the years, what locals simply call "SOGO" though there are now other outlets, has continued to be the island's most profitable department store.

Its basement connects directly to the underground East Metro Mall (10am–10pm), which is lined with retail outlets, eateries, and tasteful artworks, and runs from Zhongxiao Fuxing past Zhongxiao Dunhua MRT station.

Breeze Center ❷

The massive **Breeze Center** (Weifeng Guangchang), just north of SOGO at 39 Fuxing South Road, is a competitor in the super-mall stakes, providing a mix of upmarket facilities targeted at white-collar workers (www.breezecenter.com; Sun–Wed 11am–9.30pm, Thu–Sat 11am–10pm; tel: 0809-008888). Shopping, dining, and entertainment options are all under one roof. There is a six-screen cineplex of international caliber.

Just south of Dinghao, where the wide, tree-lined Dunhua South Road and Renai Road cross paths, is **Renai Traffic Circle** (Renai Yuanhuan), on and around which a number of big-name international designer boutiques have a presence.

Eslite Bookstore ❸

Immediately north of Renai Traffic Circle is perhaps the most popular bookstore in the city, the former flagship outlet of **Eslite Bookstore** (Chengpin Shudian), at the corner of Dunhua and Anhe roads

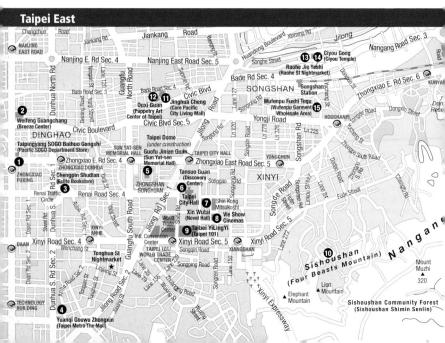

Taipei East

(www.eslite.com; daily 24 hours; tel: 02-2775 5977). It is home to the city's second-best selection of English titles, after PageOne (see page 159). Opened in the early 1990s, this venue transformed the island's book-buying scene. It was the first bookstore in Taiwan to give browsers wide aisles, a well-lit and smart-looking interior (with hardwood floors), and places to sit for more comfortable browsing. Other big outlets have been forced to follow suit to survive. This was also the world's first bookstore-chain outlet to open 24 hours. People-watching is raised to an art form in the adjoining café, which looks into the always-busy store, and on the basement levels are boutique outlets, a comfy coffee shop, and an art gallery.

Taipei Metro The Mall ❹

A few blocks south on Dunhua is **Taipei Metro The Mall** (Yuanqi Gouwu Zhongxin), in the Far Eastern Plaza Hotel complex (Sun–Thu 11am–9.30pm, Fri–Sat and the day before public holiday 11am–10pm; tel: 02-2378 6666; www.themall.com. tw). Stocked here is ritz and glamor for ladies carrying plastic and happy to flash it. Boutiques sell well-known international clothing and accessory brands, but the outlets perhaps of most interest to travelers from overseas are art workshops that have caused a splash in international art and fashion circles since the mid-1990s: Heinrich Wang's **New Chi** porcelain store (tel: 02-8773 8369, http://new-chi. com), and Loretta Yang's glass **New-workshop** (Liuligongfang) (tel: 02-2625 6559, www.liuli.com), along with a **Franz** outlet (02-2736 0799, www.franzcollection.com.tw), displaying the exquisite works of internationally acclaimed porcelain artist Francis Chen, nicknamed Franz by a teacher in college.

Patrons of the Eslite Bookstore on Dunhua Road are welcome to browse as long as they wish; the store is open 24 hours daily.

The upscale Taipei Metro The Mall (see page 149).

Sun Yat-sen Memorial Hall ❺

Address: 505 Renai Road Sec. 4,
www.yatsen.gov.tw
Tel: 02-2758 8008
Opening Hrs: daily 9am–6pm
Entrance Fee: free except for stage
performances
Transportation: Sun Yat-sen Memorial Hall

East of Dinghao is the **National Dr Sun Yat-sen Memorial Hall** (Guofu Jinian Guan), dedicated to the man called the "father of modern China" in both China and Taiwan. The memorial sits in the expansive, beautifully sculpted **Zhongshan Park** (Zhongshan Gongyuan), which is full of colorful flowers and shady groves of lushly foliaged trees. The grounds are filled at all times with people of all ages, giving it a real community feel. In the morning come to see the organized legions of tai chi practitioners, and at night and on weekends this is a popular spot for kids to fly kites. Another glimpse into local ways awaits on the north side of the building, where you'll see a long, straight pathway

of cobblestones set in cement with their ends up rather than laid flat. Using the same principles on which acupuncture is based, locals take their shoes off and walk the path, massaging their feet and improving the metabolism.

Just inside the hall's main entrance is an imposing six-meter-tall (19ft) bronze statue of the iconic "national father." In the exhibition area, visitors can watch a 30-minute multimedia presentation on his life and times, and peruse historical photos and other physical documents from his day, many of which were his personal items. Cultural performances are regularly staged at the hall.

Discovery Center of Taipei ❻

Address: 1F, 1 Shifu Road,
www.discovery.taipei.gov.tw
Tel: 02-2720 8889 ext. 4588
Opening Hrs: Tue–Sun 9am–5pm
Entrance Fee: free
Transportation: Taipei City Hall

The multilevel **Discovery Center of Taipei** (Taibei Tansuo Guan), in Taipei City Hall, takes visitors through the history of the city, with an emphasis on hands-on displays. Unveiled in 2012, the Taipei Impressions Hall on the first floor is a visual introduction to the city, featuring five screens which showcase various facets of Taipei. The second level features special exhibitions related to the city's seasons, festivals, and current issues. The third floor has displays on the city's ever-changing skyline and major thoroughfares, and its efforts to make itself a cultural capital, bring a renaissance to its old west side, and make itself a true eco-friendly living space. The fourth level is the pearl, full of educational displays such as mock-ups of the old walled city gates and cutaway models of the city's wetlands and imperial and

Taipeiers stream in and out of a busy MRT station.

colonial buildings. Scale models show the Taipei Basin's waterway-reservoir system, the city's old sections in imperial days, and a ship's hold carrying pioneers from China in the mid-1600s.

There is an abundance of vintage photographs and old film footage, including a video clip showing Chiang Kai-shek's daily open-limo ride down Zhongshan Road from his residence in Shilin District.

The 200-seat **Discovery Theater** (Faxian Juchang) is on the fourth level of the center. It features a 360-degree wraparound screen, with a quartet of short movies shown in sequence at regular times, exploring Taipei's past, present, and projected future. A virtual tour of the Discovery Center of Taipei is available free at http://vr.taipeitravel.net.

Novel Hall ⑦

Address: 3 Songshou Road, www.novelhall.org.tw
Tel: 02-2722 4302
Opening Hrs: Café and courtyard daily 9am–11pm; other areas during performances

Entrance Fee: free for café and courtyard; charge for other areas, varies with performance
Transportation: Taipei 101/World Trade Center

Just east of Taipei City Hall is the **Novel Hall for Performing Arts** (Xin Wutai), with its minimalist facade of polished stone framing a glassed-in main lobby. The facility was built and is run by Taipei's powerful Koo family, with the purpose of continuing founder Koo Xian-rong's personal mission to educate the Taiwan public in classical Chinese culture by bringing in top acts from China, especially Beijing opera. The **Fecafe**, an elegant café by the hall's sunlit lobby, has imported gourmet coffees. It is a favorite haunt of culture vultures – and not just at performance time.

Xinyi

While the Dinghao area has some retail outlets catering to families or the middle-class shopper, the **Xinyi** shopping and entertainment area (Xinyi Qu) has as its primary target the 30-somethings with ample

In the Sun Yat-sen Memorial Hall.

An interactive exhibit at the Discovery Center of Taipei that allows you to consult your "fortune."

Xinyi area's Shin Kong Mitsukoshi department store.

disposable incomes. All-in-one malls and department stores abound, filled with international brands, designer boutiques, music stores, cineplexes, performance venues, bookstores, and other amenities, all built on the largest possible scale. Since the MRT Xinyi Line opened at the end of 2013, Xinyi has become one of the fastest developing and trendy districts of Taipei. The newest landmark construction in the area is the Taipei Dome, found at the intersection of Guangfu South Rd and Zhongxiao East Rd – due for completion in 2015. The stadium will also host baseball games during the 2017 Summer Universiade, which will take place in the city. The state-of-the-art facilities will also be home to a shopping mall, cinema, hotel, and offices.

Vie Show Cinemas ❽

The Xinyi outlet of **Vie Show Cinemas** (Weixiu Yingcheng) was the first true cineplex to open in Taiwan, then going by the name of Warner Village Cinemas. It complements its 17 movie screens with lots of glitzy, flashy neon and leisure facilities such as eateries, an arcade, coffee shops, and retail outlets (online booking: www.vscinemas.com. tw). Many Western movies are shown here (undubbed, with Chinese subtitles), making this a favorite haunt for Western expat movie lovers.

Taipei 101 ❾

Address: 89F, 7 Xinyi Road Sec. 5, www.taipei-101.com.tw
Tel: 02-8101 8897
Opening Hrs: Observatory daily 9am–10pm
Entrance Fee: charge
Transportation: Taipei 101/World Trade Center

The official name of the sky-high **Taipei 101** (Taibei YiLingYi) tower is the Taipei Financial Center (Taibei Jinrong Dalou). It is located just south of City Hall.

After its opening in 2004 it was for years the world's tallest building, measuring 508 meters (1,667ft) in height. It has now been overtaken by five other constructions, with the Burj Khalifa in Dubai at the forefront. The tower has 101 floors above ground, and is designed with sections like a giant bamboo stalk, symbolizing the unbreakable strength-in-pliability of Taiwan's people. Pedestrian skybridges lead to the adjacent Grand Hyatt Taipei and New York New York department store.

Opened in early 2005, the **Taipei 101 Observatory** (Taipei YiLingYi Guanjing Tai) is located on the 89th story of the tower. The world's fastest elevators whiz visitors up at 1,010 meters (3,315ft) per minute, reaching the top in 39 seconds flat; but you won't feel a thing in the high-tech pressure-controlled shuttles. The ticket booth and elevator entrance are located on the 5th floor. Once there, be sure to take in the short documentary movie on the history of the tower. Free audio equipment is also provided for self-guided tours

in English and many other languages, detailing sights and the history of the Taipei Basin from 30,000 years ago to the present. Four powerful sets of mounted binoculars extend the range of your view.

The 89th floor has an observation deck from where visitors can enjoy commanding views of the city and the Taipei Basin, from 382 metres above the ground. There is also an interior viewing platform for the tower's massive **Tuned Mass Damper**, hanging from cables stretching between the 92nd and 87th floors. The 730-ton steel sphere holds the record for the planet's largest, heaviest, and only publicly visible damper.

The outdoor deck on the 91st floor offers an utterly different viewing experience, but it's accessible only on certain occasions and if the weather permits.

The **Taipei 101 Mall** (Taipei Yi-LingYi Gouwu Zhongxin; tel: 02-8101 7777), a building linked to the tower, is one of the newest shopping malls in the district – five massive floors with more than 100 retail and food outlets offering pretty much everything one might desire. The retail outlets that attract the most Western visitors are **PageOne**, a bookstore that stocks over 300,000 titles, about 20 percent in English, and **Jasons Market Place**, which stocks items from the globe's four corners that are quite possibly impossible to find anywhere else on the island: truffles, foie gras, caviar, cheeses, Indian delicacies, kimchi, Hokkaido catch, and about 600 types of imported health food.

Four Beasts Mountain

The Nangang Mountain Range is the line of low peaks, southeast of Taipei 101, that runs all the way to the city's eastern reaches in Nangang District. The four westernmost peaks are collectively called the **Four Beasts Mountain**  (Sishoushan), said to resemble the elephant, tiger, panther, and lion. Their peaks do not top 200 meters (600ft), making for easy hiking options.

Covering much of the hills is **Sishoushan Community Forest** (Sishoushan Shimin Senlin), so named because local residents have taken the initiative, with city assistance, to maintain the trails and other facilities. The intricate network of pathways here takes one past small temples, pagodas, and pavilions. Unlike at Yangmingshan (see page 194), which is harder to access on weekends and tends to have steeper trails, here you'll see many middle-aged folk and senior citizens from the neighborhoods immediately below, out on their daily constitutionals or doing tai chi in strategically located spots with the best views of the city sprawled below. The trailheads that are easiest to find are near the end of Zhuangjing Road, which runs south from the Taipei World Trade Center toward Elephant Mountain, the westernmost peak.

WHERE

At the Discovery Center of Taipei, a free audio is available by depositing your ID. Free English tours are available for groups of 30 or more (advance notice is required).

Evening crowds out in Xinyi.

Inside the Vie Show Cinemas.

West of Taipei 101, the Taipei World Trade Center (Shimao Zhongxin) is a regular venue for key trade events, and contains many foreign "trade offices" (euphemism for "embassy" in diplomatically isolated Taiwan).

Songshan District

North of Xinyi District and south of the Jilong River is the primarily residential **Songshan District** (Songshan Qu). In imperial days, the section along the river was a riverport and small market town based around Ciyou Temple. The Japanese made this a suburban enclave in the colonial days, renaming the area "Songshan," meaning "pine mountain," even though nary a pine grew here. They were just looking north at Yangmingshan and pining for their beloved homeland Japan.

Core Pacific City Living Mall ⓫

In the western part of Songshan is **Core Pacific City Living Mall** (Jinghua Cheng), located at 138 Bade Road Section 4 (Sun–Thu 11am–9.30pm, Fri–Sat 11am–10.30pm; tel: 02-3762 1888; http://web01.livingmall.com.tw). Its opening caused small retailers in the district to howl in protest, but consumers have been thrilled by the facilities. This is a very big place, as evidenced by the fact there is nearly 8km (5 miles) of colonnade taking

you through the shopping areas on 15 floors. The fact that it is located on a vehicle-infested road somewhat distant from MRT stations and other major retailers has not stopped shoppers from flocking. The main interests here for overseas visitors are the many upscale dance clubs, bars, restaurants, and the cineplex, providing after-hours fun for night owls.

Puppetry Art Center ⓬

Address: 99 Civil Boulevard, www.pact.org.tw
Tel: 02-2528 9553
Opening Hrs: Tue–Sat 10am–5pm
Entrance Fee: charge
Transportation: Taipei City Hall

Located next to the Living Mall, the **Puppetry Art Center of Taipei** (Taibei Ouxi Guan) has at its core a private collection of almost 5,000 string puppets, shadow puppets, glove puppets, and related objects. The first level of the large four-story center is dedicated to DIY workshops and seminars. The second houses the permanent collection. The history and different forms of puppetry are explained, and demonstrations of puppet-making and manipulation are frequently scheduled. The many puppet characters seen in the vast Chinese storytelling repertoire are also introduced. The third level is for special exhibits. In the Taiwanese Puppetry Area, special performances of the various types of local puppetry drama are staged. Guided tours in English are available with advance notice.

Raohe Street Nightmarket ⓭

The **Raohe Street Nightmarket** (Raohe Jie Yeshi) is Taipei's newest nightmarket (daily 5pm–midnight; www.raohe.com.tw), blossoming into its present form in the 1980s around the old vendors beside Ciyou Temple. It stretches the length of Raohe Street between the temple and Jilong Road. There are about 400 vendors in all, permanent outlets on either side and movable stalls in two rows down the center. The section nearest the temple concentrates on clothing, fruits, and toys. The middle offers folk arts, including paper-cuttings, calligraphy, and macramé, plus traditional food treats made on site. The far section features the many traditional Taiwanese snack foods found at all local nightmarkets.

Try the oyster vermicelli *(o-a-mi-sua)* by **Dongfa Restaurant** (Dongfa Yinshi Dian) at No. 94; they have served it since the 1930s. At No. 215, **Yuhuaxing Food Company** (Yuhuaxing Shipin Gongsi) has been making traditional pastries and cakes, including Mazu festival treats, since the 1940s. Alternatively, see how sesame oil is traditionally made at **Shandong Xiaomo Sesame Oil Shop** (Shandong Xiaomo Mayou Dian) at No. 84.

The market is best known for its medicinal stewed pork ribs. There are a number of sellers, but perhaps most popular is **Chairman Chen's** (Chen Dong Yaodun Paigu) at No. 160. The smell of the small-size ribs simmering in Chinese herbs in large pots is quite heady, the taste in no way like taking doctor's medicine, however.

Ciyou Temple

Address: 761 Bade Road Sec. 4
Tel: 02-2766 9212
Opening Hrs: daily 8.30am–9pm
Entrance Fee: free
Transportation: Songshan Railway Station

Ciyou Temple (Ciyou Gong) is located across from Songshan Railway Station, making for easy access by commuter train. In fact, elderly commuters hauling their sacrificial offerings is a familiar, comforting sight at the station; many come from outside the city. This Mazu temple dates from 1757, and was the core of the small Xikou riverport, which was long ago absorbed into the city. Today, though the Jilong River runs close by in the

north, it is out of sight behind the urban build-up. But the area still has a small-town rural feel about it; in fact, until the early 1990s, the land between here and Jilong Road was mostly open rice paddy.

This temple is the venue for what are among Taipei's loudest Mazu birthday celebrations in terms of color and cacophony. The temple roof is richly ornamented; note the flying dragon, a common motif on temples because dragons are the source of rain, always hidden behind clouds, and thus protect the wood-built complexes from fire.

Wufenpu Garment Wholesale Area

The **Wufenpu Garment Wholesale Area** (Wufenpu Fushi Tequ) is a god-send for budget shoppers seeking high-quality non-branded clothing and fashion accessories at low prices (daily 11am–10pm). This bustling, concentrated area of over 1,000 small wholesalers is located between Zhongxiao East Road and Songshan Railway Station, a 5-minute walk west of Houshanpi MRT station (exit

The circular motif is not only the "zero" in "Taipei 101," but also the shape of a traditional Chinese coin, a potent symbol of wealth.

Admiring the tower from the vantage point of Four Beasts Mountain.

WHERE

The Small No. 5 bus, which can be caught outside Kunyang MRT station, the eastern terminus of the Bannan Line, travels past Academia Sinica's front door and through the local tea-plantation area. Riders can hop on and off at any point in the latter area.

4). You'll find the full range in tastes here, from items that rival those of brand-name designers to the kitsch. Testament to the "quality at low prices" of Wufenpu is the fact that the majority of Taipei's street and nightmarket vendors selling clothing and accessories come here for stock. The items are sourced in Taiwan, Hong Kong, Korea, Japan, and other countries, and in terms of style run the gamut from demure items for 30-somethings to street fashion, grandma clothes, pop-idol Korean and Japanese fashions, hip-hop, punk, and athletic wear, and more.

Nangang

East of Songshan is **Nangang**, which means "south port." In imperial times, this was the southernmost navigable location on the Jilong River. It is primarily a residential area whose business activity centers on family-run shops and small-scale factory workshops.

The area's claim to fame is the prestigious **Academia Sinica**, Taiwan's leading academic institution, the Nangang Tea Plantations, and two new facilities that have

A view from the Taipei 101 Observatory.

Worshipping at Ciyou Temple.

sprung up since the mid-1990s as a result of a concerted city government economic-stimulus blueprint, Nangang Software Park and the sleek new Taipei World Trade Center Nangang Exhibition Hall, a massive complex with its own station on the new Neihu MRT line. The Academia Sinica sits in a valley in Nangang's south. On its grounds are two sites of interest to tourists: Hu Shih Memorial Hall, and the Museum of the Institute of History and Philology. By the end of 2016 the district will also have a new landmark – the **Taipei Pop Music Center**, which is set to be the country's most professional music performance venue.

Hu Shih Memorial Hall ⑯

Address: 128 Yanjiuyuan (Academia) Road Sec. 2, www.mh.sinica.edu.tw/koteki
Tel: 02-2782 1147
Opening Hrs: Wed and Tue–Sat 9am–5pm

Entrance Fee: free
Transportation: Taipei Nangang Exhibition Center

Hu Shih (1891–1962), philosopher, writer, academic, and statesman, was one of the foremost public figures in China in the 20th century. He served as head of the Academia Sinica in his later years, and passed away in his residence, now the **Hu Shih Memorial Hall** (Hu Shi Jinian Guan). His democratic leanings and outspokenness repeatedly got him in hot water with Chiang Kai-shek; he was recalled from his post as ambassador to the US (1938–42) and had troubles thereafter. On the first level is an exhibit hall featuring his many works, various personal effects, and explanations of his life and times. Elsewhere, his study, bedroom, and living room remain precisely as they were on the day he departed. The quiet **Hu Shih Park** (Hu Shi Gongyuan), the site of Hu's tomb, is on the slope across the street from the Institute.

Museum of the Institute of History and Philology

Address: 130 Yanjiuyuan (Academia) Road Sec. 2,

http://museum.sinica.edu.tw
Tel: 02-2652 3180
Opening Hrs: Wed and Sat 9.30am–4.30pm
Entrance Fee: free
Transportation: Taipei Nangang Exhibition Center

The **Museum of the Institute of History and Philology** (Lishi Wenwu Chenlie Guan), though not well known, showcases superb finds in archeology and ethnology made by researchers from Academia Sinica.

The first story concentrates on archeology, with artifacts of ancient Chinese civilizations from Neolithic times to the Zhou dynasty. The second story offers a cornucopia of historical records in six themes: wooden slips from the Han dynasty, rare books, imperial court archives, ethnic groups from southwest China, stele ink rubbings and historical documents from Taiwan, and special exhibits. All the artifacts have explanations on how they made their way into the collection and their academic importance.

The use of glass for the floor of the second level and connecting pathway is an impressive design concept. It gives

One of the many colorful traditional Chinese puppets on sale at the Puppetry Art Center gift shop.

A variety of street fashion for sale in the Wufenpu Garment Wholesale Area.

WHERE

Ciyou Temple and Raohe Street Nightmarket can be reached by bus from Zhongxiao Dunhua mrt station and Taipei City Hall MRT station.

the feeling of going below ground when descending to the main level, as if entering an archeological dig. On the main level is a virtual time corridor, again of glass, physically and chronologically linking the separate displays.

To get to the Academia Sinica bus stop by the main gate, take bus No. 212, 270, or Blue 25 from Kunyang MRT station.

Nangang Tea Plantations ⑱

Right by the Institute and Hu Shih Park, Jiuzhuang Road branches off from Academia Road and soon leads to the **Nangang Tourist Tea Plantations** (Nangang Guanguang Chayuan), most of which are on Section 2. Not as well known or as developed for tourism as the Muzha plantations (see page 166) directly to the south beyond the peaks of the Nangang range, these rustic locales and the numerous small teahouses are nevertheless well worth a visit. Nangang is the birthplace of Baozhong tea, one of the island's most famous varieties; its bushes were brought here by a Fujianese immigrant cultivator in 1885. The

local farmer's association has put up signs outside farms that welcome tourists, so during picking season (spring and fall), visitors can watch the picking and processing.

"Jiuzhuang" means "old village," and among the terraced fields and scarecrows are a number of old-style three-sided red-brick farmhouses with a central courtyard. See the **Yu Family Historical Residence** (Yujia Gucuo) at Lane 316, Jiuzhuang Street Section 2, the largest complex of earth-and-stone buildings still extant in Taipei (private, not open to public). Beside the now abandoned old hamlet of this tea-growing clan is a large old camphor tree said to be over 200 years old, also said to be the most painted tree in Taipei.

Nangang Tea Processing Demonstration Center ⑲

Address: 336 Jiuzhuang Road Sec. 2
Tel: 02-2786 8374
Opening Hrs: Tue–Sun 9am–5pm
Entrance Fee: charge
Transportation: Taipei Nangang Exhibition Center

Looking out over the surrounding tea plantations, the attractive and spacious **Nangang Tea Processing Demonstration Center** (Nangang Chaye Zhizao Shifan Chang) is spread out over two long, balconied tiers staggered along the slope. In an architectural style copying the traditional countryside courtyard residences of China's south Fujian, with bright red brick and white stucco, the center is devoted to the explanation and promotion of Nangang's signature tea, the half-fermented Baozhong.

There is a display on the area's rise and fall in the 19th century, a tea-processing presentation, and brewing demonstrations with tastings. Visitors are allowed to take part in the demonstrations, and in season may watch pickers at work in the center's experimental fields. The quality and quantity of printed English information is good.

The grounds of Hu Shih Memorial Hall (see page 156).

SHOPPING

Almost the entire East District is, in terms of shopping, chic, trendy, and pricey. As you move toward the area's edges, however, in the Songshan area near Jilong River and in Nangang and this area's tea-plantation hills, "tradition" seeps back in, in terms of venues, goods, and price range.

Arts and crafts

Cecilia Arts
7F-1, 59 Zhongxiao E. Rd Sec. 4.
Tel: 02-2771 7799. www.cecilia-arts.com.
p270, A2
Dedicated to preservation of traditional female sewing artistry, the works on sale here show a masterly display of arts now in danger of fading away, such as embroidery, needlework, and cloth puppets.

Ju Zi Fang
196 Raohe St. Tel: 02-2767 3378. p270, E1
This shop in Raohe Nightmarket sells standard crafts and more unusual items like cloisonné teacups and carved walnuts. It also has Balinese woodcarvings and other East Asian imports.

Taiwan OTOP
5F, 45 Shifu Rd (Taipei 101 Mall). Tel: 02-8101 7693. http://otop.tw p270, D3
OTOP stands for One Town, One Product, a government program to promote the specialty products of each Taiwan region. Here you'll find top-notch arts and crafts and food and drink items such as tea.

Baked goods

Ke Jih Pineapple Pastry Specialty Shop
836 Bade Rd Sec. 4. Tel: 02-2785 3802.
www.ke-jih.com p270, C1
Pineapple cakes are a favorite Taiwan gift item, wrapped in pretty boxes. Ke Jih's cakes have won gold twice in recent years in a contest for Taiwan's premier food products.

Books

Eslite Bookstore
245 Dunhua S. Rd Sec. 1. Tel: 02-2775 5977. www.eslite.com p270, B2
Has a good selection of English books on Taiwan and thousands of English titles. The café is great for people-watching. Open daily 24 hours.

PageOne
4F, Taipei 101 Mall, 45 Shifu Rd. Tel: 02-8101 8282. www.pageonegroup.com p270, D3
Taipei's largest bookstore, with about 300,000 titles, many in English.

Clothes

Isabelle Wen
15 Renai Rd Sec. 4. Tel: 02-2779 1150.
www.isabelle-wen.com p270, B3
Isabelle Wen is one of Taiwan's foremost fashion designers. She got her start in the area around Dadaocheng's Yongle Market, and is now an international name. Designs for women of 30 plus.

Malls

Breeze Center
39 Fuxing S. Rd. Tel: 0809-008888.
www.breezecenter.com p270, A1
An upmarket shopping center opened in the early 2000s with couture and accessories outlets. Also has a supermarket, food court, and cineplex.

Core Pacific City Living Mall
138 Bade Rd Sec. 4. Tel: 02-3762 1888.
http://web01.livingmall.com.tw p270, C1
A big complex, with hundreds of stores and over 80 eateries. There are also clubs and lounge bars on the upper floors, and the basement-level Cinemark Cineplex, open until 3am.

Pacific SOGO Department Store
45 Zhongxiao E. Rd Sec. 4. Tel: 02-2776 5555. www.sogo.com.tw p270, A2
This household name has long been Taiwan's most popular and profitable department store, with affordable brand-name fashions and domestic necessities. Connected to Zhongxiao Fuxing MRT station via the bright underground East Metro Mall beneath. Many big sales held throughout the year.

Taipei 101 Mall
45 Shifu Rd. Tel: 02-8101 7777.
www.taipei-101.com.tw p270, D3
In a six-level structure at the base of the Taipei 101 tower, this mall is a major draw with its many boutiques, restaurants, and retail outlets targeted at wealthy 30-somethings. Big names like Chanel, Tiffany, and Cartier have flagship stores here.

Taipei Metro The Mall
203 Dunhua S. Rd. Tel: 02-2378 6666.
www.themall.com.tw p270, B4
Boutiques predominate in this posh facility for the well-heeled.

Shopping areas

Dinghao
p270, B2
This area on Zhongxiao E. Rd Sec. 4 has long been called Dinghao or "top best." Has high-end and midrange clothing outlets, music stores, and eateries.

Renai Traffic Circle
p270, B3
Designer boutiques extend from the circle down Dunhua S. Rd and east on Renai Rd.

Wufenpu Garment Wholesale Area
p270, E1
Taking up a large area between Houshanpi MRT station and Songshan Railway Station, over 1,000 wholesalers, who also sell to individuals, stock clothing in all styles.

Xinyi District
p270, D3
The area around the Taipei 101 tower has a dense concentration of large, upscale malls, department stores, movie theaters, and so on, most with international brands.

RESTAURANTS, BARS, AND CAFÉS

Restaurants

Chinese

CityStar Restaurant
2F, 166 Zhongxiao E. Rd Sec. 4. Tel: 02-2777 1717. www.citystar.com.tw Open: 24 hours. **$$** p270, B2
This is a very popular late-night gathering spot. Hong Kong Cantonese dishes such as shrimp dumplings, rice porridge with sliced beef and egg, crab baked in coconut milk, and over 60 types of snacking treats prepared in traditional bamboo steamers.

Jing Yuan
2, Lane 199, Xinyi Rd Sec. 4. Tel: 02-2705

8066. Open: daily L & D. **$$** (set lunch) **$$$** p270, B3
Cantonese cuisine in an elegant classical Chinese ambience. Modest but educated selection of French wines. English-speaking staff offer good advice on ordering. Try the barbecued pork pastries and pumpkin dumplings.

Ning Chi Spice Pot
398-1 Xinyi Rd Sec. 4. Tel: 02-2703 4691. www.ning-chi.com.tw Open: daily 11.30am–10.30pm. **$$$** p270, A3
The main outlet of a "hot" chain renowned for the Sichuan specialty, *mala huoguo* ("numbingly spicy" hot pot). Cauldrons have a dividing wall to allow for a milder and a spicier broth. The larger your group, the cheaper it is; cooling beer chasers are part of the fun.

Yi Yuan Chinese Restaurant
1F, Sherwood Hotel, 111 Minsheng E. Rd Sec. 3. Tel: 02-2718 1188. www.sherwood.com.tw Open: daily L & D.

$$$ p270, G4
A classy place, the talented team here proffer Chinese regional delicacies fused with Western embellishment. Most popular are the Shanghai crab, snow frog soup with bamboo pith, and beef rolls with wild mushroom. There is a popular dim sum service at weekends, 10.30am–2.30pm. Corkage fee.

French

Tuileries French Tea House
B1, 110 Yanji St. Tel: 02-8771 0968. Open: Wed–Sun 1–9pm. **$$** p270, B2
A labor of love by a local lady who went to famed Paris teahouse Mariage Frères, and adopted its five "Golden Rules." Offers teas and light refreshments. An interesting brew is the Marco Polo Tea, a mix of Chinese and Tibetan fruit and flower teas. French and English spoken.

Amazing views at the Marco Polo Restaurant.

Indian/Halal

Aaleja
6, Alley 5, Lane 70, Yanji St. Tel: 02-2773
3227. Open: daily L & D. $$$ p270, B2
With a Pakistani head chef and his
tandoor clay oven, Aalejaserves
Pakistani and Indian dishes, and
many types of curry. The restaurant
and melt-in-your-mouth tandoori
chicken specifically have won
national awards. Has a very good,
inexpensive weekend lunch buffet.

International

B-One Buffet Restaurant
B1, The Sherwood, 111 Minsheng E. Rd
Sec. 3. Tel: 02-2718 1188. www.sherwood.
com.tw Open: daily B, L, D weekend and
afternoon tea. $$ p270, G4
Considered one of the top hotel
restaurants by many, the inexpensive, contemporary B-One has
gourmet selections streaming
from the open kitchen, including
teppanyaki, dim sum, Cantonese
barbecue, and nutritious Taiwanese soups. Corkage fee.

Italian

Capone's
312 Zhongxiao E. Rd Sec. 4. Tel: 02-2773
3782. www.capones.com.tw Open: Sun–Thu
11.30–1am, Fri–Sat until 3am. $$$ p270, C2
Capone's underworld theme is all
loud oranges and flaming reds. The
food is hearty, ranging from Chi-
cago-style steaks to Italian pasta
classics and Mediterranean-style
seafood recipes. Live music – jazz,
blues, R&B – on Thu–Sat nights.

Marco Polo Restaurant
38F, Far Eastern Plaza Hotel, 201 Dunhua S.
Rd Sec. 2. Tel: 02-2376 3156. www.shangri-
la.com Open: daily L & D. $$$ p270, B4
Try to reserve a window seat here
for the sweeping panoramas. An
extensive menu of Italian dishes
with a light modern touch and
beautifully served. Highly recommended is the home-made taglia-
telle with shrimps and
mushrooms.

Toscana
1F, The Sherwood, 111 Minsheng E. Rd Sec.
3. Tel: 02-2718 1188. www.sherwood.com.
tw Open: daily B, L & D, B, weekend brunch.
$$$ (set lunch) $$$$ p270, G4
Many say this is Taiwan's best Ital-

ian restaurant. In a solarium with
refined European decor, dine on
traditional Tuscan selections. The
grilled lamb ribs in wine is recom-
mended, as are the imported Ital-
ian smoked meats. The business
lunch is popular.

Japanese

Ibuki
7F, Far Eastern Plaza Hotel, 201 Dunhua S.
Rd Sec. 2. Tel: 02-2376 3241. www.shangri-
la.com Open: daily L & D. $$$ p270, B4
In the style of a Japanese garden,
with aquariums set into the walls,
chef talent brought in from Japan
offers sushi, sashimi, kaiseki, teppanyaki, tempura, and soups. Several vegetarian options include
vegetable tempura and deep-fried
tofu.

Irodori
3F, Grand Hyatt Taipei, 2 Songshou Rd. Tel:
02-2720 1230. www.taipei.hyatt.com Open:
daily L & D. $$$ p270, C3
With the interior of a Japanese
country manor, this self-service
marketplace-buffet has a very
good selection of different sashimi,
sushi, and tempura creations, as
well as many regional treats you
might never have sunk your teeth
into before.

Bars and cafés

Carnegie's
100 Anhe Rd Sec. 2. Tel: 02-2325 4433.
www.carnegies.net p270, B4
The core of the Anhe Road pub
area. The bar-top poles are often
used by damsels working on one of
the over 300 shooter selections.
Ladies' night Wed: free cham-
pagne for the girls from 9pm to
midnight.

Ice Monster
297 Zhongxiao E. Rd Sec. 4. Tel: 02-8771
3263. www.ice-monster.com Open: daily
10.30am–11.30pm. $ p270, B2
For those who love their shaved
ice with sweet toppings in the
summer, this is the famous stall
that created the mango ice craze
that has swept the island in
recent years. There's a line day
and night. Half a dozen toppings
are available.

Enjoying a drink at lively Carnegie's.

Organo
1, Lane 112, Anhe Rd Sec. 1. Tel: 02-2784
0555 p270, B3
Casual but sophisticated, this
lounge-bar has a smooth
soundtrack, a DJ booth, friendly
staff, chic decor, and occasional
celebrity sightings. Serves a selec-
tion of Western dishes.

Saints & Sinners
114–116 Anhe Rd Sec. 2. Tel: 02-2739
9001. p270, B4
Another mainstay, along with Carn-
egie's, in the trendy Anhe Road bar
district. Has a long horseshoe-
shaped bar, and good specials for
imported beers, wine, and spirits.
Filled with local and foreign profes-
sionals, and, on weekends, with
sports teams celebrating.

The Brass Monkey
166 Fuxing N. Rd. Tel: 02-2547 5050.
www.brassmonkeytaipei.com p272, E4
Popular sports bar with one very
big screen and numerous monitors
showing sports that Western
males prefer. Salsa night (second
Tue every month) and Ladies' night
(Thu) are also popular. The pub
food is among the city's best. The
website posts what's on.

TAIPEI SOUTH

Centered around two of the island's best colleges, this area has a slower, more bohemian, "university town" feel, despite sitting in the busy city. Further south are Muzha's popular tourist tea plantations.

The presence here of National Taiwan University and National Taiwan Normal University – the island's No. 1 and No. 3 post-secondary institutions – means that many students and faculty members reside in this area. There are also many foreigners, teaching or studying at various language institutes. The presence of this educated crowd means an unusual number of bookstores and shops that cater to the literati, selling paintings, calligraphy sets, antiques, and such. A stroll along Heping East Road Section 1, by National Taiwan Normal University, brings one past many such establishments, the proprietors of which can most often speak at least some English.

In the area's two big nightmarkets and in the neighborhood across Xinsheng South Road from National Taiwan University, countless small eateries, pubs, cafés, and teahouses have sprung up, catering to the limited-budget student crowd.

In the hills of Muzha in the far south of the city, tranquility and a slower pace take center stage – at least once you have escaped the traffic in the city below and squeezed your way into a parking spot near one of the many teahouses in the plantations. On weekends and late nights, visitors stream uphill to enjoy a little tea and scenery.

Daan

Daan Forest Park ❶ (Daan Senlin Gongyuan) is one of Taipei's newest parks, created after the homes of a long-standing squatter community of scrap-collecting families were razed in the mid-1990s after repeated warnings and much protest (daily 24 hours; free). It offers a much-welcome respite from the baking cement

Strolling in Daan Forest Park, which provides a great escape from the heat of the surrounding streets.

and asphalt of the surrounding city. At its core is an amphitheater where free concerts are frequently staged on holidays, often featuring well-known pop stars. Many exotic tree species have been planted here, most labeled, providing botanical variety and many shady spots. Like everywhere in Taipei, the place is very crowded on weekends and holidays, so come early. The Jianguo Holiday Jade and Flower markets (see page 143) are on its immediate northeast side, making for a nice weekend outing.

Yongkang Street ❷

Running south from Xinyi Road is the narrow but bustling **Yongkang Street** (Yongkang Jie), located in an otherwise very quiet residential neighborhood centered around tiny Yongkang Park. Often crowded on weekends, the street and surrounding lanes are bursting with eateries selling local food, restaurants serving cuisines from around the globe,

non-chain fashion boutiques, and shops selling traditional Chinese clothing and items such as calligraphy and tea sets. There are about 400 outlets on the street and down side alleys.

During the Japanese colonial era, this area was mostly paddy field. It had a notorious Japanese prison in the middle and the homes of personnel surrounding it. After World War II, civilians who came with the KMT moved in. Commercial development exploded in the 1970s and the paddy fields were soon gone.

Taipei Grand Mosque ❸

Address: 62 Xinsheng S. Road Sec. 2, www.taipeimosque.org.tw
Tel: 02-2321 9445
Opening Hours: daily 9am–6pm
Entrance Fee: free
Transportation: Daan Park

The large and distinctive **Taipei Grand Mosque** (Taibei Qing-zhen Si) is across Xinsheng South Road from Daan Forest Park. It serves the

The Taipei Grand Mosque is open to non-Muslims during the week in non-prayer hours. Call for confirmation.

If visiting Wistaria Teahouse in a group, request a private room with tatami mats.

10,000-plus-strong Muslim community in Taipei. Most of the island's Muslims came to Taiwan with the KMT exodus from China in the late 1940s. Family names such as Jin, Guo, Bai, and Ma – as in well-known Taiwan politician Ma Ying-jeou – are said to indicate likely Muslim ancestry. The Taipei Grand Mosque was built in the Islamic architectural style, with two minarets that are over 20 meters (65ft) tall. Many Islamic countries, including Saudi Arabia, contributed to its building, when the ROC still had formal relations with them in the 1950s.

It is said that during the 1970s oil crisis, the mosque's special relationship with King Faisal ensured continued oil supply to Taiwan, and at preferential rates. Friday prayers are held just after noon. The city declared this a heritage site in 1999 to protect it from demolition resulting from a decades-old land dispute and today the mosque is as busy as ever. Non-Muslims are invited to visit Monday to Friday outside prayer times.

Wistaria Teahouse ❹

Address: 1, Lane 16, Xinsheng S. Road Sec. 3, www.wistariateahouse.com

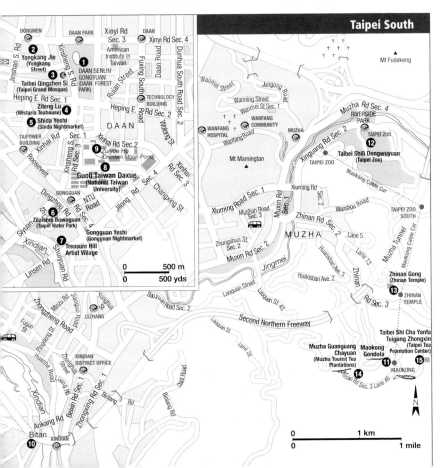

Staff pouring tea at Wistaria Teahouse.

Tel: 02-2363 7375
Opening Hrs: daily 10am–11pm
Entrance Fee: free
Transportation: Taipower Building

Southwest of Daan Forest Park is the **Wistaria Teahouse** (Ziteng Lu), one of Taipei's most popular teahouses and an important historic landmark. This heritage building draped with wistaria vines was a dormitory for mid-level Japanese officials during the colonial period. The *tatami* mats and screen doors are a legacy of this period. Later, it became a favorite meeting place for dissidents during the long terror of the martial law period. Today it is a haven for quiet conversation and contemplation. The intellectual conversation is calmer; poetry readings and other arts and literary events are often held.

All of the island's most famous teas are available here, especially Puerh teas. A decades-long dispute over ownership has finally been settled in recent years, with the government the official owner of the heritage site, but the family that has put so much money into the place allowed to run it "forever."

Shida Nightmarket ❺

The **Shida Nightmarket** (Shida Yeshi) is located west of Wistaria Teahouse on Longquan Street (daily 5pm–1am). Vendors here excel in the specialty dish of *gongwan tang* (pork meatballs in soup), among other foods. On parallel Shida Road, south of National Taiwan Normal University (colloquially known by the shortened "Shida"), is an area chock-a-block with pubs, bars, eateries, and restaurants, all moderately priced because this is a student area. Many Western language students and teachers live in the area or frequent it.

A lot of people-watching goes on at night, with guys standing about in public areas with a beer in hand (legal in Taiwan). Regular barhoppers are easy to spot, and a genial party atmosphere pervades.

Shida Nightmarket and pub area has a markedly younger and hipper feel than some of the more traditional markets elsewhere in the city.

Taipei Water Park ❻

Address: 1 Siyuan Street,
http://waterpark.twd.gov.tw
Tel: 02-8733 5678
Opening Hrs: Tue–Sun July–Aug 9am–8pm, Sept–June 9am–6pm
Entrance Fee: charge
Transportation: Gongguan

In the popular Wistaria Teahouse.

Muzha Tea Plantations

The Muzha hillsides have long been given over to tea bushes, and since the 1980s most of the plantations have opened teahouses that are very popular with day-trippers.

The hills of south Taipei come alive each night with sparkling, dancing pinpoints of light as the scores of teahouses dotting the high slopes of Muzha fill up with lovers of the golden brew. Most are open 24 hours, and the revelry reaches its fullest pitch only after midnight. Visitors come seeking a cool escape from the often steamy Taipei Basin below. The view of the big city laid out beyond like a scintillating carpet at the sippers' feet is a visual complement to the flavor of the local Oolong tea specialties: Tieguanyin (Iron Goddess) and Baozhong.

Taiwan's former president Lee Teng-hui started the tourism renaissance here in the early 1980s when, as mayor of Taipei, he re-zoned the district to allow commercial establishments (the teahouses) to be built on what had previously been land restricted to farms. The growth in revenue and number of tea bushes has since been explosive.

View from a teahouse at Muzha.

The teahouses are perched on the higher slopes of a narrow 3km-long (2-mile) valley called Maokong, or "cat's hollows" – a reference to the hollowed erosions like pawprints found in the rocks along the Zhinan Stream. Hikers come for refreshing walks during the day; students and night owls come in flocks at night to socialize.

Tea has been grown in Taiwan for more than 300 years, but it was British trader John Dodd who put Muzha on the map in the 1860s (see also page 117). Arriving after the Second Opium War, he saw that the area's conditions were perfect for Oolong tea. New bushes were brought from China and Dodd & Co. encouraged new cultivation by guaran-teeing purchase of the entire crop.

Where to taste tea

A visit to the plantations must begin at the **Taipei Tea Promotion Center** (see page 171), where visitors can see displays and live demonstrations on processing and brewing, and enjoy free tastings. English group tours can be arranged with three days' notice (per person fee). Be sure to visit the experimental plantation grounds behind the complex too for riveting views of the city.

Two of Taiwan's best teahouses are located just east of the center and it is no coincidence that they are also on the highest points of the loop road that heads up from Zhengzhi University at the valley's mouth. **Yaoyue Teahouse** ("Inviting the Moon") is at eye level just outside the restaurant and its open-air pavilions, which sit right at the edge of a promontory (6, Lane 40, Zhinan Rd Sec. 3; www.yytea.com.tw; tel: 02-2939 2025; open 24 hours, meals served daily 11am–2am, weekends until 3am; charge). This is a favorite late-night haunt for the island's pop stars. The **Big Teapot Teahouse** is known for "tea cuisine" (37-1, Lane 38, Zhinan Rd Sec. 3; www.bigteapot. idv.tw; tel: 02-2939 5615; daily 10.30am–10pm). These dishes feature locally bred free-range chicken, and are considered especially suited to being enjoyed with tea.

In general, choose teahouses on the highest slopes for the best views and quality. Further downslope, the quality tends to slide; some of the places are a bit ramshackle.

It all started with the **Museum of Drinking Water** (Zilaishui Bowuguan) housed in Taipei's first pumping station and filtration plant. In 1896 the Japanese consulted Scottish engineer William K. Burton, who suggested that water be pumped from the Xindian River and treated at this site, then stored at the facility atop the hill so that gravity would bring the water to residents. The facilities, completed in 1908, no longer provide the city with water.

A museum is now housed in the original Renaissance-style waterworks building. Exhibits show how the piping and delivery systems work, and explain the history of Taipei's water purification activities.

The museum first opened as a stand-alone attraction in 1998, but the city soon realized it had a good thing going. The **Taipei Water Park** (Taibei Zilaishui Yuanqu), targeted at children, has since come up around the museum and adjoining Gongguan Purification Plant (Taipei Water Park ticket brings entry to museum). The top draw is the new Aqua-Friendly Experience and Education Area (separate admission fee, separate entry on Lane 160, Dingzhou Road Sec. 3), where tots get to frolic in water-based amusements. Swimsuits are a must. Next in popularity is the **Pipe Sculpture Area**, where slides and tunnels have been built to mimic the waterworks piping. There are also short trails and flower gardens around and on the hill originally used to store treated water. It is very, very crowded here on hot summer days – especially weekends and during school vacation.

Treasure Hill Artist Village ❼

Address: 2 Alley 14, Ln. 230 Dingzhou Rd Sec. 3, www.artistvillage.org
Tel: 02-2364 5313
Opening Hrs: Tue–Sun 11am–9pm, exhibitions until 6pm
Entrance Fee: free
Transportation: Gongguan

This is one of Taipei's most eccentric communities. Situated on the slope of a hill overlooking the Xindian River, directly south of National Taiwan University, **Treasure Hill Artist Village** (Baozang Yan) is a community of German-built homes raised by Kuomintang soldiers after World War II, when they were posted at an anti-aircraft battery here to defend against Communist attack. Residents were evicted from the

WHERE

To get to Muzha tea plantations by MRT, travelers are advised to alight at Taipei Zoo station and take the Brown No. 15 minibus. Get off and back on the bus anywhere you wish.

View of the Xindian River at Bitan.

illegal site in 2007. The city refurbished the structures, put in sewage pipes and other amenities, and the residents have moved back in. Artists have moved in too, with an artist-in-residence program thriving, and the city is using this as a showcase for environmentally sustainable urban communities and made it an "artivist" compound, combining "artist" with "activist." It is a most unusual place, an ugly duckling with true quirky beauty, declared by the New York Times to be one of Taiwan's "must-see" spots. The Treasure Hill Artist Village opened in 2010 and is home to 14 artist's studios and exhibitions spaces, which regularly host contemporary art shows. It's a parallel project to Taipei Artist Village (see page 135). Two or three times a year an "Open Studio" is held, an event allowing guests to visit all studios in both villages and meet Taiwanese and international artists in residence.

The hillside complex of the Zhinan Temple.

SHOPPING

Save for Yongkang Street, the Taipei South area does not go in for premium-price, glitzy retail outlets. The emphasis is on affordability, as this is an area with a high student population and far enough from the downtown core that residents have more moderate disposable incomes.

Arts and crafts

Formosa Fashion
169 Jinshan S. Rd Sec. 2. Tel: 02-3393 7362. p268, D4
Opened by renowned local fashion designer Zhang Wen, specializing in displaying the essence of Taiwan native-soil regional characteristics in a wide range of goods made into mass-appeal art and objects, such as wood lamps, bags, and furniture upholstered in old-style Taiwan clothing fabrics.

Books

SMC Publishing
14, Alley 14, Lane 283, Roosevelt Rd Sec. 3. Tel: 02-2362 0190. www.smcbook.com.tw Off map
Near National Taiwan University, this is by far the best source for English books on Taiwan. Specializes in gaining rights for out-of-print books, many over 100 years old.

Clothes

Sophie Hong
4, Lane 228, Xinyi Rd Sec. 2. Tel: 02-2351 6469. www.sophiehong.com p268, E3
Sophie Hong is one of the style gurus of Chinese fashion and the most popular name in traditional Chinese attire. She uses a rich variety of fabrics, with an elegant, comfortable style of understated tones. This is her flagship store and design studio.

Nightmarket

Gongguan Nightmarket
p268, C4
Across from National Taiwan University on Roosevelt Road, this is the biggest nightmarket in south Taipei, filled with sellers of clothing, accessories, and books, all priced for student budgets.

Tea

Big Teapot Teahouse
37-1, Lane 38, Zhinan Rd Sec. 3. Tel: 02-2939 5615. www.bigteapot.idv.tw Off map
Like all the teahouses in the Muzha hills, sells the tea grown on the plantation on which it sits. The shop at this teahouse also has Oolongs from some of the other area plantations.

National Taiwan University

Often referred to colloquially by the abbreviation "Taida," the **National Taiwan University** ❽ (Guoli Taiwan Daxue) is the island's premier educational institution (www.ntu.edu. tw). Established by the Japanese as Taihoku (Taipei) Imperial University in 1928, the institution was renamed after World War II. The sprawling 110-hectare (270-acre) main campus is dotted with historic buildings in Western architectural styles, filled with tree-lined boulevards and laced by footpaths, attracting those in search of quiet and a cool, comfortable stroll. The walkways converge on a park surrounding the placid **Drunken Moon Pond** ❾ (Zuiyue Hu), where loved-up couples are serenaded by birds. The main gate of the campus is near the corner of Xinsheng South and Roosevelt roads.

Bitan ❿

A few stops south of Gongguan on the Xindian MRT Line is the recreation area of **Bitan** (daily 24 hours; free). It is centered on a wide, slow-moving, and picturesque section of the Xindian River that has the feel of a lake. The jade-green waters (*bi* means "jade green," *tan* means "lake") are nicely framed by high foliage-covered bluffs on the south and a lovely pedestrian suspension bridge on the west. A teahouse with an open-air patio and great views, very popular with locals, sits at the foot of the bridge on the south bank. A food market selling regional snacks as well as dozens of seafood eateries and tiny cafés line the two sides of the river. Some of the eateries have karaoke equipment, meaning free off-key entertainment with your meal. Paddleboats in kid-friendly shapes like Donald Duck are available for a fee at the water's edge.

Muzha

The **Muzha** area is situated in a narrow valley formed by the lazy Jingmei River on its mid-reaches. Because of its relative isolation, this was one of the last areas in the Taipei Basin to be settled by the Chinese. Despite prohibitions and formal agreements with the aboriginal inhabitants, the settlers kept moving upriver. Needless to say, the indigenous people were not amused. So, in the first half of the 1800s, the isolated settlers set up row after row of *muzha*, or wooden palisades, to protect themselves from vengeful warriors and marauding brigands. The descriptive colloquial name for the settlement soon stuck. Today the area is easily reached via the Muzha MRT Line.

Maokong Gondola ⓫

Maokong Gondola (daily 9am–9pm, Fri–Sat until 10pm, Sat–Sun from 8.30am; tel: 02-2937 8563, http://gondola.trtc.com.tw) has become immensely popularity with visitors since its opening in 2007. The cable-car line operating between Taipei Zoo and Maokong is 4.3km-long (2.7 miles) and has four stations, which also include Taipei Zoo South and Zhinan Temple, and it is worth taking a ride just for the beautiful scenery

The Museum of Water, with its grand rows of classical columns, is a favorite location for wedding shoots.

The old waterworks at the Museum of Drinking Water (see page 165).

and commanding views of the city. For a truly breathtaking sensation of gliding through the sky, go for a Crystal Cabin, which has a special glass bottom. A three-stop adult ticket for a regular cabin costs NT$50 – EasyCards can be used (see page 242).

Taipei Zoo ⑫

Address: 30 Xinguang Road Sec. 2, www.zoo.gov.tw
Tel: 02-2938 2300
Opening Hrs: daily 9am–5pm
Entrance Fee: charge
Transportation: Taipei Zoo

Located just outside the Muzha Line terminus, the **Taipei Zoo** (Taibei Shili Dongwuyuan) has undergone much upgrading since the 1990s to bring the animal habitats up to international standards. An unusual feature is the **Formosan Animals Area**, home to over 20 endemic species not likely to be spotted elsewhere. These include the Formosan giant flying squirrel and the Formosan clouded leopard. A number of species are endangered. Kids, especially, flock to the **Insectarium**, which features a two-level educational center

The multiple choices at Ice Monster.

and a 10-hectare (25-acre) valley behind with over 125 butterfly species and where educational hikes are conducted. The zoo's newest addition is the Panda House (separate admission fee; closed first Mon each month; visitor numbers strictly controlled), home to two giant pandas given to Taiwan by China in what was described as a goodwill gesture. Planned additions include an indoor rainforest pavilion, due in 2016.

Zhinan Temple ⑬

Address: 115 Wanshou Road, www.chih-nan-temple.org
Tel: 02-2939 9922
Opening Hrs: daily 4am–8.30pm
Entrance Fee: free
Transportation: Taipei Zoo

Zhinan Temple (Zhinan Gong), perched atop the mountain spur behind the zoo, is one of Taipei's most important and visited places of worship. It is also known as the Temple of 1,000 Steps, for the 1,275 steps that were long the only way up

Lü Dongbin was said to be an amorous fellow, so couples are advised to avoid Zhinan Temple, lest lusty Lü split them up to steal the girl!

to the temple – talk about dedicated followers! Popular belief suggests that conquering each step brings you 20 extra seconds of life.

The temple is dedicated to Lü Dongbin, one of the Eight Immortals who are at the core of the Chinese pantheon. Since the temple's establishment in 1891, the complex has grown in size and importance. For tourists, its unusual multistory design is an interesting variation on the traditional.

In popular lore, the Eight Immortals and other deities lead lives much like mortals. It is said that long ago, lusty Lü Dongbin chased Guanyin (the virtuous Goddess of Mercy) through the skies to Taiwan. Exasperated, she settled into the shape of the eponymous **Guanyin Mountain** – the likeness is indeed striking – and created the Danshui River to keep Lü at bay. He settled on

the Zhinan Temple spur and is said to still be looking forlornly at her.

The park area surrounding the Zhinan Temple recently added a new attraction, the golden-hued **Auspicious Dragon**. Legend has it, the dragon is the steed of the Jade Emperor. The mythical animal has traditionally been revered as a deity, and it epitomizes nobility, honor and success. The dragon has 3,600 scales and holds the ruler's seal in its left claw.

A ceramic teapot for sale at the Taipei Tea Promotion Center.

Muzha Tea Plantations

Muzha Tourist Tea Plantations ⑭ (Muzha Guanguang Cha-yuan) as well as the **Taipei Tea Promotion Center** ⑮ (Taibei Shi Cha Yanfa Tuigang Zhongxin) at 8-2, Lane 40, Zhinan Road Sec. 3 (Tue–Sun 9am–5pm; free; tel: 02-2234 0568) are perhaps south Taipei's most popular stops for those seeking a brief escape from the city.

RESTAURANTS, BARS AND CAFÉS

Restaurants

Chinese

Din Tai Fung
194 Xinyi Rd Sec. 2. Tel: 02-2321 8928. www.dintaifung.com.tw Open: daily 10am–9pm, Sat–Sun from 9am. **$$** p268, D3
Ranked way back in 1993 as one of the world's 10 best restaurants by the *New York Times*, this iconic place specializes in simple foods, notably *xiaolongbao* ("little dragon" dumplings). Busloads of gourmand Japanese tourists are a regular sight.

Shanghainese

Guangsheng Food Shop
25, Lane 38, Taishun St. Tel: 02-2363 3414.

Open: Sun–Thu 11.30am–11pm, Fri–Sat until 1am. **$$** p268, D4
Despite very low prices, this place with evocative 1930s Shanghai memorabilia has a touch of class. Highlights are the braised chicken with bamboo shoots and the yellowfish with salted cabbage. Also has good Jiangzhe dishes. Limited English spoken, but the menu is in English.

Taiwanese

Tai Yi Milk King
82, XinSheng S. Rd, Sec 3, Tel: 02-2362 3712, Open: daily 10.30am–midnight.
$–$$ p268, A2
On a Saturday night huge crowds wait in line for the shop's delicious shaved ice creations. There's an amazing variety of toppings to mix and match. Generous portions.

Vietnamese

Thanh Ky
1, Lane 6, Yongkang St. www.thanhky.com Tel: 02-2321 1579. Open: Mon–Fri 11.30am–2pm, 5.30–9.30pm, Sat–Sun

11am–3pm, 5–9.30pm. **$$** p268, D4
Always busy and popular with Vietnamese expats. Wide range of appetizers – try the fried Vietnamese spring rolls. Most of the main courses are savory rice noodle soups accompanied by spicy beef or hot and sour seafood.

Bars and cafés

45
2F, 45 Heping E. Rd Sec. 1. Tel: 02-2321 2140. p268, D4
An obligatory stop on the regular Shida weekend pub crawl, popular with expat language teachers and students. Features 1960s tunes and decor from that era.

Roxy 99
B1, 218 Jinshan S. Rd Sec. 2. Tel: 02-2351 5970. www.roxy.com.tw p268, D4
One of the varying-themed outlets of the Roxy group, a must-stop on the Shida pub crawl. The music is eclectic – jazz, rock, classics – and cover is fully exchange-able for food and drink.

Guarding the Martyr's Shrine.

TAIPEI NORTH

North of the Jilong River, Shilin is a land of museums, Tianmu is an expatriate enclave with an international flavor, Beitou has long been known for its hot springs, and Neihu's large open spaces have acquired a variety of shops and attractions.

The districts of Shilin, Neihu, and Beitou are all found north of the Jilong River, and all the main sights are within walking distance of – or a short bus ride away from – an MRT station, making for a pleasant escape from the urban crush of the city center without leaving the amenities of civilization altogether. Note that most of the museums in the area lack detailed information in English, so be sure to take advantage of English-language tours where possible.

SHILIN

Grand Hotel ❶

The **Grand Hotel** (Yuanshan Dafandian), though a bit faded and frayed at the edges today despite management's ongoing best efforts, is indeed grand (1 Zhongshan N. Rd Sec. 4; tel: 02-2886 8888; www.grand-hotel.org). Built in Ming dynasty palace style and inspired by Beijing's Forbidden City, the massive main structure supports the largest Chinese roof in the world. The facade of this 530-room behemoth is defined by towering red pillars and fronted by a pretty sculpted garden.

The ridge on which the hotel is perched was the location of the main

The Grand Hotel seen from Dajia Riverside Park.

Japanese Shinto shrine in colonial days. The shrine was torn down in anger by the KMT – as were most things too evidently Japanese – after World War II. The hotel, started in the 1950s, was a pet project of Madame Chiang Kai-shek, who sought to bring the city international stature.

There are few better spots for afternoon tea than the grand lobby. Its recessed ceiling of dragon and phoenix bas-reliefs and its grand staircase flanked by sumptuous artworks will transport you back to imperial days.

An ice-cold bowl of sweet aiyu is the perfect antidote to a grease-laden supper at Shilin Nightmarket (see page 174).

Behind the hotel is a staircase that leads to the peak of Yuanshan (Round Mountain). From here, the stirring views of the city below resemble a scale model with tiny toy planes landing at Songshan Airport.

Shilin Nightmarket ❷

Regarded by many as Taipei's best, **Shilin Nightmarket** (Shilin Yeshi) is definitely its largest and most popular, and has a history of well over 100 years (daily 5pm–midnight). It is located on the west side of Jiantan MRT station.

Long ago, a clash between immigrants from China forced a group of settlers to flee to Yangmingshan. But they periodically came down into present-day Shilin to sell produce, slipping back and forth like ghosts. As such, the market was long called "Ghost Market."

Just about every tasty traditional Taiwanese snack that exists is whipped up here for you. Enjoy cholesterol in great quantity and variety: oyster omelets, cuttlefish stew, "coffin boards" (*guancai ban*), deep-fried stinky tofu, potstickers (*guotie*), and much more. The new premises for the snack vendors were opened in 2004 and are Taiwan's first experiment with modern food centers, meant to improve sanitation and attract tourists. Traditional nightmarkets are often a challenge for the overseas tourist, with grease-coated aisles, garbage piling up by stalls, and patrons walking away from uncleaned tables as per local custom.

In the vicinity of the Shilin Nightmarket, close to MRT Jiantan Station, is the **Taipei Perfoming Arts Center**. This state-of-the-art facilities houses three theaters. The experimental, yet well-thought-out structure of the center rethinks the arrangement of space and removes traditional architectural barriers to the imagination of playwrights and directors, thus allowing to stage performances that would be impossible elsewhere.

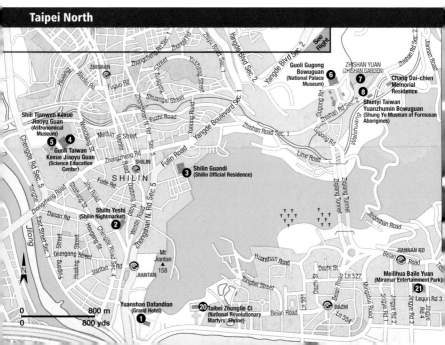

Taipei North

Shilin Official Residence ❸

Address: 60 Fulin Road
Tel: 02-2881 2512
Opening Hrs: Tue–Sun 9.30am–12pm, 1–5pm
Entrance Fee: charge
Transportation: Shilin

This expansive estate with the vague name **Shilin Official Residence** (Shilin Guandi) was one of Chiang Kai-shek's abodes during his Taipei years. Tucked at the foot of Yangmingshan's slopes, the sprawling grounds were opened as a park in 1996. The long, tree-shaded driveway opens onto pathways leading to gardens, pagodas, pavilions, and a small chapel where top KMT officials, Christian or otherwise, attended services each Sunday morning – the key to staying within the inner circle of power. There are also experimental greenhouses here from the Japanese colonial era. The grounds are 10 minutes east on foot from Shilin MRT Station.

Despite official talk about opening the house itself to public visit, objections from those KMT elements of the government loyal to Chiang Kai-shek's memory kept it out of bounds for many years. It was only in 2011 that the two-story house, where the president lived for 26 years until his death in 1975, opened to visitors.

Science Education Center ❹

Address: 189 Shishang Road, www.ntsec.gov.tw
Tel: 02-2837 8777
Opening Hrs: Tue–Sun 9am–6pm
Entrance Fee: charge
Transportation: Shilin

About 15 minutes on foot west of Shilin MRT Station is **National Taiwan Science Education Center**. Kids can run amok in this learning-is-for-fun, hands-on facility. A nine-story-high glass atrium houses permanent exhibits on the physical sciences, earth sciences, and life

During the colonial era, the Japanese brought plants from around the world for synthesis with the Taiwanese soil. The exquisite and exotic results are on display on the grounds of the Shilin Official Residence.

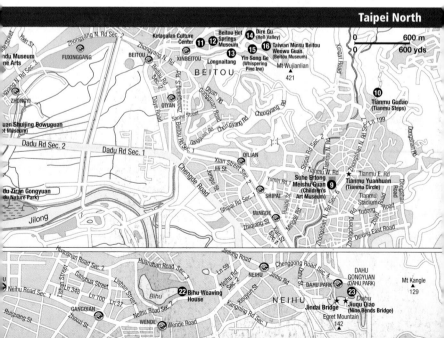

Taipei Astronomical Museum.

The SkyCycle at the Science Education Center. The center has limited written English, so try to join a free English tour (minimum 20 persons, one-week advance booking). The website has comprehensive information in English.

sciences. Additional tickets must be bought for temporary exhibitions, 3D Theater, Turbo-ride 3D Theater, Earthquake Theater, Sky Cycle, and Kid's Learning and Discovery Playground. Be warned that organization at the theaters can be somewhat chaotic. The SkyCycle, erected five stories above ground and exhibiting theories of weight distribution and balance, is also very popular. There is printed info in English, and guided English tours for groups of 20 (reservations required; ext. 1515–1517).

Astronomical Museum ❺

Address: 363 Jihe Road, www.tam.gov.tw
Tel: 02-2831 4551
Opening Hrs: Tue–Sun 8am–5.30pm; Sat 8am–9.30pm
Entrance Fee: charge
Transportation: Shilin

The **Taipei Astronomical Museum** (Taibei Shili Tianwen Kexue Jiaoyu Guan) stands right beside the Science Education Center. It has three floors of exhibits on such themes as Ancient Astrology, The Earth, Space Technology, The Solar System, and The Stars. But the star attractions are the 3D Theater (polarized 3D glasses used), IMAX Dome Theater, Cosmic Adventure theme-park ride, and the Observatory Dome with telescopes for stargazing (Tue–Sat 10am–noon, 2–4pm; additional session Sat 7–9pm). There is a separate admission fee for the first three.

Reservations are taken three days in advance for the popular Observatory Dome sessions. Most of the theater films are imported and dubbed, so check what English is available. The limited English in the regular exhibits can dampen the fun. For transportation, take a Red 30 bus from Shilin MRT station.

National Palace Museum ❻

The **National Palace Museum** (Guoli Gugong Bowuguan) is one of Taiwan's crowning glories, justly considered the world's greatest repository of Chinese artifacts (see page 190). Once part of the emperors' personal collection, off-limits to the public until after the fall of the empire, the pieces span 5,000 years. At any one time only a small portion of the 650,000 works is on display, the rest tucked away in temperature- and humidity-controlled vaults dug into the mountain behind.

The museum is far too large to take in on just one trip. English tours at 10am and 3pm daily, led by strenuously trained guides, are invaluable (online reservation needed). In 2008 the museum opened the popular Children's Gallery, helping kids aged 5 to 12 develop an appreciation of the fine arts through fun and games (free; scheduled entry times during the museum opening times).

Adjacent to the museum is the 1.5-hectare (4-acre) **Zhishan Garden** ❼ (Zhishan Yuan), an exquisitely landscaped classical Chinese garden (Tue–Sun 8.30am–5.30pm, Apr–Oct until 6.30pm; free with museum ticket).

Shung Ye Museum ❽

Address: 282 Zhishan Road Sec. 2, www.museum.org.tw
Tel: 02-2841 2611
Opening Hrs: Tue–Sun 9am–5pm; closed Chinese New Year's holidays
Entrance Fee: charge
Transportation: Shilin

With its distinctive profile, the **Shung Ye Museum of Formosan Aborigines** (Shunyi Taiwan Yuanzhumin Bowuguan) is located just east of the National Palace Museum. Perhaps Taiwan's best museum for learning about the island's native tribes, unlike other museums there is good English. This facility has played a key role in the movement to generate greater interest in and respect for the tribes' widely varying cultures.

Among the highlights are a large topographical map of Taiwan showing tribal dispersion down to village level, a section on traditional weaponry and one on beliefs and ceremonies, an Ami sea-going craft, and scale models of traditional dwellings. There are multimedia presentations, many with English versions, an English audio guide, and English-language tours can be arranged. The gift shop has many print materials hard to find elsewhere in Taipei, plus cultural products and handicrafts.

WHERE

With one-week advance notice, the National Palace Museum provides wheelchairs as well as tours for the physically and mentally disabled – a service that is rare in Taiwan.

The unusual architecture of the Shung Ye Museum.

The National Revolutionary Martyrs' Shrine.

The rooftops of hilly Beitou.

Tianmu and Beitou

Tianmu suburb lies at the northern end of Zhongshan North Road. Here one finds Taipei's densest concentration of expatriate residents, most business and diplomatic personnel and their dependants. This was an enclave for Japanese officials in colonial times. "Tianmu," or "Heavenly Mother," refers to a revered Japanese goddess. US military officers moved in after World War II, followed by international businessfolk.

The community core is **Tianmu Circle** (Tianmu Yuanhuan), at the intersection of Tianmu Road and Zhongshan North Road Section 7. To serve the foreign community, many Western-style leisure and recreational facilities exist in the area, and more English is spoken and seen here than elsewhere in Taipei.

Children's Art Museum ❾

Address: B1, No. 20, Alley 50, Tianmu W. Road, www.artart.com.tw
Tel: 02-2872 1366 ext. 14
Opening Hrs: Tue–Sun 10am–5.30pm
Entrance Fee: charge
Transportation: Shipai

West of the circle is the **Children's Art Museum in Taipei** (Suhe Ertong Meishu Guan), a private facility dedicated to children's art education and skills development. In the Magic Room, kids can "inhabit and interact" with paintings, recomposing them to stimulate the visual and tactile senses.

The Art Tunnel is a hall of mirrors that inspires new perspectives. In the Camel Exhibit Area, young masters show off their own creations. Kids must be four years or older and accompanied by an adult; advance registration is required for groups of 15 or more. Take bus Red 12, Red 15, Red 19, or 645 from Shipai MRT station.

Tianmu Steps ⑩

North of Tianmu Circle are the **Tianmu Steps** (Tianmu Gudao), leading east up Yangmingshan from Alley 1, Lane 232, Zhongshan North Road Section 7. The trailhead is clearly marked with a large signboard (with English) showing the route and main sights. The lower section weaves past apartment buildings before opening up and gliding past trees, through tall grasses, by chirping birds and cicadas, and past small temples before winding up at Chinese Culture University (Wenhua Daxue). This was once a side trail on the Pathway of the Fish, and is today one of Taipei's most popular day hike destinations, just under 2 miles (3km) long, teeming with families on non-working days.

Beitou's hot springs

Northwest of Tianmu, along the base of Yangmingshan, is Beitou District. Since the 1890s, the valley has been a favored mineral springs resort. During the 1905 Russo-Japanese War, Taiwan's Japanese governor was ordered to develop the valley on a large scale to treat Japan's wounded, in the belief that mineral springs have health benefits. Japanese officers and officials came here for R&R and to escape the Taipei Basin heat. The tradition continued in earnest during World War II when the number of military men stationed on the island ballooned. Many *kamikaze* pilots spent their last few days here, "marrying" local Beitou working girls before flying off to glory.

When the American military had a presence in Taiwan, from the early 1950s to 1979, the area developed a reputation as a red-light district. The national sense of shame was so great that at one point the government revoked the licenses of the 600 prostitutes working here. But the *zona rosa* reputation slowly faded as the popularity of hot-spring soaking among locals waned in the 1980s. In its heyday, Beitou had over 70 hotels and inns; today there are a handful.

A resurgence of interest since the late 1990s has seen old inns spruced up and new facilities built. Only a few, however, are of high enough quality to satisfy the overseas tourist.

Ketagalan Culture Center ⑪

Address: No. 3-1 Zhongshan Road, www.ketagalan.taipei.gov.tw
Tel: 02-2898 6500
Opening Hrs: Tue–Sun 9am–5pm
Entrance Fee: free
Transportation: Xinbeitou

The **Ketagalan Culture Center** (Kaidagelan Wenhua Guan) is located just 200 meters (200 yds) east of the Xinbeitou MRT station. It is dedicated to the flatland tribes that once filled the Taipei Basin. The museum building previously housed special military police forces. Today the 10-story facility contains an aboriginal culture exhibition, multimedia showroom, aboriginal theme library, conference and performance spaces, and a souvenir shop.

In the basement is a display area for arts and crafts by aboriginal

A therapeutic massage of cascading spring water at Spring City Resort.

A hot-spring soak at a spa.

Hot springs

Soaking in a mineral-rich hot spring is a very popular activity in Taiwan, and three areas within Taipei and Taipei County are particularly well known for it.

Soaking is one of the most pleasurable pastimes on Earth and, happily, is also said to alleviate a host of chronic afflictions, from arthritis to anemia and from skin to liver disease. Even the robustly healthy might benefit from a boost to the blood circulation. (Note, however, that hot springs are not recommended for pregnant women, and in general, should not replace the medical attention of a qualified physician.)

Northern Taiwan has an unusually high concentration of hot springs due to its location above an area of dormant volcanic activity. Water from underground springs is heated geothermally and forced to the surface, laden with minerals. The hot springs epicenter is undoubtedly Beitou. Xinbeitou MRT station is sometimes filled with the

A private hot spring cabin at Wulai.

smell of sulfur, and clouds of white vapor can occasionally be seen wafting through the tree-lined valley. From here, it's a short taxi ride or a 20-minute walk to the **Beitou Hot Springs Park** (6 Zhongshan Rd; Tue–Sun 9am–5pm; charge; tel: 02-2897 2260). The outdoor public baths are divided into men's and women's sections, but swimsuits are required (small fees for soaking and locker).

Choosing a hot spring

Beitou has three kinds of hot springs, green, white, and ferrous sulfur; temperatures range from 38°C (100°F) to 60°C (140°F). The green water is acidic and is said to cure rheumatism and exhaustion. The white water is sulfurous and is said to cure skin problems and liver disease. The ferrous water is clear and, in theory, drinkable. It is good for nerve strain, and clearing stuffed noses.

For a more exclusive experience, try the **Spring City Resort**. Besides its various outdoor baths, it has private indoor baths, some with modern amenities like flat-screen TVs. This luxury comes at a price, of course. For a more intimate and quaint experience, check in at the **Whispering Pine Inn**, an exclusive hotel built during the colonial era (see page 182).

The hot springs in Yangmingshan National Park are most easily reached by car. These range from outdoor springs to five-star spa resorts. **Lengshuikeng**, or "Cold Water Pit," has free male/female outdoor baths. On the northern slopes of Yangmingshan is **Tien Lai Spring Resort**, reminiscent of a 19th-century European spa resort (1–7 Mingliu Rd, Chonghe Village, Jinshan Township; www.tienlai.com.tw; tel: 02-2408 0000), with fantastic views of the mountain.

Nearer to the city is the **Landis Resort Yangmingshan**. With several dining options in house, you can enjoy tea and a warm meal in addition to a hot soak.

Not to be forgotten is the hot spring haven of Wulai. There are free **Outdoor Hot Springs** here, but for real pampering, visit the **Spring Park Urai Spa & Resort**. With stunning scenery to uplift the soul and mineral-rich waters to heat the body, hot springs are a perfect antidote to Taipei's chilly winters.

artists, including embossed leather-work by accomplished Atayal aboriginal talent Mei-mei Mashao.

On the ground level is an exhibit of historical artifacts from Taiwan's various tribes. The second level is dedicated to exhibitions of traditional artifacts and historical information on the plains peoples. Most are now completely absorbed into the Han Chinese community, and the remainder struggle for identity and recognition.

The third level has displays on all of the island's mountain tribes. The center also houses NGO offices and holds classes to help natives improve their work and language skills. Except for video clips among the displays, the exhibits are static, so call ahead to see if performances are scheduled, generally so on weekends.

Beitou Hot Springs Museum ⑫

Address: 2 Zhongshan Road,
http://beitoumuseum.taipei.gov.tw
Tel: 02-2893 9981
Opening Hrs: Tue–Sun 9am–5pm
Entrance Fee: free
Transportation: Xinbeitou

East of the cultural center, at the mouth of the valley in which all Beitou's hot-spring inns sit, is the **Beitou Hot Springs Museum** (Beitou Wenquan Bowuguan), built by the Japanese as Taiwan's first public bathhouse in 1913, and the biggest hot-spring facility in East Asia in its day. Abandoned for years, it was refurbished in 1998. The facade is reminiscent of a Tudor mansion.

Inside, the Roman-style male baths on the first level are intact but for display only. On the second level, the wood construction and *tatami*-lined floors are distinctly Japanese in style. The observation deck offers nice views. Exhibits trace the story of Beitou's love affair with soaking and give a virtual tour of Taiwan's hot springs and major mineral springs areas around the globe. Note that visitor numbers are strictly controlled, so there may be a wait on non-working days. Slippers must be worn inside; they are provided free, or new pairs can be bought.

Longnaitang ⑬

A short walk up the valley from the museum, at 244 Guangming Road, is

Tribal dress on display at Ketagalan Cultural Center.

Longnaitang, Beitou's oldest operational bathhouse (daily 6.30am–5pm; admission charge; tel: 02-2891 2236). Built in 1907, the interiors are predominantly wood and stone, and there are separate male and female pools. This is a purist establishment – patrons cannot stay overnight, nor is food available. The soaking's the thing. The sense of rustic simplicity is heightened by the primitive-looking but comfortably smooth stone pools. A favorite with local old-timers for its sense of aged familiarity, the place is in sore need of some fixing up and paint, but it is clean. During the Japanese period, this establishment was famed for its low entrance fees, just three cents; it was nicknamed "House of Three Cents."

Hell Valley

About 10 minutes on foot further up the valley, along Zhongshan Road, is Beitou's most famous site, **Hell Valley** (Dire Gu), also called Geothermal Valley in English, an ominously bubbling pit in a small cul-de-sac (Tue–Sun 9am–5pm; free; tel: 02-2893 9981). Steam rises and drifts across the surface of the

The roiling hot waters of Hell Valley.

boiling water, which can reach a temperature of 100°C (212°F). This spot is the likely source of the place name "Beitou." The aborigines that once lived in the area fearfully called the valley *Patauw*, meaning "sorceress," sure that the other-worldly phenomena seen here were the result of such dangerous, mysterious figures. The Chinese who came here in the late 1600s to extract sulfur for their munitions from one of the 27 sulfur mines in the area then bastardized the aboriginal name.

Though the main Hell Valley pool is scalding hot, a runoff channel just inside the entry gate cools the waters just enough to have once allowed the soaking of one's feet, great for athlete's foot (known in fact as "Hong Kong foot" in Taiwan, as Hong Kong was a renowned moist, malarial place before and long after the British landed there). This is no longer allowed, nor is egg boiling, a once-popular activity here. In the mid-1990s, an unfortunate visitor fell in and was scalded to death. Taking no more chances, the city has locked up all the water-access points.

Whispering Pine Inn ⑮

Nearing the top of the road that curves up the valley is the lovely all-wood **Whispering Pine Inn** (Yin Song Ge), a foliage-wreathed hideaway in a small compound wrapped on three sides by Youya Road (tel: 02-2895 1531). Inside the heritage building, built in 1931 and still a functioning business, guests can enjoy an authentic Japanese experience: shoes come off and slippers go on before one can enjoy the *tatami* floors, *shoji*, or Japanese-style sliding doors, hot-spring mineral baths in individual rooms, and ritualized tea ceremony. Outside are colorful and formal Japanese gardens in miniature. The place is now in clear need of renovation, and mold/mildew is showing up in spots; some guests report being asked to pay in full upon checking in, but insist on checking your room first.

Beitou Museum ⑯

Address: 32 Youya Road,
www.beitoumuseum.org.tw
Tel: 02-2891 2318
Opening Hrs: Tue–Sun 10am–5.30pm
Entrance Fee: charge
Transportation: Xinbeitou

Housed in a double-story wooden structure is the **Beitou Museum** (formerly the Taiwan Folk Arts Museum). Refurbished and re-opened in 2008, it is dedicated to all of Taiwan's ethnic groups, indigenous or Chinese, and contains over 5,000 pieces of embroidery, traditional apparel, and arts and crafts. The resplendent Qing dynasty bridal palanquin is a folk treasure of the most intricately carved wood. Most poignant is perhaps the display on foot-binding, a tradition that was suffered by Chinese women at all social levels for centuries except in the Hakka community.

The museum building is a former hot-spring inn built in the 1920s by the Japanese. It was a favorite military officers' club and the most popular spot in Beitou for prepping *kamikaze* pilots. Constructed in Tang dynasty style – a period during which the Japanese were greatly influenced by Chinese culture – it is set in a traditional garden with a small artificial waterfall in one corner. Slippers must be worn inside the museum, lending the place a hushed and reverential ambience.

West of the hot-springs area, in Beitou District's southwest corner where the Jilong River flows into the Danshui River, are three popular tourist destinations: GuanduTemple, Guandu Nature Park, and the Tittot Museum.

Guandu Temple ⑰

Address: 360 Zhixing Road,
www.kuantu.org.tw
Tel: 02-2858 1281
Opening Hrs: daily 6am–9pm
Entrance Fee: free
Transportation: Guandu

The **Guandu Temple** (Guandu Gong) complex is tucked under and right up the bluffs beside the Jilong River's north bank. This large, ornate place of worship was originally a small shrine to Mazu, Goddess of the Sea, set up by immigrants from Fujian Province in gratitude for her protection on the dangerous Taiwan Strait crossing. It is said to have first been built in 1661, making it Taiwan's oldest temple, though it has undergone much rebuilding in the intervening years.

The temple is known for having almost perfect *fengshui*: it faces south, with a tall "mountain" bulwark behind it, has good *qi* brought in by a slow-moving body of water moving left to right, and has a wide body of placid water in front – the waters of Guandu Nature Park – acting like a mirror to deflect baleful influences away from the front door.

Behind the temple, a cave leads up through the bluff and onto the crest, where there is a sculpted

Traditional stone lanterns are among the Japanese-style decorative touches at the Whispering Pine Inn in Beitou.

The Guandu Temple complex.

Rows of lanterns hanging at Guandu Temple carry the names of those who receive blessings for making donations to the temple.

park with terrific views. Inside the cave, visitors pass many statues of Buddhist *arhats* (saints) and a thousand-armed Guanyin statue, thus seeming to pass through a mystical subterranean world.

Guandu Nature Park

Address: 55 Guandu Road, http://gd-park.org.tw
Tel: 02-2858 7417
Opening Hrs: Tue–Sun 9am–5pm, Sat–Sun Apr–Sept until 6pm, Oct–Mar until 5.30pm
Entrance Fee: charge
Transportation: Guandu

The low-lying 60-hectare (150-acre) **Guandu Nature Park** (Guandu Ziran Gongyuan) is easily the most accessible large-scale birdwatching site from downtown. Here the Jilong River widens and flows lazily into the Danshui. The tall grasses, mangrove swamp, saltwater marsh, and freshwater ponds present the myriad endemic and migratory birds with nesting and feeding opportunities. Watch for the minuscule version of the fiddler crab native to Taiwan's mudflats. The reserve was created in 2001 after the city bought out the rice

At the Nature Center in Guandu Nature Park.

farmers here on a large scale – to the tune of NT$430 million. After two years, the wetlands and mudflats had reverted to their natural character.

The **Nature Center** has good exhibits on marshland habitats. Boardwalks and three viewing shelters allow easier human access. Numbers are limited, so get there early. There is printed info in English, and English guides can be booked ahead.

The Guandu MRT station is within 10 minutes by foot of both Guandu Temple and the nature park. A bike path zooms by the riverside, and bicycles can be brought on the trains at this station. There are also a number of bike rental shops by the temple.

Blue Highway river tours from Dadaocheng (see page 117) and Danshui (see page 206) also end here, at Guandu Wharf.

Tittot Museum

Address: 16, Lane 515, Zhongyang N. Road Sec. 4, www.tittotmuseum.com
Tel: 02-7730 4300
Opening Hrs: Tue–Sun 9am–5pm
Entrance Fee: charge
Transportation: Guandu

Just east of Guandu MRT station is **Tittot Museum** (Liuyuan Shuijing Bowuguan), which is indelibly associated with founder and artist Heinrich Wang (Wang Xiajun), a well-known former movie actor and director who famously quit the trade in the 1980s for something of more lasting value. His choice was crystal glassworks (*liuli* in Mandarin), and he has won many awards. His artworks are contemporary and functional – vases are a specialty – and the pieces created in the adjoining workshop are on display at the Tittot Museum.

The museum has two levels. The first has a classroom and workshop, and exhibits on the lost wax casting process, Wang's glassworks and artistic vision, and a selection of international work. The second has displays on the history and techniques of

A dragon detail at the Guandu Temple.

glassworking, and glass art from around the world. DIY classes are also given (extra charge; call ahead for schedule). Guided tours can be arranged in advance. In 2004, Wang established a porcelain tableware company, the New Chi (see page 73).

If you're into art, you may also like the **Kunadu Museum of Fine Arts** (www.kdmofa.tnua.edu.tw), located on the campus of the National University of Fine Arts, a 15-minute walk north of Tittot Museum.

National Revolutionary Martyrs' Shrine ⑳

Address: 139 Beian Road
Tel: 02-2885 4162
Opening Hrs: daily 9am–5pm
Entrance Fee: free
Transportation: Jiantan/Dazhi

Just north of the Jilong River, east of the Grand Hotel, three sites of interest beckon. Tucked against the city's northern hills and overlooking the river is the **National Revolutionary Martyrs' Shrine** (Taibei Zhonglie Ci). Completed in 1969, it honors the memory of the more than 300,000 killed in the 1911 revolution that ended imperial rule, the

Sino-Japanese War, and the Chinese Civil War. Tablets in Chinese testifying to their deeds are mounted on the four walls of the main building.

The main shrine stands beyond two massive doors lined with oversized brass studs. It is another public edifice in the Ming palace style of Beijing's Forbidden City, specifically the Hall of Supreme Harmony, with bold red pillars, yellow roof tiles, and colorful roof beams. The complex is spread over 3.3 hectares (8 acres) in total.

This was a favorite walking retreat for Generalissimo Chiang Kai-shek, who was portrayed as a Confucian sage of simplicity and austerity. When in the mood for a walk, the entire complex was instantaneously shut down.

Not to be missed is the precision of the 15-minute changing of the guard. It starts at 9am and takes place every hour on the hour, except for the last at 4.40pm. Visitors also love to photograph guards at the main gate, trained to stand as though frozen in time.

Miramar Entertainment Park ㉑

Miramar Entertainment Park (Meilihua Baile Yuan), at 20 Jingye

WHERE

The Red No. 2 bus from Yuanshan MRT station goes to all three sites east of the Grand Hotel: Dahu Park, the Martyrs' Shrine, and Miramar Entertainment Park.

Along the Guandu bicycle path.

3rd Road, is another of Taipei's super-malls (daily 11am–10pm; restaurants and entertainment facilities until midnight; tel: 02-2175 3456; www.miramar.com.tw). Knowing it cannot compete with the scores of brand-name outlets in the eastern district's malls, in part because it lies in an outlying suburb, the complex is positioned as an entertainment-oriented facility targeting young families and youth. Theme-park options complement its mid-range and top-end consumer products. Among the leisure and entertainment facilities here are the mesmerizing neon-lit rooftop **giant Ferris wheel**, a large-screen IMAX theater showing commercial movies, a giant merry-go-round, plus free "water dance" shows and a "seascape avenue" connecting the two main buildings.

Bihu Weaving House ㉒

The brainchild of the landscape artist Wang Wenzi, **Bihu Weaving House** (daily 6am–10pm; tel: 02-8751 1587) is a place to enjoy a unique amalgam of tranquil natural beauty and serene man-made ambience. The delicate lattice structure was weaved out of 4,000 bamboo staves by over 200 volunteers. Visit the place after dark when the construction is magically lit up and its reflection glows in the lake. When inside, sit on the "meditation platform", relax and contemplate the enchanting surroundings. Bihu Weaving House is located in Bihu Park (175 Neihu Rd Sec 2); to get there, get off at Wende MRT Station.

Dahu Park ㉓

East of Miramar is **Dahu Park** (Dahu Gongyuan), the scenic core of Neihu, and in contrast to the Entertainment "Park," a bona fide nature area, though human-embellished (31 Chenggong Rd Sec. 5; daily 24 hours; free; tel: 02-2792 7500). Amid wide swathes of soft grass is a natural lake (*Dahu* is, in

The regal splendor of the Martyr's Shrine.

fact, Mandarin for "big lake"), popular with snow-white egrets, thus explaining the park's other name, "Bailu Park." Other native waterfowl such as Mandarin ducks also flock here. Old fishermen always seem to be present, whiling away their time and landing surprisingly fair-sized catch.

The two bridges over the lake lead to a classical pavilion at the center. The **Nine Bends Bridge** (Jiuqu Qiao), which twists this way and that, calls to mind the Chinese folklore belief that ghosts cannot cross bridges that are not straight, for they can only walk in straight lines. **Jindai Bridge**, which arcs steeply above the waters, imparts a classical Chinese air. Three outdoor swimming pools of good quality are also located here (May–Sept).

On the far side of the lake is **Egret Mountain**, a squat boundary hill 142 meters (465ft) in height with shaded walking trails that pass by small, old temples.

SHOPPING

Shilin has a large student population, and the Beitou and Neihu areas are far enough from downtown that incomes are comparatively moderate and retail outlets correspondingly middle-of-the-road. The chic and glitzy, with correspondingly high prices, re-enters the picture in Tianmu, an expat enclave of higher incomes and more cosmopolitan character.

Antiques

Bai Win Antiques
2, Lane 405, Zhongshan North Rd Sec. 6. Tel: 02-2874 5525. www.baiwin antiques.com Off map
Items from Taiwan, China, and Southeast Asia, from the Han, Ming, and Qing dynasties. From furniture to lotus shoes to old collectible Shanghai posters.

Clothing

iPrefer
22 Jingye 3rd Rd. Tel: 02-2175 3201. Off map
The flagship outlet of a growing Taipei chain, sells quality handcrafted attire, and adornments that exhibit "metropolitan-style bohemianism." All design is done in-house and dyeing done traditionally.

Department store

Dayeh Takashimaya
55 Zhongcheng Rd Sec. 2. Tel: 02-2831 2345. www.dayeh-takashimaya.com.tw Off map
Tianmu's main department store (no giant malls yet), a 12-story Japanese-owned outlet, with upscale boutique brands. A favorite Tianmu gathering spot. Free shuttle buses from Shilin and Shipai MRT stations.

Food

Isaac
84 Shipai Rd Sec. 2. Tel: 02-2821 8128. www.isaac-food.com.tw Off map

A bakery, Isaac has won the prestigious annual Taipei Pineapple Cake Competition in 2009, and also been voted most popular with foreigners in the traditional-cake category. It carries many other traditional baked treats, which come in attractive packaging. Close to Shipai MRT Station on the Danshui Line.

Kuo Yuan Ye Traditional Cakes
546 Wenlin Rd. Tel: 02-2838 2700. www.kuos.com p274, C2
A bakery in business since 1867, provides traditional baked goods. Chinese "cakes" are often savory; try the delicious Dongpo Cake, with a filling of rice wine, braised Dongpo Pork, and mushrooms.

Matsusei
B1, 3 Tianmu W. Rd. Tel: 0800-023804. www.matsusei.com.tw Off map
Walk into the store and you find yourself on a small shopping street, with "outlets" stocked with specialties such as Japanese cookies, Korean treats, Chinese hams, and so on. There are items from around the globe, and many low-fat selections.

Gifts and souvenirs

National Palace Museum Gift Shop
221 Zhishan Rd Sec. 2. Tel: 02-2881 2021. www.npm.gov.tw p274, E1
An expansive space carrying over 3,500 items, including quality books on the museum's artworks and fine reproductions of many of the pieces. A clever series of moderate-price items features famous NPM works of art.

Knives

Hao He-ji Famous Shilin Cutters
74 Dabei Rd. Tel: 02-2881 2856. p274, C3
The Shilin Cutter is a special type of foldable pocket knife invented in the Qing dynasty, with a distinctive eggplant-shaped handle and blade

shaped like a bamboo leaf. This iconic outlet is considered Taiwan's best, and people buy the knives as collector pieces. Available in many sizes; other types of Chinese knives also for sale.

Mall

Miramar Entertainment Park
20 Jingye 3rd Rd. Tel: 02-2175 3456. www.miramar.com.tw Off map
A super-mall positioned as an entertainment-oriented facility for young families and youth. Its Ferris wheel and recreational options complement the mid- and top-range consumer products.

Nightmarket

Shilin Nightmarket
p274, B3
Located right outside Jiantan MRT Station, this is Taiwan's best-known nightmarket. A new facility right across from the station houses hundreds of food vendors. The streets and alleys of the surrounding neighbourhood are stuffed with vendors hawking clothes, shoes, accessories, toys, CDs, and more. Quality is generally good, prices low. Look for the brand names like Esprit, which sell off-season items at steep discounts.

Tea

King Ping Best Tea
2, Lane 124, Zhongshan N. Rd Sec. 7. Tel: 02-2871 7811. www.kingping.com.tw Off map
This firm has repeatedly won awards in Taiwan for its premium-blend teas. Displays clearly show tea leaf of different character in varying grades. The packaging used is very appealing, making its blends popular gift items.

RESTAURANTS, BARS, AND CAFÉS

Restaurants

American

Jake's Country Kitchen

705 Zhongshan N. Rd Sec. 6. Tel: 02-2871 5289. Open: daily 6.30am–midnight. **$$** p274, C1

A Tianmu institution since 1979, Jake's is a veritable home-away-from-home for the district's expats. This cozy nook specializes in US family fare and Mexican standards. Popular new menu additions include the Chicken Mole, made with chocolate and over 10 spices, blended with banana.

A sweet treat and coffee.

Balinese

Kopi Bale

43, Lane 621, Beian Rd. Tel: 02-2533 1218. Open: daily L & D. **$$** p274, E4

The wood decor here, with wicker chairs and mats for seating, calmly evokes the island paradise, the owners' homeland. The Balinese curry is popular, as are the fried noodles and rice, and the deep-fried fish and chips with tartar sauce.

Chinese

Fang's Restaurant

7 Tianmu E. Rd. Tel: 02-2872 8402. http://fangs-restaurant.modo.com.tw Open: daily L & D. **$$** p274, C1

Fang's (est. 1981) has a solid reputation for its Shanghai and Jiangzhe cuisine. There is an extensive range of *xiaolongbao* steamed dumplings. The *zuiji* ("drunken chicken") is truly delightful. Only beer and fiery sorghum spirits served.

Golden Dragon Restaurant

6F, Grand Hotel, 1 Zhongshan N. Rd Sec. 4. Tel: 02-2886 8888 ext. 1262. www.grand-hotel.org Open: daily L & D. **$$** (dim sum) **$$$** p274, C4

The Grand may no longer be the top spot to spend the night, but its Cantonese cuisine is still top-tier. Today's chefs continue to use the secrets originally passed on by the premier chefs who came to Taiwan with Chiang Kai-shek. The emphasis is on fresh seafood and dim sum. Superb views of the Taipei Basin.

Grand Garden Restaurant

1F, Grand Hotel, 1 Zhongshan N. Rd Sec. 4. Tel: 02-2886 8888 ext. 1211. www.grand-hotel.org Open: Mon–Fri B, L, afternoon tea & D, Sat–Sun L, D & afternoon tea. **$$$** p274, C4

Amidst elegant imperial-style surroundings and subtle, unobtrusive staff, you can savor both Eastern and Western dishes. The abundant afternoon tea buffet is highly recommended.

Hwa Young Gourmet and Banquet

5F, 20 Jingye 3rd Road. Tel: 02-2175 3888. Open: Mon–Fri 11.30am–3pm, 5.30–10pm, Sat–Sun 11.30am–4.30pm, 5.30–10pm . **$$** p274, E3

If you fancy the raucous dining experience in a big hall-like restaurant that locals so love, visit this spot in Miramar Entertainment Park. The dim sum and à la carte seafood selections are best. Limited English.

Silks Palace

221 Zhishan Rd, Sec. 2. Tel: (02) 2882 9393. www.silkspalace.com.tw Open: daily 11am–9.30pm. **$$/$$$** p274, E1

In a sumptuous facility on the National Palace Museum grounds, featuring glass walls three stories high, Silks Palace prepares the culinary greats of Taiwan and China. A special treat is "eating" famous NPM masterpieces, such as a chef-made version of the Jade Cabbage, Meat-shaped Stone, and White Jade Branch of Elegant

Lychee.

Yuan Yuan
1F, Grand Hotel, 1 Zhongshan N. Rd Sec. 4.
Tel: 02-2886 8888 ext. 1241. www.grand-hotel.org Open: daily 11am–9pm. **$$$**
p274, C4
In North China, wheat and millet are the starch staples rather than rice, and this is reflected in the Northern culinary delights here. Tender beef noodle soup, soft steamed dumplings, and rich broths and soups are all artfully whipped up in an attractive show kitchen.

French

Chez Jimmy
27, Lane 50, Tianmu E. Rd. Tel: 02-2874 7185. Open: daily L & D. **$$$** p274, C1
Chef Jimmy Chang was running the Sheraton Taipei's French restaurant when local fans bankrolled Chez Jimmy; you often see black limos parked outside. The chef's personal favorites are grilled sirloin with anchovy butter and tuna tartare with ginger and caviar.

Indian

Café India
1F, 30 Keqiang St. Tel: 02-2837 7365.
www.cafeindia.com.tw Open: daily L & D.
$$$ p274, C1
Serves a wide range of South Asian fare, with over 60 menu entries. Don't miss the cubed lamb or chicken *masala tawas* (*tawas* refers to the concave iron hot plates used). Good-value buffet lunches on weekends.

Italian

Davinci
1 Xueyuan Rd. Tel: 02-2891 7963. Open: daily 11.30am–9.30pm. **$$** p274, A1
Italian cuisine in an elegant setting, with good views of Taipei and the Danshui River. Try the veal with foie gras d'oie and roasted seafoods. There is also a range of good pasta dishes. Menu has English, but staff will struggle.

Japanese

Chikurintei
2F, Spring City Resort Hotel, 18 Youya Rd. Tel:

02-2892 4546 ext. 25. www.springresort.com.tw Open: daily L & D. **$$$** p274, A1
In one of Beitou's hot-spring resorts, offering splendid views of the surrounding hills and mouth-watering creations such as Taraba crab hot pot. Offers à la carte and good-value seasonal set menus.

Taiwanese

Cha for Tea
555 Zhongshan N. Rd Sec. 5. Tel: 02-2888 2929. www.chafortea.com.tw Open: daily 11am–11pm. **$$** p274, C2
A bright outlet of a growing chain. Teas, of course, are on the menu, but what is special is the "tea cuisine." Try the green-tea mango mousse, tea-leaf tempura, and tea chicken. Has outdoor seating, rare in Taipei.

Bars and cafés

Alleycat's
31, Lane 35, Zhongshan N. Rd Sec. 6. Tel: 02-2835 6491. www.alleycatspizza.com
p274, C1
Perhaps best described as a "pizza bar," has an extensive bar list, and good cocktails. Serves thick, inexpensive stone oven-baked pizzas, one of Taipei's few spots with "real" pizza outside the big international chains. With expat owners, this is a favorite late-night expat hangout.

Hsien-chu-fu Café
221 Zhishan Rd Sec. 2. Tel: 02-2881 2021 ext. 2359. www.npm.gov.tw p274, E1
In the National Palace Museum, on the first floor of the East Wing, this bright and airy space allows grand mountain views to pour in through tall French windows. Has a good selection of international coffees and light foods. Large reproductions of the museum's art treasures lend a touch of class.

Patio84
84-1 Tianmu E. Rd. Tel: 02-2873 3263.
p274, C1
Formerly known as Green Bar, this roadhouse-type place inspires loud talk and the swilling of beer. Big sports events are screened

Colorful cocktails.

and the outdoor patio is invariably packed. Kitchen open late serving mostly Tex-Mex pub food. Tap and bottled beers. Happy hour every day from 4–8 pm.

The Pig & Whistle
78 Tianmu E. Rd
Tel: 02-2873 8898. p274, C1
A perennial Tianmu favorite, this British-style pub has appropriate sports on the big screen. It is also relaxed enough in the afternoon and early evening to bring the kids along. The fish and chips with house red-wine vinegar are very good.

TNUA Cafeteria
1 Xueyuan Rd. Tel: 02-2896 1292. p274, A1
In the National University of the Arts, a good place if visiting Guandu. Open 7am–8pm, the comfy outdoor patio has superb night views of twinkling Taipei. Try the Huisun Arabica beans, long grown in Taiwan's central mountains.

THE NATIONAL PALACE MUSEUM

Not only one of the world's largest collections of Chinese artistic treasures, here is a chronicle of 5,000 years of Chinese history and heritage.

Housed within the museum (see page 176) are over 650,000 artifacts, rare books, and documents, the majority of which were the personal possession of the emperor or part of the imperial archives. The trove has its origins in the Song dynasty (960–1279), but later emperors added to the collection, which reached its zenith in the Qing dynasty, whose Manchu rulers were particularly avid at expanding the trove. When the empire fell and the Republic was established, an Exhibition Office was set up to take charge of the imperial collection.

In 1931, the Japanese began aggression against China. The best of the collection – over 13,000 crates – was hastily hauled away for safety. Shortly before the Nationalists fled the mainland, the top treasures were secretly sent to Taiwan by ship. The collection came to its current home in the 1960s. Hauled over 10,000km (6,000 miles) through 23 towns, over 32 years, it is said not a single piece was damaged. The collection is so vast that only a minor portion can be put on display at any one time. The remainder sits in temperature-controlled tunnels.

The Jadeite Cabbage with Insects is undoubtedly the museum's "Mona Lisa" – its signature piece. It was carved to match the natural colors of the jadeite block used, a response by the artist to nature's own hand. The Chinese cabbage has a white body and green leaves; it is considered to be a symbol of purity and virtue. The katydids on the leaves are a blessing for progeny, and indeed, this Qing dynasty artifact was originally part of the dowry for a concubine.

The Essentials

Address: 221 Zhishan Rd Sec.2, www.npm.gov.tw
Tel: 02-2881 2021
Opening Hrs: daily 8.30am–6.30pm; Fri–Sat until 9pm
Entrance Fee: charge, Children's Gallery free
Transport: Shilin MRT, then Red 30 bus

Crates of artifacts were stored in Taichung after arriving on the island.

On the steps at the grand entrance to the National Palace Museum.

The museum is noted for its collection of Song dynasty (960–1279) ceramics, which demonstrate an elegant simplicity very much in contrast to the ornate embellishment that defines Qing dynasty works. The Ru kiln, commissioned exclusively by the court, and a specialist in celadon wares, was the greatest of the major Song dynasty ceramics producers. Today, a mere 50 or so works from this source still exist, and the museum is home to 20 or so, including the delicate Lotus Bowl. Ru ware is known for its warm, opaque glazes, and also known for the fine crackle on the glaze surface, known as "crab claw markings." Ru ware was fired standing on spurs so that the glaze covered the entire vessel.

This sumptuous work, Four Magpies in Early Spring (only a section is shown here), was created by an anonymous artist of the Yuan dynasty (1279–1368). It is a hanging scroll of silk threads embroidered onto a deep blue base. The fineness of the threads is characteristic of the Yuan dynasty. Depicted are flowers like narcissi, plum blossoms and camellias, decorative rocks, and magpies. Taken together, the piece symbolizes the prosperous and bounteous arrival of spring. The magpies are traditionally believed by the Chinese to symbolize happiness.

This globular vase with dragon motif in underglaze blue from the Yongle period (1403–25) of the Ming dynasty is known as a "celestial globe" (tianqiu) due to its large, almost spherical body. The cobalt blue glaze has long been associated with Chinese porcelain outside of China because pieces such as these were often traded or given as gifts to foreigners during the period.

This Summer Crown is significant not only because it dates from the Qing dynasty, but also because it was worn by the Qianlong Emperor (reigned 1735–96). The study of this and other costume elements in the museum collection has yielded insight into the strict rules governing court regalia at the time.

This meter- (3ft-) long scroll painting (only a small section is shown here) by Qing dynasty (1644–1911) court painters is one of the most dazzlingly detailed paintings in the collection. Entitled Along the River during the Qing Ming Festival, it copies an earlier Song dynasty (960–1279) work, but portrays the lifestyles of the Qing dynasty, such as the lively street entertainment popular at the time. It also shows the influence of Western painting techniques.

This brilliant silk painting by an anonymous artist from the Tang dynasty (618–907) portrays 10 ladies of the inner court at leisure. Entitled A Palace Concert, it shows four ladies playing musical instruments while the others drink tea or wine.

This gilt bronze statue of Shakyamuni Buddha, dating from the Northern Wei dynasty (386–534), is one of the museum's oldest Buddhist artworks. The detail on the gilding is extremely fine. The large halo behind the seated Buddha, for instance, is decorated with flame motifs and the images of seven Buddhas. Behind the halo are scenes from the life of Shakyamuni Buddha. This piece is of Chinese provenance; the majority of the Buddhist artifacts in the museum are Tibetan, including mandalas and other objects.

Displayed on the wall is a reproduction of the priceless work of calligraphy Autobiography, by Huai Su, a monk who lived during the Tang dynasty (618–907). When it was written in 777, it captivated the scholarly class with its particularly expressive and unrestrained "cursive" style. It is prized for attaining a spirit of freedom while maintaining a controlled technique. Like other rare works classified as "national treasures," the original piece is only put on display once every three years to prevent rapid deterioration. If it is not on display during your visit, there are other works equally worth admiring. Wang Xizhi of the Jin dynasty (AD 265-420) is considered the "Sage of Calligraphy," and influenced many others. Look out for the Tang dynasty copy of his Clearing After Snowfall.

IN THE ZHISHAN GARDEN

Located on the east side of the museum is the exquisitely landscaped Zhishan Garden. Measuring some 16,000 sq meters (19,000 sq yds), the grounds consciously evoke the great classical gardens of imperial China. Shady pathways meander leisurely among carefully tended trees, shrubs, and flowers. Indeed, the philosophy of classical Chinese gardens has been to create a free-flowing, organic format that invites wandering, unlike the symmetry of buildings.

In the National Museum Palace Garden.

This is a carved red sandalwood curio chest containing 30 items, dating from the Qing dynasty (1644–1911), whose emperors were fond of them. Each chest contained tiny paintings or calligraphic works, porcelain and jade figurines, and even Western miniatures.

YANGMINGSHAN

Yangmingshan stands right on the Taipei's north doorstep and is Taiwan's crowning national park, a mountain oasis offering an accessible respite from the urban pressures of life in the relentlessly bustling city over which it looks.

The cluster of mountains that forms the westernmost end of the Datun mountain range also forms the northern wall of the Taipei Basin, in which the city sits. Known collectively as Yangmingshan, or Mount Yangming, they were formed in a period of intense volcanic activity about 2 million years ago.

The days of geological excitement are over, but the mountains still give vent to the thermal activity below, creating Yangmingshan's best-loved attractions – fumaroles and hot springs. Hot-spring inns and public pools abound, and in winter the roads are packed into the wee hours with those on their way to and from seeking relief for bones and joints.

Most tourist attractions lie along the Yang-Jin Highway (Yang-Jin Gonglu), which stretches from Shilin District in north Taipei to the fishing port of Jinshan on the North Coast. The highway is also called Yangde Boulevard on the Taipei side. It slides through the saddle between Yangmingshan's two highest peaks, the 1,080-meter (3,543ft) Mount Datun on the west and the 1,120-meter (3,739ft) Mount Qixing on the east. The journey from downtown Taipei to Yangming Park, the starting point for most visits to the national park, takes about 45 minutes by private vehicle.

Yangmingshan National Park

The primary attractions for overseas visitors are the hiking opportunities, which open up green expanses, wide vistas, and a rich variety of resident and migratory fauna. The pristine **Yangmingshan National Park** (Yangmingshan Guojia Gongyuan) takes up the middle and higher

A stunning bird's-eye view from Yangmingshan over the city.

reaches of the mountain. The core of the national park is the lovely, sculpted Yangming Park.

Lin Yutang House ❶

Address: 141 Yangde Boulevard Sec. 2, www.linyutang.org.tw
Tel: 02-2861 3003
Opening Hrs: Tue–Sun 9am–5pm
Entrance Fee: charge
Transportation: Shilin

Right beside the highway, on the lower reaches of Yangmingshan's southern slopes, is the **Lin Yutang House** (Lin Yutang Guju), former home of the renowned linguist, philosopher, poet, and inventor. Educated in the West and a prolific writer in English, Lin (1895–1976) was to the Western world a key voice representing the Chinese in the first half of the 20th century. Swept up in the great Nationalist exodus from China to Taiwan after the Chinese Civil War, he eventually settled in this self-designed villa.

The white stucco residence was built with elements of the Spanish hacienda style. There is a calm inner courtyard with a garden and a fish pond. Inside the house is a memorial library and Lin's personal effects. There is also a backyard café with bird's-eye views, perfect for enjoying fresh mountain air and solitude. Guided tours are available (advance notice).

Yangming Park ❷

Continuing uphill, **Yangming Park** (Yangming Gongyuan) is the first major destination within the national park (daily 8am–6.30pm; admission charge). During the Japanese colonial period, this was an experimental botanical garden, which the KMT government built upon when the national park was established in 1985. The grounds are magnificent – packed with ponds, waterfalls, grottoes, gardens, groves, and brilliant colors. The Feb–Mar bloom of cherry blossoms, azaleas, and camellias is especially delightful, celebrated with the Yangmingshan Flower Season festival. The place gets busy on non-working days; if possible, use public transport. When the crowds lessen, the many resident bird and butterfly species come out of hiding.

WHERE

From Taipei Railway Station, take bus 260 for all sites on the main highway to Yangming Park, the bus route's terminus.

The National Park is a popular place to unwind.

The rooms in Lin Yutang's house, including the bedroom shown here, are displayed basically in the state he left them when he passed away in 1976.

National Park Visitor Center ❸

Address: 1-20 Zhuzihu Road, www.ymsnp.gov.tw
Tel: 02-2861 5741
Opening Hrs: daily 8.30am–4.30pm (closed last Mon of the month)
Entrance Fee: free
Transportation: Shilin

About 400-meters/yds uphill via a connecting trail from Yangming Park is the **Yangmingshan National Park Visitor Center** (Youke Fuwu Zhongxin), which should be the first stop-off point for those wanting to explore the areas outside Yangming Park. Inside are valuable exhibits on the unique flora, fauna, geology, and trails of the Yangmingshan massif, with a large-scale 3D map invaluable for helping to get your bearings and understand the terrain. The English here and in the free maps and other print info is good.

This is also the place to book guide services and one of the park's few campsites.

Yangming Villa ❹

Address: 12 Zhongxing Road, www.ymsnp.gov.tw
Tel: 02-2861 1444
Opening Hrs: daily 9am–4.30pm (closed last Mon of month)
Entrance Fee: charge
Transportation: Shilin

Off the main highway north of the visitor center is Yangming Villa (Yangming Shuwu), a hot-springs inn during the Japanese era that was renovated in 1971 by Chiang Kai-shek, the last of his three Taipei residences. His summer retreat from the city heat, the expansive, heavily wooded grounds have bunkers, barracks, and at least one secret escape tunnel. The buildings are in a dark green hue for camouflage.

From the second-level balcony of the main residence, one can see the Danshui River snaking all the way to the port of Danshui. Chiang loved the views, which reminded him of China. The interior is as it was in

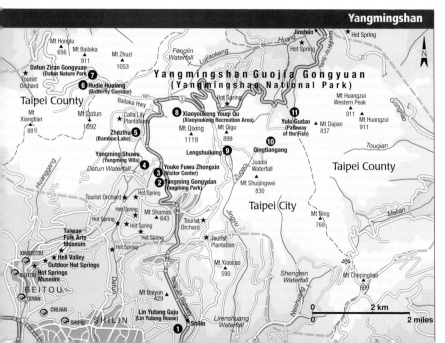

his day. Visitors can sit on the stone bench, amid his plum trees, where he and Madame Chiang sat together feeding the fish.

Caoshan, or "Grass Mountain," was Yangmingshan's original name, referring to the tall silvergrass that covers the highest slopes. Chiang renamed it Mount Yangming after his favorite Ming philosopher Wang Yangming (1472–1529). All visits beyond the visitor center are conducted with guides, on one-hour tours; tours for individuals are at 9am and 1.30pm.

Bamboo Lake ❺

About half a mile (1km) north of the visitor center, just before the Yang-Jin Highway passes through the Datun-Qixing saddle, is **Bamboo Lake** (Zhuzihu), situated in a depression created when lava flows from Mount Qixing piled up on its western side.

There is no lake today. The marshy depression was drained by the Japanese to conduct agricultural experiments. This is where the regionally famous Penglai rice was invented, making Taiwan a rice basket for the Japanese empire and China. Today the basin is filled with farms raising crops for sale in the city, and is best known for exotic flowers and, in particular, calla lilies.

Buying flowers and produce is much cheaper here than in the city. Many farms also have dedicated restaurants with courtyard and patio seating, bringing gourmands in great hordes on weekends. Expats in the know like to stroll along the depression's tree-shaded loop road on weekdays, stopping for a light meal and beer at one of the restaurants.

Yangmingshan is famous for its calla lilies (Zantedeschia aethiopica), and the Calla Lily Festival is a major part of the annual Taipei Flower Festival (Taibei Huaji) organized by the city in the spring.

SHOPPING

There is limited shopping in this area, with its low concentration of residences outside park boundaries. The venues that exist are primarily aimed at the tourist, either items such as souvenirs and mementoes or fresh foods and produce at the many recreational farms inside and outside the park's borders.

Food

Mama Yang's Pickles
118 Pingjing Rd. Tel: 02-2861 2170.
Sells fresh organic vegetables grown on the surrounding farm, as well as house-crafted preserves. Many are pickled Chinese-style in a soy-sauce base.
Wellcome Supermarket
7 Gezhi Rd. Tel: 02-2862 4435.
www.wellcome.com.tw
The only supermarket on Yangmingshan, in the only true village, just before Chinese Culture University on the main highway. Close to the national park, with many

related items for day-outings, such as BBQ foods. An extra-large wine and spirits section. Open 24 hours.

Flowers and plants

Huayushu Horticulture
51 Zhuzihu Rd. Tel: 02-2862 1791.
This is one of Bamboo Lake's biggest and best-known cash-crop farms, with great flower and plant variety. Depending on the season, pick your own calla lilies, sunflowers, or lavender, or buy them at the shop. There's also a variety of sweet grasses used in local kitchens.
Mojing Garden
54 Zhuzihu Rd. Tel: 02-2862 5109.
A splendid Bamboo Lake operation with friendly staff, specializing in bonsai and myriad other forms of potted plant life intended as home and garden ornamentation.

Gifts and souvenirs

Lin Yutang House

141 Yangde Blvd Sec. 2. Tel: 02-2861 3003 ext. 11. www.linyutang.org.tw
Stationery such as commemorative pens, postcards, letter paper, and envelopes, white porcelain tableware such as teacups, bowls, and plates, editions of Lin's books and related publications.
Yangmingshan National Park Visitor Center
1-20 Zhuzihu Rd. Tel: 02-2861 5741, www.ymsnp.gov.tw.
Publications on themes related to the park, maps and other items, plus souvenirs such as hats, T-shirts, and postcards.
Yangming Park
Located in the national park, just south of the visitor center, there is a popular food and shopping area on the park's west side. Fresh local farm foods and packaged snack foods can be purchased, along with items for having park fun such as locally made kites, umbrellas, and more.

Grazing buffalo at Qingtiangang.

The valley of Bamboo Lake.

Butterfly Corridor ❻

Just north of Bamboo Lake, on the southwestern slope of Mount Datun, the Bailaka Highway (County Highway 101) heads west off the main highway. Follow the path beside the road for about half a mile (1km) to the entrance of **Butterfly Corridor** (Hudie Hualang). This is a heavily shaded, easy 1.8km (1.1-mile) trail that gives visitors the chance to see some of the area's 151 species of butterfly. Though hot, the period of June–Sept just after the rainy season (May for higher altitudes) is a good time to visit – it is the peak nectar and pollen season for the butterflies.

Datun Nature Park ❼

The entrance to **Datun Nature Park** (Datun Ziran Gongyuan) is practically across from the entrance to Butterfly Corridor (daily 9am–4.30pm, closed last Mon of month, tel: 02-2861 7294). This reserve is laced with well-tended raised wooden walkways. One trail snakes through tall swaying silvergrass before nearing the peak of Mount Datun. The vistas from the observation platform are more than worth the walk. There is road access too to this point, as well as to most major spots in the nature park. The peak itself is off-limits, the site of a "secret" military listening post spying on China.

Xiaoyoukeng ❽

Address: 69 Zhuzihu Road, www.ymsnp.gov.tw
Tel: 02-2861 7024
Opening Hrs: daily 9am–4.30pm (closed last Mon of month)
Entrance Fee: charge
Transportation: Shilin

Back on the Yang-Jin Highway, in the Datun-Qixing saddle, is the **Xiaoyoukeng Recreation Area** (Xiaoyoukeng Youqi Qu), whose star attraction is the fuming Xiaoyoukeng, or "Little Oil Pit." The "oil" is actually acidic water, and the fumarole belches gas and steam. The **Xiaoyoukeng Visitor Center** (Xiaoyoukeng Fuwu Zhongxin) has scale models, a viewing terrace, movie on local nature topics (free), and a parking lot. If possible, avoid this place on weekends. A trail of medium difficulty leads from here to the top of Mount Qixing. The hike takes about an hour one way. Guided tours are available (booking needed).

Lengshuikeng ❾

Jingshan Road traverses the eastern mid-slopes of Mount Qixing, accessed from the main highway just below Chinese Culture University. The first major tourist spot along here is **Lengshuikeng**, or "Cold Water Pit." Here, waters heated deep beneath the surface mix with cold water gushing from

a scar in the earth created by volcanic activity, resulting in a hot spring with lower temperatures than usual. There are public baths (daily 24 hours; free), with separate male/female facilities and a wading pool for foot-soaking. There is also a visitor center with a snack shop and info displays (daily 9am–4.30pm, closed last Mon of month; tel: 02-2861 0036). Guided tours should be booked prior to the visit.

Qingtiangang

Just east of Lengshuikeng is the wide plateau of **Qingtiangang** ❿, formed by ancient backed-up lava flow from the surrounding extinct volcanoes (daily 9am–4.30pm, closed last Mon of the month; vehicle admission charge; tel: 02-2861 5404). The grass here has been chewed to putting-green

consistency by a herd of tame water buffalo. It is the highest point on the **Pathway of the Fish** ⓫ (Yulu Gudao), an old smuggling route used to get fresh catch from Jinshan port into Taipei Basin past Japanese tax officials. Some who resisted the Japanese military held out for years at Qingtiangang's fortifications. Visit the mock-up of an old gate at the top of the bluffs overlooking Jinshan. The Japanese eventually prevailed, widening the pathway for horse and cannon travel.

The pathway here follows a rushing stream and is dotted with abandoned settlers' huts and picturesque small stone-arch bridges. The rest of the path is today's Jingshan Road and connecting sections of the Yang-Jin Highway. Note that visitor numbers are high on weekends, and vehicle numbers controlled.

Xiaoyoukeng's barren moonscape is covered with bright yellow formations of crystallized sulfur.

RESTAURANTS

Chinese

Chin Tein Restaurant
Rooftop, Landis Resort Yangmingshan, 237 Gezhi Rd. Tel: 02-2861 6661. www.landis resort.com.tw Open: daily 7am–9.30pm. $$$
This rooftop venue is a Taipei rarity with wonderful views of the mountain. It is packed for breakfast on weekends. Try the purple-yam porridge and the distinctive egg-based recipes. Offers a full Chinese-style BBQ menu at night for groups (advance notice).

International

Shan Lan Café
1F, Landis Resort Yangmingshan. Tel: 02-2861 6661. www.landisresort.com.tw Open: daily 7am– 9.30pm. $$

Indoor and outdoor seating with big views, improved further with premium coffees from around the globe. Chinese, American, and Continental breakfasts, plus standard Taiwanese café selections at other times. The beef noodle soup, noodle dishes, and sandwich platters are especially good.

Tein He Restaurant
2F, Landis Resort Yangmingshan. Tel: 02-2861 6661. www.landisresort.com.tw Open: daily L & D. $$$
Fine international fusion cuisine is offered at this bay-windowed, white and cream Art Deco venue. Try the arum (calla) lily soup and salad, with all ingredients sourced from the park's Bamboo Lake.

You-Bu-Wei-Jhai Café
141 Yangde Blvd Sec. 2. Tel: 02-2861 3003 ext. 11. www.linyutang.org.tw Open: Tue–Sun 10am–9pm. $$
Situated in the Lin Yutang House, a heritage site overlooking Taipei Basin, has seating in a leafy courtyard patio. A good selection of international coffees and inexpen-

sive Chinese-style set meals, sandwiches, etc.

Taiwanese

Shanmu Lin (China Fir Forest)
55-12 Zhuzihu Rd. Tel: 02-2861 7159. Open: daily 10.30am–10pm. $$$
"Shanmu Lin" means "fir forest," and it is rare in Taipei to dine outdoors among natural growth. The vegetable dishes and soups incorporate arum lily, orchid, and other flowers from the Bamboo Lake farms.

Stone House Restaurant
63 Zhuzihu Rd. Tel: 02-2861 2453. www.stonehouse63.com Open: Tue–Sun 11.30am–10pm. $$$
The name literally means "evergreen cottage," a lovely old stone ploughman's cottage converted to serve fine free-range chicken and fresh greens from the owners' farm (they are English-speaking, having lived in the US). Wash it down with big mugs of draft. NT$850 minimum per person charge for sitting on the outdoor patio.

Relaxing by Danshui waterfront.

DANSHUI AND BALI

These two river towns – one a former military outpost and port, the other a sleepy fishing village – boast wide waterfront concourses, bike paths, old-style shops and snacks, preserved colonial and historical relics, and the world's northernmost mangrove forest.

Danshui, an old port city about 20km (12 miles) northwest of Taipei, has enjoyed a dramatic revival as a tourist attraction. In the old days, it took an hour to drive from Taipei, and once there, the congested lanes and cluttered waterfront presented formidable obstacles to even the most determined visitors.

Times have changed. The MRT now whisks visitors from downtown Taipei to Danshui in 30 air-conditioned minutes, and Danshui itself has become a tourist-friendly town with wide waterfront concourses, abundant seafood restaurants, boat rides, unique snacks, and carnival games. New attractions aside, it is still home to the colonial-era forts, embassy, and other historical sites that first made it famous.

Meanwhile, across the river, an equally remarkable renaissance has taken place in Bali, a once-sleepy town that now boasts its own tourist attractions, including a waterfront bicycle path, a well-preserved mangrove swamp, and the astounding Shihsanhang Museum of Archaeology. Ferries ply the placid Danshui River, carrying day-trippers back and forth between these two tourist hubs, now Taipei's most popular weekend getaways.

Danshui

Located at the mouth of the Danshui, this spot and the nearby city of Keelung are where Taiwan's early Western colonists – the Spanish and the Dutch – made their landings. Danshui's high bluffs provided strategic views of river and ocean, and began to be fortified in 1629. Under this protective umbrella, seaborne trade thrived, and Chinese and other seafarers made regular visits. It was also a vital watering stop (*Danshui* means "fresh water") on the trade

Colonial Fort San Domingo.

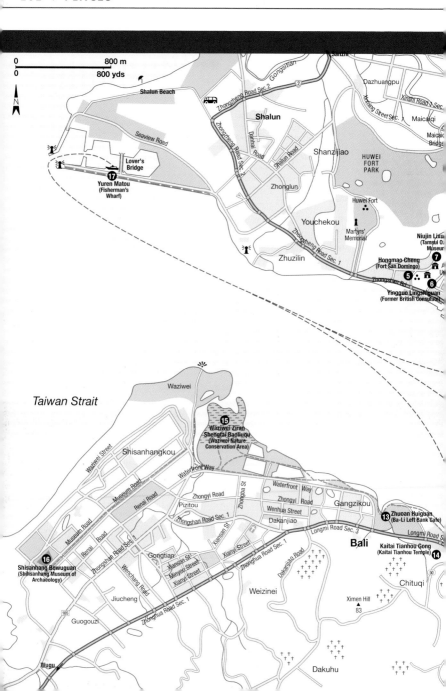

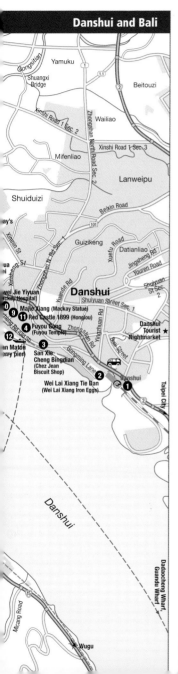

Danshui and Bali

routes that connected Hong Kong and Southeast Asia to Japan and the US. Additionally, its location on a fertile stretch of seacoast supported a thriving fishing industry.

Today, Danshui's location and history attract tourists in abundance. But instead of scouring the seas for enemy ships, visitors to old Fort San Domingo now gather to admire the sunsets. The nearby sea still supports a viable industry, but the commercial fisheries now supply the local seafood restaurants. Even the traditional snacks have historical origins. The trading companies long ago left for Taipei, but their descendants are still here, plying the tourist trade. The area surrounding **Danshui MRT station ➊** is abuzz with street musicians and artists, giving it a lively, vacation atmosphere rarely found in Taipei city.

Gongming Lane

Walking west from the MRT station along the waterfront, you reach bustling, pedestrianized **Gongming Lane**, a typically Taiwanese nightmarket street chock-a-block with grilled seafood, hot battered fishballs,

Danshui's giant ice-cream cones.

fried tofu, cheap clothes, souvenirs, and more.

Right at the entrance is **Wei Lai Xiang Iron Eggs** ❷ (Wei Lai Xiang Tie Dan). Since 1946, this shop (tel: 02-8631 0171) has been making *tie dan*, or iron eggs, a famous Danshui snack invented to preserve eggs for local fishermen. These are chicken or quail eggs cooked for many hours in a pot filled with fermented bean paste, soy sauce, sugar, and various spices, until the eggs turn jet black. They taste better than the name sounds – the outside of the egg is rubbery but flavorful, while the inside is a crumbly, tasty yolk. They come in five flavors, from sweet to very spicy.

Vacuum-packed iron eggs make for a great edible souvenir to take home.

Old Street

Gongming Lane eventually merges into Zhongzheng Road, often called **Old Street** (Lao Jie), home to wonderful renovated old trading houses. These tiend and elegant buildings are five or six stories tall, and hark back to the days when Danshui was a key trading port. Also of interest are the many little shops selling folk crafts and other items and snacks reminiscent of yesteryear.

Shopping for beach footwear and treats on Old Street.

Definitely worth a stop is **Chez Jean Biscuit Shop** ❸ (San Xie Cheng Bingdian), which has been serving dozens of traditional Taiwanese confections since 1935 (81 Zhongzheng Rd; daily 9am–8.30pm; tel: 02-2621 2177; www.sanxiecheng.com.tw). There are free samples of their sesame crisp (*zima su*), green tea biscuit (*lücha gao*), pineapple cake (*fengli su*), and other goodies. But be warned: try one, and you might get hooked.

The pumpkin pastry (*jinguarou bing*) is superb. When here, take the time to go to the basement to view the informal but impressive display of traditional Chinese confectionery molds, many of which are used to make the turtle-shaped cakes that serve as prayer offerings (turtles symbolize long life). There are no signs leading to this unofficial museum of sorts; just go down the stairs in the rear of the shop.

Further up Zhongzheng Road, at No. 200, is **Fuyou Temple** ❹ (Fuyou Gong). This venerable Taoist temple is dedicated to the goddess Mazu, patron saint of fishermen and seafarers. The temple is thick with the smell of candles and incense, and the beams are blackened with the smoke of long

BLACK-BEARD

George Leslie Mackay (1844–1901) was born in Ontario, Canada. At the age of 28, he was commissioned as the first foreign missionary of the Canadian Presbyterian Mission. He set up his mission station in Danshui, where he stayed for the rest of his life. Besides his evangelistic efforts, he was a dentist and educator, and despite being given the moniker "black-bearded barbarian" by the locals, he was well respected for his medical work and benevolence. An important figure in Danshui's history, his legacy includes a nursing school, hospital, college, and ethnography entitled *From Far Formosa: The Island, Its People and Missions.*

Sweet treats.

years. The place has an eerie, unearthly feel, especially on a rainy afternoon.

From here, a good strategy for a one-day visit to Danshui is to take a 10-minute taxi ride up to Fort San Domingo, before strolling back down to the waterfront and taking a ferry to Bali.

Fort San Domingo ❺

Address: 1, Lane 28, Zhongzheng Road, Danshui
Tel: 02-2623 1001
Opening Hrs: Tue–Sun 9am–5pm
Entrance Fee: charge
Transportation: Danshui

Fort San Domingo (Hongmao Cheng) is perhaps the most famous attraction in Danshui. From the entrance, a short walk up a garden path leads to the red stone buttresses of the ancient fort, which overlooks the mouth of the Danshui River. This sturdy building neatly timelines much of Taipei's colonial history. The Spanish built it in 1629 and the Dutch occupied it in 1642. Twenty

years later it was rebuilt by Chinese invaders, after Qing dynasty forces seized control of Taiwan. Its name in Chinese roughly means "fort of the red-haired ones," referring, of course, to the Western colonizers.

In 1867, the British leased the fort, painted it red, and turned the entire compound into a consulate. A footpath runs from the fort to the **Former British Consulate ❻** (Yingguo Lingshiguan), a Victorian structure completed in 1891. It is a fine example of colonial architecture, and its graceful verandas and vaulting bay windows evoke impressions of a distant era, when Taipei was considered an exotic posting on the remote side of the world. Because it commands such lofty views of the Danshui River and the Pacific Ocean, this was once a good place from which to fire cannons. Now it is a good place to view the famous Danshui sunsets. In 1972, after Britain officially recognized mainland China, it returned the fort and the consulate to Taiwan.

Aletheia University

After leaving Fort San Domingo, a left turn up a steep road leads to the

WHERE

Fort San Domingo can be reached by taking bus Red 26 from Danshui MRT station. This bus continues onward to Fisherman's Wharf.

The bust of George Leslie Mackay.

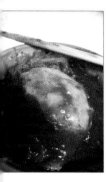

Gung ho gourmands can try the extra spicy A-Gei, which delivers a blast of peppery spice that will have you crying for a cold drink.

entrance of what is known today as **Aletheia University**, at No. 32 Zhenli Street. Founded by Canadian missionary Rev. Dr George Leslie Mackay (see page 204), it was Taiwan's first Western-style educational institution, with a broad-based curriculum. Across a garden and pond is the original Oxford College building, completed in 1882. Now it houses the small **Tamsui Oxford Museum** ❼ (Niujin Lixuetang), filled with photographs and memorabilia of Mackay, as well as information on the history of the university (open by appointment; free; tel: 02-2621 4043). Designed by Mackay, the building blends Eastern and Western elements in unique ways. The bricks and roof tiles were imported from Xiamen, China, and the symmetrical structure is laid out in the traditional Chinese format. But the doors and windows are decidedly Western, and on the roof, pagoda and cross stand side by side in perfect harmony.

Zhenli Street's A-Gei

Further down narrow Zhenli Street are hole-in-the-wall eateries, home of a famous Danshui snack called *A-Gei*. This Japanese-inspired dish consists of vermicelli crystal noodles stuffed inside a tofu skin, sealed shut with fish meat, and drenched in a savory red sauce. Try **Wenhua A-Gei** ❽, at No. 6-1 (daily 5am–3pm; tel: 02-2621 1785). One portion makes for a nice, light lunch.

Mackay memorials

At the end of Zhenli Street, cross Xinsheng Street and go down Jianshe Street until you reach a tiny, triangular park. Here is the **Mackay statue** ❾ (Majie Xiang), a large, black granite bust of the elegantly bearded man. West of the statue, narrow Mackay Street leads to **Mackay Hospital** ❿ (Huwei Jie Yiyuan), which was Taiwan's first Western hospital (no entry). It was built by Mackay, and is another example of Western colonial architecture combined with Chinese touches.

East of the Mackay statue, atop a hill reached by 106 stone steps, sits the **Red Castle 1899** ⓫ (Honglou) restaurant, a wonderfully remodeled colonial building. Built in 1899, the British structure was reopened as a restaurant in 2000. The red brick colonnades and green balustrades are punctuated by a sweeping banyan tree in the courtyard. Red Castle commands a magnificent view of the Danshui River and waterfront.

Danshui waterfront

At dusk, visitors gather to watch the sun set behind Guanyinshan across the river. The waterfront becomes a swirl of activity, with carnival games, blasts of smoke from grilled sausage and squid vendors, the shouts of happy children, and the lure of hawkers urging visitors to try their seafood.

Visitors may notice people carrying enormous ice-cream cones. These

SHOPPING

Danshui is an old port town now seeing a tourist renaissance, mostly with local day-trippers. In many forms, from old-time handicrafts to old-time foods to old-time medicines, it is "tradition" that is on sale here.

Arts and crafts

An-Ka Café
247 Zhongzheng Rd. Tel: 02-2626 0381.
The "An-Ka" means "encore," a reference to the many dolls and toys putting on a show for you. Decorated like a young girl's bedroom, all are handmade, many for sale. Good range of coffees and Taiwan-style coffee-based drinks.

Chinese medicines

Baoan Tang
89 Zhongzheng Rd.

Tel: 02-2621 2650.
The name translates as "preserve safety hall." This is a century-old Chinese medicine shop, still managed by the original family. Their ancient pharmacopeia knowledge is well known; whatever your chronic complaint, they'll have something for you.

Hand Puppets

Budaixi Specialty Hall
14 Chongjian St. Tel: 0918 371 921.
"Budaixi" translates as "Taiwan puppet theater." Filled with hand-puppets of intricate design, displaying Taiwan's many genres, all for sale, this shop has been in place for almost a hundred years, though it has a clean, bright, and modern-looking interior.

are another Danshui specialty: you can buy a 20-cm (8-inch) swirl of soft-serve atop a cone, while those with better balance and bigger appetites can buy a 50-cm (20-inch) swirl.

The Danshui **ferry pier** ⑫ (Duchuan Matou) connects Danshui to Bali and to Fisherman's Wharf. Two ferry companies serve Bali from the Danshui pier.

Bali

Bali is the quiet *yin* to the lively *yang* of Danshui. Instead of a buzzing funfair atmosphere, Bali offers a gentle riverside path that extends the 5km (3-mile) length of the waterfront, sometimes called the Bali Left Bank, and beyond into Taipei Basin. It passes the Waziwei Nature Conservation Area on the way to the Shihsanhang Museum of Archaeology. Bicycles and tandems can be rented, and the ride to the museum is flat and peaceful. Quality of bikes vary, so check them closely.

As a tourist attraction, Bali is young, and it shows in the boardwalks and young buildings and parks that dot the waterfront. From the comfortable alfresco perch of the **Waterfront Bali Restaurant** ⑬ (see page 209), Danshui looks like a small strip of lights lying at the foot of the brooding Datun peak.

A short distance away from Bali's ferry pier is the main road, Longmi Road, from where visitors can catch a bus to the Shihsanhang Museum. Across the road is **Kaitai Tianhou Temple** ⑭ (Kaitai Tianhou Gong), originally built in 1786, dedicated to the goddess Mazu, a cherished figure in a town that once made its living by fishing and trading. Even by Taiwanese standards, this temple bristles with dragons and other Taoist icons. Mazu is most commonly seen with a dark blue visage, but here has the rarer golden complexion.

About 1.5km (1 mile) west of the ferry pier, reached via Waterfront Way or bike path, is the **Waziwei Nature Conservation Area** ⑮ (Waziwei Ziran Shengtai Baoliuqu), the northernmost mangrove forest in the world. Nature-lovers flock to the area to watch the tiny fiddler crabs pop out of their holes and then scuttle back to the safety of the sand, among other ecological wonders. In Chinese, these claw-waving crustaceans are known as "the crabs who call the tide."

Shihsanhang Museum ⑯

Address: 200 Bowuguan Road, Bali Township, www.sshm.ntpc.gov.tw
Tel: 02-2619 1313
Opening Hrs: Apr–Oct Mon–Fri 9.30am–6pm, Sat–Sun 9.30am–7pm,

Danshui's waterfront is a magnet for Taipeiers of all ages.

FACT

The Shihsanhang archeological site was discovered in 1955 by an air force pilot, whose compass went crazy when he flew over the iron-rich site. The Shihsanhang people practiced the first native iron-smelting technology in Taiwan.

Nov–Mar Mon–Sun 9.30am–5pm
Entrance Fee: free
Transportation: Danshui

The US$13 million **Shihsanhang Museum of Archaeology** (Shisanhang Bowuguan), which opened in 2003, is a remarkable achievement. The building is a modern architectural masterpiece that has won widespread recognition – and the coveted Far East Architecture Award in 2003 – for its dramatic, angular design and user-friendly layouts. The exhibits boast detailed English – a rarity in Taiwan – and the museum is staffed by knowledgeable and friendly guides who speak Mandarin, English, or Japanese.

But the main attractions are the exhibits, which present a rich and moving cultural experience that illustrates Taiwan's prehistory. The museum is built atop an archeological site rich in relics from the Shisanhang people, who were occupied this fertile land some 500 to 1,800 years ago, and who first in Taiwan to have iron-smelting technology. They practiced agriculture and harvested clams and other seafood from the rich Danshui delta. Among the displays are cross sections of pits filled with clam shells, shark bones, and deer teeth – evidence of their diet.

Shihsanhang Museum of Archaeology.

They were also open to barter and trade and coexisted peacefully with the Dutch, Portuguese, and Chinese traders who frequented Danshui. But they were eventually overwhelmed by the flood of Chinese immigrants who settled in the Taipei area beginning in the 1600s. *Shisanhang* means "13 Companies," referring to the original 13 trading *hang* that operated here during the Qing dynasty.

The museum's most remarkable feature is perhaps the Timeline, an elegant suspended bridge that hovers four stories high, providing a bird's-eye view of the exhibits and a unique historical perspective.

Fisherman's Wharf ⑰

From Bali's ferry pier, visitors can take a ferry back across the river to **Fisherman's Wharf** (Yuren Matou), a long pier and harbor that has forsaken its fishing past and become another tourist attraction. The highlight of the wharf is its signature pedestrian bridge, Lover's Bridge (Qingren Qiao), an elegant suspended structure in the style of a sailing ship's mast and rigging, which spans the harbor and makes a dramatic addition to the visual esthetics of the area. This pier is a favorite with romantic couples.

RESTAURANTS

Chinese

Red Castle 1899
6, Lane 2, Sanmin St. Tel: 02-8631 1168.
www.redcastle-taiwan.com Open: daily 11am–10pm. $$$
On a hillside high above the river sits Red Castle, a beautifully renovated colonial building with a welcome blast of air conditioning. The first-floor restaurant serves old favorites like Chinese yam salad and spicy Danshui fishballs. Coffee, sandwiches, and desserts are served at the third-floor Coffee Bar. Good seasonal set menus.

Continental

Waterfront Bali Restaurant
39 Waterfront Way. Tel: 02-2619 5258.
www.waterfront.com.tw Open: daily 11am–9pm. $$
Located just north of the Bali pier is this huge two-level café with a roomy outdoor balcony, a spacious front lawn, and a peaceful view. The menu is mostly Western, with items like baked lamb chop, grilled salmon, and baked prawns in cheese. All the usual café beverages like iced coffee, espresso, and Japanese green tea are available. Menu in English.

ECoffee
69 Gongming St. Tel: 02-2626 3588.
www.ecoffee.com.te Open: 9am–midnight. $
With two floors, the first open to the street. Offers a good range of coffees for very low prices, and comfy seating that welcomes leisurely people-watching. Try the ice coffee, very sweet, a special Taiwan treat. Has Taiwanese snack foods.

No. 83 Café
83 Zhongzheng Rd. Tel: 02-2625 5100. $
This long-length, narrow-front shop opened in 2005, proving irresistible to tourists with its big original paintings of old Danshui and coffee-making machines everywhere. Has beans from around the world, its Arabica are the best and most popular.

South Train
1, Lane 51, Boai St. Tel: 02-2629 2688.
Open: daily 11.30am–10.30pm. $$
Train aficionado Wang Zhi-bi has created an establishment that is part restaurant and part museum, filled as it is with train models and paraphernalia. One half is a mock-up railroad dining car. A trained chef, Wang makes everything from scratch, and he recommends the casseroles (vegetarian, beef, or seafood) and noodles with local clams and home-made basil ketchup. Kitchen closes at 9pm.

Sunrise Café
13, Lane 56, Gongming St. Tel: 02-2621 6100. Open: daily 10.30am–11pm. $
Sunrise Café serves tea, coffee, and sandwiches alfresco. Its recommended beverages are the mango ice and the ice-cream coffee. Cooled by the gentle breezes that waft in from the Danshui River, the dining area is smack in the middle of the street life that surrounds the Danshui MRT station. Menu in English.

Italian

Pasti
233-3 Zhongzheng Rd. Tel: 02-2626 2472.
Open: Thu–Tue L & D. $$
Danshui has a heavy student population and moderate incomes, so prices everywhere are very reasonable. This airy, very casual glass-front eatery has a wide range of Italian pasta dishes. Try the seafood ones, with shrimp, scallops, or squid fresh from the harbor.

Taiwanese

Hai Feng Can Ting (Sea Breeze Restaurant)
17 Zhongzheng St. Tel: 02-2621 2365.
Open: daily 11am–11.30pm. $$$
This famous Taiwanese eatery is a legend in Danshui. There is no menu; guests select their freshly caught seafood from among the ice-covered offerings in the front. This is classic Taiwanese seafood, with flash-fried oysters, grilled snapper, stewed bamboo shoots with pork and scallions, chili basil clams, and stir-fried shrimp. Very *renao* (lively), with big crowds and lots of noise.

Ming He
5, Lane 56, Gongming St. Open: daily noon–late. $$
While not strictly a sit-down restaurant, Ming He does have a few tables and chairs. But the main event is the grilled squid, one of the classic snacks of Taiwan; nobody does it better. It is barbecued on hot coals, then slathered with a sweet-hot sauce, dusted with sesame, cayenne and "secret" ingredients, then cut up and served. Delicious. No English – just point and eat.

Danshui and Bali specialize in fresh seafood.

Local treats on Jishan Street.

Shopping for goodies at Jishan Street's food stalls.

TAIPEI'S SURROUNDINGS

Outside of the city, Taipei County offers many quick and easy day-trip options, featuring rugged coastal and mountain scenery, rejuvenating hot springs, and a glimpse of old-time, small-town life.

On the city's doorstep, and easily accessed via the efficient road and rail networks, are several day-trip options that will satisfy the demands of all visitors. Whether you are interested in exploring the island's history or delving into its religious institutions, there is plenty to see. Alternatively, those seeking to embrace nature, some time away from the crowded city, or simply a soothing soak in a mineral spring, will be spoiled for choice. All of the excursions presented in the following chapters can be reached in just an hour or so.

Rocky Heping Island.

On the North and Northeast coasts, there are sporting options in the surf, tanning and volleyball on the sands, hang-gliding opportunities, camping facilities, and explorations of coastal geology. For the history buff, some of the island's oldest ports in and off the coastal towns will provide the key to understanding the interest exhibited in Taiwan's northern region over the past 400 years by pirates and traders, Spanish, Dutch, and Japanese colonists, Chinese settlers, and Canadian missionaries, among others. In the small hill towns of Jiufen and Jinguashi on the Northeast Coast, one can dig deep into Taiwan's mining history and also discover the harsher legacies of Japan's colonization of the island through the remains of a notorious World War II prisoner-of-war camp.

Enjoying the beach at Baishawan.

Directly to the city's south, the town of Wulai enables contact with the island's northernmost aboriginal tribe and immersion in its hot-springs soaking culture. Sanxia and Yingge are two towns southwest of the city. Aside from its preserved 19th-century Old Street, Sanxia is host to one of the finest extant examples of temple architecture in Taiwan. Yingge is a center of artistic creativity and the heart of the island's ceramics production for the past 200 years.

It is no coincidence that full-day and half-day outings to all of these locations, which are located in a tight ring around the city, are run on a regular basis by Taipei's experienced tour agencies. This is your best option if you are not familiar with the island and local dialects. In general, they provide superb value.

A rocky path at Yeliu Scenic Area.

THE NORTH COAST AND KEELUNG

This region is host to the sublime and the surreal, and a synthesis of the two: a giant stone gateway formed by millennia of lapping wave action, a temple whose main deity is a dog, a hilltop tomb that sings for visitors, and miles and miles of coastline.

ncompassing the northernmost tip of Taiwan, this area is de-limited by the Danshui River in the west and Keelung Harbor in the east. It is washed by the Pacific Ocean and the East China Sea. A line of extinct volcanoes still simmering down under, the Datun Range, forms its back. This is the North Coast, with its crashing surf, blue waves, fresh ocean catches, and the most bizarre and beautiful stone sculptures crafted by Mother Nature.

NORTH COAST

In 2004 most of the North Coast was included in the newly created **North Coast and Guanyinshan National Scenic Area** (Beihaian Ji Guanyinshan Guojia Fengjing Qu), an easily accessible place of calm as well as natural ruggedness.

Baishawan ❶

Provincial Highway No. 2 is the only road that runs along the North Coast between the breakers and the mountainside. Commonly referred to as the North Coast Highway, its first few kilometers east of Danshui negotiate undulating hills. The sea appears abruptly at **Baishawan**, or "White Sand Bay," a beach tremendously popular with locals on non-working days (June–Aug daily 8am–dusk; admission

charge). The soft white sand found here is a rarity along the mainly rocky coastline. There are shower facilities and eateries. Those not keen on basting themselves in the hot sun can rent equipment for surfing and windsurfing. The winds are best when the cool northeasterlies blow from November to March. Locals avoid the place during this period, resulting in thinner crowds. The tiny, eponymous town by the beach, with cafés and pubs lining the highway, throbs into the night on weekends.

Jinbaoshan's neat rows of tombs.

At the Temple of the 18 Kings, a faux gold-plated icon of the canine deity is installed. Oddly enough, worshippers stick burning cigarettes in the incense urns rather than joss sticks. Rubbing the dog is also said to bring good luck.

Nsa Headquarters

The **National Scenic Area headquarters** (Bei-Guan Guojia Fengjing Qu Guanli Chu) is located right by the beach (daily 9am–5pm; tel: 02-8635 5100; www.northguan-nsa.gov.tw). This large new facility opened in 2009; there are good exhibits with usable English, plus useful maps available.

Shimen ❷

Sitting right by the highway a few kilometers east of Baishawan is the most unusual natural landmark on the coastal route, **Shimen**, or "Stone Gate." Shimen is a huge coral formation that was gradually pushed high above the waterline by heaving tectonic activity over the recent eons. As it rose, pounding wave action ate away its center, leaving a hole large enough to drive a truck through. A narrow and steep flagstoned path leads to the low summit and panoramic views.

Temple of the 18 Kings ❸

Tucked under a bluff beside the highway is the **Temple of the 18 Kings** (Shibawang Gong), surely one of Taiwan's most unaffected cultural experiences (daily 24 hours). Of the 18 gods celebrated here, 17 are human and one is a dog.

The story goes (there are variations galore) that a ship went down offshore here on a rough crossing from China in the Qing dynasty. Seventeen merchants drowned, and after failing to save its master, a dog came ashore, sat down here, and starved while steadfastly waiting for its master to appear. A temple was built by locals inspired by its loyalty.

As the gods were businessmen when mortals, those who worship wealth come here in droves. Members of the underworld, especially the red-light world, frequent the place late at night, making for a raucous festival atmosphere. Snack vendors, trinket sellers, and old-style games stands

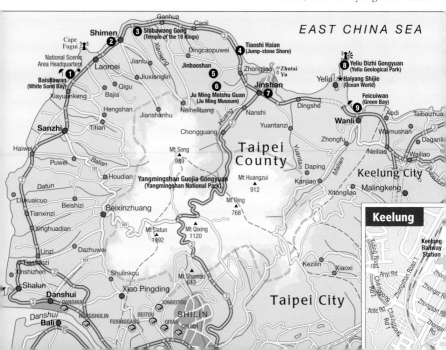

abound, as do families and young couples, making for a one-of-a-kind cultural scene that is great fun and entirely safe.

Tiaoshi Haian ❹

The highway heads southeast along a section colloquially known as **Tiaoshi Haian**, or "Jump-stone Shore," on some Chinese tourist maps. The origin of this moniker is evident from the massive boulders – some bigger than houses – that have fallen onto the beaches from the bluffs towering above the highway.

Jinbaoshan ❺

At the 34.8km or 39.7km mark on the highway, turn inland and uphill to **Jinbaoshan** (daily 24 hours; free; tel: 02-4498 5900).

This is not your average tourist site. It is a graveyard that is the nearest thing Taiwan has to Graceland. The highlight is the tomb of Teresa Teng, a Taiwanese songstress who died of

asthma in 1995 at age 43. She sang in many languages, and is revered by the Japanese, Hong Kongers, and other Asian tourists you'll see at the tomb. A special jukebox of sorts has been set up by the tomb to allow public enjoyment of Teng's musical legacy.

Teresa Teng's tomb at Jinbaoshan.

Others come here for the solitude, magnificent tomb architecture, and thrilling views. The entire upper slope is neatly lined with the tombs of Taiwan's esteemed and famous. Buried here is master puppeteer Li Tian-lu. The gardens are evocatively sculpted in mystical Buddhist style, complete with a tunnel of macabre sculptures under a pagoda, depicting man's passage from chubby new life to decrepitude and death, signifying life's impermanence.

Ju Ming Museum ❻

The roads to Jinbaoshan also lead to the **Ju Ming Museum** (Ju Ming Meishu Guan), on a nearby plateau with sweeping views (Tue–Sun May–Oct 10am–6pm; Nov–Apr 10am–5pm; admission charge; tel:

North Coast

0   3 km
0   3 miles

eelung
land
Liandong
Nanya
ing Dao
Badouzi
Mt Jilong
gyuan
Shenao   Rubin   587   Jinguashi
ing Island Park)
Jiufen
anqiao
Ershawan Paotai
(Haimen Tianxian)   Ruifang
102
aipei County
elung   Linyukeng   Sandiao
Peak
Houdong   523   102
Mt Sanguazikeng
Sijiaoting   536
Mt Wufen
Nuannuan   757

Harbor
Xinliu
Rd
Xinwu Rd
ZHONGZHENG GONGYUAN
(ZHONGZHENG PARK)
Zhongzheng Road
Xinsi Rd
Shoushan Road
Xinsan Rd
Guanyin
Statue
Xiner Rd
Yisi Rd
Xinyi Road
Yisan Rd
Yier Rd
Henyi Road
Yiyi Rd
Miaokou Yeshi
(Miaokou Nightmarket)
0   300 m
0   300 yds

WHERE

Dedicated shuttle buses leave for the Ju Ming Museum from beside the Jinshan Township Office in Jinshan. Get there via the Jinshan line bus from Danshui MRT Station. Times for the shuttle vary; check the museum website.

Lee Hu Pastry Shop (est. 1882), at No. 90 Rensan Street, is considered by many to be Taiwan's best purveyor of sweet pineapple cake (fengli su), a bite-size cube-shaped pastry shell filled with chewy pineapple paste (daily 9am–9.30pm; tel: 02-2422 3007; www.lee-hu.com.tw).

02-2498 9940; www.juming.org.tw). The 10-hectare (26-acre) museum, with Taiwan's largest outdoor sculpture garden, is filled with some 500 of the thickly sliced rock figures by Ju Ming, one of Taiwan's best-known artists. It is home to an equal number of his paintings.

Jinshan ❼

There isn't very much to see in the little fishing town of **Jinshan**, but do make a quick stop at **Jinbaoli Street** (Jinbaoli Jie) in the town's overflowing old center. It is one of the last streets in Taiwan to retain the look of its Qing dynasty origins.

There is a high viewing platform on the edge of town with views of the aptly named **Candlestick Islets** (Zhutai Yu) offshore.

Yeliu Geological Park ❽

East of Jinshan is the **Yeliu** ("Wild Willows") **Geological Park** (Yeliu Dizhi Gongyuan), where there are no willows but instead a rich grove of bizarre sandstone, lava, and coral sculptures eroded by wind and waves (daily 7.30am–5pm, May–mid Sept extended hours, tickets

Street vendor in Jinshan town.

sale until 6pm; admission charge; tel: 02-2492 2016; www.ylgeopark.org.tw). Its most famous rock is one that resembles a bust of Egyptian Queen Nefertiti.

A footpath here climbs steeply up toward the tip of the long, narrow promontory. The views from the lighthouse here are worth the ascent.

Ocean World

Between Yeliu fishing port and the promontory is **Ocean World** (Haiyang Shijie), an ocean park of average quality with a large aquarium, performing dolphins and sea lions, and an underwater tunnel (Mon–Fri 9am–5pm, Sat–Sun 9am–5.30pm; admission charge; tel: 02-2492 1111; www.oceanworld.com.tw).

Green Bay ❾

Another popular beach resort is **Feicuiwan**, or Green Bay (daily 8am–8pm; admission charge; tel: 02-2492 6565). Equipment for hang-gliding, parasailing, jet-skiing, and windsurfing is available. This is also one of the few spots in Taiwan where surfing is possible.

On weekends you'll see paragliders floating down from the bluffs behind. Riders are willing to ride tandem with thrill-seekers for a small fee. But note that these are not accredited instructors, and have no connection with the nearby resort. For more info, visit the Wings Taiwan website (www.wingstaiwan.com). One thing that heightens the soaring fun is the presence of a camouflaged hilltop Patriot missile battery and hill-bottom ammo dump; errant gliders are constantly irritating the soldiers.

KEELUNG

Keelung is Taiwan's second-busiest seaport, and the maritime gateway for the island's north. Sandwiched between high hills and saltwater, there are a number of interesting cultural and historical sites here.

Miaokou Nightmarket ⓾

Just east of the harbor's inner end is **Miaokou Nightmarket** (Miaokou Yeshi), one of Taiwan's most renowned (daily dusk–3am; www.miaokow.org). It runs for 300 meters/yds along Rener Street in front of old **Dianji Temple** (Dianji Gong). There are hundreds of delicious traditional Taiwanese snacks to try. Fresh sea-food figures prominently. Try the *tianbula*, a Taiwanese adaptation of Japanese tempura served with a slightly sweet and spicy red sauce.

Zhongzheng Park ⓫

From the harbor you can see the white statue of Guanyin, the Goddess of Mercy, standing atop a hill to the east, watching over ships, sailors, and residents. This is peaceful **Zhongzheng Park** (Zhongzheng Gongyuan), on Shoushan Road (daily 6am–10pm; free). Climb up into the 25-meter-tall (75ft) statue for the best views. Behind is a tranquil Buddhist temple.

Haimen Tianxian ⓬

Higher up the hill are the remains of **Haimen Tianxian**, better known as **Ershawan Fort** (Ershawan Paotai),

built by the Qing government in 1840 (daily 9am–5pm; free; tel: 02-2420 1122). Entry is through an impressively refurbished classical fortress gate. Quiet pathways lead through the grounds, and reproduction cannons in the original gun emplacements overlook the harbor and sea. *Haimen Tianxian* translates literally as "Sea Gate Heaven Danger," implying that those who trespassed below would call down the wrath of the heavens. The fort saw action in the 1884–85 Sino-French War, but its effectiveness was diminished because its cannons were locked in position. This is an official "First Rank" Taiwan heritage site.

Heping Island Park ⓭

Heping (Peace) Island, reached via a short bridge near the harbor mouth, is where the Spanish built their main fort in 1626. No ruins remain today, but this hilly rock is the location of **Ho Ping Island Hi Park** (Heping Dao Gongyuan), full of bizarre rock formations, wind-swept paths, and a small old-style amusement park (daily 8am–6pm, summer until 8pm; admission charge; tel: 02-2463 5999; www.hipark.com.tw).

WHERE

From Danshui MRT station, travelers can catch a bus that plies Provincial Highway No. 2, along which are most of the tourist sights. The bus route terminates at the commuter railway station in front of Keelung Harbor.

RESTAURANTS

PRICE CATEGORIES

Prices for an average meal for two persons, including drinks.
$$$$ = above NT$2,000
$$$ = NT$1,000–2,000
$$ = NT$500–1,000
$ = under NT$500

International

Blue Bay Lounge
18/19F, Evergreen Laurel Hotel, 61 Zhongzheng Rd, Keelung. Tel: 02-2427-9988. Open: B, L, afternoon tea, D. $$$
With floor-to-ceiling windows on all sides, this spot offers magnificent night views of the harbor. The 19th floor is a café and main dining

area, with a choice of buffet, set meals, or snacks. The seafood dishes are, of course, harbor-fresh.
Happy Family Seafood Restaurant
221 Wenhua Rd., Keelung, www.happy family.com.tw Tel: 02-2422-2008. Open: 11am–2pm, 5–9pm $–$$
Located at the Keelung harbor, this is a famous seafood place. The food here is fresh and tasty, while the interior of the restaurant has a classy, yet cozy ambience. Really good value for money.
Provence Café
20-5 Beishizi, Sanzhi Town. Tel: 02-8625 2298. Open: 11am–midnight. $$
A sprightly café and bar right on the beach off the main highway,

with breakers directly below. The bar is on an expansive oceanside deck. Despite the name, the menu features dishes from many cuisines, including Taiwanese hot snacking foods.
That Little Place on Fishing Road
134-5 Zhonghua Rd, Jinshan Town. Tel: 02-2498 8455. Open: daily 10.30am–11pm. $$$
A place of great character where the coastal and Yangmingshan highways meet. Opened by a fisherman, prepares first-rate seafood. Filled with antique farming and fishing tools, it looks out to sea and inland up misty Jinshan Valley. Offers many blended Italian coffees.

A dramatic evening view of the coast from Jiufen

JIUFEN, JINGUASHI, AND THE NORTHEAST COAST

Offering some of the most rugged and spectacular scenery found in north Taiwan, this area is defined by lofty mountains and surging sea. The long-isolated mining towns of Jiufen and Jinguashi, on Mount Jilong, are drenched in history and nostalgia.

Much of this area falls within the official boundaries of the **Northeast and Yilan Coast National Scenic Area** (Dongbeijiao Yilan Haian Guojia Fengjingqu).

Jiufen is reached via County Highway No. 102, the Ruijin Highway, which winds east from Keelung. Just east of Jiufen, Jinguashi sits in a steep, narrow valley on the southeast side of Mount Jilong.

JIUFEN

A town of steep lanes and steps, Jiufen has become a prime tourist destination for locals since the release of Taiwanese director Hou Hsiao-hsien's acclaimed movie *City of Sadness*, partially filmed here. The film depicts the sufferings of Taiwan's people when Chiang Kai-shek's KMT party set up its exile government in the 1940s. The town's narrow streets are lined with old red-brick, wood-frame buildings left over from the gold-rush days of the late 19th and early 20th centuries. Many have since been converted into teahouses with stunning views.

Jiufen was dubbed "Little Shanghai" at the height of the gold rush in the 1920s and 1930s, when it was jammed with theaters, seedy

teahouses, wine houses, and brothels, its glittering lights clearly visible from far out at sea. The town's only through road, called Qiche ("Car") Road, is one of the few traffic arteries wide enough for four-wheeled vehicles. Walking tours generally start at the junction of Qiche Road and Jishan Street, going downhill via Shuqi Road back to the highway.

Along Jishan Street

Along **Jishan Street ❶** (Jishan Jie), a narrow pedestrian lane with only

Jiufen's steep Shuqi Road

The design of the City of Sadness Restaurant evokes the Japanese colonial era; best of all is the open-air rooftop teahouse-cum-dining area, with the town looming above and the sea crashing below.

the occasional scooter, the sky is for long stretches almost blocked from view by the awnings of the densely packed eateries, galleries, jewelry shops, and souvenir stands. Artists seeking solitude flocked here first, followed – after *City of Sadness* fame – by tourists.

Each tourist destination in Taiwan has its *mingchan*, or local "famous products," and fish stew is one of Jiufen's. Visit **Grandma's Fish Stew ❷** (A-Po Yugeng), at No. 9 Jishan Street, for a taste (daily 10am–10pm; tel: 02-2497 6678). Other local specialties are fried taro and sweet-potato balls, and spicy beef noodle soup. Drop in at **Jiufen Old Noodle House ❸** (Jiufen Lao Miandian), at No. 45, where the secret house ingredients add a unique twist to the beef broth in which the thick beef slices and noodles are boiled (daily 10.30am–7.30pm, Sat–Sun until 8.30pm; tel: 02-2497 6316).

Shuqi Road ❹

Near the end of Jishan Street is the junction with the renowned **Shuqi Road** (Shuqi Lu), a steep and exceedingly narrow stone stairway that fairly plummets downhill (362 steps!), home to most of the picturesque shooting locations for *City of Sadness*. The lane is lined with teahouses, a number in heritage buildings, all with great views of the hills, coast, and ocean.

City of Sadness Restaurant ❺

The wood-framed, three-story **City of Sadness Restaurant** (Beiqing Chengshi Chalou), on the corner of Shuqi and Qingbian roads, was one of the main locations for the film's local shoots (35 Shuqi Rd; daily 24 hours; tel: 02-2496 9917).

Jiufen Folk Art Gallery ❻

Located at 131 Qingbian Road is **Jiufen Folk Art Gallery** (Jiufen Minsu Yishu Xiaoji; free; daily

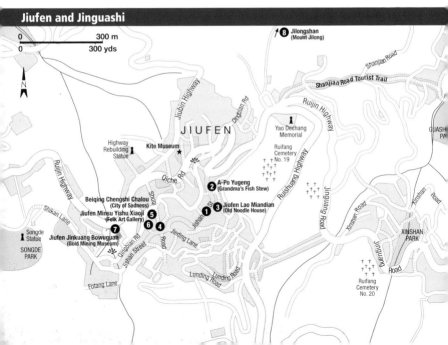

Jiufen and Jinguashi

0   300 m
0   300 yds

N

Jilongshan ❽ (Mount Jilong)

Shanjian Road

Shanjian Road Tourist Trail

Jiubin Highway

Qingbian Rd

Ruijin Highway

JIUFEN

Yao Dechang Memorial ①

Highway Rebuilding Statue

Kite Museum ★

Ruifang Cemetery No. 19 ✝

Qiche Rd

Ruijin Highway

Ruishuang Road

A-Po Yugeng ❷ (Grandma's Fish Stew)

Jinguang Road

Xinshan Road

GUASHI PA...

Shikan Lane

Ruijin Highway

Beiqing Chengshi Chalou (City of Sadness)

Jiufen Minsu Yishu Xiaoji ❺ (Folk Art Gallery)

❻ ❹

Jiufen Lao Miandian ❸ (Old Noodle House)

❶ ❸

Shuqi Road

Jishan St

Jieding Lane

Xinshan Road

XINSHAN PARK

Songde Statue

SONGDE PARK

❼ **Jiufen Jinkuang Bowuguan** (Gold Mining Museum)

Qingbian Rd

Jishan Street

Lunding Lane

Lunding Road

Ruifang Cemetery No. 20 ✝

Fotang Lane

10am–8pm; tel: 02-2497 9400). It has attractive displays tracking the town's historical transformations. The second story of this Japanese colonial era edifice has an open-air wraparound balcony where tea, coffee, and lovely views can be enjoyed from under the shade of umbrellas.

Gold Mining Museum ❼

The small but interesting **Jiufen Gold Mining Museum** (Jiufen Jinkuang Bowuguan) is off Qingbian Road and down short Shibei Lane, at No. 66 (daily 9am–6pm; admission charge; tel: 02-2496 6379). If you want to learn all that is needed to get yourself launched in gold mining and processing, there is no better place; the friendly curator teaches the art of panning and smelting, and often lets visitors try it out.

Mount Jilong ❽

At the north end of town, take the long grass-swept path that climbs up to the crest of **Mount Jilong** (Jilongshan), an extinct volcano that stands between Jiufen and the sea. The flagstoned walk ends at a few pagodas with an awe-inspiring 360-degree vista. On weekdays the area is very quiet.

JINGUASHI

A marked footpath, **Shanjian Road Tourist Trail**, guides visitors from Jiufen to Jinguashi. This valley was the site of a notorious Japanese POW mining camp during World War II. The abandoned mining and smelting facilities, the old guesthouse originally built for a visit by Emperor Hirohito, and other facilities from the bygone era of mining prosperity are now being developed for tourism, and offer stimulating walks that evoke the turbulent past.

Gold Ecological Park

Though Jinguashi's most important historical relics are all spread out through the valley, they are under the common administration of the **Gold Ecological Park** (Huangjin Bowu Yuanqu), christened in 2004 (Mon–Fri 9.30am–5pm, Sat–Sun 9.30am–6pm, closed first Mon of

The curator of the Jiufen Gold Mining Museum happily demonstrates the art of panning for gold to visitors.

The old refinery ruins near Jiufen.

Jiufen and Jinguashi

Jinshui Highway
Qitang Road
Guashan Sports Center
Wuhao Road
Road
Qitang Road
JINGUASHI
Jinguang Road
❾❿ Fuwu Zhongxin Tourist Information Center)
Shuiyi Rd
Jinguang Road
Huangjin Bowu Yuanqu (Gold Ecological Park)
❿ Huanjing Jiaoyu Guan (Environment Education Center)
⓫ Taizi Binguan (Crown Prince Chalet)
Benshan Wukeng (Benshan Fifth Tunnel)
⓬
⓭ Huangjin Bowuguan (Museum of Gold)

Tableaux at the Benshan Fifth Tunnel.

month; www.gep.tpc.gov.tw). Access to the "park" – the valley, in other words – is free, but admission is charged for the main attractions – all those introduced below and a few others.

Information Centers

The place to start is the **Tourist Information Center** ❾ (Youke Fuwu Zhongxin) at 51-1 Jinguang Road (tel: 02-2496 2800). Free parking is provided here – almost impossible to find elsewhere in the valley. Introductory displays with some English are set up and tickets to all venues sold. It is located in the old Taiwan Motor Transport bus station.

East of the Information Center is the **Environmental Education Center** ❿ (Huanjing Jiaoyu Guan), an old mining company administrative building offering fixed exhibits and multimedia presentations on Jinguashi's natural ecology and the history and culture of mining. There is also a good introductory movie shown on the park.

Crown Prince Chalet ⓫

Just south of the Environmental Education Center is the **Crown Prince Chalet** (Taizi Binguan), a

Jinguashi literally means "gold melon rocks," in reference to the yellow sulfur-coated boulders strewn along the stream that hurtles down the gorge.

villa in traditional Japanese style with a landscaped garden, archery field, and, incongruously, a mini-putt. It was built in 1922 in preparation for a grand tour of the colony by the future Emperor Hirohito of Japan, then Crown Prince. In the end, the tour did not take place. The chalet itself is not open for public visits.

Benshan Fifth Tunnel ⓬

Just before the top of the valley is **Benshan Fifth Tunnel** (Benshan Wukeng), a long shaft in which visitors can get a decidedly gloomy glimpse of life in the mines, an experience heightened by piped-in sounds of drilling, miners talking, and explosions (additional admission charge). The nine tunnels in the valley stretch 600km (370 miles) and go as deep as 132 meters (433ft) below sea level. The Japanese wanted gold to finance their war activities, and both sulfur and copper for the armaments they required. They set up the infamously brutal Kinkaseki mining camp here.

Museum of Gold ⓭

Right by the Benshan tunnel, the **Museum of Gold** (Huangjin

Bowuguan), devoted to the precious metal and its extraction, is housed in a glass-and-steel retrofit of an old Taiwan Metal Mining Co. building. In the **Gold Panning Experience**, you can try your luck and can take home anything your Midas touch reveals.

NORTHEAST COAST

Along the Northeast Coast, the majestic Xueshan (Snow Mountain) range spills into the Pacific, making for lovely vistas with blue waters in front, narrow slivers of flatland on the coast, and towering bluffs pressing in behind. Weekends and holidays see every coastal nook and cranny crowded with day-trippers from the Taipei Basin.

Fishing is the primary industry here, and all along the coast you will come across brightly painted craft packed like sardines in little harbors. A single road – Provincial Highway No. 2, commonly called the Coastal Highway – is etched into the base of the high bluffs along the shore.

If you are driving on the heavily used Coastal Highway, to get to the most southerly points and back in one day requires an early morning start.

An alternative is the new Taipei-Yilan expressway for one leg of the journey. Though tunneled and not offering a lot in terms of view, it allows you to reach Yilan County in just 40 minutes instead of two and a half hours or more, leaving more time for each coastal scenic spot.

Avoid using Provincial Highway No. 9 to Yilan, which starts from Xindian, south of Taipei. It is a windy, dangerous, and extremely unpleasant mountain traverse – though quite pretty.

Nanya

Traveling southward, **Nanya** is the first site within the National Scenic Area (NSA), at the 89km mark on the Coastal Highway (roadside markers indicate distances, calculated using the city of Keelung as the base). Strange rock formations abound here, the result of wind and water erosion of the area's sandstone. The stone, which used to be underwater long ago, has been pushed up by tectonic activity. It is laden with veins of iron, making for efflorescent striations that are quite dazzling when exposed.

At the Museum of Gold in Jinguashi, you can caress for luck the gold bar that holds the Guinness Record, weighing in at 220kg (485lbs).

A striated rock formation at Nanya.

Northeast Coast

Boardwalks here make walking between and atop boulders very pleasant. Be sure to leave time to head away from the crashing surf and line fishermen in order to sally under the highway and into the deep, narrow valley behind, where you will see farmers in traditional conical bamboo leaf hats tending stamp-size plots on steep slopes.

Cape Bitou

Cape Bitou (Bitoujiao) juts out into the ocean at the highway's 93km mark. It covers an area of almost 500 hectares (1,235 acres). Caves, plateaux, and other landforms can be found at the base of its craggy cliffs, eroded by surf and wind.

Atop the cape, watching over the crashing waves, is the gleaming white **Bitou Lighthouse** ⓯ (Bitou Dengta). It was built by the Japanese in 1896, and was given its present form after being bombed by the Allies in World War II. You can reach it along a trail that snakes up from beside the highway; the highway passes under the cape through a tunnel. Atop the bluffs you'll be rewarded with spectacular views of mountains falling into the sea, as far as the eye can see.

Longdong

One of the most popular swimming spots on the Northeast Coast and also one of Taiwan's premier diving locations – certainly the best in the north – is **Longdong Bay Park** ⓰ (Longdongwan Gongyuan), at the 95.5km mark (daily 8am–7pm; admission charge; tel: 02-2490 9445). It contains a great variety of marine life in its cool, clear waters. The recreational facilities within the park include a good range of equipment for water activities. There are also vertical cliffs good for rock climbing at the tip of the cape.

The bay was named *Longdong*, or "dragon cave," either because it seems like the entrance to a dragon's lair, or because the Mandarin name stems from a similar-sounding aboriginal word.

At the south end of Longdong Bay is **Longdong South Coast Park** ⑰ (Longdong Nankou Haian Gongyuan), its entrance at the 96km mark (daily 8am–6pm; admission charge; tel: 02-2490 1000). The naturally formed pools, once abalone ponds, are just knee-deep at low tide, but surge to 9 meters (30ft) in depth at high tide, making for good snorkeling and scuba-diving, with sightings of shrimp, crab, starfish, sea urchins, mollusks, and sea anemones. The visitor center houses an exhibition on geology and different forms of land and marine life found on the Northeast Coast. There is also a marina here. Starting at the north end of Longdong South Coast Park is a meandering, coast-hugging pathway of majestic viewpoints leading back to Cape Bitou. Note there is also a vehicle parking charge at both Longdong locations, with limited free opportunity along the highway, especially on weekends.

Jinshawan ⑱

At about the 100km mark on the highway is **Jinshawan**, the aptly named "golden sand bay." The fine 200-meter (660ft) stretch of sand is constantly packed with sun-seeking beach lovers. Facilities include a children's recreation area and beach volleyball courts.

Aodi ⑲

The fishing village of **Aodi**, at the 103km mark, is renowned for the still-flapping, still-crawling freshness of its seafood. Like the fish that pose expectantly in the tanks lined up at their entrances, the restaurants here jostle together right along the highway, which is also the town's main thoroughfare.

Yanliao

South of Aodi is **Yanliao Beach Park** ⑳ (Yanliao Haibin Gongyuan), the largest developed recreational site on the northeast coast, with golden beaches that stretch south all the way to Fulong (daily 8am–7pm; admission charge; tel: 02-2490 2991). The waterfront pond and garden here are well designed and a pleasure to walk through. No visit would be complete without some people-watching by the sea at the South Seas-theme café.

In 1976 the **Yanliao Colonial Resistance Historical Site** (Yanliao

Taipeiers flock to Aodi on weekends and holidays for the winning combination of fresh seafood and a seaside drive.

The rocky cliffs of Cape Bitou.

The Ho-Hai-Yan Music Festival, Taiwan's biggest rock festival, is held over three days at Fulong Beach each summer. Some 20,000 revelers attend at any one time. Admission is free. Trains run hourly between Taipei and Fulong, and shuttle buses to and from Fulong station

Kangri Jinian Bei) was set up to honor the fighters from Taiwan and China who tried to repel the Japanese troops who landed here in 1895 after China ceded the island upon losing the Sino-Japanese War.

Longmen Riverside Camping Resort ㉑

The **Longmen Riverside Camping Resort** (Longmen Luying Dujia Jidi) is at the highway's 107.8km mark (entry daily 8am–7pm; admission charge; tel: 02-2499 1791; www.lonmen. tw). *Longmen*, which means "dragon's gate," refers to the debouchment of the Shuangxi River, the largest waterway in the northeast. The 37-hectare (91-acre) resort offers a superb range of facilities. The campsite includes three log cabins and roofed wooden platforms. Watersports facilities are in abundance. From here Yanliao beach can be accessed by foot or bike (rentals available) along trails which bring you across a postcard-perfect suspension bridge spanning 200 meters (660ft) over the Shuangxi River. There is also a parking fee here.

Fulong Beach ㉒

Fulong Beach (Fulong Haishui Yuchang), at the 108.8km mark on

A carved rock on Caoling Historic Trail.

the Coastal Highway, is undoubtedly the Northeast Coast's most popular beach (daily 8am–6pm; admission charge; tel: 02-2499 1211). It boasts a complete range of watersports facilities. The waters are comparatively sheltered here, making it suitable for non-powered boating activities such as windsurfing, rowing, and kayaking. The **Fulong Visitor Center** (Fulong Youke Fuwu Zhongxin), located beside the National Scenic Area administration headquarters, has exhibits, print materials, video briefings, and other information on the area's natural and cultural treasures (36 Xinglong St, Fulong Village; daily June–Sept 8am–6pm; Oct–May 9am–5pm; tel: 02-2499 1210; www. necoast-nsa.gov.tw).

Cape Sandiao ㉓

The tip of **Cape Sandiao** (Sandiaojiao) is Taiwan's easternmost point.

Surfing at Honeymoon Bay.

The **Cape Sandiao Lighthouse** (Sandiaojiao Deng-ta), gleaming white on a pristine green lawn, was built in 1935 (Tue–Sun 9am–4pm; free; tel: 02-2499 1300). The lane to the lighthouse is at the 116.5km mark on the Coastal Highway. "Sandiao" is a rendering of "San Diego," a name bestowed in the 1620s by the Spanish on their first trip to scout for sites to build the forts needed in order to contest the Dutch.

Maoao Fishing Village ㉔

Just north, tucked seemingly right under the eroding cliffs of the cape, is perhaps Taiwan's loveliest little harbor, **Maoao Fishing Village** (Maoao Yucun). The *ao* means "fishing harbor" in Taiwanese. The bright fishing boats float shoulder to shoulder. There are numerous quaint old stone houses built by early settlers. Under the cliffs boardwalks have been built, and at low tide you can walk out to the breakers.

Daxi (Honeymoon Bay) ㉕

Nestled in a horseshoe-shaped cove given the popular moniker "Honeymoon Bay" (Miyue Wan), **Daxi** (131.5km mark) offers the north's best surfing. The waves are generally 2–3 meters (6–10ft) high. On weekends and holidays you'll find many aficionados who have risen before dawn to get in a full day's surfing. Non-surfers also abound, lured by the soft sand, ghost crabs, and vivid sunrises.

Beiguan Tidal Park ㉖

At the 136km mark is **Beiguan Tidal Park** (Beiguan Haichao Gongyuan), where twisting pathways sculpted out of coral and heaved high by tectonic activity lead to the top of a rugged, massive oceanside outcrop with stunning views of ocean and mountain (daily 8am–midnight; free; parking fee; tel: 03-978 0727). Below, cuesta formations and tofu-shaped rock jostle for space. Beiguan was fortified

in the late Qing dynasty to watch for enemy ships. A cannon emplacement is on display. The crowded line of small eateries, though now a bit ragged, features some very tasty and fresh seafood.

Caoling Historic Trail ㉗

The Northeast Coast also offers pleasant walks in the hills away from the surf. The **Caoling Historic Trail** (Caoling Gudao) was part of a key pathway connecting northwest and east Taiwan in the past. It was an aboriginal trail expanded by Han Chinese pioneers in the early 1800s. Today most of the original trail has returned to nature, but the Caoling section has been rescued and spruced up. The trail takes about four hours to complete, one way; there are some challenging grades.

The views along the pathway are quite inspiring, and there are also a number of protected historical relics. The southern trailhead can be accessed from Dali train station, at the 127km mark of the coastal highway.

RESTAURANTS

PRICE CATEGORIES

Prices for an average meal for two persons, including drinks.
$$$$ = above NT$2,000
$$$ = NT$1,000–2,000
$$ = NT$500–1,000
$ = under NT$500

International

Café Drizzle
3F, 32 Qiche Rd, Jiufen. Tel: 02-2406 1000. Open: Sun–Thu 10am–10pm, Fri–Sat until–2am. $$
A cozy spot with a great coastal panorama from an outdoor deck with funky umbrellas and other Art Deco touches. Quality coffees from around the globe and light snacks, local and Western.

Taiwanese

Grandma Lai's Taro Dumplings
143 Jishan St, Jiufen. Tel: 02-2497 5245. Open: daily 7am–9pm, Sat–Sun until 11pm. $
This is Jiufen's best-known spot for its famous taro balls. These are dumplings made from taro paste, served hot or cold in a sweet, syrupy soup with sweet bean.

Yan Chao Seafood Restaurant
210 Renhe Rd, Aodi. Tel: 02-2490 2729. Open: Daily 11am–11pm. $$$
On the coastal highway, one of the old stalwarts among Aodi's famously large cluster of seafood restaurants. The emphasis is all on the food, not the decor. The fried clams are very good.

The Wulai Cable Car affords a great view of the valley.

WULAI, SANXIA, AND YINGGE

At the base of the foothills just south of the city are three towns of distinctive character, offering insight into local aboriginal and hot-springs culture, age-old religious tradition, and artistic expression in ceramics.

Day trips to these three towns are a breeze via the island's modern, convenient highway system, whether one is driving oneself or with a tour group. The trio lies in valleys through which two large rivers flow north into Taipei.

Wulai lies in a narrow valley along one of the upper tributaries of the Xindian River. Sanxia and Yingge sit close to each other in a broad valley in the mid-reaches of the Dahan River. Their differing topographies meant that while Han Chinese pioneers moved up the Dahan, displacing the resident aborigines, Wulai's isolation slowed the ingress of settlers and provided protection, preserving it as the northernmost settlement of the island's Atayal tribe.

WULAI

Wulai is 40 minutes south of Taipei city along Provincial Highway No. 9A. Buses to Wulai can be found outside Xindian MRT station. Alternatively, most tour companies in Taipei offer package tours which include entry to several attractions.

Though most of Wulai's permanent residents are Atayal, most of the businesses in Wulai Village are owned and run by Han Chinese. The

town is divided into two main areas, one focused on hot-springs soaking, the other on aboriginal-theme recreation and entertainment. "Wulai" is the Chinese rendering of the Atayal term *ulai*, meaning "poisonous." The first settlers thought the rising steam from the hot springs made the air and water here unsafe.

Traffic into the town is restricted. Visitors park (for a fee) in the large lot situated just north of the bridge-cum-entrance to the town. The bus station and police station are also here.

Main Attractions
Wulai Atayal Museum
Outdoor Hot Springs
Wulai Falls
Wulai Aboriginal Culture
  Village
Cable Car
Temple of the Divine
  Progenitor
Old Street
Yingge Ceramics Museum
Old Pottery Street

Maps and Listings
Maps, pages 232, 234, 236
Restaurants, page 237

A performance at Wulai Aboriginal Cultural Village.

Rice cooked in bamboo tubes, one of the aboriginal foods on sale at Wulai Village.

The dramatic Wulai Falls.

The busy hot-springs resort area sits between the Tonghou and Nanshi rivers, which meet here. Steam rises from the waters and sand in certain spots, and one may see individuals soaking up the minerals in self-dug pits by the riverside – an age-old aboriginal practice – especially in the early mornings.

Wulai Atayal Museum ❶

Wulai's newest attraction is the attractive multi-story Wulai Atayal Museum (Wulai Taiya Bowuguan), telling the story of Taiwan's northernmost tribe, a mountain-dwelling people (12 Wulai St, Wulai Village; Tue–Fri 9.30am–5pm, Sat–Sun 9.30am–6pm; tel: 02-2661 8162; admission charge; www.atayal.tpc.gov.tw). The complex sits just before the Old Street section of eateries as you enter Wulai Village. The many displays are clearly laid out, with good English. Highlights include models of the Atayal's traditional bamboo structures, which no longer exist, exhibits on weaving complex

patterns from simple looms, for which the women are famed, and traditional facial tattooing, indicating status.

Wulai Village ❷

The hot-spring area, called **Wulai Village** (Wulai Xiang), is filled with hot-spring inns, eateries, and gift outlets along Wulai Old Street (Wulai Laojie) selling aborigine trinkets and packaged traditional snack foods. New money has come into the area, and many of the newer hot-spring resort hotels are first-rate. But they are expensive – the demand for soaking facilities far outstrips the supply in Taiwan, no matter how much concrete developers pour into the game.

Outdoor Hot Springs ❸

A walk straight through the village takes just a few minutes and leads to a bridge spanning the Nanshi River. At the far end, follow the signs on the right to get to the local **Outdoor Hot Springs** (Lutian Gonggong Yuchi) by

Wulai

| 0 | 600 m |
| 0 | 600 yds |

Taipei

Nanshi

Tonghou

Wulai Bridge

Lutian Gonggong Yuchi ❸
(Outdoor Hot Springs) ❶
Wulai Taiya Bowuguan ❷
(Wulai Atayal Museum)

Wulai Xiang
(Wulai Village)

Xiaoyi

Mini-Train Station

Jiajiuliao

M o u n t   B a q u

Wulai Pubu
(Wulai Waterfall)

Wulai Shandi Wenhua Cun
(Aboriginal Culture Village) ❺ ❹

Mt Dadao
620

Kongzhong Lanche ❻
(Cable Car)

Nanshi

Yunxian Leyuan ❼
(Yun Hsien Holiday Resort)

Wawa Gu ★
(Doll Valley)

Xinxian Waterfall

Neidong

Mt Dabaoke
1152

N

the river (daily 24 hours; free). There are three pools of different temperatures. Rocks have been used to construct walls that regulate the flow of cool river water into the natural hotspring pools. Ropes facilitate direct descent into the hot water.

Wulai Falls ❹

Return to the bridge and continue along the narrow paved road deeper into the Nanshi River valley. The vistas grow ever more dramatic as the gorge deepens and the rock walls climb higher. The spectacular **Wulai Falls** (Wulai Pubu) soon spills into view, surging down a cliff from a height of 80 meters (260ft), ending up largely as spray as the valley's winds buffet the waters about. Rainbows are often the result on sunny days.

Aboriginal Culture Village ❺

The **Wulai Aboriginal Culture Village** (Wulai Shandi Wenhua Cun) is on a plateau directly across from and below Wulai Falls, owned by tribal members (daily 9am–5pm; tel: 02-2661 6635; admission charge). In the **performance theater**, traditional songs and dances of all of Taiwan's

tribes are staged four times daily (10.40am–3.30pm). Audience members are brought up on stage, and one male is invariably selected to "marry" a native princess. There is also a **culture display area** where traditional weapons and costumes, handicrafts, and a beautiful Ami-tribe canoe are on view. Many eateries outside the culture village complex serve traditional Atayal fare, occasionally including wild boar.

Yun Hsien Holiday Resort

The **Cable Car** ❻ (Kongzhong Lanche) runs across the gorge from the culture village to the source of Wulai Falls, high on a plateau (daily 7.30am–8pm; admission charge). The car provides the only access to **Yun Hsien Holiday Resort** ❼ (Yunxian Leyuan), an amusement park completely overhauled and updated in recent years (daily 9am–5pm; entry with cable car ticket; tel: 02-2661 6386; www.yun-hsien.com.tw). Access to the natural obstacle course and nature trails is free; there is also golf, a swimming pool, paintball, and eco-tours, each with an additional charge. You can stay overnight at the attractive refurbished hotel, which has a good Chinese restaurant, a coffeeshop, pool tables, and karaoke.

TIP

Wulai is prettiest in February and March, when the hillside cherry trees burst into bloom, ushering in milletplanting time and a month-long aboriginal festival.

One of the many avian species seen in Taiwan.

BIRDWATCHING

Wulai is one of Taiwan's 10 best birdwatching areas. Follow the Tonghou River from beside the bus station and head upstream about 7km (4 miles). Even mid-elevation birds can sometimes be seen here in the winter months, making this the perfect choice for birdwatchers with limited time.

Birds are in greatest number from November to February. Common species include riverine birds such as the Formosan Whistling Thrush and River Kingfisher. Rarer types spotted include the Indian Black Eagle, Maroon Oriole, Tawny Fish Owl, and Black Kite.

The only shops are located by the trail entrance, so bring your own food and drink.

FACT

On the outskirts of Sanxia – and just about every town in Taiwan near a highway – you'll see the ubiquitous betel-nut stands. Chewing of betel-nut (binlang) parings is popular in Taiwan, especially with truckers, for its analeptic effects.

SANXIA

Only 20 minutes or so from Taipei via the Second Northern Freeway, the old town of Sanxia is in many ways still living a century ago, most evident in its old core. It sits at the base of several high hills and at the confluence of three rivers that snake out from those hills. The town name literally means "three gorges." It was long the market center for farmers hauling their produce out of the river valleys and for miners hauling coal down from the nearby mountains. But the age of truck transport meant the town could be bypassed. This was not necessarily beneficial to the town's economy, but it was a boon to tourists, as local heritage sites have lived on without threat from developers, as if the second half of the 20th century never occurred.

Qingshui Zushi Temple ⑧

The physical and spiritual heart of this historic town is the **Temple of the Divine Progenitor** (Qingshui Zushi Miao), which stands at 1 Changfu Street (daily 4am–10pm; tel: 02-2671 1031). The temple is dedicated to a patriot from the Song dynasty, Chen Chao-ying, who fought bravely against the Mongols when they swept down from the north. This inspired his people, and his descendants eventually helped overthrow the invaders. He is also said to have been a master of medicine and a sorcerer, unselfishly using his powers to help his countrymen.

An icon of Chen was brought here in 1769, it is thought, and the temple first raised. There have been numerous renovations since, leading to what is one of the most profusely adorned of all Chinese temples. It is well known for its carvings in high relief. A terrible earthquake almost destroyed it in 1834, the Japanese burned it in 1895 when they found out that the temple was the headquarters for the local resistance, and it was virtually razed again in World

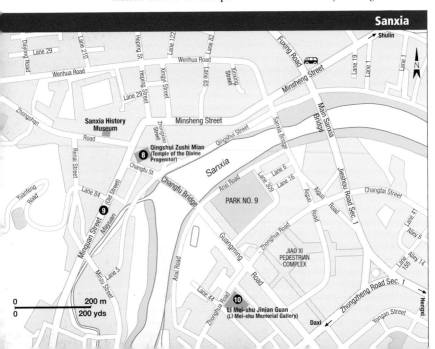

War II by Allied bombers because the Japanese were using it as local military barracks and headquarters.

The complex is always at its noisiest and most colorful just after the Chinese New Year. On the sixth day of the first lunar month, worshippers come flooding in by the hundreds bearing offerings and lighting incense to celebrate the birthday of the Divine Progenitor. Amid the smoke and firecracker blasts, elaborate decorated floats are paraded into the spacious front courtyard. A competition is held each year to grow the heaviest sacrificial pig, called a *shenzhu* (literally, "divine pig"). These monstrously proportioned beauty contestants are displayed, slain, and offered to the god as tribute. The winning family is guaranteed good fortune for a year. After the ceremonies, a huge feast is held, to which all visitors are welcome.

Old Street ❾

Sanxia's other great draw is **Old Street** (Laojie), a section of Minquan Street next to the temple. The two rows of double-story red-brick shophouses have been refurbished, creating the longest and best-preserved of the over 170 "old streets" in Taiwan. The imaginative can walk back a century and form a solid picture of what a town in northern Taiwan looked like in the years after the Japanese marched in. This was long the town's main commercial artery. In 1916 the Japanese straightened out the twisting thoroughfare to allow better troop movement, easier access for the Japanese-instituted fire brigade, and better sanitation. This was made easier by the fact that many buildings had been destroyed in the fierce resistance fighting.

As elsewhere, the Japanese incorporated diverse architectural elements into the structures, all of which are fronted by arcades. Facades carry symbols traditionally used by old samurai families, who had turned their energies

to business once their traditional martial role in society had been suppressed as part of the Meiji Restoration. The mortar used is made of glutinous rice and crushed seashells, a trick learned from the Dutch, whose engineers found themselves without mortar supplies from Batavia when they occupied Taiwan in the 1600s.

Li Mei-shu Memorial Gallery ❿

Across the Sanxia River is the **Li Mei-shu Memorial Gallery** (Li mei-shu Jinian Guan) at 10, Lane 43, Zhonghua Rd (Sat–Sun 10am–5pm; groups by arrangement Mon–Fri; tel: 02-2763 2333; admission charge; www.limeishu.org). A native son of Sanxia, Li Mei-shu (1902–83) is perhaps best-known outside Taiwan as one of its most accomplished artists, a master of Western-style naturalist painting who depicted the spirit of Taiwan's countryside.

Less well-known is that he spent 36 years of his life leading master craftsmen in renovating the town's great temple after World War II, remaining faithful to the Tang and Song dynasty

WHERE

Deeper in the lovely gorge past the culture village in Wulai is *Doll Valley* (Wawa Gu). Here one leaves the resort village day-trippers behind, entering a valley of pristine streams with sparkling small waterfalls and cool pools that has the feel of a hidden-away Shangri-La. Genuine Atayal residences dot the area, and hikers like to camp out under the stars. This is one of the best day-hiking spots in north Taiwan, a favorite with expatriates in the know. Any travel beyond the valley requires a mountain-hiking permit.

Sanxia's Qingshui Zushi Temple.

On a hill northeast of Yingge train station is *Parrot Rock* (Yingge Shi), a huge boulder with a foliage crown giving it the vague likeness of a parrot's bill and body. Hence the town's name; *yingge* means "parrot." The story goes that after liberating Taiwan from the Dutch in 1662 to set up his own regime, Ming patriot Koxinga led his army north. At Yingge they were attacked by a giant parrot, which the fearless leader killed with his magic cannon. Where it crashed, it became the boulder seen today.

motifs that dominate the important heritage site and shrine. His son carries on the intricate work – go to the rear of the temple to see the artists.

The gallery is a tribute to Li Mei-shu's talent and devotion to his culture. In one area are his favorite personal memorabilia, providing insight into Taiwanese life in the early 20th century, and in a second area are his works of art.

YINGGE

In Taiwan, the words "Yingge" and "ceramics" are close to synonymous. The town has been the island's center for pottery making for over 200 years, since it was found that the local water and clay were particularly suited to the art. This pottery town has scores of kilns, large and small, and numerous retail outlets, many fronting the factories. Locals and tourists come from far and wide to purchase items that range from the practical, such as pots and cups, to the masterfully artistic.

Yingge Ceramics Museum ⓫

With bold exterior lines and curves, the structure that houses the **Yingge Ceramics Museum** (Yingge Taoci Bowuguan) is itself a striking architectural work of art (200 Wenhua Rd; Tue–Fri 9.30am–5pm, Sat–Sun until 6pm; tel: 02-8677 2727; admission charge; www.ceramics.tpc.gov.tw).

Inside the sunlight-filled glass, concrete, and steel facility are exhibits on both historical and contemporary works and techniques, including Prehistoric, Aboriginal, and Taiwanese Works of Ceramics, and Development and Techniques of Ceramics in Taiwan. Free English audio tours are available.

The art-filled outdoor plaza is popular with families, and inside there are always kid-friendly hands-on exhibits. A visit here before strolling among the local shops is strongly suggested to enable more informed buying. Of special note is the brightly colored

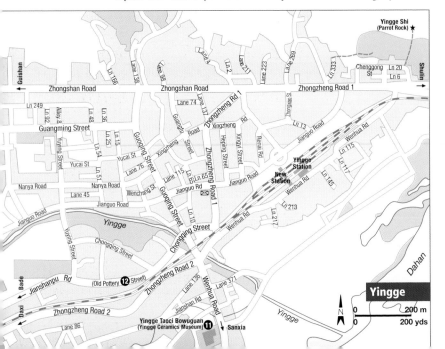

koji or *jiaozhi* ceramics, Taiwan's own unique contribution to the art form.

Temple-roof figures were traditionally made of broken tile pieces as the island's people were very poor. Items are fired at a low temperature, about 900°C (1,652°F), making them comparatively brittle. The results were so attractive that decorative pieces for the home were soon in demand. The Japanese in particular liked the style, hence the greater currency of the term "*koji*."

Old Pottery Street ⑫

The 300-meter/yd-long cobblestoned **Old Pottery Street** (Taoci Laojie) has long been the town's core production area, and is heavily imbued with an idyllic sense of history. It is lined with over 100 shops, and stuffed with tourists. The street is one section of Jianshanpu Road. The shops overflow with ceramic pieces of all sorts, including reproductions of art treasures from the Taipei National Palace Museum.

TIP

Many of Yingge's larger pottery outlets allow visits to their kilns, and also handle overseas shipping. On Old Street, a good number have open workshops and stage DIY sessions.

Traditional pottery on Old Street.

RESTAURANTS

PRICE CATEGORIES

Prices for an average meal for two persons, including drinks.
$$$$ = above NT$2,000
$$$ = NT$1,000–2,000
$$ = NT$500–1,000
$ = under NT$500

Aborigine

Taiya Po Po
14 Wulai St, Wulai. Tel: 02-2661 6371.
Open: daily 9am–11pm. **$$**
On Wulai Old Street, the name means "Atayal Grandma's." Offers wild mountain boar (not always available), banana rice, and fried wild mountain yam rolls. Don't miss the sweet millet wine.

International

Helen's Coffee
1, Lane 86, Wenquan Rd, Wulai. Tel:
02-2661 6392. Open: Sun–Thur 9am–9pm, Fri–Sat until 11pm. **$$**
Ample outdoor seating allows you to sit back, savor your coffee, take in the view, and absorb the crisp mountain air. Located just past the bridge after leaving Old Street.

Life in Between Museum Café
3F, 200 Wenhua Rd, Yingge.
Tel: 02-8677 2727. Open: Tue–Sun 9.30am–4.30pm, Sat–Sun until 5.30pm. **$$**
On the aerial platform of Yingge Ceramics Museum, a lovely, airy place looking over the museum gardens and off to Taipei 101. There is a good range of international coffees and organic mountain teas.

Japanese

Grandma's Sushi
63 Zhongzheng 1st Rd, Yingge. Tel:
02-2670 9345. Open: 5am–9pm.
$
An old and much cherished shop. The Taiwanese acquired a love for sushi during the Japanese colonial era. Inexpensive, wide variety, extremely fresh, and made right before you. Also has miso soup and classic local dishes.

Taiwanese

Changfu Eatery
17 Changfu St, Sanxia.
Tel: 02-2671 9543. Open: daily 9am–8pm.
$
Located right by Qingshui Zushi Temple, the specialty dish here is marinated chicken with braised pork. There is a good range of noodle dishes and the owner family is justifiably proud of their river shrimp and fish recipes.

Local taxis.

INSIGHT GUIDES **TRAVEL TIPS**
TAIPEI

TRANSPORTATION

GETTING THERE AND GETTING AROUND

GETTING THERE

By air

Taiwan's pivotal location means it is part of or sits below Asia's most important air routes. Thus, every major airline operating in Asia provides regular service to the island. With air travel over the Pacific growing steadily, advance reservations are advised; this is especially true around the week-long Chinese New Year holiday period, which generally falls in late January or early February.

All major US international airlines fly into Taoyuan Airport. There are no non-stop flights from the UK, but KLM operates a flight through Amsterdam, and British Airways – with cooperation partners – through Hong Kong and Shanghai. US flights through West Coast hubs and UK flights through Hong Kong take about 12–14 hours. Qantas and other airlines fly to and from Taiwan; Air New Zealand works with cooperation partners.

Taiwan Taoyuan International Airport

Formerly known as Chiang Kai-shek International Airport, this facility serves the island's northern and central areas. The original terminal, now Terminal 1, was given a makeover in the early 2000s. But most international airlines seek space at Terminal 2, which has more upscale restaurants, duty-free shopping, and dedicated lounge facilities. A shuttle links the two terminals. The construction of Terminal 3 is planned. For more info on the airport, tel: 03-273 3728 or visit www.taoyuan-airport.com.

The **Tourism Bureau** operates info counters in both Terminal 1 (baggage claim area; tel: 03-398 2194) and Terminal 2 (arrival hall exit; tel: 03-398 3341). Transit passengers with a layover of over 7 hours within a 24-hour period before their connection can enjoy a free half-day tour of Taipei by presenting their passport and ticket. Participants must have a valid ROC visa or come from a country eligible for visa-exempt entry. Visit their website for details (www.taiwan.net.tw).

Songshan Airport

This is Taipei's domestic airport, located in Songshan District at 340-9 Dunhua N. Rd (tel: 02-8770 3460; www.tsa.gov.tw). Flights go to other major cities in Taiwan and to the offshore islands of Kinmen (Quemoy), Matsu, and Penghu as well as to mainland China, Japan and South Korea. The advent of

KEY AIRLINE INFORMATION

Air New Zealand
11F, 25 Chang An E. Rd,
Sec.1 Tel: 02-2537 0146
www.airnewzealand.com

American Airlines
11F, 25 Chang An E. Rd, Sec.1
Tel: 02-2563 1200
www.aa.com

Cathay Pacific Airways
12F, 129 Minsheng E. Rd
Sec. 3
Tel: 02-2715 2333
www.cathaypacific.com.tw

China Airlines
131 Nanking E. Rd Sec. 3
Tel: 02-2537 0146
www.china-airlines.com

Delta Air Lines
Tel: 0080-665-1982
www.delta.com

EVA Airways Corporation
1F, 117 Changan E. Rd Sec. 2
Tel: 02-2501 9599
www.evaair.com.tw

KLM (Royal Dutch Airlines)
Tel: 02-7707 4701
www.klm.com

Qantas
11F-1, 111 Songjiang Rd
Tel: 02-2509 2000
www.qantas.com.au

United Airlines
Tel: 02-2325 8868
www.tw.united.com

TRANSPORTATION

the Taiwan High Speed Rail system has had a big impact on the domestic air carriers: a number have ceased operations, and the others have severely cut services. Check the airport website to be sure what routes are being offered. Save for holiday periods, bookings are easily made right at airport counters. Ticket prices for Taiwanese destinations average about NT$2,100, and no flight takes more than an hour.

There is limited English used on domestic flights. Note that flights to offshore islands are frequently canceled because of fog and other inclement weather. Direct bus services connect Songshan and Taoyuan International Airport. Flights to and from **Kaohsiung International Airport**, that city's domestic hub, enable connections to regional flights from there, including regular service to and from China.

By sea

Since 2009 there has been a ferry service between the mainland China harbor of Xiamen and the Taiwanese port of Keelung. It is operated by the **Cosco Star ferry**, which departs from Xiamen every Tuesday and Thursday, and leaves Keelung on Wednesdays and Sundays. The journey takes about 9 hours (www.coscotw.com.tw).

By train

There are two types of service available, the regular system run by the **Taiwan Railway Adminis-**

Alight at Taipei Bus Station.

ONLINE PURCHASE OF TRAIN TICKETS

The TRA allows online purchase of tickets 14 days ahead for trains, with collection of tickets within three days of booking at the train station itself. A pass-port must be presented at pickup. Use of this service is recommended for travel during holidays and long weekends. Visit www.railway.gov.tw.

tration (TRA) and the new **Taiwan High Speed Rail (THSR)** system launched in the mid-2000s. The THSR runs on its own set of tracks, elevated in dramatic fashion high above the plains.

From Taipei, the regular system has two lines running along the west and east coasts to the far south, connecting all major cities and towns. Trains are cheap and often full during holidays and long weekends, so book ahead. Those who do not mind the physical strain can opt for standing-room tickets. Though efficient and inexpensive, the system can be complicated, especially for non-Chinese speakers. Seek help from a local travel agency if you plan to use the network for more than one journey.

There are five regular train types. *Ziqiang*, *Juguang*, and *Fuxing* are air-conditioned services in descending order of speed. The *Qujian Che* are short- to medium-distance commuter trains, all air-conditioned, with no assigned seating. *Putong* is the cheapest and slowest service, with no air conditioning or reserved seating; these trains are often up to 50 years old and offer a close-up glimpse into countryside life.

For more information, call the service hotline (tel: 0800-765 888), the main ticketing office at **Taipei Railway Station** (tel: 02-2371 3558), where English is spoken, or visit the TRA website, which is useful, relatively clear, and in English (www.railway.gov.tw).

The TRA, facing heavy competition from the THSR and improved bus services, is refocusing on short and intermediate commuter travel and on tourist runs. For the tourist trains, prices often include accommodations, road transport to certain sites, and entry tickets. Details

are available on the website, including info on which travel agencies will handle bookings for you.

THSR (tel: 4066 3000; www.thsrc.com.tw) offers a high-speed link between Taipei Railway Station and Zuoying in Kaohsiung. Express trains complete the journey in 96 minutes while regular THSR trains making all eight stops along the way take two hours. There are standard and business carriages on each train; the system runs 6am to midnight.

By bus/coach

Long-distance bus travel is popular with locals because of the low cost – a bus ticket from Taichung, in central Taiwan, to Taipei is only about NT$300. In addition, since most bus terminals are right around Taipei Railway Station, connection to the MRT and city bus systems is easy. Many companies operate 24 hour-services.

A bus trip from Kaohsiung in the south normally takes about 5 hours, and costs NT$500–800, depending on the time of day. During holidays, however, it may take much longer. At these times, planes or trains are the way to go. Bus travel down the cliff-hugging east coast is not recommended.

Many private companies run inter-city services to Taipei. Ask your hotel concierge for advice on which service to use and for help in getting to the terminal. By departure time almost all buses are fully booked; it is best to buy reserved-seat tickets at the station one or two days prior to departure. Services range from standard to deluxe, with sofa chairs and large TVs in the coach. Videos are always played, often at full volume, save late at night; earplugs are advised.

ACTIVITIES

A – Z

LANGUAGE

GETTING AROUND

From Taoyuan Airport

Located in Taoyuan County, 45km (28 miles) south-west of Taipei city, Taiwan Taoyuan International Airport is linked to Taipei's north area and downtown by the Sun Yat-sen Freeway, and to the city's south and east via a link expressway and the Second Northern Freeway. Travel time to Taipei on both routes is about 45 minutes.

By taxi

Only registered airport service taxis can pick up passengers at the two terminals. A 50 percent surcharge is added to the fare displayed on the meter, and you must also pay highway tolls. A taxi to the city center from the airport will set you back about NT$1,200. By law, taxis must take you anywhere in Taiwan you wish to go.

For trips from the city to the airport, the law says travelers pay only the metered fare, but drivers generally will not agree to a trip (for which they can get no return rider) for less than NT$1,000.

By bus

Dedicated airport buses serve both terminals, stopping directly outside the arrival halls. At least four bus companies offer service to and from the airport: **Kuo-Kuang Motor Transport**, **CitiAir Bus**, **Free Go Bus**, and **Evergreen Bus**. Stops are made in the city at many fixed locations indicated by roadside airport-service signs. The ear-

liest service leaves Taipei at 4am, and the latest from the airport at 1.15am, both with Free Go Bus. One-way adult fare ranges from NT$90 to NT$145. Ticket counters are in the arrival halls, but if you need further help, approach the airport information counter. Consolidated details on bus services and 24-hour taxis are on the airport website (see page 240).

From Songshan Airport

As the airport is within city limits (10–15 min drive to downtown), there is no limo service or shuttle connections to the rail network. Scheduled taxis wait outside the terminal; a surcharge is added. Unscheduled taxis that have just let people off can pick passengers up at the western end of the terminal without surcharge. A taxi ride to/from about any point in the city should not be more than NT$230. Many city buses come right up to the terminal building, including two that connect to the Muzha MRT line; many other buses connecting to different MRT lines stop on Minquan Rd, which runs east-west in front of the terminal. A detailed map showing buses stopping at and around the terminal is given on the airport website (www.tsa.gov.tw). There are buses to Taoyuan International Airport from the station at the western end of the terminal.

Orientation

Taipei City encompasses an area of 270 sq km (104 sq miles), from the

district of Wenshan in the south to Yangmingshan National Park in the north, but its urban core is the area of roughly 56 sq km (22 sq miles) bordered by the Danshui and Jilong rivers. Local residents (including taxi drivers) often do not know their city in these terms. The majority know their own immediate neighborhoods only. For many, missing the drop-off point by one or two stops means they get a bit lost.

In general, residents tend to see the city in terms of major arteries and landmarks – large malls, a famous restaurant etc. Luckily, maps with good English are found in all MRT stations. There are also good tourist maps of the city available at all tourist service centers.

Public transportation

Taipei's public transport system is intricate, efficient, and inexpensive. The still-young and ever-expanding MRT system is your key to easy exploration of the city. Bus routes color-coded to the corresponding MRT line launch from each station to almost all points in that station's vicinity.

Metro (MRT)

Widely known as the MRT (*jieyun* in Mandarin), it is easy to reach almost all points of interest using Taipei's Metro and a short bus ride, taxi trip, or walk.

In all stations there is a bank of machines from which you may purchase single-trip tokens or day passes. The former, which can be used only on the day of purchase, can be swiped at machines beside exit toll gates to obtain a free pass for a single bus trip. The latter, which includes a refundable deposit of NT$50, allows unlimited use of the system on the day of purchase, with same-day bus transfers available each time you exit a station. The machines provide change if you only have bills. There are instructions and route charts in clear English on the ticket machines. Fares range from NT$20 to NT$65, depending on the distance traveled. A 24-hour metro

EASYCARD

The EasyCard, a stored-value contactless smartcard usable on all local buses, the MRT, all city-owned parking lots, some private lots, metered parking spots, Xinyi District automated bike-rental kiosks, train travel, and many other locations, is sold for NT$500, comprising a NT$400 stored value and a NT$100

refundable deposit. There is a maximum NT$10,000 balance. They are available at MRT stations, bus stations, and convenience stores throughout the city and Taipei County; top them up at dedicated EasyCard machines in all stations. Unused fees and the deposit are refundable. For more info, visit www.easycard.com.tw.

DRIVING ADVICE

Locally, the concept of no-fault liability has not taken hold. Each party theoretically pays according to the blame apportioned, though the reality may sometimes be different. Overseas visitors are advised to always call the Foreign Affairs Police, whatever the seriousness of an incident (http://english.tcpd.taipei.gov.tw). Locals prefer to settle on the spot, avoiding police and insurance companies for less serious incidents, though this sometimes leads to cases of manipulation.

Be advised that the number one rule of the road, whatever is written officially, is that the big guy goes first, and that anyone with his nose in a spot first gets that spot. Many local drivers seem to believe it is possible to have two moving bodies in one space, and test this theory regularly, especially in heavy traffic.

pass costs NT$200. For those staying a few days, the **EasyCard** is the best option; it brings you a discount of 20 percent off the stated adult fare for each trip. The system operates from 6am to midnight daily.

Bicycles are permitted on the end-carriages on weekends and holidays, from 6am to end of service; a single-journey ticket for a person with a bike is NT$80. Bike access to the stations is via the street-level elevators at most stations (exceptions include the whole Wenhu line); these are marked on signboards and the online route map; parking at stations is always in demand.

The MRT system extends to two major points outside the city – north to the port of Danshui and south to the city of Xindian, where buses to Wulai can be caught.

For more details visit the **Taipei Rapid Transit Corporation** website (www.trtc.com.tw) or call the **Metro Taipei Service Hotline** at tel: 1999 (when calling from Taipei) or 02-2181 2345 (24 hours).

Buses

Taipei offers a comprehensive bus network that is cheap, clean, and easy to understand. The city has implemented a GPS system, with displays showing bus ETAs. On board, upcoming stops are announced in English and shown on displays above the driver.

Routes extend through the city and often into the surrounding Taipei County as well. All buses are air-conditioned. The fare is NT$15 (for adults) for each leg of a route (longer routes are broken into separate sections; most journeys that do not cross a river involve just one section). Fares can be paid in cash by dropping the exact amount (no change given) into a glass box by the driver, though most locals use the EasyCard. Last buses leave the terminals at 11pm. For more detail and route maps, visit www.e-bus.taipei.gov.tw.

Taxis

Taxis are ubiquitous and available any time of day simply by hailing from the street. Fares are low, with the average cross-town trip no more than NT$250 or so. Charges are NT$70 for the first 1.25km (0.7 miles) and NT$5 for every additional 250 meters/yds. NT$5 is also charged for every 1 minute and 40 seconds the cab is traveling under 5kph. There is a an NT$20 surcharge for all rides that start between 11pm and 6am. These rates and fees also apply throughout Taipei County except in Danshui, Ruifang, and Wulai. For trips further afield the meter will most likely not be used; agree on a fee beforehand to avoid dispute. Starting two days prior to and including the entire Chinese New Year holidays, an extra NT$20 will be added to the total amount for all trips; there is also a standard surcharge of NT$20 added at night.

Most taxi drivers cannot converse in English, so have your destination and hotel written down in Chinese. Drivers cannot refuse an intra-city fare, no matter how short the distance. For any complaints,

the best resource is the Traffic Division, Taipei City Police Department at tel: 02-2321 4666.

Driving

The city's public transport is very efficient, and few short-term visitors rent vehicles save for longer excursions. Traffic is too heavy and parking space too difficult to find to make driving in the city worthwhile. Rental companies listed in the English papers are reliable, provide service in English, and charge reasonable rates. Outside of Taipei, English signage is unreliable except on major highways, and many a newcomer has experienced frustration on driving excursions. Only the adventurous need apply, and only if extra time is allowed for inadvertent "detours." Note that these roads are also often quite narrow, with many switchbacks and barely enough room for two vehicles, especially on curves.

An international license is required for driving in Taiwan. Driving is on the right-hand side of the road, and all vehicle occupants are required by law to wear a seatbelt.

Cycling

The city boasts an extensive network of bicycle paths as well as an automated bike-rental system, "YouBike", in operation since 2009. There are nearly 200 rental stations across the whole of Taipei, and bikes can be rented and dropped off at any one of them, which makes the system a comfortable way to shuttle through the city. For a single ride the fee is NT$10 for every 30 minutes within the first four hours, NT$20 per 30 minutes between four and eight hours, and NT$40 per 30 minutes over eight hours; a deposit, which can be paid by a credit card, is required. Long-term users (registered as members) ride free for the first half an hour. The EasyCard can be used to pay for rental. For rental instructions and a map showing the location of kiosks visit: www.youbike.com.tw; tel: 02-8978 5511.

ACTIVITIES

FESTIVALS, THE ARTS, NIGHTLIFE, SIGHTSEEING TOURS, SPORT, AND CHILDREN'S ACTIVITIES

FESTIVALS

Public holidays are marked with an asterisk (*). For more details on events, contact the Taiwan Tourism Bureau; 02-2349 1500; 0800-011 765 (24H); www.taiwan.net.tw. Or contact the Taipei City Govt. Dept. of Information and Tourism; 02-2720 8889; www.taipei.gov. tw (For a complete list of public holidays, see page 261).

January

Pingxi Sky Lantern Festival. One of Taiwan's more unique traditional festivals, and one of ethereal beauty. In the upper Jilong River valley, thousands of glowing "sky lanterns," mini hot-air balloons, are released into the night sky, each carrying personal prayers to the gods. Can occur in Feb.
Taipei Lunar New Year Shopping Carnival. Shops in five commercial clusters in Datong District, notably Dihua Street, come together during the two-week run-up to Chinese New Year with myriad special discounts, premium giveaways, snacks for shoppers, and other enticements, making the annual shopping spree something of a party.

February

Taipei Lantern Festival. A 10-day event with thousands of theme lanterns and colorful folk arts closing off the traditional New Year holidays, held at or around the Sun Yat-sen Memorial and Taipei City Hall.
Taipei Flower Festival. Also called the Yangmingshan Flower Festival, this stretches over almost two months (end of Jan–start of March), when the great army of flowers first planted on Yangmingshan by the Japanese burst in bloom, attracting a flood of admirers to the hills to enjoy special displays, artistic performances, picnicking, and more.

March

Taipei Traditional Arts Festival. Brings in top talent, mostly from Asia, specifically the Chinese world, for a series of about 30 large-scale performances stretching over two-plus months. The main venue is Zhongshan Hall. Tel: 02-2383 2170; www.tco. taipei.gov.tw.

April

Tomb Sweeping Day*. Held on April 5 (2015) or April 4 (2016 and 2017); also called Ancestor Worship Day. Cities empty and the countryside fills up as entire clans head to the hills to clean family tombs, pay ceremonial respects with time-honored rituals, and spend a half-day out together.

June

Dragon Boat Festival*. Second of the three big traditional festivals of the Chinese year. It is celebrated around the summer solstice, with city-staged dragon-boat races and traditional-arts performances at Dajia Riverside Park. The boats symbolize the escorting of high-summer pestilence out to sea. In 2016 it will actually be held in June, while in 2017 it will take place in May.
Taipei Film Festival. A platform for the promotion of local movie-makers, with showings from many other countries as well, that spans two to three weeks. Usually goes on into July. Most screenings are at Zhongshan Hall. Tel: 02-2528 9580; www.taipeiff.org.tw.

July

Yingge Ceramics Festival. A celebration of Yingge's 200 years as Taiwan's greatest center of ceramics production. The two main venues are Yingge Ceramics Museum and Old Street, with a series of kiln visits, DIY workshops, and entertainment events. Runs into August. Tel: 02-8677 2727; www.ceramics.ntpc.gov.tw.

August

Keelung Ghost Festival. Ghost Month runs the entire seventh lunar month (May start in July or extend into September), with the largest-scale celebrations to appease visiting other-worldly spirits in the coastal city of Keelung, around downtown temples, with a magical floating-lantern ceremony at Badouzi harbor to guide water spirits in. Tel: 02-2422 4170 ext. 367; www.klccab.gov.tw

Taipei Dadaocheng Fireworks and Music Festival. A one-day party in the park around Dadaocheng Wharf, with pop concerts bracketing a huge fireworks show over Danshui River. Tens of thousands fill the Dadaocheng neighborhood.

Taiwan Culinary Exhibition. A hugely popular multi-day food extravaganza staged at the Taipei World Trade Center. The main focus is on the many styles of Chinese food, with chef competitions, DIY classes, endless sampling, and a bazaar-like food court.

September

Mid-Autumn (Moon) Festival*. Third of the three big annual Chinese festivals, celebrating the harvest moon and bountiful crops. At night, open spaces will be filled with families and groups of friends feasting at hibachi barbecues and admiring the perfect moon, its roundness symbolizing the perfection of reunited families. Scheduled to be held on Sept 27 in 2015, Sept 15 in 2016, and Oct 4 in 2017.

October

Double Tenth National Day*. The October 10 (Double Tenth),

LOCAL LISTINGS

Visitors can obtain information on the arts, nightlife, shopping, and eating out through several publications available free at hotels or tourist information counters of the Taipei City Government and Tourism Bureau. *This Month in Taiwan* and the bimonthly *Travel in Taiwan* and *Discover Taipei* are

all magazines chock-full of useful information. The weekend editions of the two local English newspapers are also useful, especially the Friday editions.

The Taiwan Fun website, at www.taiwanfun.com, is also one of the best sources of listings and information.

1911 uprising in China that created the Republic is celebrated before the Presidential Office Building with a full-day menu, including the National Day Parade, ceremonial military review, folk performances, and hours of night-sky color with the National Day Fireworks Display.

Taipei Hakka Yimin Festival. Celebrates the unique cultural legacy of the Hakka people with traditional temple processions, shoulder-pole performances, Hakka-style lion dance parade, food bazaars, traditional "tea-picking" opera, and more. Main venues are The Red House, National Concert Hall, and Zhongshan Hall. Sometimes staged in November.

December

Taipei New Year's Eve Countdown Party. Centered on Citizen Plaza at the front of Taipei City Hall, the entire district pedestrian-only, this is a massive party with pop stars performing non-stop, traditional food and folk-art areas, and a terrific fireworks show over Taipei 101 at midnight.

THE ARTS

There has been a real explosion of creative expression since the lifting of martial law in 1987, with myriad private initiatives complementing government-sponsored groups. Many have garnered critical acclaim internationally. In the spring each

year, the city government sponsors the Taipei Traditional Arts Festival in support of age-old art forms.

Art galleries

Taipei's private galleries represent a wide range of styles, from traditional landscapes to modern abstract and installation art. Most of the artists are local. If time is limited, the best option to explore is the **Apollo Building** (actually a complex of five buildings) in the upscale Dinghao shopping area, which houses a number of the island's most important galleries; most other key venues are also found in the East District.

Apollo Gallery
2F, Apollo Building A, No. 218–6, Zhongxiao E. Rd Sec. 4
Tel: 02-2781 9332
www.artgalleryapollo.com
One of Taipei's most venerable and respected galleries. Pan-Asian contemporary art complements Taiwanese oil paintings.

Asia Art Center
177 Jianguo S. Rd
Tel: 02-2754 1366
www.asiaartcenter.org
In the business since 1982, this is a display space for Chinese artists, both traditional-style masters and contemporary artists. Housed in a bright and airy refurbished facility with three floors of displays.

Digital Art Center Taipei
180 Fuhua Rd
Tel: 02-7736 0708
www.dac.tw
A sleek new venue dedicated to

The smart Vie Show Cinema.

"R&D, experimentation, creation and incubation" in the digital arts, fusing digital technologies and arts, with a heavy focus on performance projects. Local and international talent. Near Zhishan MRT Station.

Songshan Cultural and Creative Park
133 Guangfu S. Rd
Tel: 02-2765 1388

BUYING TICKETS

Tickets for performances at the National Concert Hall or Theater can be purchased at the venues or at CKS Cultural Center outlets. Tickets for many other events can be obtained at ERA outlets.
ERA outlets: Caves Books, FNAC, Kingstone Bookstore, and the New Schoolmate Books branches on Tianmu E. Rd and on Renai Traffic Circle. Service personnel will likely not speak English. Tel: 02-2341 9898; www.ticket.com.tw.

www.songshanculturalpark.org Taipei's creative hub opened in 2011 in a former tobacco factory in the Xinyi District. Now one of the most energetic cultural institutions in the city.

Cinema

The Taiwanese tend to prefer big blockbuster Hollywood hits or Hong Kong's mass-market movies. The local movie-making industry has suffered as a result over the years, with movies rarely doing well at local theaters if they are given cinema screen-time at all. There are exceptions – in 2009 *Cape No. 7* broke records, becoming the second-highest grossing movie of all time in Taiwan (see page 60).

Most movie-watching venues are cineplexes. Overseas movies are shown in the original language, with Chinese subtitles. Note that local audiences will talk more during a movie, and eat substantial foods with stronger aroma than Western moviegoers

may be used to – though this is now more prevalent at older theaters rather than the swanky new stand-alone cineplexes such as **Vie Show Cinemas** (www.vs cinemas.com.tw) or those in new department stores such as **Core Pacific City** (http://web01.living mall.com.tw).

The local English-language newspapers have daily listings of screenings and theaters. Adult tickets are about NT$250, with discounts for morning showings.

If you are keen to see local movies, **SPOT Taipei Film House** has an intimate arthouse-film screening center for 98 people (see page 136). In 2005, when director Tsai Ming-liang's award-winning *The Wayward Cloud* proved too risqué for local censors, this was the only public venue where you could see it.

Each year the city government hosts the **Taipei Film Festival** (www.taipeiff.org.tw), showing the works of young directors, especially non-mainstream and independent movies, made both locally and overseas. The movies are shown at a number of venues, including Zhongshan Hall.

New high-end performing venues include Taipei Performing Arts Center, which houses three theaters and Taipei Pop Music Center, due to open in 2016.

Performing arts venues

Huashan 1914 Creative Park
1 Bade Rd Sec. 1
Tel: 02-2358 1914
www.huashan1914.com
Opened in 2007 in a restored factory building, Huashan is a creative arts' center which hosts a number of cultural events including music festivals and art shows.

National Concert Hall
21-1 Zhongshan S. Rd
Tel: 02-3393 9888
http://npac-ntch.org
Home of the Taipei Symphony Orchestra. Classical and pop talents, frequently from overseas.

National Dr Sun Yat-sen Memorial Hall
505 Renai Rd Sec. 4
Tel: 02-2758 8008
www.yatsen.gov.tw
Large-scale musical and dramatic performances, local and international, are staged here.

National Theater
21-1 Zhongshan S. Rd
Tel: 02-3393 9888
http://npac-ntch.org
Chinese and Taiwanese opera, Chinese folk arts, Western opera, and ballets are staged. The Experimental Theater hosts small-scale events.

Novel Hall for Performing Arts
3 Songshou Rd
Tel: 02-2722 4302
www.novelhall.org.tw
Dedicated to the promotion of traditional Chinese stage arts, with regular performances of Chinese drama, including Beijing, Taiwanese, and Hakka opera. Troupes from China are often invited to perform here.

The Red House
10 Chengdu Rd
Tel: 02-2311 9380
www.redhouse.org.tw

On the second floor of a lovely heritage building, small-scale traditional Chinese art forms such as puppetry, children's theater, and folk singing are some of the highlights.

TaipeiEYE
113 Zhongshan N. Rd Sec. 2
Tel: 02-2568 2677
www.taipeieye.com
Traditional Taiwanese, Chinese, and aboriginal performance arts each Mon, Wed, Fri–Sat night, with a sampling of many forms in an exciting 60–90-minute visual and aural kaleidoscope specially tailored for the tourist. Takes care to explain each form's evolution in the past century. Located in the heritage "Taiwan Cement Hall."

Zhongshan Hall
98 Yanping S. Rd
Tel: 02-2381 3137
www.tco.taipei.gov.tw
This is the main venue for the Taipei Traditional Arts Festival, sponsored by the city each spring. Traditional Chinese instrumental music, Chinese opera forms, hand puppetry, and various other folk-art performances are also staged here year-round.

NIGHTLIFE

From homey British-style pubs to upscale dance clubs with the best international DJs brought in for special shows, Taipei pulses each night into the early hours. Pubs and bars are often open as early as 11.30am for lunch, and clubs with kitchen facilities open around 6pm. The majority close between 1am and 3am. In general an imported bottle of beer will cost NT$150–200, a glass of wine about the same, and mixed drinks NT$200 or more. Pubs and bars for each area are listed in the Places chapters; venues focused on music are listed below.

One of the most popular nightlife areas with the younger crowd is Shida Road. A more expensive – the word "upscale" is not quite appropriate – entertainment dis-

trict is the "Combat Zone" (see page 82). Most of the establishments here are girlie bars, the clientele primarily middle-aged or older bar-hopping men.

Clubs and discos

It is the under-30s, of course, who go clubbing, and Taipei has the requisite number of venues and themes to bring them in. The attraction is dance, and most spots offer a mix of canned dance music and DJs, both local and imported.

Wanhua
Paris Night Club
5F, 89 Wuchang St Sec. 2
Tel: 02-2331 6067
A venerable club in place for three decades now. Great vintage disco decor, though no disco music; instead it ranges from local pop to Western. Sometimes presents live bands, including from overseas.

Taipei East
Babe 18
18 Songshou Rd
Tel: 0930 785 018
In the Vie Show Cinemas complex, run by the same group that handles Room 18 nearby. Targeted at a very young (but legal age) crowd. The music is hip-hop. Open Wed to Sun, there is a cover, and there are constant theme parties.

DV8
385 Fuxing S. Rd Sec. 2
Tel: 02-2733 9039
www.dv8taipei.com
A new club run by a DJ billing himself "king of night-market hard house," ie, very, very fast beats. DJ Tim from Massachusetts plays on Wednesday nights. Happy hour everyday 6–9pm.

Lava
B1, 22 Songshou Rd
Tel: 933 893 189
www.lava-club.com.tw
A newer spot beside Room 18, this is perhaps Taipei's hottest all-you-can-drink club (Wed, Thu, Sun). On Fri and Sat the cover

NIGHTMARKETS

The nightmarkets of Taipei are regularly among the top four most popular attractions for overseas visitors. In addition to a smorgasbord of traditional Taiwanese snacks, peddlers hawk cheap clothing, accessories, handicrafts, and more. There are nightmarkets all over the city (refer to the Places section for details).

goes up, but just covers drinks of the same value. It Is jammed to the rafters on weekends.

Luxy
5F, 197 Zhongxiao E. Rd Sec. 4
Tel: 02-2772 1000
www.luxy-taipei.com
One of the sleekest and ritziest of the city's glitzy dance clubs. In fact it is two clubs in one, each with a very different ambience, top DJs, VIP rooms and lounges. Cover of NT$500–600 Wed to Sat, with free entry before 11pm. Ladies' night is Wed, and there is a house dance party on Thu.

Myst
9F, ATT4Fun, 12 Songshou Rd
Tel: 02-7737 9997
www.club-myst.com
An immensely popular night club, the number one night spot in recent years, hence the fact that it's usually jam-packed. It's located right next to Taipei 101 tower, which can be admired from the club's external balcony.

Primo
2F, 297 Zhongxiao E. Rd Sec. 5
Tel: 0958 783 838
A very stylish club, and likely Taipei's most exclusive, with a club membership scheme. Charges NT$1,000 entry Wed–Sat for non-members. Everyone is dressed to kill, and local pop star sightings are common. The music is hip-hop and house.

Room 18
B1, 88 Songren Rd
Tel: 02-2345 2778
www.room18.com.tw

Bring lots of plastic to this dance club party haven for local rich kids. Everyone is ultra-cool and the DJs are über hip. There's hip-hop in one room, house in the other. Cover charge Wed, Fri, Sat, with irregular live sets.

SPARK
12 Songshou Rd
Tel: 02-7737 9885
www.sparktaipei.com.tw
One of Taipei's most popular dance clubs has hip-hop, R&B, electro, and house music. It is a visually stunning spot, with a translucent glowing dance floor and ceiling, LCD screens everywhere, and a giant rectangular bar.

Ziga Zaga
2F, 2 Songshou Rd
Tel: 02-2720 1200 ext. 3198
This joint in the Grand Hyatt leads a double life – restaurant by day, live jazz club after the witching hour (7.30pm in this case). Attracts a mostly 30-something professional crowd. Brings in premium overseas bands.

Taipei South

Club W
67 Roosevelt Rd Sec. 2
Tel: 02-3365 3041
Near the corner of Roosevelt and Heping roads, this is a gritty venue with DJs in a basement, featuring many folk who never seem to see the light. NT$500 cover on weekends gets you all you can drink. Has wet T-shirt contests, pole dance contests, and such.

Gay and lesbian venues

While not as hedonistic as, say, Bangkok, Taipei still has a solid gay nightlife scene – less raunchy, but more friendly than many of Asia's hipper cities. There is no single area of concentration for gay nightspots. Foreigners are more than welcome. At clubs, be prepared for techno remixes of Taiwanese hits, which patrons will enthusiastically sing along to. Stranger yet is the spontaneous "cha cha"

that breaks out as the night wears on. The websites www.fri-dae.com, www.gaytie.info and www.utopia-asia.com have listings and updates.

Wanhua

Bon T-Bar
B1, 9 Boai Rd
Tel: 02-2381 3849
A women-only venue that is always filled to the brim when the next day is a day off. Open 10pm to 7am. Bar has a good selection of local and imported beverages. Light foods available; canned music.

Café Dalida
51, Lane 10, Chengdu Rd
Tel: 02-2370 7833
Foreigner-friendly gay bar in the courtyard at The Red House. The Red House area has emerged as Taipei's hottest rainbow district. Alfresco bar open during the day and well into the night.

G-Mixi
51, Lane 10, Chengdu Rd, www.facebook.com/Gmixibar
Tel: 02-2388 2069
Extremely friendly bear bar, run by loquacious Singaporean Donny, also in The Red House. Mostly Taiwanese, Japanese, and mainland Chinese, the bar staff pass your personal info along on the back of the house business card to those you may want to meet.

Central Taipei

Body Pub
6, Lane 135, Zhongshan N. Rd Sec. 1
Tel: 02-2565 1072
A small and cozy space for wine, music, and karaoke. Gay-owned and very friendly. Designed by the owner, it is one of the city's more visually attractive nightspots. Mixed drinks are NT$250–300.

Funky
B1, 10 Hangzhou S. Rd Sec. 1, www.funky.club.tw
Tel: 02-2394 2162
In business for two decades. Popular club with overseas partygoers and also a mainstay of the scene. Also features karaoke.

Seen in the Taiwanese hit movie *Formula 17*.

G*star
B1, 23 Songjiang Rd
Tel: 02-2721 8323
A dance club opened in 2009, flowing with lasers and black curtains. Plays Taiwanese pop tunes. Has a cover charge, and happy hour from midnight to 2am.

IT Park
2F, 41 Yitong St, www.itpark.com.tw
Tel: 02-2507 7243
A chic, comfy art gallery-cum-bar, there is a cozy terrace here that is perfect for tea or coffee and a chat.

Taipei East

Jump
B1, 68 Keelung Rd Sec. 1, www.club-jump.com
Tel: 02-2756 0055
A big underground gay club, with friends also welcome. Features frequent theme parties and dancing, dancing, dancing, the focus on thumping electronic dance music and house music.

Taipei South

Fresh
2F, 7 Jinshan S. Rd Sec. 2
Tel: 02-2358 7701
A gathering place with a bar on the first floor, a disco on the second, and a rooftop garden with sofas perfect for lounging. Cover charge Fri–Sat night.

Gin Gin Bookstore
8, Alley 8, Lane 210, Roosevelt Rd Sec. 3, www.ginginbooks.com
Tel: 02-2364 2006
A well-stocked gay bookstore with the usual mix of books, music, videos, and more risqué merchandise. The gay Hours café is next door, and Love Boat lesbian specialty shop across the street (www.lesloveboat.com).

Jazz and live music

As elsewhere, it seems, Taipei's jazz audience cannot match its pop and rock audiences in terms of size, but it certainly

does so in terms of passion.

Over the course of an evening or on alternating nights, jazz venues will often range into R&B and even pop, while rock venues may move into soft rock and pop. Alternative venues, on the contrary, brook no mainstream diversions, staying true to its spirit.

Central Taipei

The Farmhouse
5, Lane 32, Shuangcheng St
Tel: 02-2595 1764
One of the old venerables in the Combat Zone, not in the girlie bar vein, but in an English yeoman cottage style. A dinner club/live music venue is on the ground floor, and a British pub below. Has a different band each day.

Taipei East

Brown Sugar
101 Songren Rd
Tel: 02-8780 1110
www.brownsugarlive.com
The live band each night is usually local but overseas groups are sometimes brought in. The music is mainly jazz and blues, with some soft rock. Check the website for events, artists, and menu.

EZ5
211 Anhe Rd Sec. 2
Tel: 02-2738 3995
www.ez5.com.tw
If you love Canto pop, come to this live-music club-cum-restaurant venue in the hot Anhe Road entertainment district. Two to three recognizable regional stars take to the stage each night, starting after 9.30pm, many throwing off some of the usual syrupy style for more throaty tunes.

Taipei South

Blue Note
4F, 171 Roosevelt Rd Sec. 3
Tel: 02-2362 2333
On the south edge of the Shida area, Blue Note has live jazz each night, with the audience invited to jam when the house band plays. In the day, slide on headphones and groove to thousands of album selections.

Riverside Music Café
B1, 2, Lane 224, Roosevelt Rd Sec. 3
Tel: 02-2368 7310
www.riverside.com.tw
Live band performances nightly 9.30–11.30pm. All music styles, from jazz to fusion to pop and alternative rock. Open mike on Mon. Cover charge includes one free drink (NT$250 Mon–Fri, NT$300 Sat–Sun).

Witch House
7, Lane 56, Xinsheng S. Rd Sec. 3
Tel: 02-2362 5494
www.witchhouse.org
A small café-cum-restaurant that becomes a venue for alternative live art at night. Live musical acts are the main attraction, but there are also stage shows, poetry readings, and other activities.

Karaoke (KTV)

Karaoke singers in Taiwan get their own soundproof den-like room, small to very large, which loosens the inhibitions of those too shy to sing in front of an open crowd. Rooms are equipped with a large-screen TV and high-quality sound system. A group pays a base fee, which allows a specific number of song selections; additional tunes are available with an extra charge. Teas, juices, pop, alcohol, and snack foods are served, and each person gets a complimentary beverage. Mandarin, Taiwanese, and Japanese tunes are abundant, but the selection of Western tunes will vary. Two chains of good repute, Cash Box Partyworld (www.cashboxparty.com) and Holiday KTV (www.holiday.com.tw), have large selections of English songs. Most KTV lounges are open 24 hours or almost till dawn. Be aware that a number of tragedies in the past have raised general concerns about fire safety. Inspection is now much stricter, especially within city limits, but be sure to check fire exits and extinguishers when visiting.

Old Walled City and Zhongzheng

Holiday KTV
34 Guanqian Rd
Tel: 02-2381 9208

Central Taipei

Cash Box Partyworld
312 Linsen N. Rd
Tel: 02-2537 2235
Cash Box Partyworld
3 Nanjing E. Rd Sec. 2
Tel: 02-2560 2111

Taipei East

Cash Box Partyworld
22 Zhongxiao E. Rd Sec. 4
Tel: 02-2771 5000
Holiday KTV
29 Fuxing S. Rd Sec. 1
Tel: 02-2751 2508

SIGHTSEEING TOURS

Customized tours

All Taipei-based travel agencies accredited by the Tourism Bureau for English-language tours handle customized excursions suiting specific needs, with experienced guides that provide insights you likely won't come across in guidebooks or other sources. A listing of agencies can be found on the bureau's website www.taiwan.net.tw.

DIY walking tours

The Tourism Bureau has a good brochure with easy-to-follow maps introducing Taipei's two oldest areas, **Dadaocheng** and **Wanhua**, available at the bureau's main office and its travel information center in the city (see page 262). Ask for the *Taipei Walking Tours: Heritage*.

If you plan to tackle one of the many hiking trails surrounding the city, three fine books will prove invaluable. Written by long-term expat Richard Saunders, *Taipei Day Trips 1* and *2*, and *Yangmingshan the Guide*, direct you to trailheads and introduce what you'll see on the

way, with clear maps and instructions provided. The books are available at most **Eslite Bookstores**, **Caves Books**, **PageOne** Bookstores, and the **Community Services Center**.

Guided bus tours

A number of local travel agencies accredited by the Tourism Bureau provide scheduled half-day tours of the main sites within the city, as well as to the destinations explored in the Excursions chapters. The itineraries of the different companies are remarkably similar, as are the prices. General details and links to agencies can be found on the Tourism Bureau's special Taiwan Tour Bus website www.taiwantourbus.com.tw.

Pickups are available at most international hotels. Buses are air-conditioned, and qualified guides are proficient in English. You can contact the agencies directly or have your hotel do it.

There are two very popular tours within the city, both daytime outings, one to the National Palace Museum, Martyrs' Shrine, and Longshan Temple (NT$900), the other to Dihua Street, Lin An Tai Historical House and Museum, and Baoan Temple, with a Chinese kung fu show and a visit to a foot-massage parlor included (NT$1,300). A nighttime adventure to Snake Alley, Longshan Temple, and Taipei 101 starts with a Mongolian barbecue dinner (NT$1,300; excludes ticket to Taipei 101 observation deck). There is also a hot-springs tour to Beitou and Yangmingshan (NT$1,300). Half-day excursions include visits to Wulai (NT$1,300), the North Coast (NT$1,000), and the Northeast Coast plus Jiufen (NT$1,100).

Pickup is about 8.30am for morning and full-day tours, and 6pm for evening tours. Avoid tours on weekends, when roads and venues are crowded. Below are the most popular operators.

Bobby Travel Service: 11F, 88 Changan E. Rd Sec. 2, tel: 02-8500

3034, www.bobby.com.tw.
Edison Travel Service: 4F, 190 Songjiang Rd, tel: 02-2563 5313, www.edison.com.tw.
Golden Foundation Tours: 5F, 142 Zhongxiao E. Rd Sec. 4, tel: 02-2773 3266, www.gftours.com.tw.
Have Fun Travel Service: 3F, 38 Nanjing E. Rd Sec. 2, tel: 02-2536 3782, www.havefuntravel.tw.
South East Travel Service: 60 Zhongshan N. Rd Sec. 2, tel: 02-2522 1000, www.settour.com.tw.

EXCURSIONS

Directions to day-trip destinations are found in the Places chapters, but due to limited English outside the city, tours are advised.

Nature tours

The **Community Services Center** (see page 255) periodically sponsors nature-exploration tours, generally in English, led by knowledgable individuals. Check the website for upcoming events.

River tours

Originally the term **Blue Highway Tours** was used in Taiwan to refer to coastal tours on blue ocean waters. It is now used to refer to river tours as well, though waters of blue you will not see. Taipei has ten tour routes from five wharves, including from Dadaocheng Wharf to Fisherman's Wharf at coastal Danshui (90 minutes); from Dadaocheng Wharf to Guandu Wharf (45 minutes); and from Guandu Wharf to Fisherman's Wharf (30 minutes). Some, but not all, trips between Dadaocheng and Danshui stop at Guandu. You are allowed to bring bicycles on the boats, meaning sections of the riverside bike-path network can be skipped if desired. Bikes rented at kiosks at Dadaocheng and Guandu can be dropped off at the other location after use. The Taipei

City Govt. also promotes a Blue Highway run on the Jilong River between Guandu and Dajia Riverside Park, but there are relatively few customers because the banks are often high and vision thus restricted. The service is often sporadic to non-existent, especially during the cool winter months.

From Fisherman's Wharf there are also true Blue Highway tours (about 45 minutes) off the coast but always in view of the river mouth. All cruises are on privately owned yachts. Reservations are possible but not necessary; show up at the ticket kiosks by the respective piers and line up. Departures are frequent during daylight hours. Note that service is sometimes suspended in the cool winter months due to lack of business. Services run daily from 10am to 7pm.

Tour operators do not speak English (and often do not answer phones), so your best sources of assistance or information are the city-run tourist counters around the city and, during the week, the city's Dept. of Information and Tourism (tel: 02-2720 8889). Blue Highway's website: www.riv-

erfun.taipei.gov.tw.

General information is broadcast on speakers during tours, but in Chinese and almost impossible to hear over the engines. However, since 2014 there have been English speaking tour-guides on some of the routes.

SPORT

Participant sports

Adventure sports

Two-thirds of Taiwan is comprised of rugged mountain. Though it offers unlimited outdoor adventure thrills and spills, it is not recommended that you head out alone. Reliable clubs with trained guides and personnel, especially ones that speak English, are almost impossible to find. Government oversight is sporadic or non-existent, though the tourism promotion offices will still promote the sport. Bungee jumping and paragliding are examples where no official body oversees the certification for guides or instructors. Whether for high-mountain hiking,

trekking, climbing, sea kayaking, river tracing, or others, you are strongly advised to hook up with an experienced organizer, for example **FreshTreks** (www.freshtreks.com), **TaiwanAdventures** (www.taiwan-adventures.com), or **In Motion Asia** (http://inmotionasia.com). All these companies are founded and run by expats, and handle everything from pick-up and drop-off to equipment provision and passes. They offer prepackaged and custom excursions.

Bowling

Yuanshan Sports Complex
6 Zhongshan N. Rd Sec. 6
Tel: 02-2881 2277
Open daily 8.30am–2am. Also has good table tennis facilities, with automatic servers, sauna facilities, and other amenities.

Camping

Close to Taipei are a number of campgrounds that cater to group camping. Note that in these spots the main areas tend to fill up on weekends and holidays with young people who stay up late and quite possibly sing lustily or listen to loud music. When you wake up the next morning, most will already be gone. The edges of these campgrounds will provide more quiet; ask ahead.
Jinshan Youth Activity Center
Tel: 02-2498 1190
http://chinshan.cyh.org.tw
Located on the North Coast just west of the town of Jinshan. Has both campgrounds and hotel rooms. Six-person tents can be rented for NT$800 per night.
Jingshan Camping Area
16, Alley 71, Lane 101, Jingshan Rd
Tel: 02-2862 3666
This is the only area where camping is allowed in Yangmingshan National Park, close to the Qingtiangang plateau. It costs NT$600 per night for six persons without rental of gear. Rental of the site and tent will cost NT$900, and each sleeping bag costs NT$50. There are also barbecue units and gas cylinders for rent.

Karaoke is hugely popular.

TRANSPORTATION

ACTIVITIES

A – Z

LANGUAGE

Cycling

Taipei has a network of bicycle paths following the Jingmei, Xindian, Danshui, Shuang, Keelung and Jilong rivers. Bike-rental facilities are placed at strategic points. Your best bet is **Dajia Riverside Park**, because dedicated shuttle buses travel to and from the Danshui MRT line; also the Jilong section is the most picturesque.

The paths on the north bank of the Jilong River stretch to Guandu Nature Reserve, pass Hongshulin Mangrove Swamp along Danshui River, and end at Danshui MRT station. From there you can take the ferry to Bali and take the bike path to the Shihsanhang Museum.

There are now also dedicated bike lanes in the city's core, most concentrated in the Xinyi District around such sights as Taipei 101, Taipei City Hall, and Four Beasts Mountain. A system of automated bike-rental kiosks "YouBike" has been set up in Xinyi to make convenient on/off touring in the district by bike. There are also rental kiosks at Taipei MRT stations as well as in the old and central districts of city. Bike-rental fees are NT$10 for every 30 minutes within the first four hours; a deposit is required. Bikes do not need to be returned to the original kiosk. For a map showing the location of rental stations and instructions visit: www.youbike.com.tw.

The affirmation of the city's efforts to promote cycling is perhaps the fact that it has been chosen to host the Velo-city Global 2016 event, the world's largest international cycling forum.

Diving

It is difficult to find reliable, up-to-date information on diving opportunities and facilities, especially in north Taiwan. The best first step is to contact the Taiwan Tourism Bureau; its website ("Travel Information/Links" section) has a list of Taipei outfits to link up with. Note that diving along the North Coast is not optimal because of rugged seas; good diving sites are at the

Northeast Coast National Scenic Area. Diving in the Taiwan Strait is almost non-existent because of extensive silting and mudflats.

Golf

At golf courses near Taipei, fees generally run about NT$3,000 for an 18-hole round. Prices go up on weekends, generally to around NT$4,000 at a top-flight course, when they get very crowded. This includes the caddy fee. Though most are private, clubs allow non-members to play without member sponsorship, but with restrictions. Have your hotel concierge arrange things, for there is little chance English will be spoken. As with clubs around the world, they are open from sunup to sunset.

Formosa First Country Club
50, Lin 7, Gezhu Village, Maowei Qi, Luzhu Township
Taoyuan County
Tel: 03-324 5291
Designed by Arnold Palmer, featuring a classical American hill-course terrain. Non-members welcome at all times.

Miramar Linkou Golf & Country Club
9 Xiafu Rd, Xiafu Village, Linkou Town, Taipei County
Tel: 02-2606 3456
Located west of Taipei, in the hills between the city and Taiwan Taoyuan International Airport, this course was designed by Jack Nicklaus. Has a top-flight clubhouse, with restaurants, a sauna, fitness center, and pool tables. Non-members are welcome, but members tee off first.

Ta Shee Golf and Country Club
166 Rexin Road, Yongfu Ward, Daxi Township, Taoyuan County
Tel: 03-387 5699
www.tasheeresort.com.tw
Guests of Ta Shee Westin Resort have automatic access to the course. Others pay for entry. Also offers hiking trails and a top-flight sports and fitness facility, with outdoor tennis.

Taiwan Golf and Country Club
32, Lane 6, Zhongzheng Rd, -Danshui
Tel: 02-2623 0114

In the hills overlooking Danshui, this is Taiwan's oldest course, being well over 100 years old. Non-members tee off before 10am on Sat and all hours weekdays; no access on Sun.

In-line skating

Taipei Youth Activity Center
B1/B2, 17 Renai Rd Sec. 1
Tel: 02-2342 2388
The in-line skating park on the basement levels features open rinks, cones for technique skating, and a long, winding course that slopes from upper to lower level. Admission NT$150 weekdays, NT$200 holidays, no time limit.

Martial arts

Every morning starting at about 6.30am, you'll find tai chi practitioners moving through the forms at the CKS Memorial, Sun Yat-sen Memorial, and 228 Peace Park. Little or no formal teaching is done, and novices are welcome to join in and follow along. For formal instruction, contact one of the below:

Wu Jian Taekwondo and Martial Arts Center
10F, 293 Songjiang Rd
Tel: 02-2503 4667
Certified head coach Albert Wang, who speaks English, has over a quarter-century of experience teaching foreigners. Prices are moderate, all visitors are welcome, and no experience is necessary.

Yan Nian Daoguan
2F, 32 Fuguo Rd
Tel: 02-2837 1779
www.ymti.org
Master Wang Yan-nian taught the Yang style of tai chi. He passed away in 2008, but the renowned school continues. Foreign assistants teach in English or French.

Mountaineering

Certain mountain areas are restricted and require a special mountaineering permit. This can be obtained at the Foreign Affairs section of any local police department, or at the police detachment in any national park. An application form must be submitted and a passport, visa, or Alien Resident Certificate must be submitted for inspection. The processing fee is NT$10, and the application is evaluated immediately. There are two levels of restricted area; for the more highly restricted zones a guide is necessary. The **Chinese Taipei Alpine Association** (www.mountaineering.org.tw) can arrange an experienced English-speaking guide for a group of four or more members. Visit the Tourism Bureau website (www.taiwan.net.tw) for more details or call the National Police Administration (tel: 02-2357 7377).

Rock climbing

The most popular outdoor cliffs near the city are at Longdong on the Northeast Coast. With the best surface variations in the north, they are suitable for both beginners and experienced climbers. There are no developed facilities, so unless you are experienced and familiar, it is best to hook up with a local association.

Beitou Sports Center
100 Lane, 39 Shipai Rd Sec. 1
Tel: 02-2820 2880
Chinese Taipei Climbing Association
http://climbing.org.tw
Civic Bouldergym
552, Civic Blvd. Sec. 8
Tel: 02-2788 6220
Gonguang Bouldering Rockgym
Near 43-45, Xizhou Rd
Tel: 0972-980-592
Neihu Sports Center
12 Zhouzi St.
Tel: 02-2656 0052
Wanhua Sports Center
6-1 Xi'ning S. Rd
Tel: 02-2880 6066

COOKING CLASSES

The **Community Services Center** (see page 255) offers cooking classes, introductory courses on various regional Chinese cuisines, and visits to local nightmarkets, wet markets, and dry markets.

Swimming pools

Taiwan Aqua Fitness Association
3F, 13-2, Lane 97, Xinsheng N. Rd Sec. 1, www.aquatafa.org.tw
Tel: 02-2731 2296
Taipei City Neihu Sports Center
12, Zhouzi St
Tel: 02-2627 7776
www.nhsports.com.tw
Taipei Song Shan Sports Center
1 Dunhua N. Rd
Tel: 02 6617 6789
www.sssc.com.tw
Taipei Xinyi Sports Center
100 Songqin St
Tel: 02-8786 191
http://xysc.cyc.org.tw
Taipei Nangang Sports Center
69, Yucheng St
Tel: 02-2653 2279
http://ngsc.cyc.org.tw

Tennis

Space is at a premium in Taipei. Private clubs have courts, and the city has been hard at work to build tennis and other facilities in outdoor green areas. Ask your hotel concierge to find a facility and set you up. Among the city hotels, the Grand Hotel and Landis Resort Yangmingshan have courts restricted to guests. **Taipei Youth Park**, at 199 Shuiyuan Rd, between the Old Walled City and Wanhua, has seven public courts. No reservations; first come first served.

For additional advice, contact:
Taipei Sports Office
10 Nanjing E. Rd Sec. 4
Tel: 02-2316 7586
www.tms.taipei.gov.tw

Windsurfing

In north Taiwan, generally only adventurous foreigners hit the waves during the cool winter months, for this is when the winds are most blustery.

Spectator sports

Attendance at sporting events in Taiwan is limited. Most venues do not seat more than 10,000. There is, however, significant TV viewership for the local pro baseball and basketball leagues, and for inter-

national meets in these sports. There are also strong TV followings for pool, martial arts, and whichever sport local talent is doing well internationally in at that moment in time.

Baseball

The four teams in Taiwan's pro league, the CPBL, do not always play in their home-base cities. Instead teams often play in other cities in an effort to maximize their fan base. Doubleheaders featuring four different clubs are sometimes staged to maximize turnout and league exposure. Each team has talent from the Americas, who play here 2–3 times per week during the 9-month season (no games in the cool, wet winter months). Expect exuberant spectators to cheer the entire game and urge their favorite team on. International championships are occasionally hosted.

Tianmu Baseball Stadium
77 Zhongzheng Rd
Tel: 02-2873 6548
A 10,000-seat facility with the Yangmingshan hills as backdrop. Site of Taiwan's pro baseball games. Tickets rarely cost more than NT$300, and games are played weekends only because of noise restrictions in what is a high-end residential neighborhood.

Basketball

Most of the teams in the island's pro basketball league are based in Taipei, and consist of local players. Lacking the height and speed of international basketballers, the league takes pride in its take-no-prisoners style.

Taipei Arena
2 Nanjing E. Rd Sec. 4, www.taipeiarena.com.tw
Tel: 02-2578 3536
An attractive multi-function sports complex opened on the corner of Nanjing and Dunhua roads in 2005. Hosts many major international sporting events and is the main base for the island's Super Basketball League, with seating for 13,000 to 15,000.

A – Z

AN ALPHABETICAL SUMMARY OF PRACTICAL INFORMATION

A

Accommodations

Upper-end hotels in Taipei are expensive in comparison to North American and European prices, but not unduly so. They are renowned for gracious and attentive service, in keeping with the Confucian ethic of striving to be the perfect host.

The Tourism Bureau divides top-end hotels into two categories: International Tourist and Regular Tourist. The International Tourist hotels provide a superior range of luxury services and amenities. Don't expect special services from the Regular Tourist hotels, but facilities are fully up to international standard.

Taipei being the island's main center for business and one of the globe's most wired cities, the majority of hotels are oriented toward the business traveler. The better venues almost certainly have free, in-room broadband access and it is possible in more basic venues too.

Smoking is prohibited in all hotel rooms, as well as in all enclosed public spaces (except where a designated smoking area has specifically been set aside).

The city's hotels do not, as a rule, provide complimentary breakfasts, but the International Tourist and Regular Tourist venues will have a restaurant or bar that serves Western-style breakfast foods; with hotels in other categories it is hit and miss. Rooms will contain kettles along with packets of tea, coffee, creamer, and sugar.

The one area in which service can be said to be flawed is in the English-language capability of lower-level staff, but it must be said that the hotels work hard to make up for it. In any event, whatever your need, an English speaker will be close at hand.

Since the vast majority of visitors from Western countries come to Taipei on business, by far the majority of the hotels are in the city's core business areas, on and near Zhongshan North Road, the old downtown, and the eastern district, which is the new center. Hotels in the Beitou and Yangmingshan areas primarily cater to travelers there for the hot springs. For the most part, there is a dearth of accommodations of international caliber in Taipei South, Zhongzheng, the Old Walled City, and the old districts by the Danshui River, but inexpensive, clean, and pleasant accommodations are generally available there.

In International Tourist hotels, rooms will generally cost NT$7,000–12,000, while those in Regular Tourist places will range from NT$4,000–7,000. Otherwise, rooms in non-tourist-designated hotels with good, clean, basic amenities can be had for NT$2,000–4,000 per night. These establishments cater especially to the businessperson, and managerial staff will be able to speak English. There are few budget hotels; those that do exist are concentrated in the crowded older areas of the city.

When making reservations directly with the hotel – even from the airport – ask for discounts or special rates. Most establishments will grant a discount of up to 30 percent if you book ahead, even more for online bookings. Major hotels have counters in both terminals of Taiwan Taoyuan International Airport; the Tourism Bureau service counters in the two terminals can also help. All rates are subject to a 10 percent service charge. All Taipei hotels accept major credit cards.

Addresses

Taipei's address system may at first appear a bit complicated, but once you get the knack of it, you'll find it is quite logical and negates the need to memorize countless names in this dense metropolis.

Most addresses have a building number, lane and alley number (if applicable), street name, and section. An example is "No. 15, Lane 25, Zhongxiao East Road Section 3." The city is organized into a grid, with Zhongshan Road and Zhongxiao Road serving as main north-south and east-west axes respectively. All long arteries are divided into sections which are numbered higher the further they are from the central axis. Thus, Section 1 of Zhongxiao East Road is closest to Zhongshan Road, Section 2 further east, and so on. The pattern is mirrored westward for Zhongxiao West Road.

On each section, building numbers start at "1." So there can be a No. 1 on Zhongxiao E. Rd Sec. 1, on Zhongxiao E. Rd Sec. 2, and so on. Lanes branch off from main arteries, and are numbered like buildings. For instance, to find the sample address above, go to Sec. 3 of Zhongxiao E. Rd and find building No. 25; beside it will be a Lane 25. Go down that lane and find building No. 15. Alleys branch off from lanes, so something like "No. 15, Alley 6, Lane 25" means: go down Lane 25 and find building No. 6. Alley 6 will be beside it. Go down the alley to building No. 15.

This efficient system allows one to guess the location of any address quickly.

If you expect to be in Taiwan for any length of time, invaluable orientation is conducted for newcomers by the local expat-run non-profit **Community Services Center** at No. 25, Lane 290, Zhongshan N. Rd Sec. 6, tel: 02-2836 8134, www.communitycenter.org.tw.

Admission charges

All museums, cinemas, and other leisure and recreation facilities will offer discounted admission for children, seniors, students, and the disabled. Groups are also offered discounted entry. In Taiwan museums do not tend to have special free-entry days.

Age restrictions

The legal drinking age in Taiwan is 18, as is the age at which one can obtain a driver's license, even if you hold a valid license from another country. Any person with a valid driver's license and ID may rent a vehicle. The legal age of consent is 16.

B

Budgeting for your trip

Accommodations of international caliber usually cost NT$4,000 or more per night, though discounts can be had by booking online and well ahead. Taxis are inexpensive, with a cross-city run of about 9 km not likely to go over NT$250.

Hotel meals are not cheap, but Western-style restaurants found in them will generally offer set meals at a discount of around 25 percent compared to ordering items à la carte. Good, inexpensive local fare can be had at nightmarkets and local eateries, which serve simple dishes.

Business travelers

Traveling to Taipei on business is a pleasure. All international tourist hotels have full business facilities, and provide in-room Internet access. Taxis are available any time, day or night; simply stand by the street and raise your hand to hail one. The city provides taxi drivers who have passed official English exam with special stickers for display on windshields. There is also a hotline for foreigners on English-speaking taxi service tel: 0800-024-111. But be prepared to expect language obstacles, so have your destination and hotel written in Chinese beforehand. If you need a receipt, just say "shouju" and draw an imaginary rectangle in the air. A large logo on the outside of a vehicle in the shape of a plum blossom (neon-lit at night) indicates excellent cab drivers who need to meet several requirements set by the Taipei City Transportation department in order to use it.

Traffic can be heavy, especially during the rush hours, so allow extra time for delays when going to meetings. Most locals are used to people showing up as much as 20 minutes late, but phone if you anticipate a longer delay and apologize when you arrive.

Always have your business card ready; it is seen as your badge of identity, and is always exchanged when meeting people formally. Receive it with both hands, take a real look at it to show respect, do not put it away immediately, and when you do, slide it into a place that demonstrates the new relationship is being taken seriously.

C

Children

Taipei has a fair amount of green space and a number of attractions that will appeal to kids. Bus fares and admission fees to most attractions are discounted for children. Some venues declare a height limit of 120cm (4ft) for kids, but this is not vigorously enforced except at locations where safety is an issue, such as at amusement-park rides. Have your child's ID on hand just in case, however.

Traffic is very heavy at rush hour, so avoid moving about with young ones at this time, or leaving them unsupervised at any time. The problem is not crime, but heavy vehicle and foot traffic.

The use of strollers is not very convenient, except in the eastern district of the city, where pedestrian walkways are wider, flatter, and generally unblocked, and many new buildings have wheelchair access. Local mothers prefer carrying toddlers in front. The city is working very hard to flatten and straighten out sidewalks throughout all neighborhoods, but this is still hit and miss. Note that down all lanes and alleys there are in fact no sidewalks.

Washrooms in many newer buildings (but certainly not all), and specifically in department stores and international hotels, will have diaper-changing facilities, as do washrooms in all MRT stations. Rooms set aside for nursing, however, are non-existent. Malls and department stores are good places to bring picky eaters, as all have a good selection of restaurants and a food court with much variety.

For more assistance, a call to the **Community Services Center**, staffed mostly by the wives of expatriate businessmen, is recommended.

Climate

When to visit

Taipei is located in the subtropical region. The average annual temperature is 22°C (71°F), the average annual rainfall is 2,152mm (85ins), and the average number of rainy days is 181.

The hot season stretches from June to early September, and can hit 40°C (104°F) on the baking street. Perhaps "hottest season" is more accurate, as it is over 25°C (77°F) and humid from mid-March to mid-October. This is the period of the southwest monsoon. Being at the northern tip of the island, Taipei is somewhat sheltered from the storms by the island's north-south mountain spine.

Typhoon season stretches from July to October, and Taipei can be deeply impacted by the powerful winds and heavy rains. Flooding is a constant menace, especially in foothill areas of the Taipei Basin. Rigorous prevention measures are taken to minimize damage.

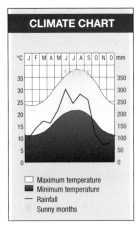

In winter, the weather is often chilly. The air is moisture-laden, and it often rains in late January and early February. Cold fronts move in from the Asian continent, and this is the season of the northeast monsoon.

Spring rains fall from March to April, and "plum rains" (*meiyu*) from May to June. During this period, it tends to drizzle rather than rain heavily.

What to wear

In the hot season, bring your lightest and loosest clothing. Most local businessmen go without jacket and tie during the period, opting for short sleeves and open collars. For formal occasions such as meetings, note that hotels, restaurants, and offices are air-conditioned, so tie and jacket can be put on just before arrival and taken off after introductions.

In winter, bring warmer outer clothing that you can quickly take off and carry. Most locals go without raingear, preferring to carry umbrellas to handle the rains, which seem to burst and finish at a moment's notice. Umbrellas are sold everywhere.

Crime and safety

Taipei is an exceedingly safe place. It is fine to walk around even late at night. Violent crime against tourists is almost unheard of, and overseas visitors almost never suffer abuse, physical or verbal.

Stories of snatch theft and pickpocketing are occasionally heard, so take commonsense precautions. The heavy bars often seen on the windows and doors of private homes are to prevent break-ins, but homeowners do not fear violent crime and travelers are in no way affected.

Drivers in Taipei, however, are often quite aggressive, notably during periods of heavy congestion, and despite systematic local government action to eliminate the practice, still too often nudge their vehicles through pedestrians at crosswalks and run red lights. So be alert when crossing the street.

Customs regulations

Individuals aged 20 and over have a duty-free allowance of 1 liter (2 pints) of alcoholic beverages and up to 25 cigars or 200 cigarettes or 450 grams (1lb) of tobacco products only. Foreign currency above US$10,000 will be confiscated if found after not being declared. There is also a restriction concerning the import of the Chinese currency, maximum amount allowed is RMB20,000.

Items which are prohibited and will result in a substantial fine or imprisonment include publications espousing communism, pornography, illicit and narcotic drugs, endangered animals or animal parts, copyright-infringed goods, weapons (including gun-shaped toys), counterfeit currency or forging equipment, gambling apparatus, or foreign lottery tickets.

An Outbound Declaration Form is required when departing the country if a traveler is taking out the following: over $10,000 in US currency (or equivalent in other currencies), over $60,000 in New Taiwan dollars, gold, antiques, or dutiable items such as personal computers and professional photographic equipment that may be brought back into Taiwan for sale.

For more details, contact the **Directorate General of Customs**, Ministry of Finance, at 13 Dacheng St, Taipei, tel: 02-2550 5500 ext. 2116, http://eweb. customs.gov.tw. The Taiwanese Immigration Agency also runs a special website for foreigners who are going to spend lengthier time or go to live in Taiwan (http://iff.immigration.gov.tw).

D

Disabled travelers

Taipei is not an easy place to maneuver in for the physically impaired. The city has worked hard in the past decade to rectify this by smoothening sidewalks, providing ramps, and adding tactile paving surfaces for the visually impaired to follow. The problem is that there are often no sidewalks, or only very narrow ones.

Most of Taipei's large, modern public buildings (including government buildings and museums) have wheelchair-access ramps. This is only occasionally the case for modern residential buildings. They are not required by law in older buildings. The city's international hotels will have more facilities, but this should be confirmed prior to arrival. Most are good at handling special requests. Many big museums offer wheelchairs and some now have special guided tours for visitors using them.

Each MRT station provides elevator access from street level. There is also a reserved spot for wheelchairs in the first and last car of each train. Avoid using the MRT system during rush hour, when it becomes extremely crowded.

By law, guide dogs are given access to all locations. However, be advised that many citizens are not aware of this and not

used to these dogs, which they may view as unclean. The city administration is working hard to advise citizens of the law and promote access.

Pedestrian crossings at major intersections have audio countdown signals to help the visually impaired. Be aware, however, that drivers are often less than patient with pedestrians.

E

Electricity

Taiwan uses the same standards as the US. Electrical mains supply 110 volts, 60 Hz AC. Connection is via standard flat two-pin plugs. International hotels will be able to supply adapters if required. Many newer non-residential buildings have 220 volt sockets.

Embassies and consulates

Taiwan, ie the Republic of China (not to be confused with People's Republic of China), has formal diplomatic relations with 21 UN member states and the Holy See. Countries outside this group set up trade offices, which are quasi-embassies that handle matters such as visa insurance and replacement of lost or stolen passports.

Australia
Australian Office in Taipei
27F, President International Tower, 9-11 Songgao Rd
Tel: 02-8725 4100
www.australia.org.tw
Canada
Canadian Trade Office in Taipei
6F, Hua-Hsin Building,

EMERGENCIES

Fire/Ambulance: 119
Police: 110
Taipei Foreign Affairs Police: 02-2556 6007
Directory Information in English: 02-2311 6796

1 Songzhi Rd
Tel: 02-8723 3000
www.canada.org.tw
New Zealand
New Zealand Commerce and Industry Office
9F, 1 Songzhi Rd
Tel: 02-2720 5228
www.nzcio.com
United Kingdom
British Trade and Cultural Office
26F, President International Tower, 9-11 Songgao Rd
Tel: 02-8758 2088
www.ukintaiwan.fco.gov.uk
United States
American Institute in Taiwan
7, Lane 134, Xinyi Rd Sec. 3
Tel: 02-2162 2000
www.ait.org.tw

Etiquette

Long-held traditions are still in force in Taiwan, but if you act courteously, and ask in advance what to do when unsure, you'll do fine. The Taiwanese are very tolerant of non-locals who seek to understand and respect local ways, even if mistaken in particulars.

Dress. Bare feet are generally considered dirty in public places, though no one will accost you. Sleeveless shirts and exposed feet are not permitted on the MRT. Nude bathing is illegal.

Eating. Food is usually served on round tables with a lazy Suzan in the center. Pick modest portions when the food reaches you; piling up your favorite is in bad taste. Do not stick your chopsticks straight up in your rice, as this resembles incense sticks in urns at temple funeral rites; it may bring bad luck. Placing chopsticks across the top of your bowl indicates you are full.

Entertaining. In Chinese culture, it is essential for the good host to entertain guests. If in town on business, you'll thus be taken out almost every night. For proper long-term relations, you should reciprocate at least once before departure to express appreciation.

Most entertaining is not done in the home because of cramped quarters, but often at banquet restaurants in hotels. According to tradition, the host sits across the round table from the guest of honor, not beside, though this is not rigorously observed today.

Chinese tradition is to "fight" jovially to pay the bill even if one is the guest, though all know the host will "win" the argument in the end. If you are really intent on paying, get it done on the quiet before the bill is brought to the table.

When offered a formal toast, raise your glass to chest level with both hands.

At the end of formal occasions, the serving of tea indicates the party is over. Though your host may insist the fun continue, the insistence is a polite form only.

Gifts. Always present gifts with both hands, palms facing up. (In ancient China, a palm facing down might conceal a weapon.) Do not give clocks or watches, which suggest the recipient's demise. Handkerchiefs or towels are only given at funerals; at other times, they would be construed as wishing the recipient grief. Do not give knives or scissors, for sharp objects indicate you wish to sever the relationship, as do objects that come in pairs such as chopsticks.

Greetings. The Western handshake has taken hold, so to speak, generally given with a slight nod of respect. Other forms of touch like hugging, backslapping, and so on are not common. A man laying hands on a woman in any way can quickly earn him the unflattering label "*se lang*," or lecher.

Names. In Chinese, a person's family name comes first, followed by a given name. So the family name of Ma Ying-jeou is "Ma" and the given name is "Ying-jeou." On formal occasions, an honorific like *nüshi* (Ms), *xiansheng* (Mr), or a title like *jingli* (Manager) may be used after a surname, e.g. *Li Jingli* (Manager

Li). But this will usually only occur when Mandarin is the spoken medium. In any case, it is considered overfamiliar to use someone's given name until the person initiates informality.

G

Gay and lesbian travelers

Homosexuality has traditionally been frowned upon in Chinese society due to the Confucian concern with marriage and progeny. This rarely, if ever, takes the form of physical violence, however, so gay travelers are safe. Open displays of affection will draw looks – no different from many other places.

Most local gays still hide their orientation from colleagues and relatives, but things are changing, and they now voice their concerns publicly in an organized manner. Taipei has an annual gay-pride parade, Taiwan Pride. Clubs are discreet but now operate openly and are no longer subject to raids. In 2003, a bill to legalize same-sex marriages was mooted – a first in Asia – but it was rejected three years later. However, Taipei is more tolerant of gays than many other Asian cities. In polls about three-quarters of respondents state they feel homosexual relations are acceptable. Nearly 70,000 participants attended the annual LGBT pride parade in October 2014 in Taipei (http://twpride.org), one of the largest in Asia.

The **Taiwan Tongzhi Hotline Association** (tel: 02-2392 1969; www.hotline.org.tw) provides counseling, support, and a community resource center. (See page 248 for nightlife info.)

H

Health and medical care

Taipei has made great strides in the past decade or so in ensuring

a clean living environment. Rest assured that the food in small eateries and nightmarkets is safe to eat, even though they may be crowded, sometimes greasy, and somewhat dirty, especially during peak hours. Tap water is treated, but it is recommended that it be boiled before consumption. Bottled water can be found at convenience stores and supermarkets.

The medical treatment available in Taipei hospitals is of a high standard. If you fall ill, have your hotel call a hospital for you. Care is always available on short notice – most hospitals have 24-hour emergency and outpatient service.

It is best to stick with large hospitals and avoid local clinics. The doctors at the latter are highly trained, and most have passable English, but because of the healthcare compensation system, they tend to process patients too quickly. The government is hard at work trying to rectify this well-known deficiency in the system.

Visitors staying more than three months in Taiwan must have an HIV test conducted. Certificates of cholera inoculation are required for travelers coming from certain countries or who have spent five days or more in infected areas.

The country has emerged virtually unscathed from the epidemic scares of the 2000s such as SARS, bird flu, and swine flu, a testament to its public-health system.

Hospitals with more experience dealing with foreigners are:
Chang Gung Memorial Hospital 199 Dunhua N. Rd, www.cgmh.org.tw
Tel: 02-2713 5211
Mackay Memorial Hospital 92 Zhongshan N. Rd Sec. 2, www.mmh.org.tw
Tel: 02-2543 3535
Taiwan Adventist Hospital 424 Bade Rd Sec. 2, www.tahsda.org.tw
Tel: 02-2771 8151

TRANSPORTATION

Veterans General Hospital
201 Shipai Rd Sec. 2, http://wd.
vghtpe.gov.tw
Tel: 02-2875 7628

I

Internet

All international hotels provide Internet access for guests in business centers, and all international hotels now have broadband or wireless access in rooms, with more going wireless throughout the facility. The city also has a great many Internet cafés, but be advised that most cater to teen video gamers and are quite loud.

Fees average about NT$30 per half hour due to heavy competition among outlets, but this also means places open and close with impressive speed.

The city has a comprehensive public wireless-access network. Free wireless access can be enjoyed in most public areas of the city, around major hospitals, Taipei Public Library branches, the city's administrative-district office buildings, MRT stations, and throughout the Xinyi Planning District. If you have a Taiwanese mobile phone number, register an account on the Taipei Free Public Wi-Fi Access website: www.tpe-free.taipei.gov.tw. Otherwise you should visit one of the Taipei information centers where it will be done for you. There is also a paid Wi-Fi service called WIFLY, which is found at restaurants, coffeeshops, hospitals, and shopping centers, Taipei Railway Station, in the Ximending, Xinyi, and Zhongxiao/Dunhua commercial districts, at all well-known fast-food franchise outlets, and at all 7-Eleven convenience-store outlets. For this, log onto the WIFLY website (www.wifly.com.tw) to register and set up your prepaid account, or obtain a prepaid stored-value card or member's card at a Starbucks or 7-Eleven outlet.

L

Left luggage

Left-luggage services (self-service) are available at Taoyuan International Airport in the Arrival Hall of Terminal 1 (1F) and in the Arrival Hall (1F) and the Departure Hall (3F) of Terminal 2. There is a charge per piece.

Lost property

Locals will most likely turn found property in at the local police precinct. Your best bet is to contact the Foreign Affairs Police, who speak English, and can attempt to trace the valuables on your behalf.

M

Media

Magazines

There is a decent selection of local English-language magazines of interest to tourists.

Discover Taipei is a City Government bimonthly, available at the city hall bookstore, the city's visitor info centers, MRT stations, and other sites popular with expatriates and foreign tourists. It focuses on sights and events of interest to visitors. Also at www.taipei.gov.tw.

Travel in Taiwan is a Tourism Bureau bi-monthly found at its visitor centers and at hotel counters. It has feature articles and practical info on Taipei specifically and the country in general. Also at www.tit.com.tw.

This Month in Taiwan, available at hotels and newsstands, is also targeted at the tourist. Also at www.thismonthintaiwan.com.

Taiwan Panorama, available at large bookstores, is a glossy bilingual monthly on culture, society, and politics. Also at www.taiwan-panorama.com.

Taiwan Review, a Government Information Office monthly, cov-

Taiwan has a vibrant press.

ACTIVITIES

ers general affairs and is available at major bookstores. Once independent editorially, it is today more of a government mouthpiece, notably in topics that might negatively affect Taiwan's image abroad. Also at http://taiwan review.nat.gov.tw.

Newspapers

There are two local English newspapers, the *Taipei Times* (www.taipeitimes.com) and *China Post* (www.chinapost.com.tw), none of international caliber. The *Taipei Times* is the most professional. Its website is free and requires no subscription. All two carry local, regional, and international news, and are available at newsstands, convenience stores, and hotels. *Taiwan News* used to be a third English newspaper until September 2010 when it transformed into digital news portal www.etaiwannews.com. Daily editions of a good selection of international papers, including the *Asian Wall Street Journal* and *International Herald Tribune*, are available at hotels, major bookstores, and some newsstands.

A – Z

Radio

The only English-language station in Taiwan is the Taipei-

LANGUAGE

based ICRT – International Community Radio Taipei (www.icrt.com.tw). The FM channel 100.7 is the more popular, with chatty DJ shows, a mix of Western and local pop music, short news broadcasts, the BBC World Report, and so on.

Television

All hotels have cable television, with around 100 channels available. International channels carried as basic service are CNN, Discovery, ESPN, National Geographic, and HBO. Daily schedules are published in the local English papers.

Money

The country's currency is the New Taiwan dollar (NT$). At time of press, US$1 was equal to NT$30. Coins come in denominations of NT$1, NT$5, NT$10, NT$20, and NT$50; paper notes in NT$100, NT$200, NT$500, NT$1,000, and NT$2,000, though you'll almost never see NT$2,000 bills.

Changing money

Major foreign currencies can be exchanged for Taiwan dollars at large banks. The website of the Tourism Bureau www.taiwan.net.tw provides a list of banks (in the Before You Go section). International hotels will exchange currency, but offer the least attractive rates. Travel agencies that cater to overseas visitors may change money, and a few large-scale

MAPS

There are plenty of good maps of the city in Chinese, but fewer in English. The free maps available at tourist information centers around the city are, however, more than adequate for sightseeing purposes. The Community Services Center also sells a comprehensive map (www.communitycenter.org.tw).

department stores have exchange counters. Taiwan Taoyuan International Airport has exchange booths in both terminals, but arriving visitors should note they are only accessible before one passes immigrations and customs. You will not find the licensed private money changers found elsewhere in Asia.

Receipts are given when currency is exchanged, and must be presented in order to exchange unused NT dollars before departure. If possible, wait to exchange at the airport, where the counters carry a wider range of currencies and staff have greater familiarity with the process. It may be difficult to exchange NT dollars overseas, with very unattractive rates given.

Credit cards and ATMs

The major credit cards (American Express, MasterCard, Visa, and Diners Club) are accepted by most merchants except where cash-only transactions are the rule (small eateries, nightmarkets, and such).

Many ATMs allow withdrawals of local currency using major international cards. ATMs have clear English. Use only those at banks, some MRT stations, convenience stores, and other major institutions. Forgo freestanding units of any kind to avoid periodic scams by organized crime.

Traveler's checks

Traveler's checks are handled solely by major banks, some tourist-oriented businesses, and international hotels. Most banks will levy a processing fee. Hotels offer less attractive rates, and will handle such checks only for guests.

Tipping

Tipping is not common or expected in Taiwan. Hotel bellhops generally get NT$20 per piece of luggage. The majority of hotels add 10 percent to food and beverage as well as room charges, as do more upscale res-

taurants these days. Taxi drivers do not expect tips.

O

Opening hours

Most corporate businesses are open from Monday to Friday, 9am–5pm or 5.30pm. Government offices are open Monday to Friday, 8.30am–5.30pm, with an official lunch hour from 12.30–1.30pm.

Department stores generally open every day at 10–11am and close at 9–9.30pm. Most open on national holidays except for the first few days of Chinese New Year. Other retail outlets mostly open at 9–10am and close at about 10pm. Outlets of major convenience-store chains, including the ubiquitous 7-Eleven, almost all stay open 24/7, and certain large supermarkets will also stay open into the wee hours.

P

Postal services

Taiwan's postal service is speedy and reliable. Regular airmail will reach North American destinations in about 6–7 days. **Chunghwa Post** (www.post.gov.tw), the national service, also offers express delivery that costs less than international courier services. Delivery of mail takes about 24 hours within Taipei and 48 hours within Taiwan. Hours for post offices are 8am to 6pm Monday through Friday, with the largest office in each area also open Saturday from 8am to 4pm.

Taipei's **Central Post Office** (tel: 02-2361 5752) is located in front of the old North Gate, on Zhongxiao W. Rd Sec. 1. Staff in the international section speak decent English (staff at other post offices speak Chinese only). Packaging materials can be purchased at the central branch.

TIME ZONE

Taipei and all of Taiwan is +8 GMT, +13 EST (+12 with daylight savings).

When using streetside mailboxes, place domestic mail in the green boxes – intra-city items in the right-hand slot and others in the left-hand slot. International airmail goes into the left-hand slot of the red boxes.

Public holidays

The dates of traditional holidays are based on the Chinese lunar calendar, and thus vary each year in the Gregorian calendar. There is a minimum of four days of holiday during Chinese New Year, and depending on where in the week these days fall, up to a full week off work may be granted. Taipei is comparatively sleepy at this time, and most shops remain closed.
Foundation Day of the Republic of China: Jan 1
Chinese New Year: Jan/Feb (1st day of the lunar year)
Peace Memorial Day: Feb 28
Tomb-Sweeping Day (Qing Ming Festival): Apr 5
Dragon Boat Festival: May/June (5th day of the 5th lunar month)
Mid-Autumn Festival: Sept/Oct (15th day of the 8th lunar month)
National ("Double Tenth") Day: Oct 10
Regarding dates, note that the Republic (*Minguo*) system of reckoning years is used on official documents in Taiwan. The founding of the ROC in 1912 is considered year 1, so *Minguo* 104 is 2015 on the Gregorian calendar.

Public toilets

The city provides relatively clean public washrooms in the larger parks, but not the smaller ones. If nature calls, your other options are temples, fast-food outlets, shopping malls, MRT stations, and the larger hotels. A few

things to remember: only the hotels and the MRT stations always provide toilet paper, so carry some if you're going out for a while. Unlike some places in Asia you'll never be charged for washroom use here. And remember that parks and temples will most likely have only squat toilets.

R

Religious services

There are about 10,000 Muslims in Taipei (not including about 4,000 workers from Indonesia), served by **Taipei Grand Mosque** (tel: 02-2321 9445) on Xinsheng S. Rd by Daan Forest Park.
About 6 percent of the Taipei population is Christian, 80 percent of whom are Protestant, mostly Presbyterian. The rest are Roman Catholics, as are the 130,000 or so workers from the Philippines. The following churches conduct services in English:

Anglican/Episcopalian
Church of the Good Shepherd
509 Zhongzheng Rd
Tel: 02-2873 8104
www.goodshepherd.com.tw
Sunday English service at 9.30am. Combined English/Chinese service at 9.30am, 4th Sunday each month.

Roman Catholic
Mother of God Church
171 Zhongshan N. Rd Sec. 7
Tel: 02-2871 5168
www.catholic.org.tw
English services on Sunday at 10am, 12.15 and 7pm, Wed at 7pm.

S

Smoking

Smoking indoors in public places was banned throughout Taiwan in early 2009. Places

like restaurants may provide special smoking areas if completely insulated from the non-smoking area.

T

Tax

Taiwan levies a 5 percent VAT on purchases. Refunds are available to foreign travelers (see page 70). For more details, visit the **Taipei National Tax Administration** (TNTA) website www.ntbt.gov.tw. All outbound passengers have to pay an airport departure tax of NT$300. This is incorporated in the air ticket price.

Telephones

Taiwan's **international dialing code** is 886. For overseas calls to Taipei, add the prefix 2 before the local number. To make a domestic call to Taipei from outside the city, add 02. No area code is required when dialing within the city.
Dial 002 for **international direct** dialing (IDD)
For **operator assisted international calls**, dial 100
For **international information**, call the toll-free number 0800 080 100
To place **reverse-charge calls**, dial 108
For English-language **directory assistance**, dial 106

Cell/mobile phones

These can be used as long as your phone operates on the GSM network which is common to most countries except the US and Japan. To cut costs, buy a SIM card, which gives you a local number and an allotted quantity of usage time. They are available at cell-phone retail outlets. Prices for prepaid cards start at NT$100. Mobile network operators in Taiwan include Chungwa Telecom (www.cht.com.tw), which is the largest, FarEasTone (www.fetnet.net), Taiwan Mobile (www.taiwanmobile.com), and Vibo Telecom (www.vibo.com.tw).

Public phones

Both local and international calls can be made from public phones. The rate for local calls is NT$1 per minute. There are coin-operated machines (a disappearing breed) and phones that require magnetic-strip stored-value cards. These are sold at convenience stores, railway stations, bus stations, and major scenic sites.

For overseas calls, use one of the public phones marked as IDD capable in English. Visa, Master-Card, and JCB cards can be used at major hotels, and IDD cards can be bought at convenience stores.

Tourist information

The central government's **Tourism Bureau** (www.taiwan.net.tw) has both local and overseas information centers. Locally, the bureau approves and monitors tour agents and works with them to set up appropriate package tours.

The **Taipei City Government** (www.taipei.gov.tw) has information centers with service in English and other languages.

Local tourist offices

Tourism Bureau Main Office
9F, 290 Zhongxiao E. Rd Sec. 4
Tel: 02-2349 1500
Open: 9am–5pm
Travel Information Service Center
240 Dunhua N. Rd
Tel: 0800-011 765 (24H)
Taipei Railway Station
3 Beiping W. Rd
Tel: 02-2312 3256
Songshan Airport
340-9 Dunhua N. Rd
Tel: 02-2546 4741
East Metro Mall
77 Daan Rd Sec. 1
Tel: 02-6638 0059

Beitou MRT Station
1 Guangming Rd
Tel: 02-2894 6923
Specializes in Beitou's hot springs.
Jiantan MRT Station
65 Zhongshan N. Rd Sec. 5
Tel: 02-2883 0313
Ximen MRT Station
B1, 32-1 Baoqing Rd
Tel: 02-2375 3096
Tamsui MRT Station
1 Zhongzheng Rd
Tel: 02-26267613
Taipei 101 MRT Station
B1F, 20 Xinyi Rd Sec. 5
Tel: 02-2758 6593

V

Visas and passports

A stay of 90 days without a visa is available to citizens of 42 countries, including the US, UK, Canada, Japan, New Zealand, and the European Union nations; citizens of Australia can obtain 30-day landing visas instead. Passports must be valid for at least six months. All visitors must have a valid visa for their next destination, if required, and the necessary tickets for onward travel. Visitors can apply for a visa upon arrival by filling out a form, providing two passport photos, and paying NT$1,600 for a single-entry visa, NT$3,200 for a multiple-entry visa.

For visa extensions, overstays, and all relevant details, contact the **Bureau of Consular Affairs**, Ministry of Foreign Affairs, at 3F, 2-2 Qinan Rd Sec. 1, tel: 02-2343 2888, www.boca.gov.tw.

W

Women travelers

Taipei is much safer for women out on their own at night than the average Western city. However, caution is always advisable.

Within the MRT system, there are monitored safety zones at platforms for women, clearly marked in English. Telephone numbers are given at phone terminals for special taxi services (though operators speak little or no English).

Women are on exceedingly rare occasions subjected to surreptitious photo-taking or peeking, with cameras or mirrors hidden in shoes, briefcases, and so on. There have also been instances of secret cameras set up in public washrooms, so keep an eye out.

Though a Confucian patriarchy is still dominant in the home, the concept of the independent career woman has gained solid social acceptance; female business travelers can expect full respect.

WEBSITES

www.etaiwannews.com/dtn: Taiwan News portal, including a directory of Taiwan online, the bible for English contact info for organizations, businesses, and other entities.
www.romanization.com: Eclectic info, including guidance on transliteration, street names, and out-of-print books on Taiwan.
www.gio.gov.tw: The Government Information Office site, with useful links.

www.taipei.gov.tw: The official City Government website, with useful general information.
www.taiwan.net.tw: The official Tourism Bureau website.
www.taipeitravel.net: Run by the city's tourism-related dept, practical info on dining, shopping, shows, etc.
www.taiwanfun.com: Reviews of restaurants, bars, and nightclubs.
www.tit.com.tw: Issues of *Travel in Taiwan* bimonthly online.

LANGUAGE

UNDERSTANDING THE LANGUAGE

GENERAL

Most Taiwanese are descendants of immigrants who came in the 1600–1800s from China's southern Fujian Province. Their mother tongue, *Minnanyu*, or Southern Min (sometimes also called "Taiwanese"), is often spoken at home, but somewhat less so in official spheres. This is the result of a century-long history of official suppression by first the Japanese and then the Kuomintang administration. Since the lifting of martial law, restrictions have given way to a lively localization movement (encompassing the Hakka and aboriginal languages as well), and today you'll hear announcements on the MRT in four languages.

But **Mandarin Chinese** (called *Guoyu* in the ROC) remains the official language of Taiwan, the native tongue of the large number of "mainlanders" in Taipei and Taiwan generally, and the most useful language to learn for tourists. (Note that the various Chinese "dialects" are mutually unintelligible.)

As for English, despite official initiatives to improve proficiency, most people you walk up to on the street will wilt from the challenge. If in trouble, your best bet is to use the telephone assistance

numbers or to speak to the staff at international hotels.

WRITTEN CHINESE

Chinese writing is well known for using logograms – symbols to represent each "word" – rather than an alphabetic system. It developed from an ancient practice of using pictographs to write. Though advocates say that this complex system carries the weight of a great Chinese cultural legacy, and that it circumvents the problem of Mandarin's many homophones, it is generally agreed that the system is difficult to learn, requiring the memorization of thousands of separate characters – not practical for short-term visitors. Fortunately, all streets in Taipei have signs with their romanized names.

ROMANIZATION

From the time Westerners first came into contact with the Chinese language, various systems for romanizing the language have been created. Hanyu Pinyin was adopted by the PRC in 1958, and has come to be the international standard. Prior to this, the de facto standard in the West was the Wade-Giles system. Note that these systems are viewed by the

Chinese as pronunciation aids, and not replacements of the traditional writing system.

Romanization in Taiwan was long a mess. The Wade-Giles system had been used since the early 20th century, and the Yale system widely used too, but with the widespread adoption of Hanyu Pinyin worldwide there was pressure to do so here as well. Pro-independence factions were opposed to this because it is associated with China. In the early 2000s the DPP central government adopted Tongyong Pinyin, a Taiwanese innovation, but the city of Taipei went ahead with Hanyu Pinyin under former mayor Ma Ying-jeou. With the return of a KMT national government in the 2008 elections the demise of Tongyong was guaranteed, and in January 2009 Hanyu was declared the official system in Taiwan. Non-Hanyu transliterations persist, however, especially with older individuals more comfortable with the other systems.

GRAMMAR

Chinese is relatively straightforward in this respect. One finds no conjugations, declensions, tense changes, or other complicated bits to memorize. The subject-verb-object word order is used (as in English).

SPOKEN MANDARIN

The Chinese have long considered the basic unit of the language to be the *zhi*, a monosyllable that corresponds to a single written Chinese character. Because there are comparatively few sound combinations in Mandarin, this leads to many *zhi* having the same pronunciation. A linguistic device that has evolved to distinguish *zhi* is the tonal system. Every *zhi* has one of Mandarin's four pitch contours (listed here in the traditional order): high and level, rising, low (or falling then rising), and falling. For example, the syllable *fa* means "emit" with the first tone, "punish" with the second, "method" with the third, and "hair" with the fourth. These tones are usually the greatest stumbling block for non-native speakers learning the language.

Another common difficulty is the use of aspiration to distinguish certain consonants. Aspiration is the audible exhalation that comes after the "t" in English "top" but not in "stop". This distinction is what differentiates *pai* (to delegate someone) from *bai* (to worship someone). Retroflexion, the curling back of the tongue for certain consonants, is what separates "riches" (*cai*) from "kindling" (*chai*).

The trickier speech sounds of Mandarin are as follows (Hanyu Pinyin, Wade-Giles, Tongyong):
b, **p**, **b** "p" in "spot"
p, **p'**, **p** "p" in "pot"
d, **t**, **d** "t" in "stop"
t, **t'**, **t** "t" in "top"
g, **k**, **g** "c" in "score"
k, **k'**,**k** "c" in "core"
j, **ch**, **j** "g" in "Swiss gene" said quickly
q, **ch'**, **c** "ch" in "mischief"
x, **hs**, **s** "ss" in "kiss her" said quickly
zh, **ch**, **jh** "j" in "jowl"
ch, **ch'**, **ch** "ch" in "chore"
r, **j**, **r** US English "r"
z, **ts/tz**, **z** "ds" in "reds"
c, **ts'/tz'**, **c** "ts" in "cats"
a, **a**, **a** "a" in "far"
e, **e/o**, **e** "ur" in "curse"
i, **i**, **i** "i" in "elite"

i, **ih/u**, **ih** "i" above but with the tongue further back
o, **o**, **o** "o" in "shore"
u, **u**, **u** "ue" in "blue"
ü, **ü**, **yu** German ü
ye, **yeh**, **ye** "ye" in "yes"
ei, **ei**, **ei** "ei" in "reign"
ie, **ieh**, **ie** "ye" in "yes"
iu, **iu**, **iou** "you"
ian, **ien**, **ian** "ien" in "Oriental"
ou, **ou**, **ou** "ow" in "blow"
ong, **ung**, **ong** "owe" with the "ng" of "sing"
ui, **ui**, **uei** "way"
uan, **üan**, **yuan** German ü with the "an" of "man"

USEFUL TERMS AND PHRASES

Greetings

Hello Ni hao
Goodbye Zai jian
See you tomorrow Mingtian jian
Thank you Xie xie
You're welcome Bu keqi
No problem Mei wenti
I; we wo; women
You ni; nin (polite); nimen (plural)
He/she/it; they ta; tamen
Who shei
My name is… Wo jiao…

Numbers

One yi
Two er (ordinal); liang (cardinal)
Three san
Four si
Five wu
Six liu
Seven qi
Eight ba
Nine jiu
Ten shi
Eleven shiyi
Twelve shier
Twenty ershi
One hundred yibai
One thousand yiqian
One million yibaiwan

Time and place

What time? Jidian zhong?
What day? Libai ji?
Yesterday zuotian

Today jintian
Tomorrow mingtian
One o'clock yidian zhong
Two o'clock liangdian zhong
Where is…? …zai nali?
Very far/near Hen yuan/jin
I want to go to… Wo yao qu…

Transport and lodging

Airport jichang
Airplane feiji
Train huoche
Bus bashi
Bus (public) gonggong qiche
Taxi jichengche
Telephone dianhua
Reservation dingwei
Hotel lüdian/jiudian
Room fangjian
Key yaoshi
Luggage xingli

Basic sentences

I want Wo yao…
Do you have…? Ni you meiyou…?
We don't have… Women meiyou…
I like… Wo xihuan…
I don't like… Wo bu xihuan…

Food and drink

Restaurant canting
Bar jiuba
Alcohol jiu
To eat; let's eat chifan
To drink he
Water shui
Fruit shuiguo
Tea/coffee cha/kafei
Hot/cold re/leng
Sugar tang
Salt/pepper yan/hujiao
Hot (spicy) la
Bottoms up!/Cheers! Ganbei!
Settle the bill jiezhang

Shopping

Money qian
How much does it cost? Duoshao qian?
Too expensive tai gui
Credit card xinyong ka
Old lao (aged); jiu (not new)
New xin
Big/Small da/xiao
Black/white/red hei/bai/hong

FURTHER READING

BUSINESS AND PRACTICALITIES

Taipei Living 10th Edition. Updated every two years, this handy reference book published by the Community Services Center helps Taipei expats settle in.

CULTURE

An American Teacher in Taiwan by Ken Berglund. A personal account of work, life, and love in Taiwan, written from a perspective of a Southern Californian.
Culture Shock! Taiwan: A Guide to Customs and Etiquette by Chris and Ling-li Bates. A concise primer for confused foreigners on the ins and outs of getting on with the locals.
Culture Taipei! A Guidebook for Thinking Travelers by Teresa Hsu and Chris Logan. Practical details on the city's every nook and cranny.
Dos and Don'ts of Taiwan by Steven Crook. A light-hearted guide which gives insight on cultural differences and offers a number of practical hints, ideal for the uninformed first-time visitor.
Formosan Odyssey: Taiwan, Past and Present by John Ross. An entertaining and insightful account of a New Zealander's north-south trek down the island.
Getting Along with the Chinese: For Fun and Profit by Fred Schneiter. A splendid romp through the region, filled with business and personal insights and anecdotes, by an old regional hand.
Keeping Up with the War God by Steven Crook. A well-written no-holds-barred look into the local culture from a long-time expat

resident who loves the island.
Reflections on Taipei: Expat Residents Look at their Second Home by Rick Charette. Taipei's people, culture, and development in modern times through the eyes and experiences of long-term expats.
Taiwan A to Z: The Essential Cultural Guide by Amy C. Liu. Written by a Taiwanese who lived in the US, and fully understands both Western and Eastern cultures, a great primer for anyone wishing to learn more about Taiwan.
Trademarks of the Chinese I and II. These "trademarks" refer to distinctive cultural features, ranging from lion dancing to ancestral spirit tablets, *fengshui* to the Chinese zodiac.
Window on Taiwan by Mark de Fraeye. Beautiful photography by Mark de Fraeye, with essays by experts.
Why Taiwan Matters: Small Island, Global Powerhouse by Shelley Rigger. A comprehensive study and an enjoyable narrative on Taiwan's society, economy and politics.
Vignettes of Taiwan by Joshua Samuel Brown. A rollicking compilation of articles on Taiwan life, often witty and insightful, by a writer who worked as a local-paper reporter.

HISTORY

China's Island Frontier: Studies in the Historical Geography of Taiwan edited by Ronald G. Knapp. Intriguing academic essays on unusual topics such as sugar, walled cities, and pushcar railways.
From Far Formosa: The Island, Its People and Missions by George

Leslie Mackay. A look at Formosa by a respected 19th-century missionary well known in Taiwan.
Forbidden Nation: A History of Taiwan by Jonathan Manthorpe. Because of its strategic geographic location Taiwan has always been coveted by others, and is doggedly struggling to free itself.
The Island of Formosa: Past and Present by James Davidson. A reprint of a thick and detailed 1903 tome, the first comprehensive study of Taiwan in English.
Statecraft and Political Economy on the Taiwan Frontier, 1600–1800 by John Robert Shepherd. A dense, scholarly dissertation, this is the single best English source available on the period.
Taiwan: Nation-State or Province by John F. Copper. Introduction to the island's geography, economy, history, and more.
Taiwan: A Political History by Denny Roy. A comprehensive, readable account of Taiwan's road to democracy that puts modern developments in historical context.

OTHER INSIGHT GUIDES

More than 180 **Insight Guides** and **Insight City Guides** cover every continent, providing information on culture and all the top sights, as well as superb photography and detailed maps.
Insight Guide Taiwan explores the country further and is an ideal companion to this book.
Insight Fleximap Taipei combines clear, detailed cartography with essential travel information. A laminated finish makes the map durable, weatherproof, and easy to fold.

INSIGHT GUIDES

INSPIRING YOUR NEXT ADVENTURE

Insight Guides offers you a range of travel guides to match your needs. Whether you are looking for inspiration for planning a trip, cultural information, walks and tours, great listings, or practical advice, we have a product to suit you.

www.insightguides.com

TAIPEI STREET ATLAS

The key map shows the area of Taipei covered by the atlas section. An index of street names and places of interest shown on the maps can be found on the following pages. For each entry there is a page number and grid reference

Map Legend

Highway with Junction	
Highway (under construction)	
Freeway	
County Highway	
Township Highway	
Road	
Track	
International Boundary	
County Boundary	
National Park/Reserve	
Ferry Route	

✈	Airport
† ⛪	Church (ruins)
†	Monastery
🏰 🏛	Castle (ruins)
∴	Ancient Site
∩	Cave
★	Place of Interest
🏠	Mansion/Stately Home
※	Viewpoint
⚑	Beach

	Freeway
	Highway / Main Road
	Main Roads
	Minor Roads
	Railway
	Pedestrian Area
	Important Building
	Park
	Transport Hub

Ⓜ	Metro (MRT)
🚌	Bus Station
❶	Tourist Information
✉	Post Office
🏛	Cathedral/Church
☾	Mosque
✡	Synagogue
🗽	Statue/Monument
🏛	Tower
🗼	Lighthouse

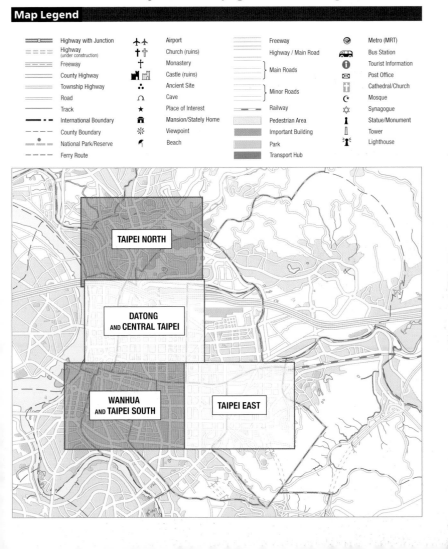

TAIPEI NORTH

DATONG AND CENTRAL TAIPEI

WANHUA AND TAIPEI SOUTH

TAIPEI EAST

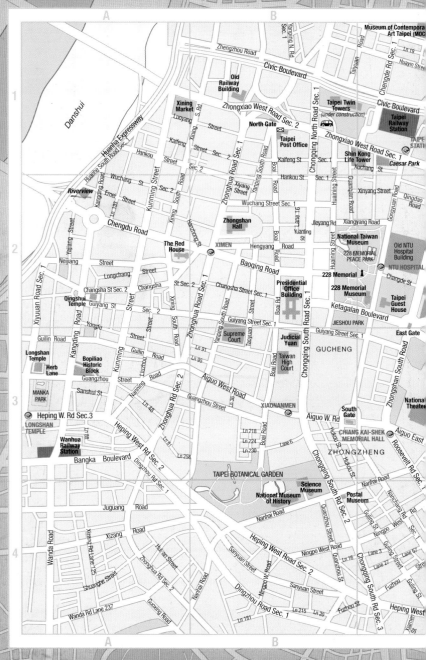

D · E

0   600 m
0   600 yds

Lane 147
Lane 119
Lane 107
Lane 85
Lane 83

Jilin Road
Lane 90

Linsen North Road
Tianjin Street
North Rd Sec. 1

Lane 53
Lane 33
Changan West Road
Lane 53
Zhengzhou Road

Changan E. Rd Sec. 1

Lane 57
Su Ho Memorial
Paper Museum

Lane 45

Songjiang Road
Jianguo North Road Sec. 1

Sun Yat-sen
Historic Events
Memorial Hall

Taipei Artist
Village

Beiping East Road

Zhongshan

Civic Boulevard

Beiping   East   Road

Ln 25

Xixong Street

Lane 23

Tianjin
Beiping
Linsen North Road

SHANDAO
TEMPLE

Shaoxing N. Rd

Hangzhou N. Rd

Jinshan North Road

Weishui Road

Bade Rd Sec. 1

Lane 40

Zhongxiao East Road Sec. 1

Jinan
Presbyterian

Sheraton
Taipei

Shandao
Temple

Ln 45

Lane 64

Taipei
Information
Park
(under construction)

Guang Hua
Digital Plaza

Civic Boulevard

Bade Road Sec. 1

National Taipei
University of Technology

Lane 192

Qingdao East Road

Ln 6

Chinese
Handicraft
Art

Zhongxiao East Road Sec. 2

ZHONGXIAO
XINSHENG

Zhongxiao East Road Sec. 3

Lane 40

Jinan Road Sec. 1

Lane 6

Qidong Street

Lane 71
Lane 64

Lane 3

Lane 197

Jinan
Road Sec. 1

Lane 37

Lane 25

Xinsheng South Road Sec. 1

Lane 103

Xuzhou Road

Shaoxing South Road

Hangzhou South Road

Xuzhou Road

Jinan Road Sec. 2

Tongshan Street

Jinan Road Sec. 2

Lane 32

Jinan Road Sec. 3

Lane 212

National Taiwan
University Hospital

Linsen South Road

Lane 71

Danyang Street

Lane 77

Lane 45

Sec. 1

Lane 119

Lane 51

Renai Road Sec. 1

Renai Road Sec. 2

Taipei Youth
Activity Center (Y17)

Shaoxing S. Rd

Lane 101
Lane 105
Lane 111

Lane 57

Lianyun Street

Ln 133
Ln 137

Lane 24

Jianguo Elevated Road

National
Concert Hall

Xinyi Road Sec. 1

Lane 131
Lane 141

Lane 61
Lane 63

Jinshan South Road

Lane 40

Lane 139

CKS Memorial
Hall Plaza

Hangzhou South Road Sec. 2

Ln 69

Lane 145

Lane 304

Lane 111

Lane 90

Chiang Kai-shek
Memorial Hall

Ln 71
Ln 75

Lianyun Street

Lane 157

Lane 318

Lane 160

DONGMEN

Xinyi Road Sec. 2

Lane 161

Xinsheng South Road Sec. 2

DAAN PARK

Xinyi Road Sec. 3

Lane 165

Lane 170

Ln 4

Lane 222

YONGKANG
PARK

Lishui Street

Yongkang Street

Lane 31

Dingkang Street

Ln 30

DAAN FOREST PARK

Lane 160

Lane 78

Aiguo East Road

Ln 21

Jinshan South Road Sec. 2

Lane 102

Lane 59

Lane 190

Jinhua Street

Lane 71

Minquan St

Lane 59

Jinhua Street

Lane 132

Ln 13

Jinhua Street

Lane 222

Chaozhou Street

Ln 59

Ln 141
Ln 159

Chaozhou Street

Ln 54

Lane 226

Roosevelt Road Sec. 1

Hangzhou South Road Sec. 2

Ln 93

Ln 21

Ln 185

Lishui Street

Chaozhou Street

Ln 9

Chaozhou Street

Shida Rd

Ln 11

Taipei
Grand
Mosque

Ln 11

Rd Sec. 1

GUTING

Nanchang Rd
Sec. 2

Heping E. Rd Sec. 1

National Taiwan
Normal University

Heping East Road Sec. 1

Lane 12

Lane 141

Jinshan South Road Sec. 2

Ln 191

D · E

1

2

3

4

A

B

Lane 60

Taipei Sports
Office & Gymnasiam

Taipei
Arena

Taipei
Municipal
Stadium

Lane 120
Lane 100
Lane 80

Lane 105
Lane 216

Guangfu North Road

Zhulun   Street
Longliang Road

Lane 4

Lane 55

Lane 256

Lane 45
Lane 51

Lane 45

Cultural
Center

Lane 1

1

Lane 45

Road

Lane 45 2

Sec. 2

Metropolitan
Hall

Bade Road Sec. 3

Changan N. Rd Sec. 2

Dunhua North Road

Lane 106

Lane 1

Lane 21

Fuxing

Lane 12

Lane 6

North

Bade

Ln 33

Lane 22

Lane 3

Road

Yilan

Lane 32

Lane 4

Ln 366

Lane 30

Lane 74

Lane 46

Lane 5

Street

Lane 300

Ln 31

Lane 45

Lane 100

Lane 80

Lane 58

Breeze
Center

Alley 70

Alley 57

Civic Boulevard

Civic Boulevard

Lane 40

Lane 79

Lane 131

Lane 1

Daan Road

Lane 107

Lane 160

Lane 62

Yanji Street

Lane 180

Lane 1

Anding Street

Lane 217
Lane 237

Lane 52

Lane 187

Lane 181
Lane 205
Lane 233

Lane 200

SUN YAT-SEN
MEMORIAL HA

Pacific SOGO
Department Store

2

Zhongxiao East Road Sec. 4

ZHONGXIAO
FUXING

ZHONGXIAO
DUNHUA

Zhongxiao East Road Sec. 4

Lane 248

Fuxing South Road Sec. 1

Lane 232

Lane 260

Lane 22

Lane 236

Lane 27

Daan Road Sec. 1

Lane 170

Lane 280

ZHONGS
PARK

Lane 290

Lane 143

Lane 71

Lane 252

Lane 308

Lane 26

Eslite
Bookstore

Anhe Road Sec. 1

Lane 151

Lane 346

Guangfu South Road

Lane 270

Renai Road Sec. 3

Renai Road Sec. 3

Renai
Traffic
Circle

Renai Road Sec. 4

Fuxing South Road Sec. 1

Lane 253
Lane 169

Dunhua South Road Sec. 1

Anhe Rd Sec. 1

Lane 266

Lane 147

Lane 175

Lane 22

Lane 25

YANJI
PARK

Lane 4

3

Lane 157

Dongfeng

Street

Yanji Street

Lane 364

Lane 111

Daan Road Sec. 1

Siwei Road

Lane 295

Lane 122

Lane 90

Lane 127

GUOAN
PARK

ZHON

Ln 220

Lane 76

Lane 329

Ln 102

Lane 135

Lane 99

Ln 139

Lane 141

Xinyi Road Sec. 3

Xinyi Road Sec. 4

Xinyi Road Sec. 4

XINYI ANHE

DAAN

Siwei Road

Wenchang Street

Wenchang Street

Guangfu South Road

Jilong Ro

Lane 78

Anhe Rd Sec. 2

Tonghua Street

Daan Road Sec. 2

Lane 154

Lane 39

Linjiang Street

Lane 131

Dunhua South Road Sec. 2

Lane 98

Ln 101

Linjiang Street

Ruian Street

Fuxing South Road Sec. 2

Ln 120

Ln 123

Lane 160

Ln 140

Ln 143

4

Lane 71

Siwei Road

Lane 106

Anhe Road Sec. 2

Ln 162

Ln 144

Lane 151

Lane 170

Lane 5

Tonghua Street

Jilong Road Sec. 2

Jiaxing Road

Lane 160

Lane 178

Tonghua Street

Lane 107

Ln 186

Far Eastern
Plaza Hotel

Lei Road

Ln 42

0   600 m

0   600 yds

TECHNOLOGY
BUILDING

A

B

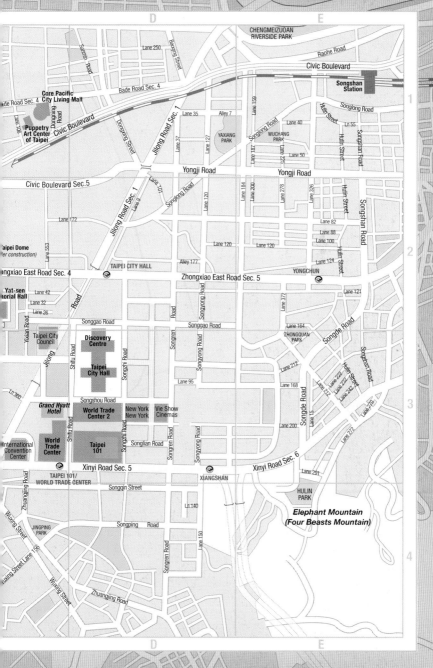

CHENGMEIZUOAN
RIVERSIDE PARK

Raohe Road

Civic Boulevard

Songshan
Station

Lane 250

Baoqing Street

Songlong Road

Bade Road Sec. 4

Core Pacific
City Living Mall

Bade Road Sec. 4

Dongxing Road

Civic Boulevard

Puppetry
Art Center
of Taipei

Dongxing Street

Jilong Road Sec. 1

Lane 35

Alley 7

Lane 159

Songlong Road

Lane 40

Hulin Street

Songlong Road

Ln 55

Songshan Road

Lane 37

Lane 127

YAXIANG
PARK

WUCHANG
PARK

Lane 187

Lane 222

Lane 50

Yongji Road

Yongji Road

Civic Boulevard Sec.5

Jilong Road Sec. 1

Lane 9

Lane 101

Songlong Road

Lane 184

Lane 200

Lane 278

Lane 326

Hulin Street

Songshan Road

Lane 172

Lane 120

Lane 120

Lane 82

Lane 353

Lane 88

Lane 100

Taipei Dome
(under construction)

Lane 120

Lane 120

Hulin Street

Lane 124

ngxiao East Road Sec. 4

Alley 177

YONGCHUN

TAIPEI CITY HALL

Zhongxiao East Road Sec. 5

Yat-sen
morial Hall

Lane 42

Songlong Road

Lane 372

Lane 121

Lane 32

Lane 26

Road

Songde Road

Songgao Road

Songren

Songgao Road

Lane 164

Yixian Road

Taipei City
Council

Shifu Road

Songzhi Road

ZHONGQUAN
PARK

Discovery
Centre

Lane 212

Lane 222

Hulin Street

Songshan Road

Jilong

Taipei
City Hall

Lane 95

Lane 168

Lane 212

Lane 242

Lane 270

Ln 300

Songyong Road

Songde Road

Songshou Road

Lane 200

Lane 15

Lane 272

Grand Hyatt
Hotel

World Trade
Center 2

New York
New York

Vie Show
Cinemas

World
Trade
Center

Shifu Road

Songzhi Road

Taipei
101

Songren Road

Songlian Road

Songyong Road

International
Convention
Center

Xinyi Road Sec. 5

Xinyi Road Sec. 6

Lane 261

TAIPEI 101/
WORLD TRADE CENTER

XIANGSHAN

HULIN
PARK

Zhuangjing Road

Wuxing Street

Songqin Street

Ln 140

Elephant Mountain
(Four Beasts Mountain)

JINGPING
PARK

Songping   Road

Songren Road

Lane 150

Wuxing Street Lane 156

Wuxing Street

Zhuangjing Road

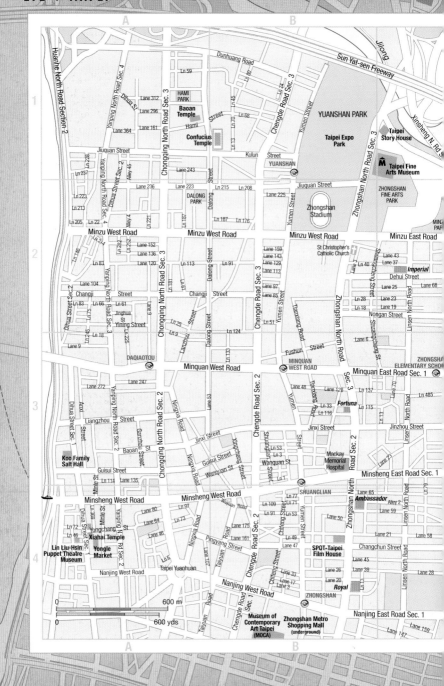

Huanhe North Road Section 2

Dunhuang Road

Sun Yat-sen Freeway

Jilong

Xinsheng N. Rd S

Ln 59

Yanping North Road Sec. 4

Dihua St.

Lane 312
Lane 296

Chongqing North Road Sec. 3

HAMI PARK

Baoan Temple

Ln 24
Ln 45
Ln 68
Ln 70

Chengde Road Sec. 3

Yumen Street

YUANSHAN PARK

Taipei Story House

Lane 364
Lane 161

Hami

Street

Ln 13

Taipei Expo Park

Zhongshan North Road Sec. 3

Taipei Fine Arts Museum

Ln 237

Jiuquan Street

Confucius Temple

Kulun

Street

YUANSHAN

ZHONGSHAN FINE ARTS PARK

MIN PAF

Yanping North Road Sec. 4

Alley 45

Lane 243

Jiuquan Street

Lane 225

Ln 223
Ln 213

Lane 236

DALONG PARK

Lane 223

Dalong Street

Ln 215

Ln 208

Zhongshan Stadium

Ln 205
Ln 22

Ln 187

Ln 176

Minzu West Road

Ln 214

Minzu West Road

Minzu West Road

St Christopher's Catholic Church

Minzu East Road

Imperial

Lane 282
Lane 252

Lane 152
Lane 136
Lane 120

Dalong Street

Ln 113

Ln 91

Lane 159
Lane 143
Lane 129
Lane 113

Shuangcheng St

Lane 43
Lane 37

Ln 83

Chengde Road Sec. 3

Lane 97

Dehui Street

Lane 68

Changji

Street

Lane 104

Ln 181

Changji

Street

Ln 61

Yanping North Road Sec. 3

Ln 66

Jinghua

Yining Street

Ln 25

Lanzhou

Dalong Street

Ln 124

Ln 51

Tiandong Road

Zhongshan North Road

Lane 25
Ln 28
Ln 18

Lane 23
Lane 19

Nongan Street

Linsen North Road

Ln 245
Ln 18

Ln 9

Ln 225

Ln 133

Lane 6

Lane 9

DAQIAOTOU

Minquan West Road

Fushun

Street

MINQUAN WEST ROAD

Minquan East Road Sec. 1

ZHONGSHAN ELEMENTARY SCHOOL

Lane 272

Lane 247

Yanping North Road Sec. 2

Chongqing North Road Sec. 2

Lane 53

Baoan Road

Chengde Road Sec. 2

Lane 48

Tiandong Road

Yumen

Lane 128

Zhongshan North Road Sec. 3

Ln 137

Ln 33
Ln 116

Fortuna

Ln 115

Ln 113

Linsen North Road

Ln 485

Dihua Street Sec. 1

Anxi

Liangzhou

Street

Gangqian Street

Ninghua Road

Jinxi Street

Jinxi Street

Jinzhou Street

Koo Family Salt Hall

Baoan

St

Ln 114

Guisui Street

Ln 135

Guisui Street

Wanquan St

Ln 53
Ln 3
Ln 1

Chongqing North

Zhongshan North

Mackay Memorial Hospital

Road Sec. 2

Lane 23

Minsheng East Road Sec. 1

Wanquan St

Minsheng West Road

Minsheng West Road

SHUANGLIAN

Ambassador

Lane 65

Alley 2

Lane 80

Ln 97

Ln 109
Ln 77
Ln 91
Ln 71
Ln 53

Lane 59

Linsen North Road

Ln 79

Lane 64

Yongchang N. St

Ninghua Road

Lane 175

Yumen Street

Lane 50

Lane 21

Lane 58

Lin Liu-Hsin Puppet Theatre Museum

Ln 72
Ln 46

Dihua Street Sec. 1

Yanping N. Rd Sec. 2

Ln 6

Xiahai Temple

Yongle Market

Lane 46

Pingyang Street

Lane 161

Chengde Road Sec. 2

Chifeng Street

Ln 49

Ln 47

SPOT-Taipei Film House

Lane 45

Lane 26

Changchun Street

Lane 39

Lane 28

Nanjing West Road

Taipei Yuanhuan

Taiyuan Road

Lane 33
Lane 3

Lane 20

Ln 13

Royal

0   600 m

0   600 yds

Nanjing West Road

Chengde Road Sec. 1

Chifeng Street

ZHONGSHAN

Museum of Contemporary Art Taipei (MOCA)

Zhongshan Metro Shopping Mall (underground)

Nanjing East Road Sec. 1

Taiyuan Road

Lane 147

Lane 159

D **E**

Mingshui Road

Jilong

Dazhi Bridge

DAJIA RIVERSIDE PARK

YINGFENG
RIVERSIDE
PARK

1

Riverside Park Road

Binjiang Street

Lin An Tai
Homestead

Binjiang Street

Taipei Expo
Park

XINSHENG
PARK

Songshan Airport

Minzu East Road

Minzu East Road

Ln 461

Lane 412 Lane 457

Alley 31

3

Ln 447 Ln 167

Alley 19 Lane 394 Lane 443

7 Ln 105

Ln 443 Lane 152

Alley 2 Lane 384 Lane 420

ui Street

Road

Dehui Street

2

25 Ln 407

Lane 370 Lane 415

Lane 356 Lane 514

Jianguo North Road Sec. 3

Lane 75 Lane 328 Lane 387

Ln 80 Ln 227

Lane 53

Lane 318

Ln 161 Ln 488

Nongan Street

Road

9

Nongan Street

Wuchang Street

Lane 329

Alley 30

Road

Lane 71

Alley 20

Longjiang Street

Lane 345 Ln 430

Lane 315 Lane 402

Lane 357

Ln 39

Fuxing North Road

Ln 103

3 Lane 299 Lane 372

Lane 331 Ln 75

Xingtian
Temple

RONGXING
GARDEN

Minquan East Road Sec. 2

Minquan East Road Sec. 3

Ln 352 Ln 362

Lane 258

Street

ZHONGSHAN JUNIOR
HIGH SCHOOL

Ln 137

Lane 330

Jilin Road

Lane 231

Jianguo North Road Sec. 2

Lane 170 Lane 127 Lane 295

3

Ln 175

Lane 297 Lane 226

Street

Jinzhou Street

Jinzhou Street

Street

Jinzhou

Lane 259

Lane 144 Lane 105 Lane 281

Lane 218

Lane 161

XINGTIAN

Lane 130 Lane 93 Lane 271

Longjiang

Ln 73

Lane 200 Lane 239

TEMPLE

Lane 235

Lane 116 Lane 83 Lane 249

Liaoning

St John
the Baptist

Lane 102 Lane 73 Lane 248

Minsheng East Road Sec. 2

Minsheng East Road Sec. 3

Lane 194

Lane 164

Lane 174

Lane 184

Xingan Street

Xingan Street

ane 168

Ln 188

Lane 154

Lane 184

Lane 58 Ln 41

Road

ane 144

Lane 170

Lane 258

Fuxing North Road

Qincheng Road

Lane 160

Lane 20 Lane 17 Lane 179

Ln 174

Changchun Road

Changchun Road

Changchun Road

Jilin Road

Yijiang Road

Songjiang Road

Lane 115

Street

Jianguo North Road Sec. 2

Shuhan Rd.

Longjiang

Liaoning

Lane 197

Changchun Road

4

Ln 51 Ln 140

Yitong

Siping Street

Ln 141

SONGJIANG
NANJING

NANJING EAST
ROAD

jing East Road Sec. 2

Nanjing East Road Sec. 3

Lane 108 Lane 52

Lane 76 L. 91

D **E**

Chengde Road Sec. 6

Huang

Wenlin Road

Fuhua Road

ZHISHAN

Fuguo Road

Zhongshan North Road Sec. 6

Yusheng St.

Zhicheng Rd Sec. 6

Shuangxi Street

Fulin
Bridge

Shuangxi St

Waishuang

Waishuang

Wenlin Rd.

Wenlin
Bridge

Front St

Back St

Fuzhi

Wenchang Street

Meilun Street

Meilun Street

Taipei
Astronomical
Museum

Hsiating Street

Huaguang Street

Meile Street

Wenlin Road

Fushou St.

Zhongshan North Road Sec. 5

National Taiwan
Science Education
Center

Jihe Road

Zhonghua St

Hsiaming St.

Zhongzheng Road

Chengde Road Sec. 5

Xiashulin St

SHILIN

Tonghe East Road Sec. 1

SHEZI
SPORTS
PARK

Fude Road

Wenlin Road

Daxong Road

Dart Road

Xiaobei Street

Shezheng St

Zhongzheng Road

Xiaoyi Road

Xiaobei Road

Dabei Road

Yanping Nth Rd Sec. 6

Shezeng Road

Bailing Bridge

Danan Road

JIHE PARK

Shejiang Street

Jihe Road

Danan Road

Xiaonan Street

Zhongshan North Road Sec. 5

Danan

Road

Chengde Road Sec. 4

Shilin
Nightmarket

Xiaonan Street

Wenlin Road

Jiliong

Tonghe East Road Sec. 1

Fugang Street

Hualing Street

Hougang Street

Taipei Sea
World

Daxing Road

BAILING WEST
RIVERSIDE
PARK

BAILING EAST
RIVERSIDE
PARK

Qiangang Street

QIANGANG
PARK

Taipei Performing
Arts Center
(under construction)

JIANTAN

Zhonggang North Road Sec. 4

Fugang Street

Hualing Street

Qiangang Street

Qiangang Street

Mt Jiant
1

Yanping North Road Sec. 4

Tonghe East Road Sec. 1

Hougang Street

Hualing Street

Jiantan Road

Chengde Road Sec. 4

Jihe Road

Zhongshan North Road Sec. 4

Xinsheng St.

Yanping North Road Sec. 5

HUALING
PARK

Tonghe Street

0   600 m

0   600 yds

Chengde Bridge

Tonghe Street

Jihe Rd

Grand Hotel

Sun Yat-sen Freeway (National Freeway 1)

A   B

STONE
PARK

ZHISHAN
PARK

ZHISHAN
GARDEN

Yusheng
Street

Yangde Blvd Sec. 2

Yangde Blvd Sec. 2

Yangde Blvd Sec. 1

Zhiyu Road Sec. 1

icheng Road Sec. 1

Yunong Rd

Zhongyong St

Fulin Road

SHUANGXI
PARK

SHUANGXI
PARK

Lane 254

National
Palace
Museum

Zhishan Road Sec. 2

Zhishan Road Sec. 1

Gugong Road

Lixing Street

xing Road

Rd Yunong

Guchua Street

Waishuang

ngzheng Rd

n Road

**Shilin Official
Residence**

Linxi Road

Ziqiang Tunnel

Ziqiang Tunnel

Ziqiang Tunnel

Huanshan Road

Tongbei Street

Dazhi Street

Lane 527

SHOU
RK

Tongbei Street

Sihai

Tongbei Street

Dazhi Street

Beian Road

Lane 501

**National
Revolutionary
Martyrs' Shrine**

Beian Road

DAZHI

Dazhi Street

Beian Road

Mingshui Road

Mingshui Road

Jilong

STREET INDEX

ART AND PHOTO CREDITS

Chris Stowers/Apa Publications
6MR, 6ML, 6MR, 6BL, 7MR, 6/7M,
6/7B, 7MR, 8R, 8L, 9BR, 9TR, 8/9T,
10T, 10B, 10/11, 12/13, 19, 20,
21, 22B, 22T, 22/23, 24, 25R,
24/25, 26L, 26R, 27TR, 27BR,
26/27T, 30T, 31T, 38, 40R, 42T, 47,
48B, 48T, 49B, 50, 50/51T,
50/51B, 51BR, 52/53T, 52/53M,
53TC, 54, 55, 56, 62, 63, 64, 65R,
64/65, 66, 67R, 66/67, 68R, 68L,
68/69, 70, 70/71, 71R, 72, 72/73,
73R, 74, 75, 76, 77, 78, 78/79,
79R, 80, 81, 82, 83R, 82/83, 84R,
84L, 86R, 86L, 87TR, 86/87T,
87MR, 86/87M, 86/87B, 88/89,
92/93, 94, 95, 98, 99, 101B,
100/101T, 102T, 102B, 103B,
102/103T, 104B, 104T, 104/105T,
105B, 106/107B, 107T, 108T,
108B, 108/109, 110MR, 110MR,
110BL, 111R, 112, 113, 114/115,
116B, 116T, 117B, 117T, 118,
120B, 120T, 122, 123, 125T,
124/125B, 126T, 126B, 127,
129B, 129T, 130B, 130T, 132, 133,

135B, 135T, 136, 137T, 136/137B,
138, 139T, 139B, 140, 140/141T,
141B, 143, 144, 146, 147, 148,
149T, 149B, 150, 150/151, 152T,
152B, 153, 154T, 154B, 155T,
155B, 156T, 156B, 157T,
156/157B, 158, 160, 161, 162,
162/163, 164, 164/165T, 165BR,
165TR, 166, 166/167, 168, 169T,
169B, 170T, 170B, 171, 172, 173,
174, 175, 176T, 176B, 176/177,
178, 179T, 179B, 180, 180/181T,
180/181B, 182, 183T, 183B, 184T,
184B, 184/185T, 185B, 186, 188,
189, 190T, 191TR, 190/191T,
192/193B, 194, 194/195, 196,
197T, 197B, 198, 199, 200, 203,
204T, 204B, 204/205T, 205B, 206,
207, 208T, 209, 210/211, 212,
213T, 212/213B, 214, 215, 216,
217B, 217T, 218T, 218B, 220, 221,
222, 223B, 223T, 224T, 224B,
225T, 224/225B, 227B, 227T,
228B, 228T, 229R, 228/229, 230,
231, 232T, 232B, 235, 236/237,
238, 240, 240/241, 244, 246,

250/251, 254, 259, 261, 264
City Archives 34R, 34/35
Corbis 37, 38/39, 39R, 40/41,
42B, 43
Deni Chung 110/111T
Getty Images 4/5, 7TR, 6/7T,
14/15, 16/17, 18, 28/29, 30B,
31B, 44/45, 46, 53MR, 58/59, 85,
90/91, 193MR
**Government Information Office,
ROC** 40L
iStock 1, 48/49T, 110/111, 201,
233, 266
Jim Smeal/BEI/Rex Features 58T
Kobal 60
Malibu West 144/145
National Palace Museum 190B,
191MC, 190/191M, 192ML,
192TL, 192BC, 192/193T, 193BR
National Taiwan Museum 28, 32,
33, 34L, 36
Outlookxp 208B
Taipei Tourism 52MR, 52MR, 52BL
Tsai Jui-yueh Dance Festival 61
Yang San-lang Fine Arts Museum
56/57

Cover Credits

Front cover: Mengjia Longshan
Temple *Alamy*
Back cover: (top) skyline *iStock;*
(middle) CKS Memorial Hall *iStock;*
(bottom) Martyr's Shrine Guard
Chris Stowers/Apa Publications

Front flap: (from top) jade market
Chris Stowers/Apa Publications;
Carnegies *Chris Stowers/Apa
Publications;* Dajia Riverside Park
Chris Stowers/Apa Publications;
Dragonboat Festival *Chris Stowers/*

Apa Publications
Back flap: Ximending *Chris
Stowers/Apa Publications*
Spine: jade figure *iStock*

INDEX

RESTAURANTS

BARS AND CAFÉS

Travel guides, ebooks, apps and online
www.insightguides.com

INSIGHT GUIDES

TAIPEI

ABOUT THIS BOOK

Project Editor
Sarah Clark
Author
Katarzyna Marcinkowska
Update Production
AM Services
Picture Editor
Tom Smyth
Map Production
original cartography Wadsworth
Graphics and Nelani Jinadasa,
updated by Carte. Several source
maps were generously provided by
the Department of Transportation,
Taipei City Government
Production
Rebeka Davies and Aga Bylica

Distribution

UK
Dorling Kindersley Ltd
A Penguin Group company
80 Strand, London, WC2R 0RL
sales@uk.dk.com

United States
Ingram Publisher Services
1 Ingram Boulevard, PO Box 3006,
La Vergne, TN 37086-1986
ips@ingramcontent.com

Australia and New Zealand
Woodslane
10 Apollo St
Warriewood NSW 2102
Australia
info@woodslane.com.au

Worldwide
**Apa Publications GmbH & Co.
Verlag KG (Singapore branch)**
7030 Ang Mo Kio Avenue 5
08-65 Northstar @ AMK
Singapore 569880
apasin@singnet.com.sg

© 2015 Apa Publications (UK) Ltd
All Rights Reserved

First Edition 2006
Third Edition 2015

What makes an Insight Guide different? Since our first book pioneered the use of creative full-colour photography in travel guides in 1970, we have aimed to provide not only reliable information but also the key to a real understanding of a destination and its people.

Now, when the internet can supply inexhaustible (but not always reliable) facts, our books marry text and pictures to provide that more elusive quality: knowledge. To achieve this, they rely on the authority of locally based writers and photographers.

This new edition of *City Guide Taipei* was commissioned and edited for the second time by **Sarah Clark**. The entire book was comprehensively updated by **Katarzyna Marcinkowska**, an experienced travel writer, editor and photographer.

This book retains the detailed work written for its last edition by Canadian **Rick Charette**, who has lived in Taipei since 1988 and knows the city intimately. Other original contributors include **Brent Hannon** and **Chris Taylor**.

Taipei-based **Chris Stowers**, a widely published photographer in the region, built on his previous images for this book with a stunning new shoot.

SEND US YOUR THOUGHTS

We do our best to ensure the information in our books is as accurate and up-to-date as possible. The books are updated on a regular basis using local contacts, who painstakingly add, amend, and correct as required. However, some details (such as telephone numbers and opening times) are liable to change, and we are ultimately reliant on our readers to put us in the picture.

We welcome your feedback, especially your experience of using the book "on the road". Maybe we recommended a hotel that you liked (or another that you didn't), or you came across a great bar or new attraction that we missed.

We will acknowledge all contributions, and we'll offer an Insight Guide to the best letters received.

Please write to us at:
Insight Guides
PO Box 7910, London SE1 1WE
Or email us at:
hello@insightguides.com